T0234027

ABAP in Eclipse

Install, Configure, Use, and Enhance Your ADT

Łukasz Pęgiel

Apress®

ABAP in Eclipse: Install, Configure, Use, and Enhance Your ADT

Łukasz Pęgiel
Tychy, Poland

ISBN-13 (pbk): 978-1-4842-6962-6   ISBN-13 (electronic): 978-1-4842-6963-3
https://doi.org/10.1007/978-1-4842-6963-3

Managing Director, Apress Media LLC: Welmoed Spahr
Acquisitions Editor: Divya Modi
Development Editor: Matthew Moodie
Coordinating Editor: Divya Modi

Cover designed by eStudioCalamar

Cover image designed by Pixabay

Distributed to the book trade worldwide by Springer Science+Business Media New York, 1 New York Plaza, New York, NY 10004. Phone 1-800-SPRINGER, fax (201) 348-4505, e-mail orders-ny@springer-sbm.com, or visit www.springeronline.com. Apress Media, LLC is a California LLC and the sole member (owner) is Springer Science + Business Media Finance Inc (SSBM Finance Inc). SSBM Finance Inc is a **Delaware** corporation.

For information on translations, please e-mail booktranslations@springernature.com; for reprint, paperback, or audio rights, please e-mail bookpermissions@springernature.com.

Apress titles may be purchased in bulk for academic, corporate, or promotional use. eBook versions and licenses are also available for most titles. For more information, reference our Print and eBook Bulk Sales web page at http://www.apress.com/bulk-sales.

Any source code or other supplementary material referenced by the author in this book is available to readers on GitHub via the book's product page, located at www.apress.com/978-1-4842-6962-6. For more detailed information, please visit http://www.apress.com/source-code.

Printed on acid-free paper

For my wife Zosia, I couldn't have written this book without your support and patience.

Table of Contents

About the Author

 **Łukasz Pęgiel** is IT manager for SAP applications at Hager Group. He has been active in the SAP community for more than ten years. He mostly shares his knowledge on his blog (`https://abapBlog.com`). He is a creator of the following Eclipse plugins: ABAP Favorites, ABAP Extensions, and ABAP Quick Fix. He also shares his ABAP projects or frameworks on GitHub as fidley; these include: Fast ALV Grid, JSON2ABAPType, Customers, and ALV Grid in a Nutshell. He was a speaker at the last four #sitWROs and attended a few others around Europe. He was also named a SAP Developer Hero in 2016 and a SAP Champion in 2019. He can also teach you how to brew a beer.

About the Technical Reviewer

Enno Wulff has been a passionate ABAP programmer since 1995. He focuses on documentation and knowledge transfer, clean code, and modularized development. Making the best of stable technologies using robust programming, clean code, and design patterns are Enno's goals. Starting as a freelancer, Enno has worked since 2007 for Inwerken AG in Hanover, Germany. With his Inwerken colleagues, he published the ABAP Kochbuch. Enno shares his knowledge and insights on his own website at `https://tricktresor.de` as well as on his blog at `https://blogs.sap.com`.

Acknowledgments

I never thought that writing a book would be so exhausting. I was sure that it will be much easier for someone that has experience in blogging. That is why I am extremely grateful to my wife, Zosia, for all the patience and support she gave me while I was writing this book. She took all home duties on herself, which in the era of Covid-19 and remote education for our three sons, was not an easy task to do.

I would like also to thank my sons, Szymon, Michał, and Kamil, for understanding why I was not always available these last few months.

This book wouldn't be written, if some years ago Thomas Fiedler would not have motivated me to write my first plugin for ADT. He has supported me many times since that moment, helping me whenever I needed it. I hope I will be able to pay him and his team back someday.

A very special thanks to Andreas Gautsch, Ludwig Stockbauer-Muhr, and Akysh Baymuhammedov, for finding the time to discuss their ADT plugins and Eclipse extensibility. Their contribution to the SAP community is priceless.

Without a good technical reviewer, it is hard to find mistakes. That is why I am very happy that my friend Enno Wulff was able to check each character in this book.

If work-life balance was not important to my employer Hager Group, I would not have had the time and energy to write a book. I would like to explicitly thank my boss Frank Helbing and my dearest colleague Pilar Ibarz for believing in me and giving me the motivation to take this on.

ACKNOWLEDGMENTS

To Divya Modi and Matthew Moodie and all the Apress team, for convincing me to write a book and for the support I was given during that time.

Finally, to my family, friends, and SAP community. Your warm words about the book you have not read yet motivated me to make it as good as possible. I hope you will enjoy reading it as much as I enjoyed writing it.

Introduction

It has been eight years since the first release of the ABAP Development Tools for Eclipse (ADT), yet many developers still stick to ABAP Workbench in SAP GUI (SE80). That is why this book was written.

There are many aspects that make it difficult to switch from SE80 to ADT, especially if you are still using functional programming. In this book, you will learn about the huge benefits of using ADT in your daily developer life. I assure you that after reading this book, you will never look at Eclipse and ADT in the same way.

When I was thinking about the concept of the book, I faced the problem of whether I should concentrate on the usage of ADT or assume that readers have a basic understanding of the tool, and so focus only on the extension part. In the end I decided that the book would serve the whole population of the ABAP developers—those who have never developed in Eclipse and those who use it on a daily basis. All of you should find something useful in this book.

CHAPTER 1

Installation and Basic Information

This chapter shows you how to install Eclipse and ABAP Development Tools for Eclipse (ADT). You'll also start using them, by creating your first ABAP project. I also describe the Eclipse perspectives that are installed with ADT and explain how you can customize them or create perspectives that fit your needs. Hopefully, you will be more comfortable with ADT after reading this chapter.

Installation Process

In order to use ABAP Development Tools, you need to install Eclipse and the Java Runtime Environment, which can be installed before or after installing Eclipse.

Java Runtime Environment

When you use your company notebook or PC, it is quite probable that you don't have administrator privileges that will allow you to install the Java Runtime Environment (JRE) by yourself. In such a case, you should contact your user service or any other responsible person in order to install the proper JRE.

© Lukasz Pegiel 2021
Ł. Pęgiel, *ABAP in Eclipse*, https://doi.org/10.1007/978-1-4842-6963-3_1

If you are allowed to install JRE on your own, select one of the runtime environments listed here, considering all the advantages and disadvantages. You can also show this part of the chapter to your user service, to let them decide which JRE version to install on your computer.

There are many distributions of JRE and JDK (Java Development Kit). In this chapter, I focus on the following ones:

- Oracle JRE

- OpenJDK

- SapMachine

- Eclipse JustJ

Note   It is very likely that you already have a JRE installation on your PC, managed by your environment administrator. In such a case, you can skip this part of the chapter and move to installing Eclipse. Additionally, as of Eclipse version 2020-09, you can install the Eclipse JustJ JRE directly during its installation.

Oracle JRE

Before April 2019, you did not need to think about which version of JRE to install. You simply went directly to https://www.java.com/en/download/ and installed the latest available version. But since then, as you can see in Figure 1-1, Oracle has changed its license policy. You can use the versions available there for free, if they are for personal or development use. In the case of commercial use, you or your company needs to pay a licensing fee.

Using the official Oracle JRE definitely pays when there are security issues, as Oracle provides long-term support for its releases. Releases do not change that often; they are scheduled every three years. This is a good argument for paying the licensing fee.

Figure 1-1. *Oracle Java download site*

OpenJDK

You may think that Oracle has changed their licensing model in order to make more money. Maybe you are right, but at the same time, Oracle is releasing OpenJDK under a GNU license. OpenJDK is the base for Oracle JRE/JDK, as well as for all the other distributions of JRE described in this chapter. The difference with Oracle JRE/JDK, besides licensing, is that OpenJDK is released in six-month intervals and support for the current version ends exactly when the new version is released. This might be a point against using OpenJDK, but if you can upgrade it frequently, there should not be any issue with it.

One additional point against OpenJDK is that there are no installation files for any of the OSs. You need to download TAR.GZ or ZIP files from `https://jdk.java.net/`, unpack then to the final destination folder, and set the `JAVA_HOME` parameter on your OS to the value of selected path.

3

However, you can also find prebuilt binaries from this website: `https://github.com/ojdkbuild/ojdkbuild`. This can make the installation easier and faster.

If you don't have authorization to set up your OS parameters, you still can use OpenJDK by unpacking it to the Eclipse main installation folder (after installation) under the name `jre`. This JDK will work only for this particular Eclipse instance.

SapMachine

The SAP distribution of OpenJDK is a good option, as you have one provider for your ABAP Development Tools and JRE.

As with many other OpenJDK distributions, SapMachine provides a long-term support version, which is based on OpenJDK 11, and a short-term support version, which is based on OpenJDK 15. Go to the download website at `https://sap.github.io/SapMachine/` (Figure 1-2) and you can choose not only the version and the platform, but also the type of distribution (JDK or JRE).

SapMachine should not differ much from OpenJDK, but SAP recommendations you use this distribution when using Eclipse. Personally I think it works a bit faster and is more stable than OpenJDK and GraalVM (which is another of Oracle's children in the Java world).

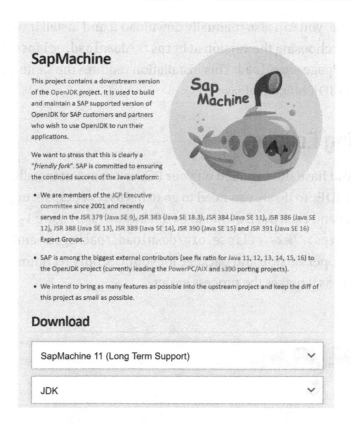

SapMachine

This project contains a downstream version of the OpenJDK project. It is used to build and maintain a SAP supported version of OpenJDK for SAP customers and partners who wish to use OpenJDK to run their applications.

We want to stress that this is clearly a *"friendly fork"*. SAP is committed to ensuring the continued success of the Java platform:

- We are members of the JCP Executive committee since 2001 and recently served in the JSR 379 (Java SE 9), JSR 383 (Java SE 18.3), JSR 384 (Java SE 11), JSR 386 (Java SE 12), JSR 388 (Java SE 13), JSR 389 (Java SE 14), JSR 390 (Java SE 15) and JSR 391 (Java SE 16) Expert Groups.

- SAP is among the biggest external contributors (see fix ratio for Java 11, 12, 13, 14, 15, 16) to the OpenJDK project (currently leading the PowerPC/AIX and s390 porting projects).

- We intend to bring as many features as possible into the upstream project and keep the diff of this project as small as possible.

Download

SapMachine 11 (Long Term Support)	⌄

JDK	⌄

Figure 1-2. *SapMachine download website*

As with OpenJDK, there are no binary installation files for SapMachine, so you need to follow the same steps in order to use it with your Eclipse installation.

Eclipse JustJ

This distribution is discussed here because, since Eclipse version 2020-09, it can be installed together with the Eclipse IDE installation (I will come back to this in the next part of this chapter). It is also based on OpenJDK and can be helpful, especially if you not only use Eclipse for ABAP development, but also for Java development. It contains fully-functional Java runtimes that can be redistributed by Eclipse projects.

Of course, you can also manually download it and install it yourself. You do so by choosing the version at `https://download.eclipse.org/justj/www/?page=download`. This installation requires the same steps as for the OpenJDK official release.

Installing Eclipse

Now that you have JRE installed on your PC, you can start installing the Eclipse IDE. To do so, you need to go to `https://eclipse.org/downloads/` and click the Download 64-Bit button (see Figure 1-3). You can also go to `https://www.eclipse.org/downloads/packages/` and directly select the proper version and package for your OS, but I recommend using the installer, as it makes the process easier.

Figure 1-3. *Eclipse installer download page*

You don't need administrator rights in order to run the installer. Just navigate to your browser download folder and run the Eclipse setup file. Once the installer opens, you can choose the Eclipse package you want to install. As you can see in Figure 1-4, each package is prepared for different purposes and contains different tool setups. There is no special package for ABAP development there, so I recommend selecting one of the two first packages: Eclipse IDE for Java Developers or Eclipse IDE for Enterprise Java Developers.

If you need any other tools inside your IDE, you can always install then later from the Eclipse Marketplace or from the Eclipse update site.

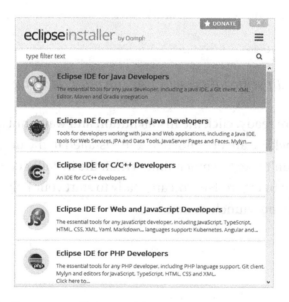

Figure 1-4. *Eclipse installer: package selection*

After you choose the package version, you'll be asked to select which JRE you want to use with your Eclipse IDE. You can choose from the installed JREs on your PC. From Eclipse version 2020-09, you can choose to install JustJ JRE at this stage. In my example, I chose to run Eclipse with SapMachine. As you can see in Figure 1-5, during this step, you have to also choose the installation folder.

Figure 1-5. *Eclipse installer: selecting the path and Java VM*

When you're ready, click the Install button and wait until all parts of your Eclipse package are downloaded and installed in the destination folder. It shouldn't take too much time. When the installer colors turn green, as shown in Figure 1-6, you are ready to start your Eclipse IDE. You can do so using the Launch button.

Figure 1-6. *Successful installation of Eclipse IDE*

You will first see the IDE splash screen, as shown in Figure 1-7. Normally I do not care much about splash screens, but in the case of Eclipse, it holds very important information, which is the version. Since the Eclipse Organization has changed the release intervals from one year to three months and I have set up my installation to upgrade automatically, the version information is important. You may of course read the upgrade package list each time, but I never remember which internal version number is current. The splash screen can also help you if you keep several instances of Eclipse on your computer.

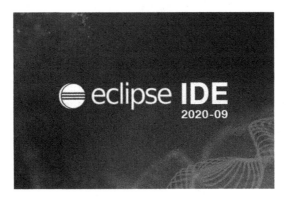

Figure 1-7. *Eclipse splash screen*

The workspace selector will appear next (Figure 1-8). You can choose where your workspace will be stored on your hard drive. Before you do so, let me explain what a workspace is.

A *workspace* is a set of projects and preferences, where projects can repeat themselves in several workspaces. You can run several workspaces at the same time, each one on a separate OS thread, but you cannot run the same workspace in parallel on several Eclipse instances.

In the case of ABAP development, a *project* is a link to a SAP instance with a specific client, user, and language. I describe ABAP projects in more detail in the following parts of this chapter.

You can choose a workspace at this stage or hold the decision for later, if you want your first workspace to be the default one. This is common choice when you do not plan to have more than one workspace.

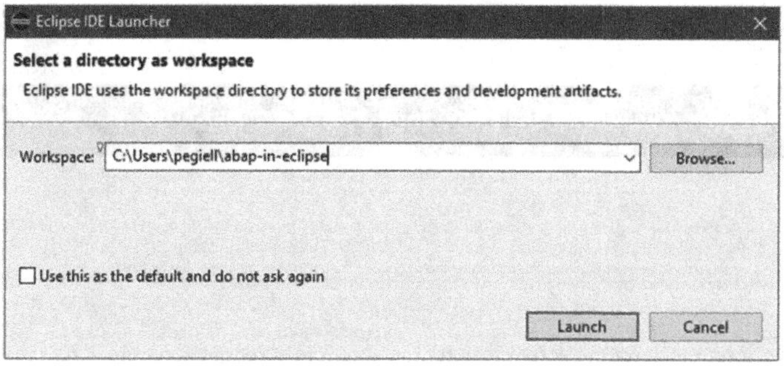

Figure 1-8. *Eclipse IDE launcher: workspace selector*

Tip   In some cases, deciding where to keep your workspace can be tricky. For example, if you keep it in a place that's synchronized to the cloud drives, such as OneDrive, Google Drive, etc., and then you want to synchronize the workspace on a few devices, it is always slower to copy many small files to the cloud, than to copy one big file. If the files are not synchronized fully, because for example you closed your PC just after you closed Eclipse, when you launch Eclipse and the workspace is not fully synchronized on other device, it can simply crash the workspace.

Once you know where you want to store your workspace, you will see the Eclipse IDE welcome screen, as shown in Figure 1-9. You can of course start using it immediately, except for ABAP development. You need to install the ABAP Development Tools plugin in order to start your journey with ABAP in Eclipse.

11

Figure 1-9. *Eclipse IDE welcome screen*

Installing ADT

Now that Eclipse is installed, it's time to install the ABAP Development Tools provided by SAP. All the information about prerequisites and Eclipse version support can be found at `https://tools.hana.ondemand.com/`. In order to use the tools properly, you also need to have SAP GUI installed if you work with on-premise SAP installations and Microsoft VC Runtime, which I assume is already installed on your PC as this is common prerequisite.

As the next step, go to the Eclipse menu bar and choose Help ➤ Install New Software. Enter the URL `https://tools.hana.ondemand.com/latest` into the Work With input field and press Enter.

You should now see which plugins versions are available for installation, as shown in Figure 1-10. You can select all of them by selecting ABAP Development Tools or you can just simply select ABAP Core Development Tools if you are interested only in the pure ABAP tools.

Tip My experience shows that in the end you will use all the available plugins, so it is better to install them all at this stage.

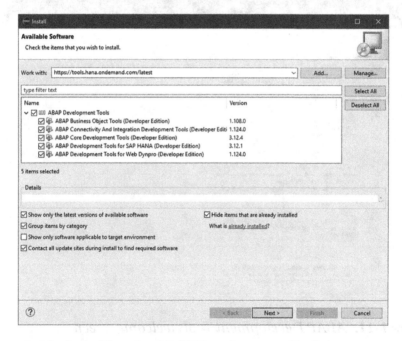

Figure 1-10. Installing the ABAP Development Tools

When you are ready with the selection, simply click Next and follow the instructions on the screen. You will be asked to accept the license agreements and to approve trusting the Eclipse Organization's certificates. After confirming all of this, the installation will start.

When all of the installation packages are downloaded and installed, Eclipse will ask you to restart the application so the new components can be loaded and used. After restart, you should get the new welcome screen shown in Figure 1-11. The links shown on the screen will lead you to the ADT help, but I recommend you close this overview and start using Eclipse directly.

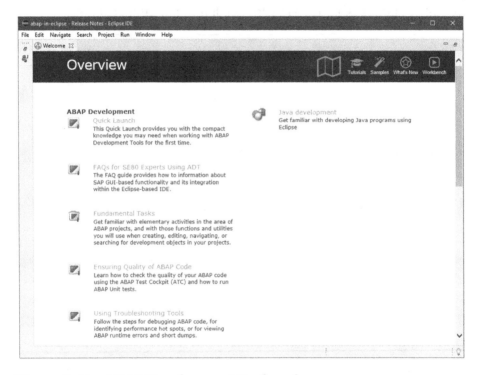

Figure 1-11. *ABAP Development Tools welcome screen*

After closing the overview tab, you will be moved to the default Eclipse *perspective* (set of views), where you will see some standard views like Package Explorer, Problems, and Outline. Additionally, you should see the Release Notes for ADT on your main screen. For the moment you can close this view, as I will explain the basics of ADT usage.

> **Note**   Release Notes appear each time the ADT is updated to the
> next minor release. You can also always come back to them using
> the Help ➤ Help Contents menu option and selecting SAP – ABAP
> Development Tools Release Notes.

Creating an ABAP Project

Creating a project is the first step you need to take in order work with
ABAP in Eclipse. A project, in the case of ABAP, is the representation of
the connection to your SAP system with a fixed client, user, and language.
There are two ABAP project types: ABAP project and ABAP Cloud project
(see Figure 1-12). As you probably assumed, ABAP project is dedicated to
on-premise systems and ABAP Cloud project is used with the SAP Cloud
Platform ABAP Environment. The next sections explain how to create each
kind of ABAP project.

Figure 1-12. *ABAP project types*

ABAP On-Premise Project

When you worked with SAP Logon Pad, you had a list of SAP systems (or connections), from which you had to choose the one you wanted to log on to. Each time you logged in to the system, you could choose the user, client, and language of the logon. When you're working with Eclipse, this list will be useful only when you're creating a new project.

Go to File ➤ New ➤ Project, expand the ABAP folder, and select ABAP Project. Click Next. You will see the connections list that you are familiar with from the SAP Logon Pad, as shown in Figure 1-13. You can use the existing connection by double-clicking the row with the chosen system, or you can provide the connection details manually.

Figure 1-13. *SAP system connections*

In the corporate world, you will probably not be able to use custom connections, as the network is usually secured by external SAP systems. That is why I focus on creating an ABAP project from existing Logon Pad entries. However, if you would like to use custom connections here, you need the same information as when creating a SAP Logon Pad entry:

- System ID

- Connection Type

- Message Server

- Group

- Message Server Port

- Application Server

- Instance Number

- SAP Router String

- SNC settings

The next steps are the same for existing SAP Logon Pad connections as for custom connections. You need to provide the client, user, password, and language for the project (see Figure 1-14). Once you create a project, you cannot change the client, user, or language, so be sure you choose wisely. The password will not be stored anywhere and you will have to enter it each time you run Eclipse.

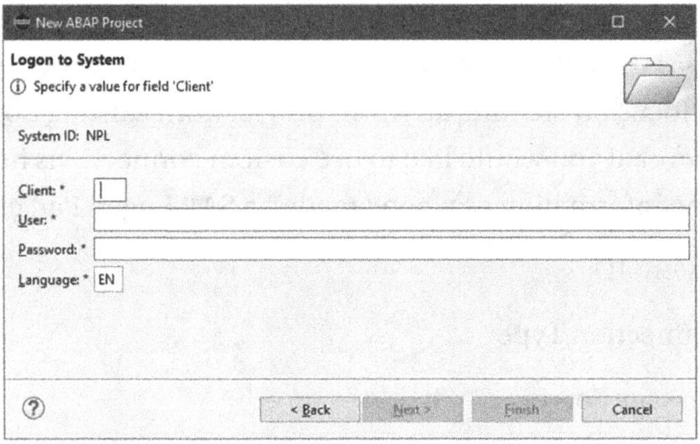

Figure 1-14. Creating an ABAP project: logon to system

I am using the Developer Edition of SAP NetWeaver, so I chose the client 001, user Developer, and English as the logon language. After providing the correct credentials, click the Next button instead of the default Finish. This will give you the opportunity to adjust the project name and to add this new project to your working sets.

The default project name proposed by ADT, as shown in Figure 1-15, is a concatenation of system ID, client, user, and language. Depending on the setup of the system you want to connect to, it may be reasonable to keep this as the default name or to remove some parts of it. For example, when you use only one client, there is no point in including the client name. The same for language and user. Personally I use as short a name as possible, for example NPL. However, if you have multiple client systems, you should add those to the project name.

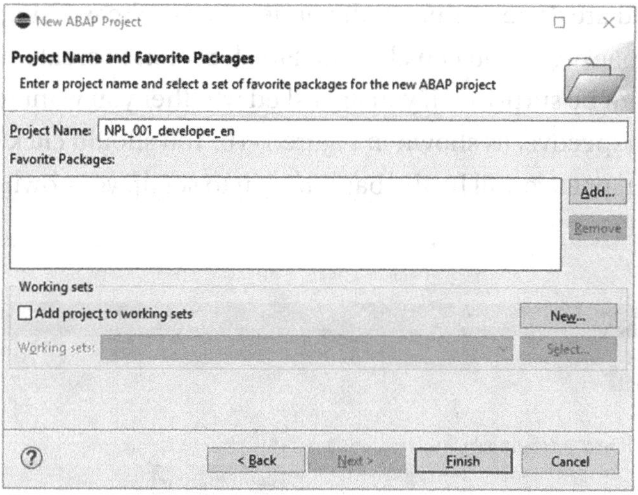

Figure 1-15. *Creating an ABAP project: project name*

The working set (a group of Eclipse projects) can be specified here or at a later stage. You can either create a new one or select one from the previously created list. They are very helpful when you work on one Eclipse workspace with several ABAP projects. For example, say you work for a consulting company and have access to many customer systems. You can use working sets to group projects by customer. The other common example is to group projects by type, such as development, integration, or production. I use working sets to split ABAP projects from Java projects.

One additional thing you can do here before clicking the Finish button is add some of the packages you will work with to the Favorite Packages. To do so, just click the Add... button. In the popup that appears, enter part of the name of the package. Select one or more packages that you want to have as your favorites.

Tip   When entering the name of the package, you can use asterisk (*) for pattern searches, for example *Z*_AC* or just *Z**.

When you are done setting up the project name, the working sets, and any favorite packages, you can click the Finish button to create your ABAP project. Do not be surprised if you are asked whether you want to open the ABAP perspective, as shown in Figure 1-16. You should click Open, as the ABAP perspective will be the base for you to set up your own working environment.

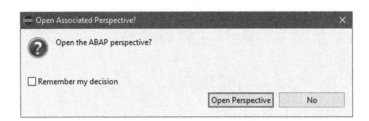

Figure 1-16. *Perspective switch for ABAP projects*

Once you're done, you will be able to finally see your newly created ABAP project in the Project Explorer view, which should be visible on the top-left side of Eclipse. As you can see in Figure 1-17, I created project named NPL. In the brackets you can see all details: system ID, client, user, and language. When you expand the project folder, you will be able to see the Favorite Packages and System Library folders. In the following sections, I will cover more details about Project Explorer and the other views.

Figure 1-17. *Project Explorer view and Favorite Packages*

ABAP Cloud Project

The second type of ABAP project is the ABAP Cloud project. You will use this kind of project when working with the SAP Cloud Platform ABAP environment. You can't use SAP GUI with this kind of ABAP environment, so you are forced to use Eclipse in order to do development there. Additionally, you will not be able to use all of the classes, types, and other development objects, that you have used in the on-premise ABAP environment, but Eclipse will help you manage these differences.

First, let's see how to create the ABAP Cloud project in your Eclipse workspace. You need to go to File ➤ New ➤ Project and choose ABAP Cloud project from the ABAP folder. You will get a popup screen to choose how you want to establish the connection to the SAP Cloud Platform Environment. You can choose from one of two options, as shown in Figure 1-18:

- SAP Cloud Platform Cloud Foundry Environment

- Service Key

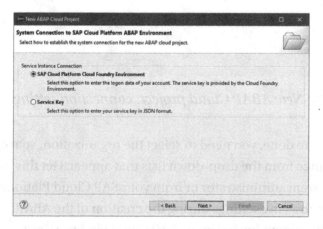

Figure 1-18. *New ABAP Cloud project: selecting a way to connect to your system*

Log On Using SAP Cloud Platform Cloud Foundry Environment

The first option allows you to set up the connection by passing and/or selecting all needed connection information, starting from region, email address, and password you use for SAP Cloud Platform. You should get the region information from your system administrator if you are connecting to your company system. If you want to connect to your trial system, the region information is in your SAP Cloud Platform Trial account, in the Subaccounts section. Once you have it, select the proper region from the drop-down list and add your credentials, as shown in Figure 1-19.

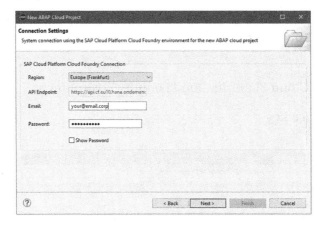

Figure 1-19. *New ABAP Cloud project: connection settings*

Once you're done, you need to select the organization, space, and service instance from the drop-down lists that appear. Get this information from your system administrator or from your SAP Cloud Platform account. Figure 1-20 shows my settings during the creation of the ABAP Cloud project for the system hosted in the SAP Cloud Platform Trial.

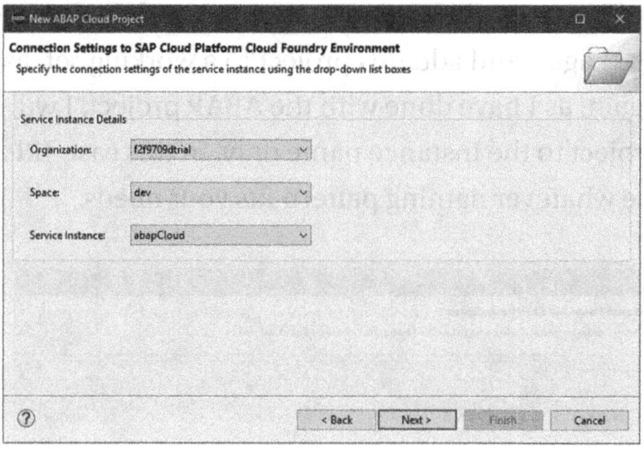

Figure 1-20. *New ABAP Cloud project: service instance details*

The next steps are very similar to the on-premise ABAP projects. First, you see a window where you confirm all the connection settings. This is also where you can adjust the language settings, as you can see in Figure 1-21. I encourage you to click Next instead of Finish.

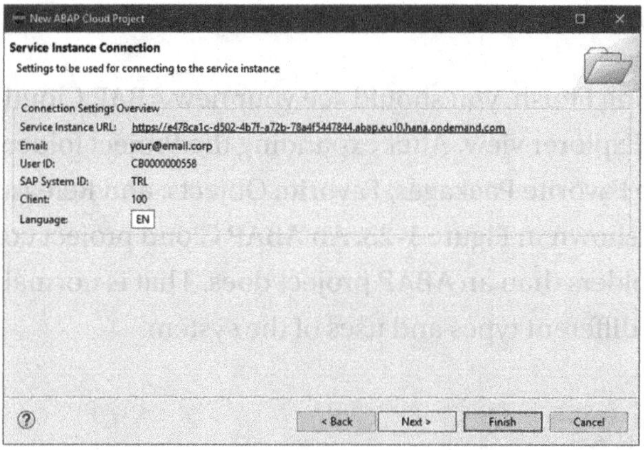

Figure 1-21. *New ABAP Cloud project: settings overview and language selection*

If you click Next, you will be able to change the default project name, add Favorite Packages, and add this project to a working set, as shown in Figure 1-22. Again, as I have done with the ABAP project, I will shorten the name of the project to the instance name only, in this case TRL. However, you can choose whatever naming pattern fits your needs.

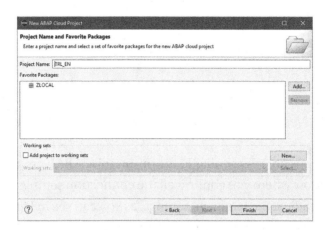

Figure 1-22. *New ABAP Cloud project: project name, working sets, and favorite packages*

After clicking Finish, you should see your new ABAP Cloud project in the Project Explorer view. After expanding the Project folder, you should see the Favorite Packages, Favorite Objects, and Released Objects subfolders, as shown in Figure 1-23. An ABAP Cloud project contains different subfolders than an ABAP project does. That is normal and is caused by the different types and uses of the system.

Figure 1-23. *Project Explorer with an ABAP Cloud project*

Log On Using a Service Key

The second way to create an ABAP Cloud project is to use a service key. A service key can be obtained from your system administrator or from the SAP Cloud Platform if you have access and authorization to do so. When you create a project this way, you need to paste the service key JSON into the text field available from the window, as shown in Figure 1-24. Or you can use Import... button in order to get the JSON file from your hard drive.

Figure 1-24. *New ABAP Cloud project: service key*

When you switch to the next window, you may see two different behaviors of the new project wizard. If you are logged into a SAP Cloud Platform account, you will most likely see the successful authentication message, as shown in Figure 1-25. The window will close itself and you will be redirected to the next window, shown back in Figure 1-21.

If you are not logged onto your SAP Cloud Platform account, you will see a place to put your credentials. You can also choose to log on with a browser. You will then be redirected to your default browser to continue the logon procedure.

Figure 1-25. *New ABAP Cloud project: authentication*

Once you have successfully logged on, you will see the exact the same windows as when logging on using SAP Cloud Platform Cloud Foundry Environment. Mainly, you'll see the Settings Overview (Figure 1-21) and Project Name and Favorite Packages (Figure 1-22).

This way of creating ABAP Cloud projects is easier and faster and gives you less chance of selecting the wrong entries if your company cloud environment contains more than one ABAP instance. It's also a good way to create the ABAP Cloud packages once your company works with the SAP Cloud Platform ABAP Environment.

Perspectives

In the previous sections, when I showed you how to create your first ABAP projects in Eclipse, I mentioned perspectives and views. Now it is time to describe them in a more detailed way. The next sections help you get familiar with the basic perspectives of Eclipse and ABAP Development Tools. But before we do that, take a look at Figure 1-26 to become familiar with the different application parts.

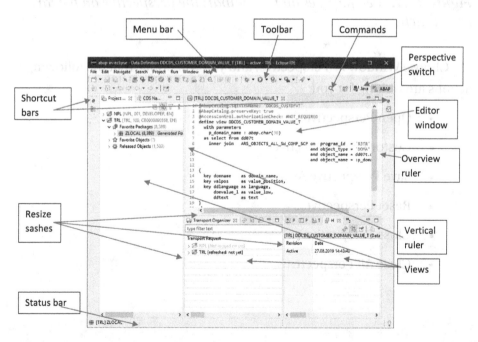

Figure 1-26. *Eclipse layout*

When you launched Eclipse the first time after installation, you saw the default Java perspective. Perspective is a layout of your workspace with adjustable views. Perspective contains one or more views. There are built-in perspectives that can be changed (we will cover them later), or you can create your own perspectives to fit different the scenarios and environments you are working with.

Perspectives can be found in two places in Eclipse, the first is in the top-right corner of the toolbar, as shown in Figure 1-27. The second is by choosing Window ➤ Perspective. If you followed the steps I have described, you should have two perspectives open: Java and ABAP. The current perspective button always looks like it's pressed down, so it should be easy to determine which perspective is active.

Figure 1-27. *Perspectives on the toolbar: the perspective on the far right is active*

Choose Window ➤ Perspective, and you will notice that the following actions are waiting for you:

- Open Perspective

- Customize Perspective...

- Save Perspective As...

- Reset Perspective...

- Close Perspective

- Close All Perspectives

You can access by toolbar the same actions you can choose from the menu bar. You can also determine whether open perspectives should be shown with or without description text, but only from the toolbar. You do this by right-clicking one of the icons of an open perspective and choosing Show Text. The perspective description can be useful when you create perspectives of the same type and with the same icon. For example, you can have separate perspectives for 4K and for FHD resolution displays. It can also be good when beginning work with Eclipse, before you get familiar with all the icons that are used in the IDE. Just look at Figure 1-28. It's clear which perspective you are in and which others are open.

Figure 1-28. *Perspectives with descriptions*

Built-in Perspectives

When you choose Window ➤ Perspective ➤ Open Perspective ➤ Other... or click the Open Perspective button on the toolbar, you will see all existing perspectives prepared by Eclipse and SAP teams. From the ones shown in Figure 1-29, which are available in my installation, I will focus on ABAP-related perspectives: ABAP, ABAP Profiling, Debug, and ABAP Connectivity & Integration.

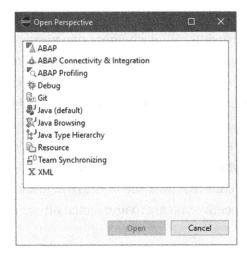

Figure 1-29. *Perspectives available after a fresh installation*

These perspectives were prepared by SAP in order to provide users with a smooth start with the Eclipse IDE and to show that you can switch perspectives during different tasks.

ABAP

This is the base perspective that was opened directly after the creation of the first ABAP project. This is usually the base perspective to start with ADT. It contains 11 views:

- Editor

- Project Explorer

- CDS Navigator

- Outline

- Problems

- Properties

- Templates

- Bookmarks

- Feed Reader

- Transport Organizer

- Feature Explorer

This perspective is suitable for standard ABAP development, especially on the small resolution screens (up to full HD). During the work, you will notice that some additional views will be opened, such as Search, History, ATC Problems, or ABAP Unit, so be prepared for this adjustment.

ABAP Profiling

One of the most common tasks of a developer is optimizing the performance of development objects. This perspective is prepared to focus on that task and the views needed for it. It contains four views:

- Editor

- ABAP Traces

- ABAP Trace Requests

- Properties

Don't be fooled by the small number of views in this perspective, they are enough for doing traces and checks. Once you find the place that needs fixing, you will switch back to the ABAP perspective in order to adjust the code.

Debug

Debugging code sometimes takes more than 50% of the total work time, especially if you do not use Test Driven Development (TDD). If you are maintaining old and legacy code, the percentage can be even higher. That is why a correct debugging environment is so important for developers. Many developers find debugging ABAP code in Eclipse very trying, especially casual Eclipse users.

I am one of its supporters, although I also was not a big fan of it in the beginning. It deserves at least a few days try before making any decision about future usage.

This perspective contains the following views:

- Debug

- Project Explorer

- Console

- Problems

- Debug Shell

- ABAP Internal Table (Debugger)

- Variables

- Breakpoints

- Expressions

- Editor

When you set up your first breakpoint in ADT and run your code, you will be asked to switch the perspective to Debug, as shown in Figure 1-30. If you work with screen resolution up to FHD, I recommend you allow switching the perspective and select the Remember My Decision checkbox. This will ensure that each time a breakpoint is met, the perspective is switched automatically. It is quite convenient, although unfortunately, after finishing the debugging process, the perspective does not switch back to the original perspective automatically. You need to switch it back manually.

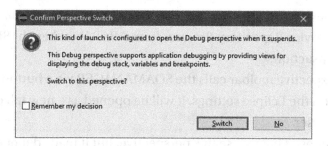

Figure 1-30. *Debug perspective switch*

When you work at higher resolutions, like 2K or 4K, you can disagree and add the missing debugging views from your ABAP perspective. This process is explained later in this chapter.

Tip   When you change your mind and want to adapt the behavior for the Debug perspective, you have to close Eclipse and navigate to your workspace folder to manually change the configuration in the preferences files.

Open the `org.eclipse.debug.ui.prefs` file, which can be found at `.metadata\.plugins\org.eclipse.core.runtime\.settings\` in any text editor (for example, Notepad++). You will find the following setting: `org.eclipse.debug.ui.switch_perspective_on_suspend=xxx`

You can adapt the setting using following values: `always`, `ask`, or `never`.

ABAP Connectivity and Integration

For Process Integration and Orchestration, as well as for web service developers, this perspective may bring some joy, especially if they worked on these topics inside SAP GUI. Among the other views, it contains the

Enterprise Service Browser and the Service Registry, which replace the Enterprise Service Repository Browser from ABAP Workbench (SE80) or SPROXY transaction.

The perspective toolbar calls the SOAMANAGER via a button and depending on the Eclipse settings, it will be opened as a new tab or in selected browser.

To be honest, I barely use this perspective, but it really depends on what your main tasks at work are.

Here is the full list of views contained in this perspective:

- Editor

- Project Explorer

- Enterprise Service Browser

- Service Registry

- Properties

- Transport Organizer

- Problems

- Outline

Preparing Your Own Perspectives

You might want to come back to this part of the book, when you are familiar with all of the Eclipse and ADT features. However, it is good to know now what can be customized in a perspective when you will be discovering all the functionalities, so you can build a plan in your head about the things you can adjust according to your needs or preferences.

Caution   A lot of changes in Eclipse are stored in workspace preference files when the application is closed. So if your instance freezes and you close it by killing the OS process, your changes in the perspective will probably be lost.

Save As

You can customize existing perspectives or create new ones by choosing the Window ➤ Perspective ➤ Save Perspective As... function. It will create a copy of the currently opened perspective with your own customized name.

The icon of the perspective will be copied as well from the existing one, so in case you do not feel comfortable changing the icon manually in the preferences file (it will be described later), make sure that you use the Show Text function to more easily switch perspectives.

When you use the Save Perspective As... function, your newly created perspective will be directly opened and you can start customizing it right away.

Removing Unnecessary Views

You may see it directly or after a while, that some of the views are not needed in your perspective. The easiest way to get rid of views is to close them using the close button on the tab with the view name. The view will be closed and it will not appear until you or a plugin opens it again.

You can of course close multiple views at once if the views belong to the same view area. Just right-click the tab with the view name and choose one of these options:

- Close Others

- Close Tabs to the Left

- Close Tabs to the Right

You can determine if the views belong to the same area simply by the alignment of the view names. When they are in the same area, the tabs appear one after another.

If you accidentally close one of the views that you already customized, don't worry about lost changes. When you open it again, its position and size will be restored.

Resize

First of all, be aware that you can change the position and size of most views. With some perspectives and views, the developer makes them non-movable and non-resizable, or they might have a minimum size set, so you cannot make them smaller. But in most cases, you can adapt them freely. The changes in view size will be saved separately for each perspective.

To change a view size, simply click one of the sashes that separates the views on the top, down, left, or right and pull it in the direction you want.

Minimize and Restore

You can also minimize the whole view area, and then it will be shown on the shortcut bar on the left or right side. This is useful when you want to hide some views for a short while, but you still want to have them in your perspective. Each view of the area will be represented by separate icons on the shortcut bar. You will be able to click the view's icon on the shortcut bar to use it, but until the whole area is restored, it will remain minimized.

In order to restore the view area to its place, simply click the Restore button visible above the views icons. When the area is restored, it will return to its previous position and size.

Maximize and Restore

When you can minimize, usually you also can maximize. This is the case in Eclipse as well. Why do I mention this in a book? Well, when you start to use it, you will notice that sometimes when all the views are open, you do cannot see the editor or any other view properly. You can then maximize the view in two different ways, by double-clicking the view tab name or by using the maximize button.

My experience tells me that you will use only the first way, which is by double-clicking the view name. I know it because it is always faster to navigate and to see the view tab instead of the maximize button. Additionally, when you double-click the view name while it is maximized, its state will be restored to the previous one. In this case, you can use the same function to maximize and to restore the size of the window. Of course, you can still use the Restore button to return to the previous view size.

Detach

You could see so far that all the views are available on a single screen and that, when you were resizing one of the view areas, the others were also resized. But you can also unlink (or detach) a view from the main layout screen.

To do so, right-click the view name and choose the Detach option. The view is shown on top of the views that are still attached to the main screen. You can manipulate the size and the placement of the view, as if it were a separate application. For example, you can move it to other screen. This view will be active on the screen only when the main Eclipse screen is also active; otherwise, it will be hidden.

You can also click the selected view and drag it over the Eclipse main screen. The behavior will be the same as when you choose the Detach option, but the view will land directly in the right place.

Tip   My advice is to detach only less important views, especially in a separate screen. When you focus your cursor on a MS Word file, for example, your detached view can disappear from focus until you move your cursor back to the Eclipse screen.

Adding a New View

Normally, you have to add new views to your perspectives manually. To do this, you need to choose Window ➤ Show View ➤ Other... You can also call a command or function that will automatically open a view related to that particular command or function.

When you choose Window ➤ Show View from the menu bar, you will see some views that can be opened. These views are preconfigured by perspectives to be visible there. You can of course use this shortcut if the view that you want to open is available there.

Customizing

The previously described possibilities are usually standard in every IDE, and customizing the toolbar, menu bar, shortcuts, and action sets is not always allowed. You can customize perspectives in Eclipse by choosing Window ➤ Perspective ➤ Customize Perspective... or by right-clicking the currently opened perspective icon and choosing the Customize... action.

The popup that opens will contain the following tabs:

- Toolbar visibility

- Menu visibility

- Action set availability

- Shortcuts

Toolbar Visibility

As you can figure out from the tab name, this tab allows you to modify the visibility of the toolbar buttons. Normally the perspectives are prepared in a way so that you have only the needed buttons on the toolbar. However, when you are creating perspectives that have limited purposes and you are working mostly with the mouse, you may want to disable some of these buttons.

As you can see in Figure 1-31, the buttons are grouped by function. The ones that are possible to hide or to display are highlighted. You can simply select one button or the whole group and decide if you want to have them in your perspective or not.

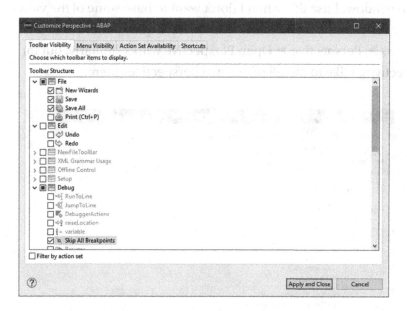

Figure 1-31. *Customizing perspectives: toolbar visibility*

Menu Visibility

You have the same options from the menu bar as you do from the toolbar. You can customize the appearance of the menu bar entries or whole groups. Just expand every available tree node to check the available functions.

My favorites here are the File ➤ New, Windows ➤ Show View and Windows ➤ Perspective ➤ Open Perspective options. In File ➤ New, which you can see in Figure 1-32, you can find all object types that can be created by your Eclipse IDE, so you can easily add object types that you use often. From Windows ➤ Show View, you can decide which views are available on the menu bar directly, without having to open a separate popup window. I use this when I don't want to have some of the views permanently on the screen, but I want to have quick access to them. Windows ➤ Perspective ➤ Open Perspective works similarly, but for perspectives. I like to put all of my own perspectives there.

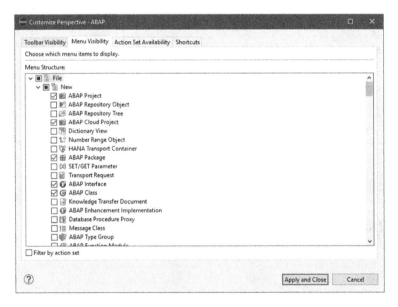

Figure 1-32. *Customizing perspectives: menu visibility*

Action Set Availability

When you were looking at the toolbar or menu visibility settings, you might have noticed that some of them were disabled. Some of these menu and toolbar entries need to be enabled on the Action Set Availability tab.

You will not find all the available toolbar and menu entries, but some of them might be helpful, especially if you work not only with ABAP but with other programming languages and you want to use one perspective for them.

You can see in Figure 1-33, that when you select one of the action sets, you will see directly which menu bar entries and which toolbar buttons will be available when you enable it for the current perspective. Of course, after you enable the action sets, you can come back to the Toolbar and Menu Visibility tabs and remove the unnecessary ones.

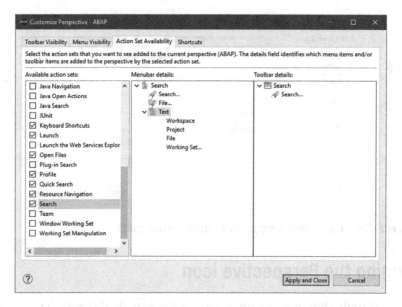

Figure 1-33. *Customizing perspectives: action set availability*

41

Shortcuts

This tab repeats what was shown in the Toolbar Visibility tab using the File ➤ New, Windows ➤ Show View and Windows ➤ Perspective ➤ Open Perspective paths, but in a bit different way. Here, you can also see the shortcut categories.

This small change, as seen in Figure 1-34, makes it easier to select the objects or views linked to a specific category, such as authorizations, CDS, or WebDynpro. It might also give you additional ideas for how you can split the perspectives for different object types.

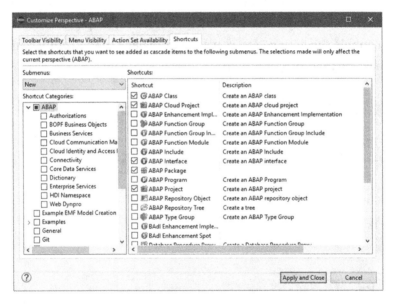

Figure 1-34. *Customizing preferences: shortcuts*

Changing the Perspective Icon

Once you create one or more own perspectives using the Save As... function, you will probably think about customizing the icons so they aren't so long. When configuring the perspective, you were not able to customize the icon, but you can do so in a different way.

I mentioned earlier about manipulating the Eclipse configuration directly in the config files. You need to do the same this here, but it will be trickier, as you need to know the URI of the icon that works with your Eclipse.

Selecting the Icon

Not knowing what is possible, one might assume that we could just create our own icon and then, in the configuration, pass the local path to this icon. But it is not that easy, because if you haven't created your own plugin that is already installed in your IDE, you'll have no idea about the possible path for icons. They are built inside the plugin's packages.

In order to get the proper icon URI, I suggest you install Eclipse Plug-in Development Environment, which contains a view called Plug-in Image Browser. To do so, you need to choose Help ➤ Install New Software... You don't need to remember the path to the installation. Just select the Eclipse Project Updates from the drop-down menu, expand the Eclipse Plugin Development Tools, and select Eclipse Plug-in Development Environment. Figure 1-35 shows how this looks for version 2020-09.

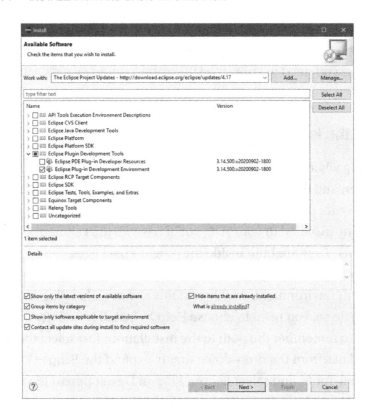

Figure 1-35. *Installing the Eclipse Plug-in Development Environment*

After installation the plugins and restarting Eclipse, you need to open the Plug-in Image Browser view, which can be found in the views inside the Plug-in Development folder. Once you're done, you will be able to see all the icons that are available in your Eclipse installation from this view. That means all the icons that are included in plugins. It doesn't matter if they were included in the standard installation of Eclipse or not. Figure 1-36 shows many icons from different Eclipse plugins. When you select an icon by clicking it, you will find a path in the Reference field, which can be found at the bottom of the view. That path can to be used to change the perspective icon.

When you find a suitable icon, copy the value from the Reference field and close the Eclipse instance.

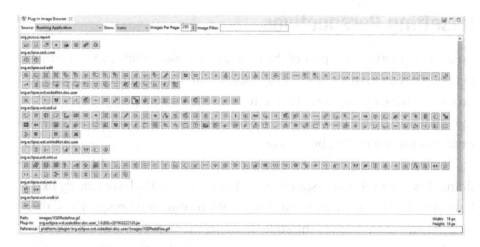

Figure 1-36. *Plug-in Image Browser view*

Changing Icons

Now it's time to open the workbench configuration file and update the icon of your own perspective. You already have the icon reference in your clipboard, so it is time to open the configuration file.

This time, go to your workspace path and open the .metadata\.plugins\ folder. Then locate the org.eclipse.e4.workbench file and open the workbench.xmi file in any of the text editors available on your OS. Use the search function to find these tags:

<children xsi:type="advanced:Perspective"

and

<snippets xsi:type="advanced:Perspective"

Each tag will contain an element called iconURI. Now paste the reference to the icon instead of its current value in both places.

Once you're done, start your Eclipse, and you will notice that the selected icon is displayed for your own perspective.

Resetting Perspectives

Errors and mistakes are part of the human condition, that is why you might need to start a perspective's configuration from the beginning. In order to do so, you have two options. One is to reset the current perspective, and the other is to delete and recreate it from scratch. You might think this is exactly the same action, but it is not.

Resetting a perspective takes it back to its initial status, which if you are doing this to a built-in perspective, makes it look and behave exactly like it would a few seconds after installation. With your own perspectives, this option takes them back to the state of saving them as your own. It means nothing more than if you make some changes to the standard perspective, let it be ABAP, then save it as the ABAP MINE perspective and continue to make changes inside this new perspective. In that case, the reset function would restore the version of the perspective that was used when saving the ABAP perspective to ABAP MINE.

To reset the perspective again, you can choose several paths. One is to choose Window ➤ Perspective ➤ Reset Perspective.... The second is to right-click the currently opened perspective from the perspective switch toolbar and choose Reset.

Deleting Perspectives

One last thing you can do with your own perspective is delete it, perhaps when you don't need it anymore, or you made it by mistake. There is only one way to do this from Eclipse. You need to choose Window ➤ Preferences, then choose General ➤ Perspectives. You will see all the perspectives there, but you will be able to delete only the ones you created.

To delete one, select one of your perspectives. The Delete button will be enabled, as shown in Figure 1-37, where I have selected Perspective to Delete.

Figure 1-37. *Perspectives preferences*

Summary

After reading this chapter, you should be able to:

- Install the Eclipse IDE and the Java Runtime Environment

- Install the ABAP Development Tools plugin

- Create your first ABAP project

- Understand, configure, and create own Eclipse perspectives

In the next chapter, you will get detailed information about the available views—either Eclipse standard ones or the one installed together with the ADT plugin.

CHAPTER 2

Views

Views are the single tabs (windows) that you can see inside your Eclipse perspective. For example, when you created your first project, you saw the project in the Project Explorer view. This view has a tree of projects and objects. There are many different types of views, such as form base views, table views, browser views, etc.

There are built-in standard Eclipse views and many others that you installed with the ABAP Development Tools. This chapter covers the most important views for ABAP developers. When I describe the standard views, I describe how they work with ABAP. This does not mean they will act the same way in other programming languages. The behavior of the view depends on the Editor view, which is different for each language supported by Eclipse.

Project Explorer

When Chapter 1 described the creation of the ABAP and ABAP Cloud projects, the Project Explorer view was introduced. This is the base view that will probably stay open in most of your perspectives, as it allows you to navigate through all the objects using the package or object type folders.

As you might remember, each ABAP project is a virtual representation of the SAP instance, with a fixed client, user, and language. There are on-premise ABAP projects and ABAP Cloud projects. As you can see in Figure 2-1, these project types display different content, as the systems are also different.

© Lukasz Pegiel 2021
Ł. Pęgiel, *ABAP in Eclipse*, https://doi.org/10.1007/978-1-4842-6963-3_2

Figure 2-1. *Project Explorer with ABAP and ABAP Cloud projects*

ABAP Repository Trees

When you expand the project on a system that's based on SAP NetWeaver release lower than 7.51 and/or without the SAP HANA database, you will see the following repositories: Favorite Packages and System Library. Favorite Packages can be added during the creation of the project as well as by using the context menu of the Project Explorer. The System Library contains all the packages of the current SAP instance. Each package in this view can contain zero or several subpackages and folders assigned to the current package objects. Its hierarchy is very similar to the SE80 one, which you can see in Figure 2-2. As in SE80, using the context menu on a folder, package, or object will allow you to create or delete new objects, activate them, or change the package assignment.

Figure 2-2. *Comparing E80 and Project Explorer*

The default Favorite Packages folder contains the $TMP package with the user's local objects linked to the project. By using the context menu (right-click the Favorite Packages node), you can add other packages to your favorites as well as add other users' local objects to your favorites. To do so, use the context menu, then choose Add a Package... or Add Local objects of User....

The Add a Package action will open a separate popup window, which you saw when creating the project. It will allow you to search for the packages by name.

Add Local Objects of User will also open a separate popup window, but only to select the user whose local objects you want to see in your favorites.

The Favorite Packages folder is extremely helpful if you work on a larger development, and if you use one or several packages only for the purpose of this project. When you have huge packages in your company that contain development objects for one big module, for example, it's no longer useful to use the Favorite Packages folder. Too many unconnected objects make it difficult to navigate through.

Systems that already work on SAP NetWeaver 7.51 or higher and with the SAP HANA database have a different structure. By default, they have Favorite Packages, Favorite Objects, and Released Objects repositories. Of course, the Favorite Packages node works exactly the same as before.

Favorites Objects works very similarly to Favorite Packages, but it contains only the single repository objects, not the packages. This means you can add function groups, function modules, classes, programs, and

51

other repository objects there, but not packages. You can add objects to the favorites by selecting them from the Project Explorer, either from Favorite Packages, Released Objects, or any other ABAP Repository Tree.

Released Objects contains all released objects in the cloud environment. These objects can be released by SAP or by anyone else from your company.

There are some more repositories that you could use. To use one, right-click the project and choose New ➤ ABAP Repository Tree.. Or, if that option is not available in your installation, choose New ➤ Other ➤ ABAP ➤ ABAP Repository Tree. A new window will appear with all the possible repository templates for the current system, as you can see in Figure 2-3.

Figure 2-3. *New ABAP Repository Tree*

Those repositories are much more powerful than the ones in older SAP releases, as they allow additional filtering by type and name. If you choose, for example, the My Objects template, you will get the property filter set to your username. As you can see in Figure 2-4, the tree structure can be defined in here. It is preconfigured for the My Objects template that the structure will be Package ➤ Object Type. But if you want to, you can remove one or both and choose any other tree level from the available levels found on the left side of the window.

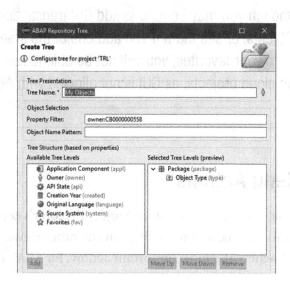

Figure 2-4. *My Object template for the ABAP Repository Tree*

All the available property filters can be found in Figure 2-5. It can be extremely helpful to combine filters together. For example, you can filter the repository by package, owner (creator), and type (like class or CDS).

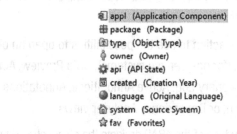

Figure 2-5. *Property filters of the ABAP Repository Tree*

The property filter, together with the naming filter, allows you to create useful repositories for your daily work.

Caution   Although you may be able to add GUI transactions to the Favorite Objects, or see them if you add one of the standard SAP packages to your favorites, you will not be able to use the GUI transactions in cloud projects, as GUI is not allowed with ABAP Cloud projects.

Context Menu Actions

There are many actions you can do from Project Explorer's context menu. Some of them are obvious, and some of them call other views. Let's take a look at Table 2-1, where the most important actions for ABAP developers are described.

Table 2-1. *Project Explorer Context Menu Actions*

Action	Usage
Duplicate	This action can be triggered not only on ABAP repository objects, but also on the projects themselves. It will copy the chosen object under the new name.
Open With	Expand this action to see the possibilities to open an object in SAP GUI (for on-premise systems), Data Preview, Activation Graph, Dictionary Log, Active Annotations, Annotations Propagation, or Dependency Analyzer views.
Open in Project	Choose in which of the ABAP projects the object should be opened.

(continued)

Table 2-1. (*continued*)

Action	Usage
Open ABAP Type Hierarchy	Open the selected object in ABAP Type Hierarchy view.
Coverage As	When you expand this action and you see ABAP Unit Tests, this means you can run a unit test for the selected objects and open the ABAP Unit & ABAP Coverage views at the same time.
Run As	You will use this action to run the object in the SAP GUI (ABAP Application), call ABAP Test Cockpit with default or selected check variant, and run ABAP Unit Test or ABAP Application in Console (for cloud development).
Get Where-Used List	With this function, a use of the selected object will be shown in the Search view.
Share Link	You can share the object using HTTP Link or ADT Link. HTTP Link will display the object in any browser for display only purposes, and ADT Link will be opened by Eclipse.
Profile As	Activate the profiling of the object using one of the three methods—ABAP Application for GUI or Console and as ABAP Unit.
Change Package Assignment	A very useful function to switch the package of the objects.
Change API State	Change the API state for example to released.
Compare With	You can compare the selected object with the previous revisions (versions) or between systems. The compared source code will be displayed in a separate view.
Export	Export the ABAP Doc documentation into HTML files. It is very similar to JAVA Doc. Just run the action, expand the ABAP folder, and select ABAP Doc.

(*continued*)

Table 2-1. (*continued*)

Action	Usage
Expand Folder By	Available only on the releases in which you can create your own ABAP Repository Trees. Allows you to switch the type of expansion from current one to owner, object type, API state, and some more.
Configure Tree	Available only on the releases in which you can create your own ABAP Repository Trees. Gives you the possibility to customize the current tree.
SQL Trace	You can activate or deactivate SQL Trace from here.
SQL Console	You can launch SQL Console view for the current project, which allows you to test SQL statements outside of ABAP objects.
Properties	Run the project specific configuration.

Toolbar and View Menu

If you thought we were done covering Project Explorer, then you were wrong. There are still a few important functionalities that you can run from the toolbar and the View menu.

The toolbar can always be found close to the view tab. If there is enough space, it is visible on the right side of the view tab name; in other cases, it can be found below the tab. This behavior is the same for any view.

Besides the toolbar it is common to have the View menu, which is accessible from the toolbar. You can see the toolbar and the View menu in Figure 2-6.

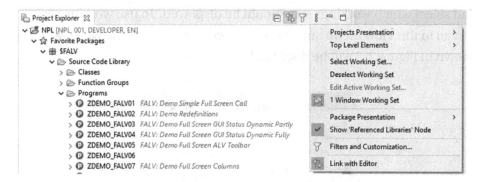

Figure 2-6. *Project Explorer toolbar and View menu*

In the Project Explorer view, the toolbar consists of Collapse All, Link with Editor, Filter, View menu, and the Minimize and Maximize buttons.

Collapse All is helpful when you have opened several projects during the day and you want to collapse every node. When this is used, all tree nodes will be collapsed.

The Link with Editor function is quite common in Eclipse views. The behavior can be a bit different between the views, but basically the content of the view will change to show information linked to the active editor. In the Project Explorer, the aim of the linking is to navigate through the whole structure of the project to the currently opened object.

It may not be clear to you yet that you can open objects in several ways, not only from the Project Explorer. That is why, when you open the object using other ways, the Project Explorer can show you the place where the object is placed. Depending on whether I am working from home using VPN or at office, I switch this option on or off, as it can be very frustrating on a slow network connection.

The filter is not useful in ABAP projects, but it can be with other ones. Here you can set up what kind of content you want to see in your project.

The View menu, in the case of ABAP Projects, could be shortened only to the working sets part and the top-level elements. I mentioned working sets during the creation of the projects. You can group projects in them, and select which workings sets should be displayed. To use working sets, just go to the View menu and choose Select Working Set. The window shown in Figure 2-7 will be displayed.

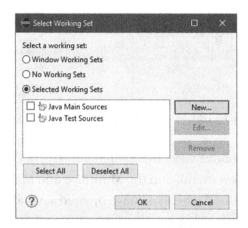

Figure 2-7. *Selecting working sets*

There are no built-in ABAP working sets, so you need to create your own. To do so, just click the New... button and select Resource as the working set type. In the next step you will be able to give it a name and select which projects should be included in it.

In my example, I created two working sets. On-premise, which contains the project NPL, and Cloud, which contains TRL. You can create different working sets, and the split and grouping depends only on you. In order to display your working sets, you need to select the checkbox close to their names from the working sets list.

You may be surprised that nothing has changed in the Project Explorer after you confirm all the steps. In order to display working sets, you need to go to the View menu and choose Top Level Elements ➤ Working Sets. Now your Project Explorer view should look similar to the one shown in Figure 2-8.

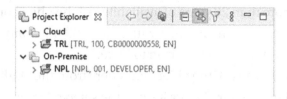

Figure 2-8. *Project Explorer with working sets*

Outline

This view is available in the ABAP perspective from the beginning and is one of the most commonly used (Figure 2-9). It helps you navigate through the code of the currently opened objects. It allows you to see all the members of the currently opened object.

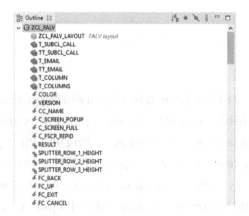

Figure 2-9. *Outline view*

This may be strange, but you should know it from the start: you will not see the components of the `includes` here if your editor currently handles the main object (program). But of course you will see the list of the `includes` and you will be able to navigate to them. You will see types, variables, local classes, events, friends, forms, and methods, but only for the current object. This might seem a disadvantage, but in most cases, it is not. After more than 20 years of availability of the object orientation in ABAP, I hope that you are familiar with it and will miss only inherited members on this view, in comparison to SE80.

When you select any of the object members from the Outline view, the code editor will navigate to the position of the selected member.

You can choose to sort the displayed members. By default they are sorted by type, visibility, and placement in the code, but you can use the Sort button on the toolbar to sort them by type and name only.

You can also show only public members of the object using the Hide Non-Public Members button.

By default, this view is linked to the editor, which means when you switch the editor tab to another object, it will be refreshed and members of the selected object will be displayed. You can unlink it from the View menu.

Problems

This view is also one of the basic. It is helpful during programming, as all messages will be visible here. You will see syntax errors and warnings here, as well as error messages found when activating an object (Figure 2-10).

When you double-click the message, you will be navigated to the problem line. When you right-click and select Problem Description, a new view called ABAP Problem Description will open with additional information. Once you fix the problem, it will disappear from the list.

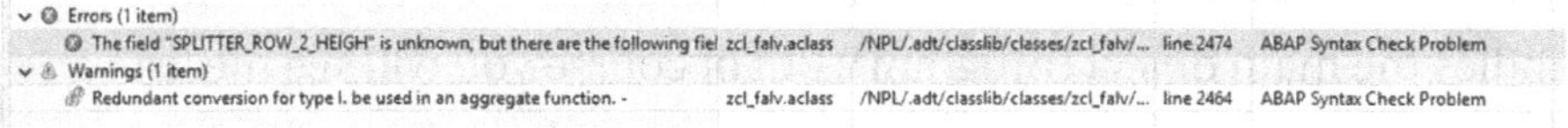

Figure 2-10. *Problems view*

By default, this view shows all the errors of the objects opened in the workspace. You can customize it by clicking the Filters button on the view toolbar or selecting it from the View menu. You can customize the filters, as shown in Figure 2-11, by choosing the scope of the view, setting the severity of the messages, and setting the types of the issues. This can be quite useful when you work with several systems and are mainly in maintenance mode, or when you use Eclipse to create Java or another type of application and you keep all of them in one workspace.

There are four predefined configurations:

- Errors/warnings on project

- Errors/warnings on selection

- Warnings on selection

- All errors on workspace

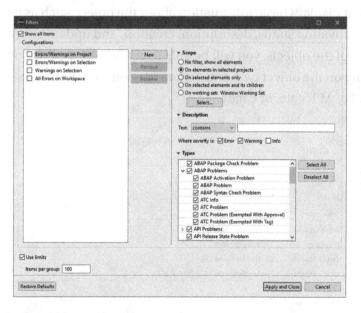

Figure 2-11. *Filters of Problems view*

You can switch between this configuration using the Show action of the View menu, where all configurations will be listed. You can also create your own configurations using the New button on the Filters area.

One last thing you can do, besides sorting and grouping, is create an additional Problems view. You can do this by using the View menu and choosing the New Problems View action. You will be able to give the view a name and set up its configuration, but this additional view will only be available in the current perspective.

Properties

Usually, we do not make many changes to the attributes of ABAP objects, but if you need to change the object description or some specific object type settings, you need to use the Properties view.

Figure 2-12 shows the General tab, which you will always find inside that view. It displays basic information about the object, such as its package, activation status, description, creation, and update information. With most of the objects, you will be able to change the description. Depending on the object type and system version, you may also see tabs like Specific, API State, or Chart.

Figure 2-12. *General tab of properties for the ABAP class*

The Specific tab shows different attributes for different object types. For example, in the case of classes, it will show ABAP Language Version, Fix Point Arithmetic, Shared Memory Enablement, Status, and Message Class. For function modules, you will find Processing Type (Normal, RFC, Update) and Release State here. In the case of programs, it will show the ABAP Language Version, Fix Point Arithmetic, Start Using Variant, Status, Authorization Group, Logical Database, and Selection Screen Number. Unfortunately, the visibility of the attributes depends on the NetWeaver stack.

The API State will be visible in classes, CDS views, and function modules, but only if your system is using a HANA database.

It's the same with the Chart tab: if you're using systems with a HANA database, you can see the graphical representation of the object type differentiation. This tab will be visible if you select a package or any of its subfolders in the Project Explorer.

Templates

When you are reusing parts of your code, but naming objects and variables differently, and you want to speed up the code-writing process, you can use templates. They allow you to prepare code snippets and containers for quick refactoring.

SAP prepared some default templates, but you are free to create some on your own. I bet you will create at least one—a program or class signature that your company or client wants to have at the beginning of each object.

Figure 2-13 shows an example of the template called lcl, which is used to create local classes more quickly. In order to use it, just double-click it and it will appear in the last place of the cursor in the active editor. (There is a quicker way to insert a template directly from the editor, but I will explain that later.)

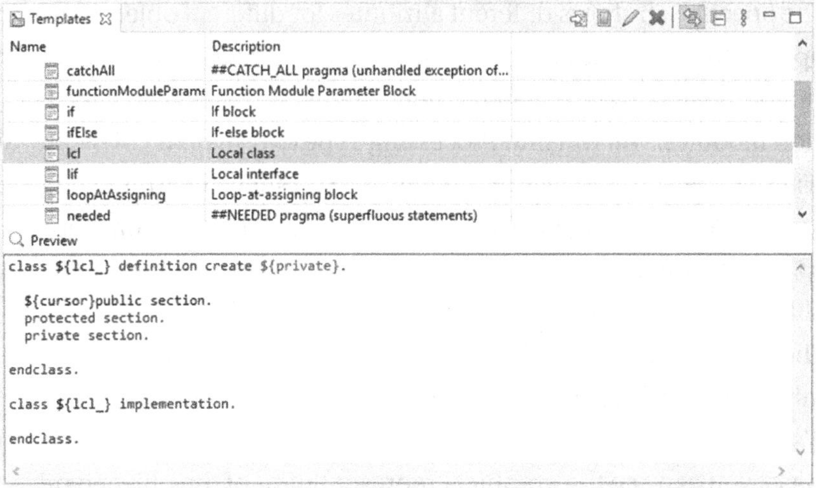

Figure 2-13. *Templates view*

Creating new templates is quite simple; you need to click the Create New Template button on the view toolbar, then fill out the name, description, and pattern. The pattern can be simple, static text, or you can use variables that enter some default values for you or allow you to rename them after inserting the template into your object.

Listing 2-1 shows a very simple template of an object signature, which will add comment lines with the object name, creation date and time, current user, and original system. It allows you to enter a description.

Listing 2-1. Sample Template for Object Signature

```
*************************************************
* ${enclosing_object}
* Created on : ${d:date('YYYY-MM-dd')} ${time}
* Created by : ${user}
* Original system: ${system_id}
*
* Purpose: ${Description}${cursor}
*************************************************
```

This template will give the result shown in Figure 2-14. As you can see, the variables were directly replaced during inserting, the description was highlighted and will be overwritten upon pressing any character on your keyboard. And last but not least, when you press the Enter button, the cursor will move to the end of the description. If you had more than one variable that is not automatic, you can switch between them using the Tab key.

```
1  ***********************************************
2  * ZCL_Z001_MPC_EXT
3  * Created on : 2020-10-19 22:42:20
4  * Created by : DEVELOPER
5  * Original system: NPL
6  *
7  * Purpose: Description
8  ***********************************************
```

Figure 2-14. Template after inserting it into the code

If you want to use your own variables in the template, just give them a name that is not the same as one of the built-in variables (see Table 2-2). In this example, ${Description} was my own variable. In the standard template lcl, it was ${lcl_} and ${private}. Also notice that the variable ${lcl_} appears twice in the standard template. Renaming the variable in one place will likewise rename the other.

Table 2-2. *Possible Eclipse Variables in Templates*

Variable	Description
${date}	Enter the date. When used in short form ${date} it will put it in default system locale, but you can force the format using any of the `java.text.SimpleDateFormat`. For example, `${iso:date('yyyy-MM-dd HH:mm:ss Z')}` will insert the date in the format `2020-10-19 23:12:15 +0200`, `${d:date('EEEE dd MM yyyy', 'en_GB')}` will insert `Monday 19 10 2020`
${time}	Insert the current time.
${year}	Insert the current year.
${user}	Insert the current user name (sy-uname).
${enclosing_ object}	Insert the current object name, for example class or program name.
${enclosing_ package}	Insert the package of the current object.
${system_id}	Insert the system ID (sy-sysid).
${word_selection}	You can also use a selected piece of code as a part of your template. To do so, use `${word_selection}` in the template, and before inserting, select the code that you want to include and insert the template. If you want to have some default text inserted if the selection is not done, use the following syntax `${currentWord:word_selection('"Default text"')}`

(*continued*)

Table 2-2. (*continued*)

Variable	Description
${line_selection}	It works exactly the same as ${word_selection}, but for multiple lines. If you want to use this with a default text value, you need to use the following syntax ${currentLine:line_selection('"Default text"')}
${cursor}	Specify where the cursor will be placed after you leave edit mode of the inserted template.
$$	Insert a $ sign.

Bookmarks

When I was describing the Project Explorer, I mentioned a context menu function called Add Bookmark, which you could use to store the object for later use. They are stored in Bookmarks views, which can be used as a kind of favorites list.

You can add each object from the Project Explorer as a bookmark. They will be added with the name that matches the resource name. When you right-click the bookmark entry and choose Properties, you will be able to change the description. When you double-click the bookmark entry, the object it points to will be opened in the associated editor.

You can also create bookmarks directly from the Editors vertical ruler, by using the context menu. That link will point directly to the selected line of an object. Figure 2-15 shows an example of Bookmarks view with five entries, including links to classes, a table, and a SAP GUI transaction.

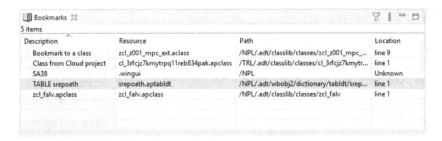

Figure 2-15. *Bookmarks view with a few items*

As it was with the Problems view, you can set up filters to change the scope of the view, or you can create several Bookmarks views, each with a different configuration.

This view is handy with small numbers of entries. However, because there is no search functionality and no way to group entries, it is very difficult to handle many entries in this view.

Search

Using the where-used list is very common task in a developer's life. There are many use cases for it and it is nice to have a good tool for it. You can call it from the Project Explorer view or from the editor by using the Get Where-used List function.

As a result, you receive a tree with all occurrences of the selected object or its part (field of table, attribute of class, etc.). The Tree view is a nice solution here, as it shows the objects in which at least one occurrence of the searched object was found. You can expand the object to see the next level, which can be a method, a function module, an include, or the place of occurrence.

Figure 2-16 displays the results of a search for the ZCL_FALV class. These results are expanded on this example only in the first occurrence. You can see that there are five matches in the three lines of the CHANGE_ SETTING method and there are a few more in other parts of the ZCL_FALV_ COLUMN class.

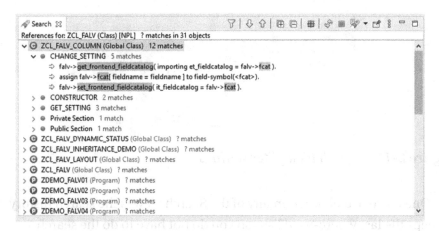

Figure 2-16. *Where-used list of the ZCL_FALV class*

When you double-click the line with the occurrence, the editor will open the place of occurrence. You can also navigate through the results using the up and down arrow buttons from the view toolbar, or using the Ctrl+, and Ctrl-. keyboard shortcuts. Using them will switch to the next/ previous result and directly open the result in the editor.

If you want to scroll down quickly through all of the results, you can use the Expand All button. It will call the SAP backend to get details for all results and will expand the tree to the last level, giving you information about the total number of occurrences.

You can filter the results by package, object type, and creator. To do so, click the Filter button and add your criteria to the filter window. In Figure 2-17, you can see that I set up a filter for the $FALV package and

CLAS/OC object type. You can find the description and possible entries by using the Ctrl+Space shortcut on the input fields. After the filter is applied, only the classes from the local $FALV package are displayed.

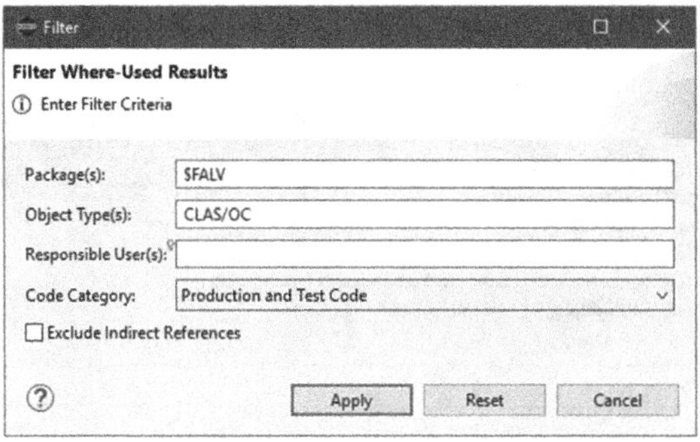

Figure 2-17. *Search view filter settings*

One more useful functionality of the Search view is the search history. It keeps the last where-used lists, so you do not have to do the search again. This option can be found under the Search History button on the toolbar, as shown in Figure 2-18. You can set the number of searches to keep by choosing Search History ➤ History... ➤ Configure.... By default, it keeps 10 entries.

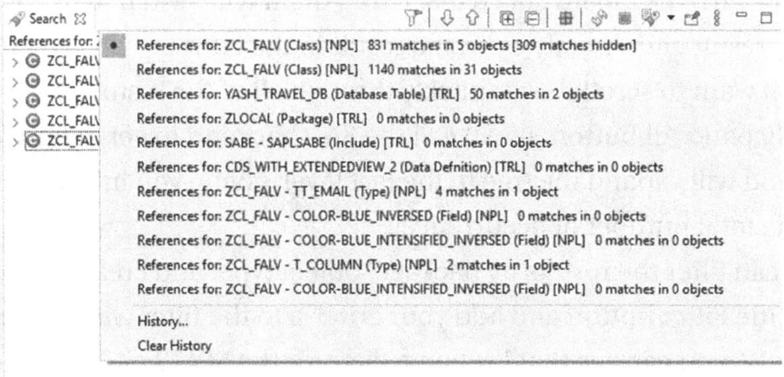

Figure 2-18. *Search history*

By using the Pin button, you can ensure that the current results stay in the current view when you use the where-used functionality again. The results for the new search will be opened in a separate view.

History

Say you want to check the last changes in the object, to see if part of the code was removed. In SE80, you used Version Management for that purpose, but in Eclipse you use the History view. Like the Outline view, it can be linked to the editor, so whenever you change an active editor tab, the view will be updated with the history of the active object. As with the Search view, it allows you to pin it and to see the previously displayed results.

As it is presented in Figure 2-19, the view contains a list of all versions, release dates, linked transport requests, and descriptions. Once you choose the version to open, just double-click it. A new tab will appear in the editor area.

Revision	Date	Author	Transport Request	Description
Active	20.10.2020 23:08:05	DEVELOPER (John Doe)	NPLK900080	Refactoring
1	20.10.2020 23:04:49	DEVELOPER (John Doe)	NPLK900077	Initial import

Figure 2-19. History view for the ZJSON2ABAPTYPE program

Figure 2-20 shows the comparison tab with current version on the left and the historical version on the right. You can navigate through the changes using the toolbar buttons or the overview ruler. What can be really helpful is that in the current version part, you can edit your code. When you find a part of the code that was deleted in the past and you want to put it back in, you can simply copy and paste it. Or you can use Copy Current Change From Right To Left button.

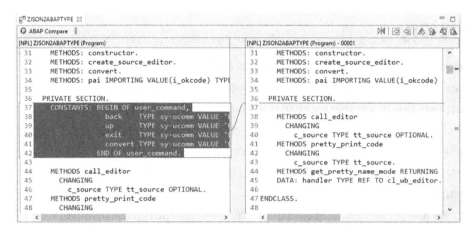

Figure 2-20. Comparing two revisions

Debug

This view is very small, but it's always used during debugging. It will always show up when an ABAP breakpoint is reached. If you have more than one debugging session open, all of them will appear here.

The example shown in Figure 2-21 contains one debug session on the NPL system. You can see on it information about the line and place of breakpoint, as well as the whole call stack. You can use this call stack to navigate to the previous levels of the call by simply clicking them.

Figure 2-21. *Debug view with a call stack*

When you want to terminate the session, you need to right-click the breakpoint description and choose one of these actions:

- Terminate: Stop current debugger session and close application

- Disconnect: Stop current debugger session, but continue with application

- Terminate and Remove: Stop debugger, close application, and remove the session from the Debug view list

- Terminate/Disconnect All: Stop all active debugger sessions and close all applications

I am not sure why the terminated debugger sessions are still kept in the view, but if you want to get rid of them, simply choose the Remove All Terminated action from the context menu.

Breakpoints

When you set up a breakpoint in the editor using the vertical ruler (not by using the BREAK-POINT statement in ABAP), all the breakpoints will be collected into the Breakpoints view. They will be visible there, no matter if you are logged onto the system or not.

All of the breakpoints set in Eclipse are external breakpoints, but in comparison to SAP GUI, they last until you remove them by demand. Figure 2-22 shows the checkboxes on the left side of the view. You can use them to deactivate the breakpoint until you want it back. Deactivated breakpoints will have a white icon as well. You can also delete certain breakpoints using the Remove Selected Breakpoints button or remove all of them at once using the Remove All button.

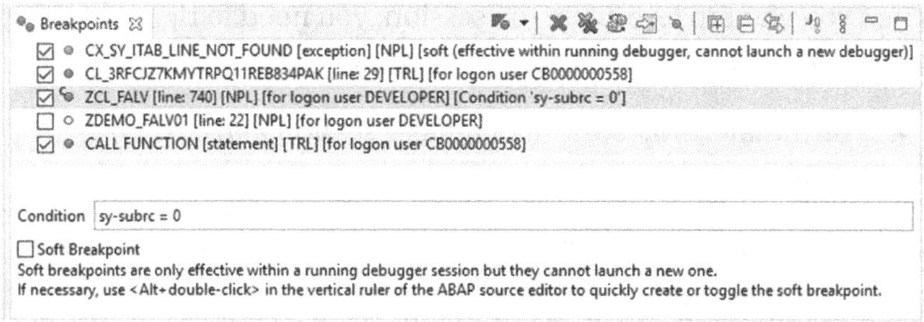

Figure 2-22. *Breakpoints view with default settings and four breakpoint types*

You can also create statement and exception breakpoints. To do so, click the Add ABAP Breakpoint button and choose one of the two breakpoint types. If you have a statement breakpoint, you will need to select one of the existing ABAP statements. Whenever this statement is called, the debugger will stop in this place. It works similarly to the exception breakpoints. You choose where the debugger should stop and whenever it will be raised, it will stop.

Conditions are a very nice feature of the Eclipse debugger. You can set them for each standard breakpoint (manually added in the editor). They work like the watchpoints in the SAP GUI debugger, so they stop only on certain conditions. That means you don't need to click the F7 key repeatedly and check the variables' values in order to see where your code is failing. In order to set them, you simply select the existing breakpoint in the view. Then, in the Condition input field, you set up the rules for this breakpoint. The rules are logical expressions, which can use variables, literals, and some built-in functions; see Table 2-3.

Table 2-3. *Possibilities for Breakpoint Conditions*

Type	Usage
Variables	You can use any variable, field symbol, structure or structure component, internal table or static class attributes that are available in the current scope of code. For example: • `variable = 5` • `<field-symbol> CP 'AB*'` • `structure-component > 15` • `structure-string(1) = 'A'` • `object->attribute IS NOT INITIAL` • `itab[9]-component CS 'PP'` • `{C:class_name}-static_attr = 'X'`
Literals	There are three literals you can use: • `' '` for character literals • `` ` ` `` for string literals • Numeric literals with or without the '-' sign
Built-in functions	So far only four functions are available for conditions in breakpoints: • `LINES( itab )`: Returns the number of table lines • `STRLEN( string )`: Returns the string length • `XSTRLEN( xstring )`: Returns the xstring length • `INEXACT_DF( )`: Returns 'X' when the result of an operation (for example, `COMPUTE` or `MOVE`) is inexact due to rounding

(continued)

Table 2-3. (*continued*)

Type	Usage
Operators	Possible types of operators are:
	• Comparison: =, <, >, <=, >=, <> or EQ, LT, GT, LE, GE, NE
	• Logical: NOT, AND, OR and brackets ( ) to combine several conditions
	• String analysis: CO, CN, CA, NA, CS, NS, CP, NP
	• Binary: IS [NOT] INITIAL, IS [NOT] BOUND, IS [NOT] ASSIGNED

Knowing the possibilities, you could create a condition for your breakpoint similar to the one in Listing 2-2.

Listing 2-2. Sample Breakpoint Condition

```
( sy-subrc <> 0 AND lines( sales_orders ) > 0 AND
sales_orders[1]-auart CS 'ABC' ) OR ( <header>-waers = 'EUR' )
```

Two last possibilities of the Breakpoints view are to skip all breakpoints and to group them. Skipping All Breakpoints is nice when you want to continue running your code until the end, but you don't want to remove the breakpoints. You just activate this by using the button on the toolbar. Until you deactivate it, the debugger will not care about the set breakpoints.

Grouping allows you to keep some order in your breakpoints, as in other cases it could be a bit messy. One of the grouping types that I use is Grouping by Projects, which in the case of ABAP means by system. You can see an example of this grouping in Figure 2-23.

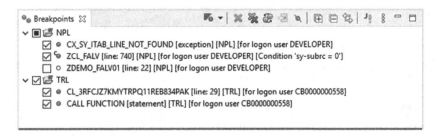

Figure 2-23. *Breakpoints with grouping by project*

Variables

This view is available during debugging. You can watch and change variables values from here. When it starts, you will have the following entries: SY-SUBRC, Locals and/or Globals nodes, ME (if the debugger stopped in a class object), and the <Enter Variable> field, which allows you to enter variable names manually.

Locals will show you the local variables in the method, form, and function module. Globals will show the global variables for the program or function group. ME will show you the whole object and all of its attributes.

You can add the variables manually to the view or by double-clicking the variable name in the editor during debugging. When you add them manually, you can use dirty assignments or table lines directly. For example, Figure 2-24 shows the dirty assignment of (ZDEMO_FALV01) SFLIGHT, table line FCAT[1], or directly via the component NO_OUT of the first line of FCAT.

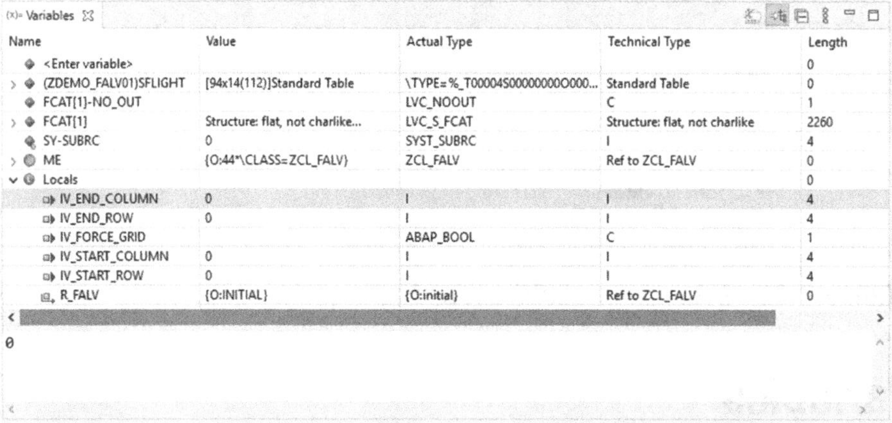
(x)= Variables
Name
Value
Actual Type
Technical Type
Length
<Enter variable>
0
(ZDEMO_FALV01)SFLIGHT
[94x14(112)]Standard Table
\TYPE=%_T00004S00000000O000...
Standard Table
0
FCAT[1]-NO_OUT
LVC_NOOUT
C
1
FCAT[1]
Structure: flat, not charlike...
LVC_S_FCAT
Structure: flat, not charlike
2260
SY-SUBRC
0
SYST_SUBRC
I
4
ME
{O:44*\CLASS=ZCL_FALV}
ZCL_FALV
Ref to ZCL_FALV
0
Locals
0
IV_END_COLUMN
0
I
I
4
IV_END_ROW
0
I
I
4
IV_FORCE_GRID
ABAP_BOOL
C
1
IV_START_COLUMN
0
I
I
4
IV_START_ROW
0
I
I
4
R_FALV
{O:INITIAL}
{O:initial}
Ref to ZCL_FALV
0
0

***Figure 2-24.** Variables view on a class object with a few variables*

When you have the proper authorizations, during debugging you should be able change the variable value. To do so, just click the Value field next to the variable name. This will highlight the value and you will be able to put in your desired value. Confirm the change by pressing the Enter button.

When you are debugging a class in the default view, the ME node shows only the attributes that can be found directly in this class. No inherited attributes or constants will be shown. You can change that behavior by going to the View menu and choosing ABAP ➤ Show Inherited Attributes or ABAP ➤ Show Constants. You can see an example of the Variables view with this settings turned on in Figure 2-25.

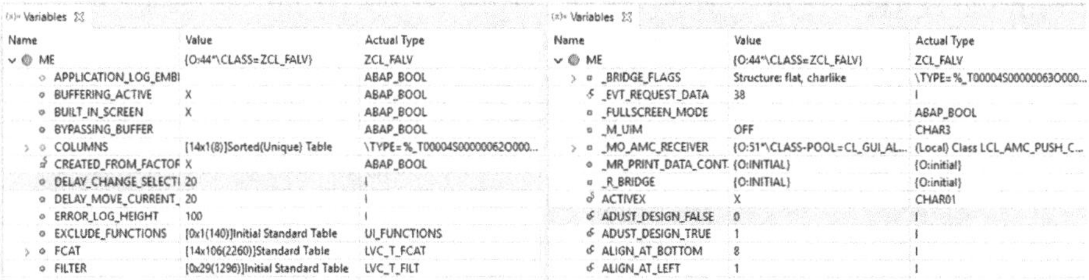
(x)= Variables
Name
Value
Actual Type
ME
{O:44*\CLASS=ZCL_FALV}
ZCL_FALV
APPLICATION_LOG_EMBI
ABAP_BOOL
BUFFERING_ACTIVE
X
ABAP_BOOL
BUILT_IN_SCREEN
X
ABAP_BOOL
BYPASSING_BUFFER
ABAP_BOOL
COLUMNS
[14x1(8)]Sorted(Unique) Table
\TYPE=%_T00004S00000062O000...
CREATED_FROM_FACTOF
X
ABAP_BOOL
DELAY_CHANGE_SELECTI
20
I
DELAY_MOVE_CURRENT_
20
I
ERROR_LOG_HEIGHT
100
I
EXCLUDE_FUNCTIONS
[0x1(140)]Initial Standard Table
UI_FUNCTIONS
FCAT
[14x106(2260)]Standard Table
LVC_T_FCAT
FILTER
[0x29(1296)]Initial Standard Table
LVC_T_FILT
(x)= Variables
Name
Value
Actual Type
ME
{O:44*\CLASS=ZCL_FALV}
ZCL_FALV
_BRIDGE_FLAGS
Structure: flat, charlike
\TYPE=%_T00004S00000063O000...
_EVT_REQUEST_DATA
38
I
_FULLSCREEN_MODE
ABAP_BOOL
_M_UIM
OFF
CHAR3
_MO_AMC_RECEIVER
{O:51*\CLASS-POOL=CL_GUI_AL...
(Local) Class LCL_AMC_PUSH_C...
_MR_PRINT_DATA_CONT
{O:INITIAL}
{O:initial}
_R_BRIDGE
{O:INITIAL}
{O:initial}
ACTIVEX
X
CHAR01
ADUST_DESIGN_FALSE
0
I
ADUST_DESIGN_TRUE
1
I
ALIGN_AT_BOTTOM
8
I
ALIGN_AT_LEFT
1
I

***Figure 2-25.** Variables with (right side) and without (left side) additional settings*

ABAP Exception (Debugger)

Exception debugging can be useful to get an idea where an exception was raised. If you're catching a few exceptions at a time and want to see the type and text without going into exception object details, this is the way to go.

In order to activate the update of the view, you need to add the name of the exception object to the input field and press or click Enter. When you stop the debugger inside the catch statement, the exception object name, text, and raise location will be shown in the view, as shown in Figure 2-26. The most common name for the exception object is E, and this is also used here.

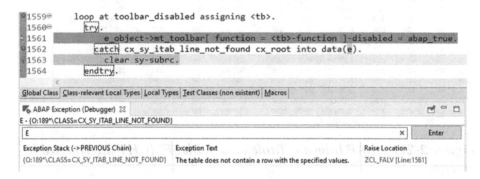

Figure 2-26. *ABAP Exception view while in a catch statement*

When you use the context menu of the object, you can jump into the raise location or you can add the object to the Variables view from here.

ABAP Internal Table (Debugger)

One of the most common things you'll do while debugging is check the internal table entries after a SELECT statement or after its manipulation some other way. The ABAP Internal Table view comes in handy here.

This view, if not already visible in your perspective, is activated when you double-click the internal table name during debugging. You can, of course, manually change the name of the table to watch the one here. As shown in Figure 2-27, the column headers are always internal field names and descriptions are not used.

Row	MANDT	CARRID	CONNID	FLDATE	PRICE	CURRENCY	PLANETYPE	SEATSMAX	SEATSOCC	PAYMENTSUM	SEATSMAX_B
1	001	AA	0017	20171219	422.94	USD	747-400	385	371	191334.22	31
2	001	AA	0017	20180309	422.94	USD	747-400	385	365	189984.86	31
3	001	AA	0017	20180528	422.94	USD	747-400	385	374	193482.55	31
4	001	AA	0017	20180816	422.94	USD	747-400	385	372	193127.31	31
5	001	AA	0017	20181104	422.94	USD	747-400	385	44	23908.86	31
6	001	AA	0017	20190123	422.94	USD	747-400	385	40	20347.70	31
7	001	AZ	0555	20171219	185.00	EUR	737-800	140	133	32143.75	12
8	001	AZ	0555	20180309	185.00	EUR	737-800	140	137	32595.15	12
9	001	AZ	0555	20180528	185.00	EUR	737-800	140	134	31899.55	12
10	001	AZ	0555	20180816	185.00	EUR	737-800	140	128	29775.75	12
11	001	AZ	0555	20181104	185.00	EUR	737-800	140	0	0.00	12
12	001	AZ	0555	20190123	185.00	EUR	737-800	140	23	5392.75	12
13	001	AZ	0789	20171219	1030.00	EUR	767-200	260	250	307176.90	21
14	001	AZ	0789	20180309	1030.00	EUR	767-200	260	252	306054.20	21
15	001	AZ	0789	20180528	1030.00	EUR	767-200	260	252	307063.60	21
16	001	AZ	0789	20180816	1030.00	EUR	767-200	260	249	300739.40	21

Figure 2-27. *ABAP Internal Table view with SFLIGHT internal table entries*

From this view, you can also delete or add rows, you can sort the entries and filter them (but only on certain NetWeaver releases), and you can export the table into TXT, CSV, or XLS files. All these functions are available from the View menu and/or from context menu for the row entry.

There are two buttons that can be very useful. The first one is the Pin button, which will help you see the table entries all the time. The second one is the Automatic Refresh button, which may help if you have a slow connection.

> **Tip**   Eclipse debugger refreshes this view each step, so this can be very expensive, especially if you have a slow connection. That is why, if you don't need to see the updated values during each step, you can disable the automatic refresh and you will see a huge difference in the performance of the debugger.

Transport Organizer

There is no work in ABAP without transport requests and tasks. They have been with us since the beginning and will probably stay with us until the end. The Transport Organizer view helps you check and manage the transport requests you are involved with.

The view shows a list of all ABAP projects. They will not show an entry until you expand the project folder on it. Once you do this, you will see all the transport requests that you can find with an SE01 transaction. The only difference is that you will not be able to see all the released transports requests on demand there, but the one that was released during last two weeks will be visible in a separate subfolder. You can see all of this in Figure 2-28.

When you start to expand the transport orders, you will notice all the objects that are currently in it or inside the task. But that is not the only way to find the objects inside transport orders. What you can do is use the filter field. You can put the full or partial name of the object that you want to find. If any transport requests are in it, it will be shown on the view.

Figure 2-28. *Transport Organizer view with two projects*

Of course, you can do much more with this view. For example, you can create new transport requests, change the owner and the type of the request, add a task for any user, and release the task and request. Not all of these functions are available in each system, availability depends on the backend as usual.

If your system is newer, when you double-click the transport request, it opens in Eclipse view, as shown in the Figure 2-29, not in SAP GUI.

Figure 2-29. *Transport Request details in Eclipse*

Note that the creation button is active on the view toolbar. Once it's used, you will be moved to the Transport Request wizard, which you can also see in Figure 2-30.

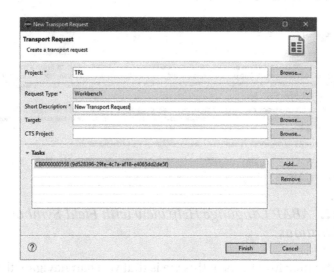

Figure 2-30. *New transport request window*

ABAP Language Help

Whether you are a newbie or an experienced ABAP developer, you will need to use the ABAP syntax help from time to time, either to learn how to use the syntax or to remind yourself about any additions you can use.

The ABAP Language Help view can be called by pressing the F1 button on any ABAP statement. You can also open it manually from the list of available views and use it on demand. When used with F1, it will directly show the help for the selected statement. When you have it open, you can manually type the statement or any other text into the search field and the view will open the information for you. As an example, Figure 2-31 shows the help for the FIELD-SYMBOL inline declaration.

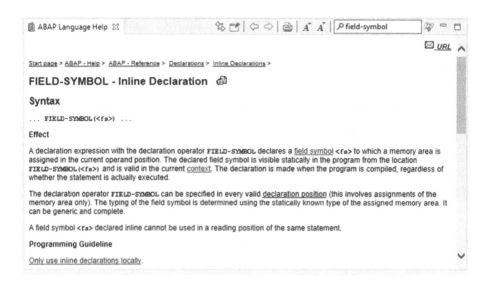

Figure 2-31. ABAP Language Help view with Field-Symbol help for inline declarations

One of the nice functions of this vie is that you can navigate through it like a web page, using the breadcrumbs and hyperlinks in the text.

Console

With ABAP development, you probably will use the Console view only when developing the cloud systems, or when developing the class if you want to test the output in addition to the unit tests. It is also useful during Eclipse plugin development, but this process is described in the next chapters.

To use the console with ABAP, you need to implement the MAIN method of the IF_OO_ADT_CLASSRUN interface, and use the OUT object to put values into the console. IF_OO_ADT_CLASSRUN has been available since NetWeaver 7.51 and can be also used on-premise systems.

Listing 2-3 shows a sample code for a class that outputs data to the Console view. When you copy it to the Eclipse editor and run it using the F9 button, it will display the output shown in Figure 2-32.

Listing 2-3. Sample Console Application in ABAP Using IF_OO_ ADT_CLASSRUN

```
CLASS zcl_console_app DEFINITION
  PUBLIC
  FINAL
  CREATE PUBLIC .

  PUBLIC SECTION.
    INTERFACES if_oo_adt_classrun .
ENDCLASS.

CLASS zcl_console_app IMPLEMENTATION.
  METHOD if_oo_adt_classrun~main.
    out->write_text( 'This is the first line'  ).
    out->write_text( 'This is the second line'  ).
    out->write_text( 'This is the third line'  ).
  ENDMETHOD.
ENDCLASS.
```

Figure 2-32. *Console view output*

ABAP Element Info

This is one of my favorite views, although you can get the same information directly from the editor using the F2 key on any ABAP object. What makes me like it so much? Well, I like to get rid of unnecessary steps when coding and debugging and I also like to have all the information available directly. This view enables me to have direct information about selected objects.

Of course I use it with the Link with Editor function enabled; that is why whenever I put the cursor on a function module, method, variable, constant, table, structure, data element, or any other ABAP object, I see the details and description of that object.

The details can be the method or function signature, including ABAP doc comments, or simply the components of the structure. If long text documentation is available, you can also navigate to it from this view, as shown in Figure 2-33.

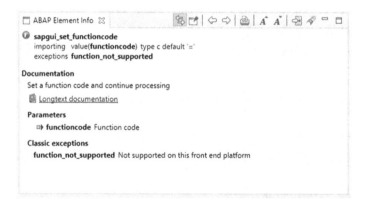

Figure 2-33. *ABAP Element Info with the SAPGUI_SET_ FUNCTIONCODE function module*

In the case of structures or dictionary tables, you will see all the components and their type and description, as shown in Figure 2-34. Of course, each ABAP object type will show information that relates to its type. So with classes, for example, you will see methods and attributes.

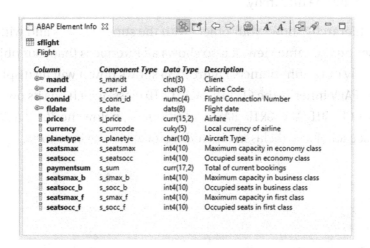

Figure 2-34. ABAP Element Info with SFLIGHT table

In addition to the displayed information, you can navigate through the elements of the view to get more detailed information about that part of the object.

ABAP Type Hierarchy

When you are wondering what the whole hierarchy of a class is, there is no better view than ABAP Type Hierarchy. You can learn from this view the clear information about the classes that are super-classes to yours, or you can see where your class is inherited from.

This view allows you to see the type hierarchy in three ways:

- Type hierarchy

- Supertype hierarchy

- Subtype hierarchy

Type hierarchy shows your object with the super-classes and with subclasses on the same view. It also shows all interfaces that your object uses directly or by inheritance. Figure 2-35 shows how it will be displayed; class ZCL_FALV inherits the CL_GUI_ALV_GRID class, which has its own superclass CL_GUI_ALV_GRID_BASE. Additionally, below the ZCL_FALV class, you can see all of its subclasses, including local classes in reports.

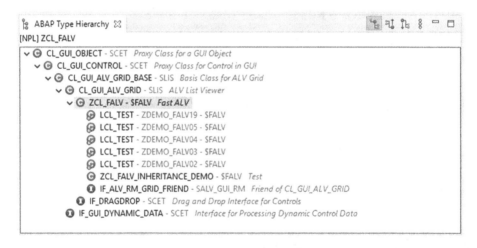

Figure 2-35. *ABAP Type Hierarchy with type hierarchy for class ZCL_FALV*

When you choose to see only the Supertype hierarchy, then as shown in Figure 2-36, you will see your class at the top of the tree. Each lower level represents a superclass of the upper level. You can also see all the inherited interfaces.

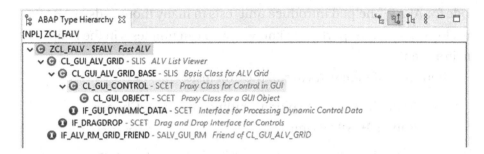

Figure 2-36. *ABAP Type Hierarchy with supertype hierarchy of class*
ZCL_FALV

The last way to display data in this view is by Subtype hierarchy,
which will display only subclasses of the checked class. This behavior is
presented in Figure 2-37, where you see all the subclasses of ZCL_FALV.

Figure 2-37. *ABAP Type Hierarchy with subtype hierarchy of class*
ZCL_FALV

ABAP Unit

ABAP developers finally started to recognize the added value that Test
Driven Development (TDD) and unit tests bring to the development and
maintenance processes. The OpenSAP course titled "Writing Testable

Code for ABAP[1]" helped introduce unit tests to many thousands of ABAP developers, so it is important to know how to run unit tests in the Eclipse environment.

There are different ways to run the unit tests:

- From the Project Explorer, Outline, or Editor: Choose Run As ➤ ABAP Unit Test.

- From the Eclipse menu bar: Choose Run ➤ Run As ➤ ABAP Unit Test.

- From the Eclipse toolbar button: Choose Run ➤ Run As ➤ ABAP Unit Test.

- Use the Ctrl+Shift+F10 shortcut.

Once you select an object or package that contains test classes, you will see the results of the test in this view. You will be able to see how many tests were successful, how many failed, and how many were not executed. You can also see all test methods in this view and you can navigate to the source of the test by double-clicking. To show you the results of the unit tests, I ran the checks for package $ABAP2XLSX, which is my local package for the abap2xlsx[2] project. This package contained 30 test methods, but only 18 were executed. As you can see in Figure 2-38, in one of the test classes LCL_TEST of the ZCL_EXCEL_READER_HUGE_FILE class, no risk level information was given, which is why the execution of all 12 test methods were not completed and its state was set to *warning*.

---

[1]This OpenSAP course can be found at https://open.sap.com/courses/wtc1. OpenSAP+WTC1_W1U5+Writing+Testable+Code+for+ABAPComent

[2]This is an open source project of the SAP Community for creating, updating, and reading XLSX files in ABAP. More info is found at https://github.com/ sapmentors/abap2xlsx

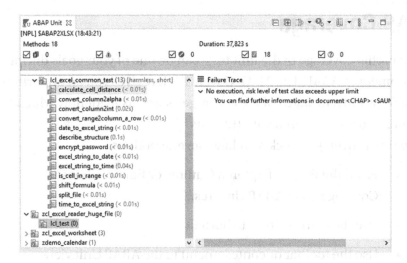

Figure 2-38. *ABAP Unit run results for the abap2xlsx project package*

When test methods fail, their icon will turn red and the status bar in this view, which in Figure 2-38 was yellow, will turn red. You will have to correct the part of code that's checked by the test method or update the test method itself. Once you fix it, you can use the context menu of the view to rerun the selected tests.

If you use the context menu to rerun the tests, you will see that there are some additional options: Rerun with Coverage and Rerun with Profiling. Rerun with Coverage runs the tests again and opens a new view called ABAP Coverage, which displays information about the percentage of the code that is covered with unit tests. You can read more about the ABAP Coverage view in the next section of this chapter.

Rerun with Profiling is useful when your tests are taking a long time and you want to determine what could be corrected to get better performance. When you use this option, after completing the tests run, Eclipse will open a new view called ABAP Trace Requests, on which you will find the request for your test methods. ABAP Trace Requests and linked ABAP Trace views are described in more detail in the next sections.

ABAP Coverage

Full or partial coverage of the unit tests can be one of your goals during development in ABAP. The ABAP Coverage view gives you an opportunity to check the current status of the coverage as well as to identify which statements are not covered with the tests.

To run a coverage check, you have several options:

- From the Project Explorer, Outline, or Editor: Choose Coverage As ➤ ABAP Unit Test.

- Use the Ctrl+Shift+F11 shortcut.

- Use the toolbar or context menu in the ABAP Unit view and choose the Rerun with Coverage function.

As a result, the standard run of the ABAP unit tests will be done. Additionally, you will notice detailed information in the ABAP Coverage view about each part of the development, for both global and local parts. Figure 2-39 shows the result of the Coverage run. Here you can see the methods of the ZCL_EXCEL_COMMON class, coverage with the progress bar, and detailed information about what was covered and what was missed by the checks statements. Using the More button, you can switch to show the branch and procedure coverage.

Element		Statement Coverage	Covered Statements	Missed Statements	Total Statements
✓ ⊙ ZCL_EXCEL_COMMON==============CP	▭	71.62%	356	141	497
✓ ⊙ ZCL_EXCEL_COMMON	▭	71.62%	356	141	497
● CALCULATE_CELL_DISTANCE	▭	100.00%	7	0	7
● CHAR2HEX	▭	100.00%	6	0	6
● CLASS_CONSTRUCTOR	▭	100.00%	2	0	2
● CONVERT_COLUMN2ALPHA	▭	93.75%	15	1	16
● CONVERT_COLUMN2INT	▭	80.85%	38	9	47
● CONVERT_COLUMNROW2COLUMN_A_ROW	▭	100.00%	4	0	4
● CONVERT_RANGE2COLUMN_A_ROW	▭	85.71%	24	4	28
● DATE_TO_EXCEL_STRING	▭	100.00%	6	0	6
● DESCRIBE_STRUCTURE	▭	100.00%	28	0	28
● DETERMINE_RESULTING_FORMULA	▭	0.00%	0	3	3
● ENCRYPT_PASSWORD	▭	100.00%	14	0	14
● ESCAPE_STRING	▭	0.00%	0	7	7
● EXCEL_STRING_TO_DATE	▭	75.00%	6	2	8
● EXCEL_STRING_TO_NUMBER	▭	0.00%	0	2	2

Figure 2-39. *ABAP Coverage for the ZCL_EXCEL_COMMON class of abap2xlsx*

But that is not all that the ABAP Coverage view can give you. Directly after the coverage run, your code in the editor will be highlighted depending on the selected coverage type (statement, branch, procedure). The covered code will be highlighted in green, and code that's not covered is in red. Figure 2-40 shows this highlighting, where only the CATCH statement is so far left without test coverage. When you do not want to see the highlighting, you can switch it off by closing the ABAP Coverage view or by clicking the Hide Highlighting button on the view toolbar.

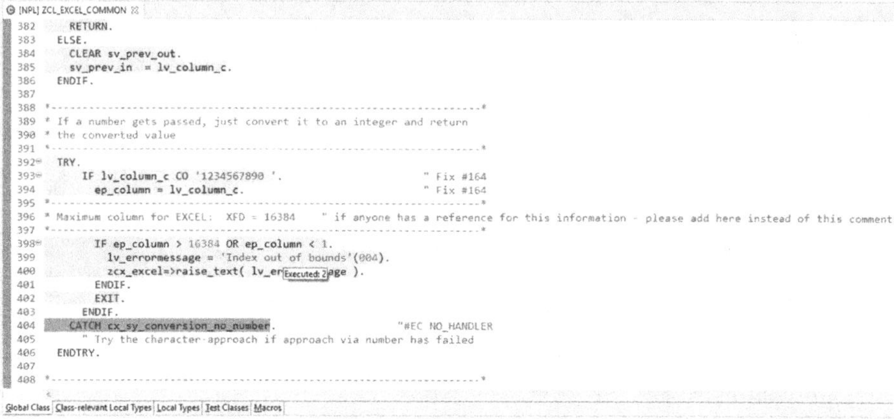

Figure 2-40. *ABAP Editor with coverage highlighting turned on*

ATC Problems

Among other things, the ABAP Test Cockpit (ATC) helps developers follow company rules and find performance issues inside the code. Depending on the system configuration, you may be forced to use it, but even if the ATC findings are not blocking you from releasing your transports, it is still good to run it in order to correct your code according to best practices.

ATC can be run in similar ways to the ABAP unit test:

- From the Project Explorer, Outline, or Editor: Choose Run As ➤ ABAP Test Cockpit or Run As ➤ ABAP Test Cockpit With....

- From the Eclipse menu bar: Choose Run ➤ Run As ➤ ABAP Test Cockpit or Run ➤ Run As ➤ ABAP Test Cockpit With....

- From the Eclipse toolbar button: Choose Run ➤ Run As ➤ ABAP Test Cockpit or Run ➤ Run As ➤ ABAP Test Cockpit With....

- Use the Ctrl+Shift+F2 shortcut.

After you run ATC, the ATC Problems view will be shown automatically. After the ATC run is finished (it can take some time), you will be notified about all findings. There are three types of findings: error, warning, and information. They correspond to the priority 1, 2, and 3.

Besides the finding type, you will also see the finding message, the check group, the place where the finding was recognized, and information about the exemption status. After selecting the message, you will also see the detailed text of the message, where you can often find the pragmas or pseudo-comments that you can use to hide the finding, or the information about how you can change your code to fulfill the rule.

Figure 2-41 shows the default ATC Problems grouping, which is by priority. Using the View menu, you can change the grouping to object or check.

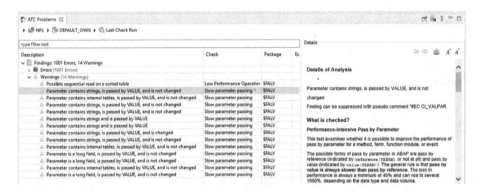

Figure 2-41. *ATC Problems view with error and warning findings*

If you double-click the finding, you can navigate to the place of the finding, which helps you more easily correct the code. Once you're done, you can use the context menu and the Recheck function to rerun the ATC and see the updated results.

If you are working on a S/4HANA custom code adaptation project, you may find a very helpful functionality in the context menu, called Recommended Quick Fix. This function calls the wizard to help you adjust the findings to the state in which they will no longer stop you from using your code on S/4HANA system.

Another very important option on the context menu is to ask for an exemption. To do so, you just select the Request Exemption function. The exemption wizard will open, as shown on the left side of Figure 2-42. You will then be able to select the scope of the exemption.

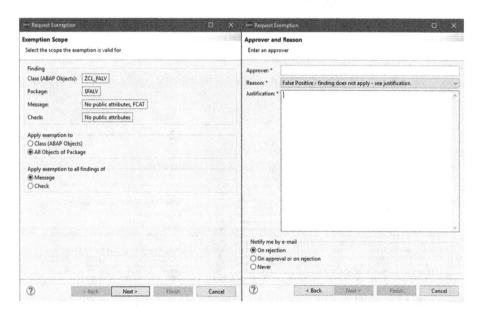

Figure 2-42. *Request Exemption wizard screens (scope and approver selection)*

The next step is to select the approver and give justification for the exemption. You can indicate if you want to be notified after the exemption status changes.

ATC Result Browser

When you want to come back to an earlier ATC check, you can use the ATC Result Browser view. It will show you the ATC checks for your user (Local Check Runs), as well as the results of Central Check Runs if you have access to the central ATC system. Information is presented in the form of a tree, as shown in Figure 2-43.

This view is useful when you want to come back to earlier results of an ATC because you were interrupted when solving the findings and additional ATC runs might take a long time in your environment.

Being able to view central ATC runs is also helpful when you are responsible for the code quality at your company or during an S/4HANA conversion project, as this can give you overall information about code quality.

Description	Errors	Warnings	Infos	Check Variant	Executed On	Run Series Name
ATC Result Browser						
type filter text						
⌄ NPL						
No active result available						
⌄ Results of Local Check Runs [created by: DEVELOPER, contact person: *]						
⌄ Today (5)						
ZCL_FALV	1001	14	0	DEFAULT_OWN	24.10.2020, 19:31	
ZCL_FALV	1001	14	0	DEFAULT_OWN	24.10.2020, 19:20	
ZCL_FALV	0	14	0	DEFAULT	24.10.2020, 19:18	
ZCL_FALV	0	14	0	DEFAULT	24.10.2020, 19:02	
ZCL_FALV	0	14	0	DEFAULT	24.10.2020, 19:00	
Yesterday (0)						
⌄ Older (1)						
ZCL_FALV_COLUMN ZCL_FALV_LAYOUT ZCL_FALV ZCL_FALV_INHE	0	24	4	DEFAULT	17.10.2020, 23:27	
⌄ TRL						
No active result available						
⌄ Results of Central Check Runs [created by: *, contact person: CB0000000!						
Today (0)						
Yesterday (0)						
Older (0)						
⌄ Results of Local Check Runs [created by: CB0000000558, contact person:						
Today (0)						
Yesterday (0)						

Figure 2-43. ATC Result Browser for local and central runs

When you double-click the run (local or central), details about all the findings for the run are displayed in this view.

Data Preview

As a developer, you will occasionally need to look at database entries. When you are using SAP GUI, you run transaction SE16 or SE16N for that. But in Eclipse, there is no point in launching these transactions, as we have Data Preview view.

To run Data Preview view, you must have the database table, database view, or CDS view opened in your editor and then press the F8 button. The other option is to use the Project Explorers context menu. You do this by selecting any of these objects and choosing Open With ➤ Data Preview. By using one of these two ways to open Data Preview, you will see a new tab with 100 entries from the selected object.

Once it is displayed you can change the number of displayed rows up to 99,999 and adapt filters to display only data that you want to see. You can also select which columns should be displayed, check the total number of entries, open the preview of the data in another system, or export entries into local files. You can do all of this by choosing the proper button on the view toolbar, which you can see in Figure 2-44.

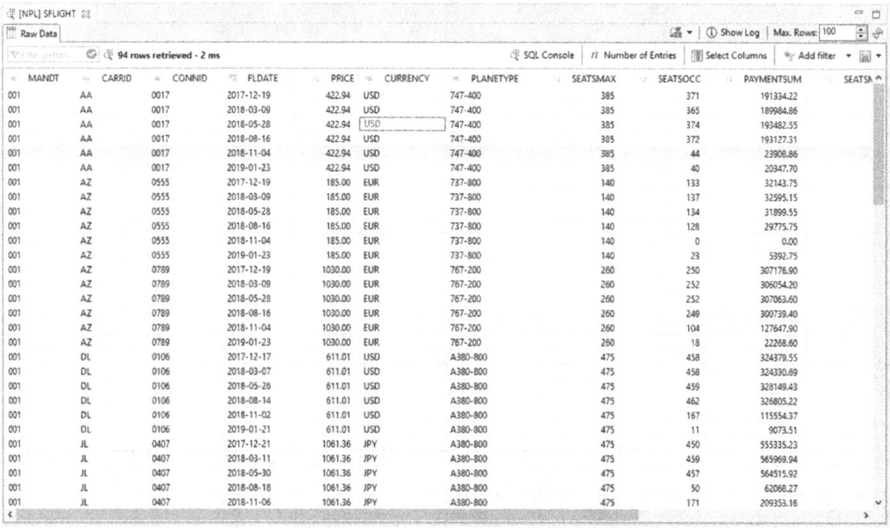

MANDT	CARRID	CONNID	FLDATE	PRICE	CURRENCY	PLANETYPE	SEATSMAX	SEATSOCC	PAYMENTSUM	SEATSM
001	AA	0017	2017-12-19	422.94	USD	747-400	385	371	191334.22	
001	AA	0017	2018-03-09	422.94	USD	747-400	385	365	189984.86	
001	AA	0017	2018-05-28	422.94	USD	747-400	385	374	193482.55	
001	AA	0017	2018-08-16	422.94	USD	747-400	385	372	193127.31	
001	AA	0017	2018-11-04	422.94	USD	747-400	385	44	23908.86	
001	AA	0017	2019-01-23	422.94	USD	747-400	385	40	20347.70	
001	AZ	0555	2017-12-19	185.00	EUR	737-800	140	133	32143.75	
001	AZ	0555	2018-03-09	185.00	EUR	737-800	140	137	32595.15	
001	AZ	0555	2018-05-28	185.00	EUR	737-800	140	134	31899.55	
001	AZ	0555	2018-08-16	185.00	EUR	737-800	140	128	29775.75	
001	AZ	0555	2018-11-04	185.00	EUR	737-800	140	0	0.00	
001	AZ	0555	2019-01-23	185.00	EUR	737-800	140	23	5392.75	
001	AZ	0789	2017-12-19	1030.00	EUR	767-200	260	250	307176.90	
001	AZ	0789	2018-03-09	1030.00	EUR	767-200	260	252	306054.20	
001	AZ	0789	2018-05-28	1030.00	EUR	767-200	260	252	307063.60	
001	AZ	0789	2018-08-16	1030.00	EUR	767-200	260	249	300739.40	
001	AZ	0789	2018-11-04	1030.00	EUR	767-200	260	104	127647.90	
001	AZ	0789	2019-01-23	1030.00	EUR	767-200	260	18	22268.60	
001	DL	0106	2017-12-17	611.01	USD	A380-800	475	458	324379.55	
001	DL	0106	2018-03-07	611.01	USD	A380-800	475	458	324330.69	
001	DL	0106	2018-05-26	611.01	USD	A380-800	475	459	328149.43	
001	DL	0106	2018-08-14	611.01	USD	A380-800	475	462	326805.22	
001	DL	0106	2018-11-02	611.01	USD	A380-800	475	167	115554.37	
001	DL	0106	2019-01-21	611.01	USD	A380-800	475	11	9073.51	
001	JL	0407	2017-12-21	1061.36	JPY	A380-800	475	450	555335.23	
001	JL	0407	2018-03-11	1061.36	JPY	A380-800	475	459	565969.94	
001	JL	0407	2018-05-30	1061.36	JPY	A380-800	475	457	564515.92	
001	JL	0407	2018-08-18	1061.36	JPY	A380-800	475	50	62068.27	
001	JL	0407	2018-11-06	1061.36	JPY	A380-800	475	171	209353.16	

***Figure 2-44.** Data Preview of the SFLIGHT table*

You can also use the context menu to set a quick filter on the selected cell or see the decomposition of the values in a selected column. For example, Figure 2-45 displays distinct values of the CARRID column.

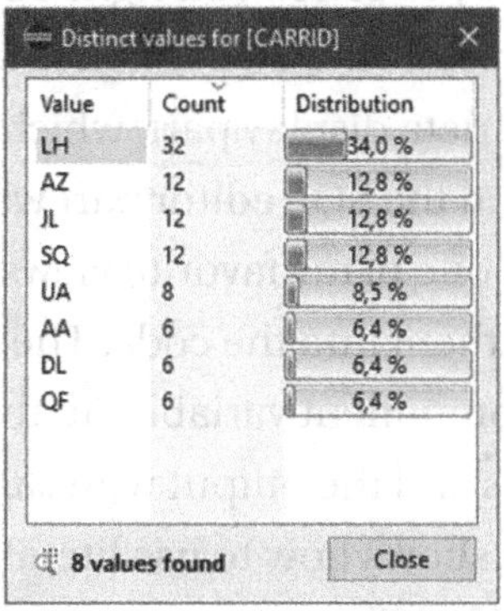

***Figure 2-45.** Distinct values on the CARRID field of the SFLIGHT table with 100 entries*

There is one more very powerful function, which allows you to copy all displayed rows as a ABAP VALUE statement. You can do that from the context menu or you can save them in a text file using the Export button. When you are not using unit tests, you may find this function less than useful. It's a perfect way to prepare mockup data for your test classes. As an example, Figure 2-46 shows the inline declaration of the mockup table with the SFLIGHT table entries that was created using this function.

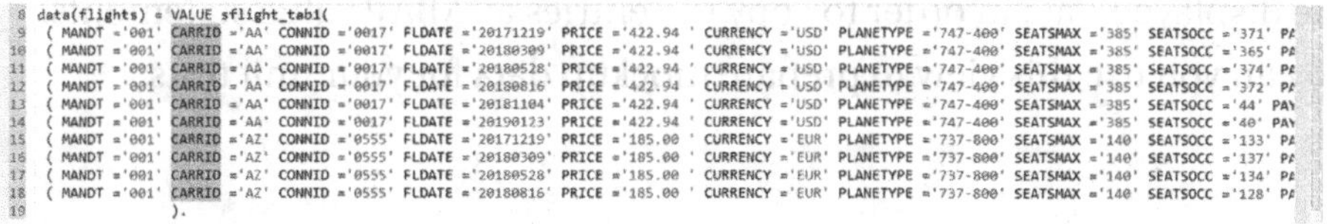

```
data(flights) = VALUE sflight_tab1(
 ( MANDT ='001' CARRID ='AA' CONNID ='0017' FLDATE ='20171219' PRICE ='422.94 ' CURRENCY ='USD' PLANETYPE ='747-400' SEATSMAX ='385' SEATSOCC ='371' PA
 ( MANDT ='001' CARRID ='AA' CONNID ='0017' FLDATE ='20180309' PRICE ='422.94 ' CURRENCY ='USD' PLANETYPE ='747-400' SEATSMAX ='385' SEATSOCC ='365' PA
 ( MANDT ='001' CARRID ='AA' CONNID ='0017' FLDATE ='20180528' PRICE ='422.94 ' CURRENCY ='USD' PLANETYPE ='747-400' SEATSMAX ='385' SEATSOCC ='374' PA
 ( MANDT ='001' CARRID ='AA' CONNID ='0017' FLDATE ='20180816' PRICE ='422.94 ' CURRENCY ='USD' PLANETYPE ='747-400' SEATSMAX ='385' SEATSOCC ='372' PA
 ( MANDT ='001' CARRID ='AA' CONNID ='0017' FLDATE ='20181104' PRICE ='422.94 ' CURRENCY ='USD' PLANETYPE ='747-400' SEATSMAX ='385' SEATSOCC ='44' PAY
 ( MANDT ='001' CARRID ='AA' CONNID ='0017' FLDATE ='20190123' PRICE ='422.94 ' CURRENCY ='USD' PLANETYPE ='747-400' SEATSMAX ='385' SEATSOCC ='40' PAY
 ( MANDT ='001' CARRID ='AZ' CONNID ='0555' FLDATE ='20171219' PRICE ='185.00 ' CURRENCY ='EUR' PLANETYPE ='737-800' SEATSMAX ='140' SEATSOCC ='133' PA
 ( MANDT ='001' CARRID ='AZ' CONNID ='0555' FLDATE ='20180309' PRICE ='185.00 ' CURRENCY ='EUR' PLANETYPE ='737-800' SEATSMAX ='140' SEATSOCC ='137' PA
 ( MANDT ='001' CARRID ='AZ' CONNID ='0555' FLDATE ='20180528' PRICE ='185.00 ' CURRENCY ='EUR' PLANETYPE ='737-800' SEATSMAX ='140' SEATSOCC ='134' PA
 ( MANDT ='001' CARRID ='AZ' CONNID ='0555' FLDATE ='20180816' PRICE ='185.00 ' CURRENCY ='EUR' PLANETYPE ='737-800' SEATSMAX ='140' SEATSOCC ='128' PA
                   ).
```

***Figure 2-46.** Table data inline declaration for entries copied from Data Preview*

One last option of Data Preview, which we should not forget, is calling the SQL Console view.

SQL Console

I just mentioned that you can call the SQL Console from the Data Preview, but there is also another way to call it. You right-click the project name in Project Explorer view and select the SQL Console function.

This view contains the data display part, which looks exactly like the one in the Data Preview and the SQL editor part where you can test your SELECT statements. This is one of my favorite views, as I can test my SQL statements before putting them into the code. The SQL editor can only use literals and SY structure component variables in the WHERE clause, but it is enough to check your joins and the output with sample WHERE conditions. As an example, Listing 2-4 shows how to use literals and the current date inside a WHERE clause of a SELECT statement.

Listing 2-4. Sample SQL Statement That Will Work with the SQL Console

```
SELECT * FROM sflight
  WHERE fldate LT @sy-datum
  AND   carrid = 'AA'.
```

When you use the code in Listing 2-4 in the SQL Console and click the Run button, you should see similar entries on the right side of the view, as shown in Figure 2-47. On Data Preview, you can use the context menu on the displayed data in order to copy the entries as ABAP value statements. So can you use this view to prepare mockup data for your unit tests.

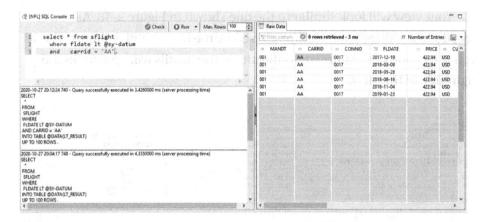

Figure 2-47. *SQL Console view with a sample SQL statement*

You can also see the historical SQL calls here, which will be cleared after you close the view. They will remain in the history of the calls, which you can check and reuse from the Down Arrow button next to Run. You can also save your current SQL statement as a favorite for future use.

Feed Reader

When you start using Eclipse and you are logged onto several systems, you will notice that from time to time, a small popup in the bottom-right corner of the Eclipse window will inform you about your recent short dumps or short dumps of objects that you have created. This information comes from the Feed Reader and can be customized according to your preferences.

When you open Feed Reader, you will see all the systems that you are currently logged onto. When you expand one of them, you will see that you have three groups of feeds:

- Runtime errors caused by me

- Runtime errors for objects I am responsible for

- System messages

Your view will look similar to the one shown in Figure 2-48. As you can see, there are three short dumps caused by me on the NPL system. When you select one of the unread notifications, the details will appear on the right side of the view.

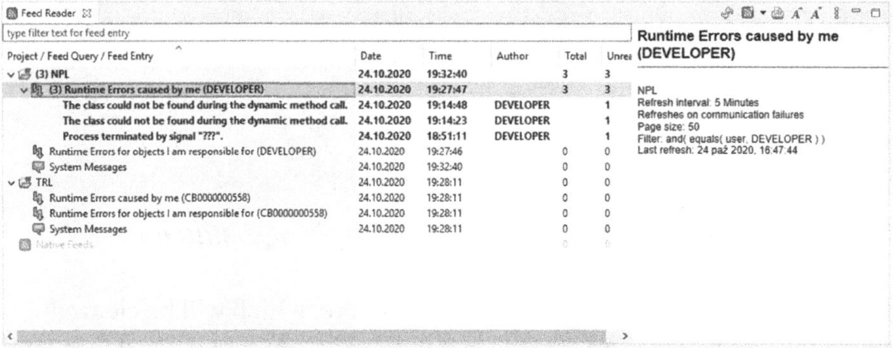

Figure 2-48. *Default Feed Reader view*

You can resize the preview of the message view to see more details. If you do, with short dumps, you will see the same information that you can get with transaction ST22, but in HTML view, you can navigate through hyperlinks. A sample short dump is shown in Figure 2-49; it presents the top of the message that contains the links to all areas of the short dump and two additional links:

- Show in SAP GUI
- Show where terminated

When you click the Show in SAP GUI link, the embedded GUI screen will appear in the place of the editor and the short dump will be opened, just like you would navigate through ST22.

When you click the Show Where Terminated link, the object in which the dump occurred will be opened on the line of termination in the Eclipse ABAP editor.

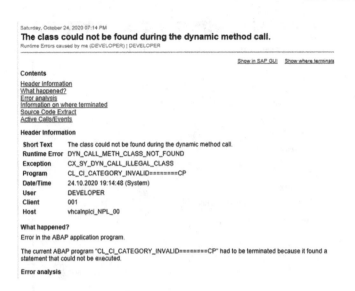

Saturday, October 24, 2020 07:14 PM
The class could not be found during the dynamic method call.
Runtime Errors caused by me (DEVELOPER) | DEVELOPER

Show in SAP GUI   Show where terminals

Contents

Header Information
What happened?
Error analysis
Information on where terminated
Source Code Extract
Active Calls/Events

Header Information

Short Text	The class could not be found during the dynamic method call.
Runtime Error	DYN_CALL_METH_CLASS_NOT_FOUND
Exception	CX_SY_DYN_CALL_ILLEGAL_CLASS
Program	CL_CI_CATEGORY_INVALID========CP
Date/Time	24.10.2020 19:14:48 (System)
User	DEVELOPER
Client	001
Host	vhcalnplci_NPL_00

What happened?

Error in the ABAP application program.

The current ABAP program "CL_CI_CATEGORY_INVALID========CP" had to be terminated because it found a statement that could not be executed.

Error analysis

Figure 2-49. *Short dump view in Feed Reader*

I do not know how about you, but I usually know when I created a dump, so I do not need the notification from Eclipse. Fortunately, there is a way to switch off these notifications, or even completely delete the feed so they are not refreshed by Eclipse's background jobs. To do so, simply select the feed that you want to change and right-click it to bring up the context menu. You will then have the options to delete it or to edit the feed.

When you use the Edit the Feed function on the runtime errors feeds, you can not only disable the notifications display and change the refresh interval, but you can also set these filters: user, package, package hierarchy, package owner, object owner, person responsible, object name, component, runtime error, or exception. Those filters, which you can see in Figure 2-50, are set to your username. You can create a filter combination using OR and AND logic, so you should be able to adjust this to your needs.

Figure 2-50. *Edit of the Runtime Errors feed*

Nevertheless, I'm deleting those two standard feeds for runtime errors and keeping the System Messages feed, where system admins inform me about restart of the system or the next system copy.

I also activated the SAP Gateway Log and native RSS feeds to follow the SAP Community.

Activating the SAP Gateway Log is very helpful when you develop or deploy a Fiori application or oData services. Select the Down Arrow button from the view toolbar and choose Add Feed from Repository. When you do this, you will have to select the project (system) from which you want to receive the error log and select from the available feeds' SAP Gateway Error Log. This is shown in Figure 2-51.

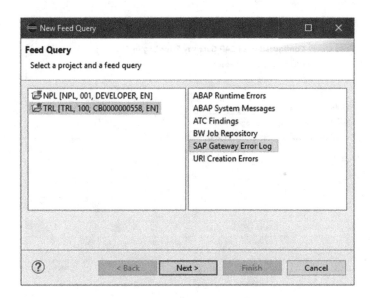

Figure 2-51. *New Feed query from the ABAP Repository*

The next step is to configure how frequent you want to get the information about the gateway errors. I set this to one minute during the testing phase and disable it after it is on a productive system for a while.

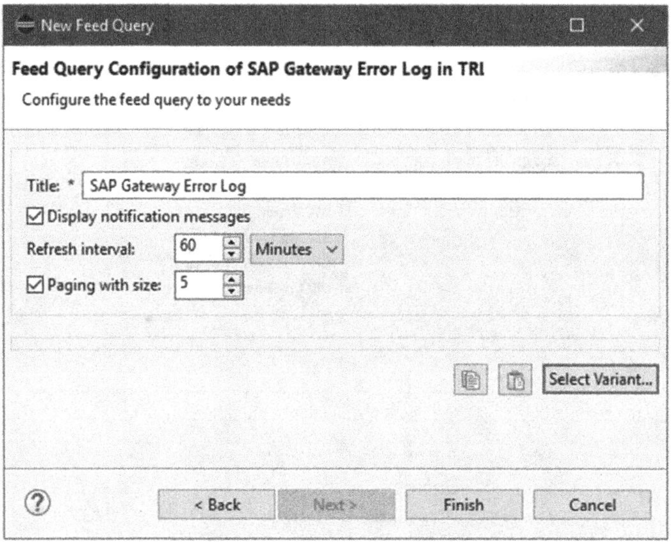

Figure 2-52. *Configuring the SAP Gateway Error Log*

After you set up all the preferences and click the Finish button, you will notice the SAP Gateway Error Log feed in the folder of the applicable system.

But using Feed Reader for only backend feeds would be a sin. You can also use it to read the standard RSS feeds and I do follow the SAP Community using it. If you want to do the same, you need to find the proper RSS feed link of the SAP Community website and use the Down Arrow button on the Feed Reader toolbar. But this time, choose Add Atom/ RSS Feed from URL. A popup will appear where you will have to enter the proper URL, as shown in Figure 2-53. In my example, I used RSS for the ABAP Development tag of the SAP Community.[3]

---

[3]The RSS ABAP Development tag of the SAP Community can be found at `https://content.services.sap.com/feed?type=blogpost&tags=83375557026073866192 4709785639136&title=Latest%20blog%20posts%20for%20ABAP%20Development`

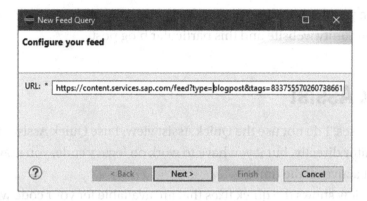

Figure 2-53. *New Feed Query for the RSS of the SAP Community*

When you set up the refresh interval and you confirm the creation of the feed, you will see it in the Native Feeds node of the Feed Reader, together with the last 20 feeds from that tag, as shown in Figure 2-54. This is one of the ways I stay in touch with all the new blog posts that are posted on the SAP Community.

Project / Feed Query / Feed Entry	Date	Time	Author	Total	U
∨ 🔊 (20) Native Feeds	24.10.2020	19:38:00		20	20
∨ 🗐 (20) Latest blog posts for ABAP Development	24.10.2020	19:38:00		20	20
Benefit from The Help Content in ADT	23.10.2020	17:19:15	Wolfgang Woehrle	1	
$Skiptoken System Query Option In SAP ODATA	23.10.2020	15:09:22	Anupam Behera	1	
Stay Informed About the Latest ADT Release Notes	23.10.2020	15:03:54	Wolfgang Woehrle	1	
Easy Handling of Complex Selection Screen	22.10.2020	22:32:04	Namasivayam Mani	1	
CI/CD Tools for SAP Cloud Platform ABAP Environment	22.10.2020	14:48:12	Daniel Mieg	1	
Nellie the ABAP Elephant	22.10.2020	03:10:13	Paul Hardy	1	
Creating Association and Parameterized Association Using BOE	21.10.2020	11:05:15	saraswathi purini	1	
SM49 & SM69 Wildcard external commands error	21.10.2020	05:05:54	kotamreddy satish redc	1	
ABAP Custom Code Migration | Hands-on Video Tutorials	20.10.2020	22:10:41	Denys van Kempen	1	
Append fields to IW38 (and maybe some other tcodes)	20.10.2020	12:01:16	V.X. Lozano	1	
Automatically generate issues from source code [abapGit]	20.10.2020	11:48:23	Enno Wulff	1	
How do I find out if the suffix of my choice is already used in a	20.10.2020	08:35:07	Andre Fischer	1	
Flexible Workflow: Custom Flexible Scenario – Part 3	19.10.2020	23:06:06	Mohammed Aymen	1	
Flexible Workflow: Custom Flexible Scenario - Part 4	19.10.2020	23:04:32	Mohammed Aymen	1	
Continuous quality using plugins and Jenkins (ABAP & UI5)	19.10.2020	00:33:08	Jacek Wozniczak	1	
something to learn from the Unix philosophy	18.10.2020	20:27:55	Michael Keller	1	
ABAP RESTful Application Programming Model (RAP) - FAQ	16.10.2020	14:37:02	Carine Tchoutouo Djom	1	
ABAP tips: Typed inline field symbol declaration	15.10.2020	18:20:16	Mike Pokraka	1	

Figure 2-54. *The latest blog post about ABAP developments on SAP Community*

When you double-click a native feed entry, you will be moved to the SAP Community website and this particular blog post.

Quick Assist

In most cases, I do not use the Quick Assist view. I use Quick Assist on the ABAP editor directly, but if you have to work on legacy code, you may want to have it active all the time.

This view shows the quick fixes that are available for your code when you place the cursor on a line, as shown in Figure 2-55. You would get the same list of proposals by using the Ctrl+1 shortcut on the code, but then you have to call it on demand.

Figure 2-55. *Quick Assist view*

Once you select the proposal that you want to accept, it will be applied to your code. In some cases, a popup will appear before the change in order to confirm all changes that will be applied in the current object and all that are affected. This is very visible, especially when refactoring the public class attributes or methods that are used in several places in your SAP environment.

The proposals that come from the ABAP backend can differ between the SAP NetWeaver versions, but all of the systems should contain several basic functions like renaming, changing visibility, pulling up or down, extraction of methods, and extraction of literals and constants. Quick Assist is covered in more detail in later chapters.

Relation Explorer

When your system is at least on NetWeaver version 7.54 or you are using SAP CP ABAP Environment 1908 or higher, you can use the Relation Explorer to get an overview of relations between the objects. The relations are displayed as a tree and grouped by the type of the related objects, which you can see in Figure 2-56.

You can open the object in Relation Explorer in a few different ways:

- By using the Alt+Shift+W shortcut in the editor

- By using the editor context menu Show In ➤ Relation Explorer

- By selecting the object using the Other Object view toolbar button

- By linking the Relation Explorer with the active editor

- By using the History List button on the view toolbar, to use previously used objects

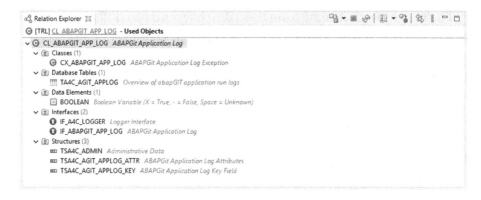

Figure 2-56. *Relation Explorer with used object context for the CL_ ABAPGIT_APP_LOG class*

The following contexts are available on this view:

- Business objects (for Data Definition Language Sources, Behavior Definitions, Behavior Implementation Classes, and CDS Views)

- Core data services (for CDS Views and Access Controls)

- Used objects (for most of the objects)

- Using objects (for most of the objects)

- Extended objects (for enhancement implementations)

- Extending objects (for objects that support the Enhancement Framework)

Each context displays different relation types; they can be selected from the toolbar menu using the Other Context button. You will not have to remember which of the contexts you can use for which object, because the list of the contexts are limited only to the ones that you can use.

ABAP Communication Log

You will not likely run into this view until you want to create your own plugin for Eclipse that communicates with the ABAP backend. This view displays information about communication between Eclipse and your SAP instance.

The log is not collected automatically, but you can manually launch it with the Start Logging button on the view toolbar. Once you activate it and start using the ABAP editor or other views that are fetching data from the backend, you will notice a HTTP session appearing, as shown in Figure 2-57. In addition to the request message, you can see information such as the status of the call, elapsed time, server time, and request and response size.

Time	Session	Request Message	Status	Thread	Elapse...	Server ...	Comm...	Request Siz...	Response S...	Version
17:07	NPL (140), s	GET /sap/bc/adt/runtime/dumps?$query=and%28%20(	200	Worker-2!	19	14	4		0,632	HTTP/1.1
17:07	NPL (139), s	GET /sap/bc/adt/runtime/dumps?$query=and%28%20(	200	Worker-3!	30	26	3		0,639	HTTP/1.1
17:07	NPL (138), s	GET /sap/bc/adt/runtime/systemmessages	200	Worker-37	8	4	3		0,519	HTTP/1.1
17:06	NPL (137), s	POST /sap/bc/adt/debugger/batch		Worker-38	0	0	0	0,462		HTTP/1.1
17:06	NPL (137), s	POST /sap/bc/adt/debugger?method=getVariables	200	Worker-2!	8	5	2	0,209	0,749	HTTP/1.1
17:06	NPL (137), s	GET /sap/bc/adt/debugger/stack?emode=_&semanticl	200	Worker-3!	27	24	2		1,277	HTTP/1.1
17:06	NPL (137), s	POST /sap/bc/adt/debugger?method=setDebuggerSett	200	Worker-3!	7	4	2	0,237	0,247	HTTP/1.1
17:06	NPL (137), s	POST /sap/bc/adt/debugger?method=attach&debugg-	200	Worker-3!	50	37	12		1,459	HTTP/1.1
17:06	NPL (136), s	POST /sap/bc/adt/debugger/listeners?debuggingMode		Worker-14	0	0	0			HTTP/1.1
17:06	NPL (135), s	POST /sap/bc/adt/debugger/breakpoints	200	Worker-3!	269	212	56	2,094	2,096	HTTP/1.1
17:06	NPL (134), s	GET /sap/bc/adt/runtime/traces/abaptraces/paramet;	200	Worker-28	513	468	44	0,829		HTTP/1.1
17:06	NPL (133), s	GET /sap/bc/adt/security/reentranceticket	200	Worker-2!	761	8	752		0,5	HTTP/1.1
17:06	TRL (57), sto	POST /sap/bc/adt/debugger/listeners?debuggingMode		Worker-4:	0	0	0			HTTP/1.1
17:04	NPL (130), s	POST /sap/bc/adt/debugger/listeners?debuggingMode	200	Worker-14	112263	112261	1		1,258	HTTP/1.1
17:02	TRL (53), sta	POST /sap/bc/adt/debugger/listeners?debuggingMode	200	Worker-4:	240126	240028	97			HTTP/1.1

Figure 2-57. ABAP communication log with activated logging

When you double-click the HTTP session line, you will access the details of the call, which include the request, response, stack trace on Eclipse side, and destination properties. Details of a sample call are shown in Figure 2-58. This should be your first place to check if something is wrong with the communication between your plugin and the backend.

111

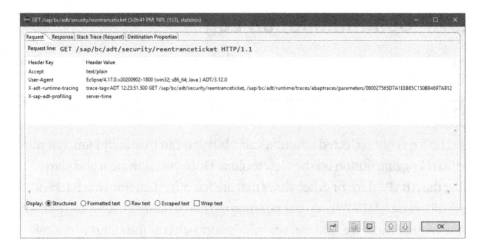

Figure 2-58. *Details of an HTTP call to the SAP backend*

If this fails, use the View menu or toolbar button to activate ABAP tracing for the HTTP calls. While activated, it will generate trace requests and collect the trace information in the system. You can use ABAP Traces view to read the trace information.

Even if everything is going correctly with your calls, you can test the behavior of Eclipse when only a slow connection to the system is available. To do so, use the Snail button on the view toolbar and select one of the preconfigured delays, or set up your own custom delays for the calls. This might help you determine if you want to do your HTTP call synchronously or asynchronously.

ABAP Trace Requests

Every ABAP developer has to check the performance of the code, but sometimes you are not able to repeat the steps the user took on the production system. In this case, you need to activate tracing in order to get detailed information about the runtime of the code.

The ABAP Trace Requests view was prepared to create and manage tracings, especially when you cannot run profiling directly on an object. To create a new request, simply click the Create Trace Request button and the wizard for trace scheduling will open, as shown in Figure 2-59.

You first need to select the scope of the tracing between the following:

- Web requests (HTTP)

- Reports and transactions (dialog)

- Remote function calls (RFCs)

- Background jobs (batch)

- Shared objects area

- Any (trace object with all possible scopes)

When you choose the proper scope, you will need to select the object type from the following:

- Report

- Transaction

- Function module

- Area constructor

- Any (which you will be able to use, for example, for class tracing)

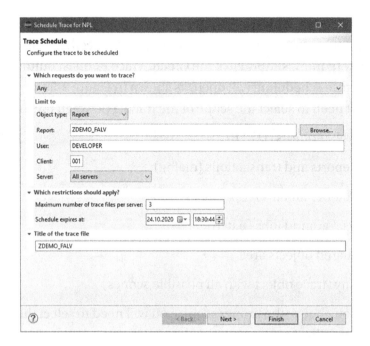

Figure 2-59. *Scheduling a new trace request: scope selection*

After object type selection, you will have to choose which object you want to trace, for which user and client, and on which server. If you want to run tracing for any user, just leave the user field empty. Additionally, you need to choose for how long the tracing will be active and after how many catches of the trace will the system stop collecting them. It is also important to set a proper name for the tracing, especially if you run lots of traces at the same time.

There are six trace parameter groups that you can use to customize your trace request. They are presented in Figure 2-60. They allow you to set the aggregation type, ABAP statements scope, time of the trace start, its maximum size and execution time, or AMDP tracing with HANA-based systems. Most of these settings should be familiar from the SAT transaction, which is used for profiling in SAP GUI.

Figure 2-60. Scheduling a new trace request: parameters

You can also set up default profiling parameters by using the Configure Defaults hyperlink on that screen, which is quite helpful if you are focused only on parts of the ABAP statements.

The trace request will appear on the requests list with all basic configuration information and with the number of trace executions; see Figure 2-61. The executions are not refreshed automatically when the view is open, so you need to click the Refresh button to see whether new executions took place.

Project / Server	Description	Time	Date	Object	Executions	Expires at	Object Type
⌄ 🖫 NPL [user filter: DEVELOPER, refreshed: 17:33:55, 24.10.2020]							
vhcalnplci	ZDEMO_FALV01	17:33:55	24.10.2020	ZDEMO_FALV01	0 / 3	18:30 24.10.2020	Report
vhcalnplci	ZDEMO_FALV01	21:59:08	05.10.2020	ZDEMO_FALV01	1 / 3	22:55 05.10.2020	Report
🖫 TRL [user filter: CB0000000558, refreshed: 17:30:34, 24.10.2020]							

Figure 2-61. ABAP Trace Request view

In order to see the trace details, you need to open ABAP Traces view or double-click the trace request. Then the ABAP Traces view will be opened automatically, highlighting the linked traces on the view.

ABAP Traces

Traces can be created in several ways in ADT. I already mentioned that they can be created from the ABAP Communication Log and from the ABAP Trace Requests view, yet there are some additional options:

- From the Project Explorer, Outline, or Editor using the context menu: Choose Profile As ➤ ABAP Application or Profile As ➤ ABAP Unit Test.

- From the Eclipse menu bar: Choose Run ➤ Profile As ➤ ABAP Application or Run ➤ Profile As ➤ ABAP Unit Test.

- From the Eclipse toolbar button: Choose Profile As ➤ ABAP Application or Profile As ➤ ABAP Unit Test.

- Use the Ctrl+F9 shortcut, which will call profiling as an ABAP application.

After a successful run, the trace will be listed on the ABAP Traces view with basic information about it, including the date and time of execution, checked object, aggregation or runtime, and size information. The columns visible in Figure 2-62 are exactly the same as in a SAT transaction. Traces created in ADT are also visible in a SAT transaction and vice versa.

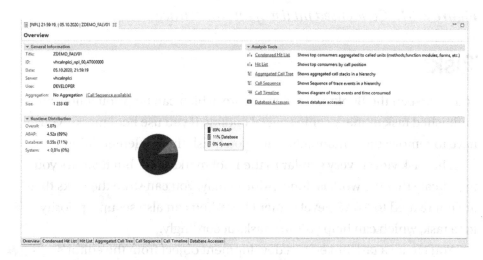

Figure 2-62. *ABAP traces lists*

You are not limited to your own traces; you can change the user filter
by using the context menu on the project name and choosing the Change
User Filter option.

When you double-click the trace, a new window will open with the
details of the trace. This window contains two or more tabs, depending
on the aggregation level of your trace. The Overview tab, which is shown
in Figure 2-63, will give you general information about trace, like the time
spent on ABAP, and the database and system calls.

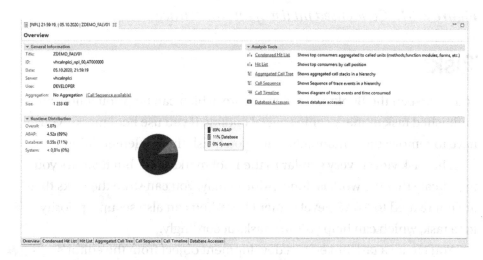

Figure 2-63. *ABAP Trace details*

The rest of the tabs show detailed information, just like the SAT tool does. For example, Figure 2-64 displays a condensed hit list of the ZDEMO_ FALV01 program, with accumulated information about the number and runtime of the called units (methods, forms, function modules, screens, etc.).

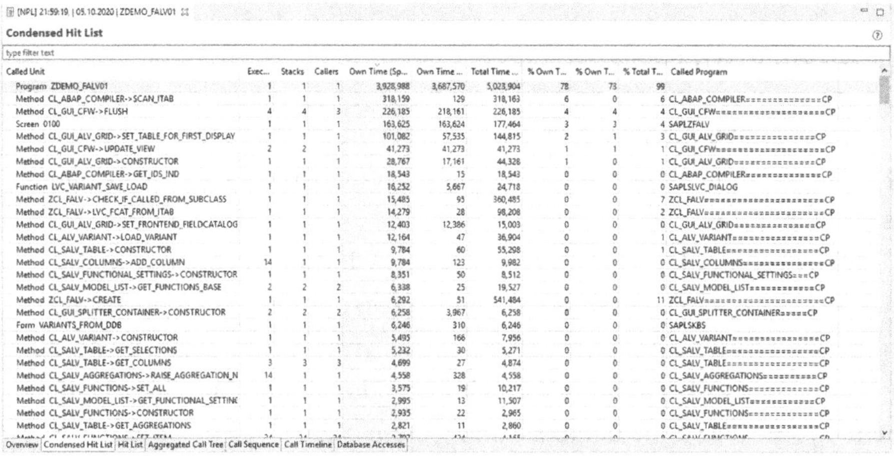

Figure 2-64. *Condensed hit list of an ABAP trace*

Tasks

You have seen the Bookmarks view before, which can help you follow an unfinished task or mark some special coding. If you use bookmarks, you have to remove them manually when you finish the implementation.

The Task view is very similar to the Bookmarks view, but it allows you to indicate that the work is done. Additionally, you can store the tasks that are not related to ABAP development here. You can also set up a priority for a task, which can help you sort tasks accordingly.

You create a task linked to a development object from the editor's vertical ruler. You right-click in the line for which the task should be created. A new window will appear; it allows you to set up a task description and priority. Looking at Figure 2-65, you can see that the link to the development object is filled and grayed out to avoid manual modifications. After clicking the Add Button, your task will appear on the list with details.

Properties
Description:
TODO: xxxx
Priority:
Normal
Completed
On element:
zcl_falv.aclass
Path:
NPL/.adt/classlib/classes/zcl_falv
Location:
line 1742
Add
Cancel

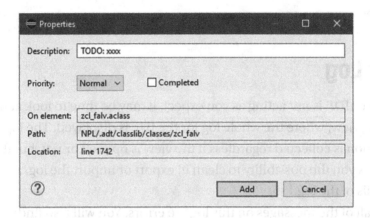

Figure 2-65. *New task linked to an ABAP Development Object*

From the view, you can create tasks that are not linked to development objects. To do so, use the context menu and choose the Add Task... option. The same window as in Figure 2-65 will appear, but this time with the element, path, and location fields empty. On the list of tasks, you will see that the resource and path entries are empty and the location is set to Unknown, just like the second task in Figure 2-66.

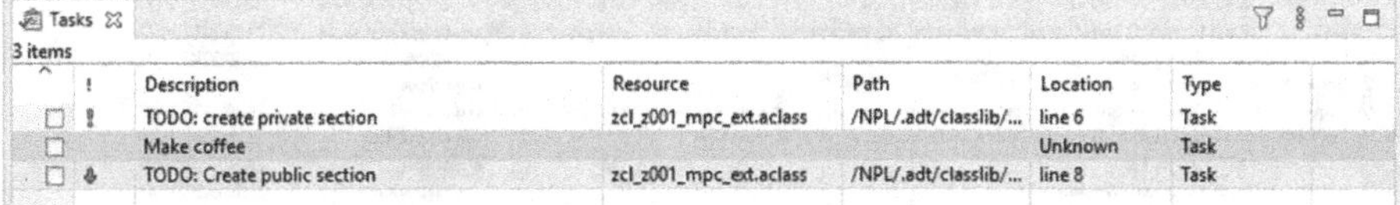

Tasks
3 items
Description
Resource
Path
Location
Type
TODO: create private section
zcl_z001_mpc_ext.aclass
/NPL/.adt/classlib/...
line 6
Task
Make coffee
Unknown
Task
TODO: Create public section
zcl_z001_mpc_ext.aclass
/NPL/.adt/classlib/...
line 8
Task

Figure 2-66. *Task view with tree tasks of different priorities*

As I mentioned, you can sort the task by priority, as well as by any other column available on the list. You can also filter the entries to show tasks that include specific text, or create a separate view with a customized filter. You should not be surprised that after double-clicking a task that's linked to a development object, you will be moved into the linked line of the object.

Error Log

When your IDE is not acting as you expect, it may be time to look at the Error Log view, where the whole log for the IDE is displayed. The log information is collected regardless if the view is opened or not, but the view gives you the possibility to clean it, export or import the log, and view the details of the log.

Not all of the messages on this log are errors. You will also find warnings and information, which you can see in Figure 2-67. You will also see the plugin that raised the message and the date of the error.

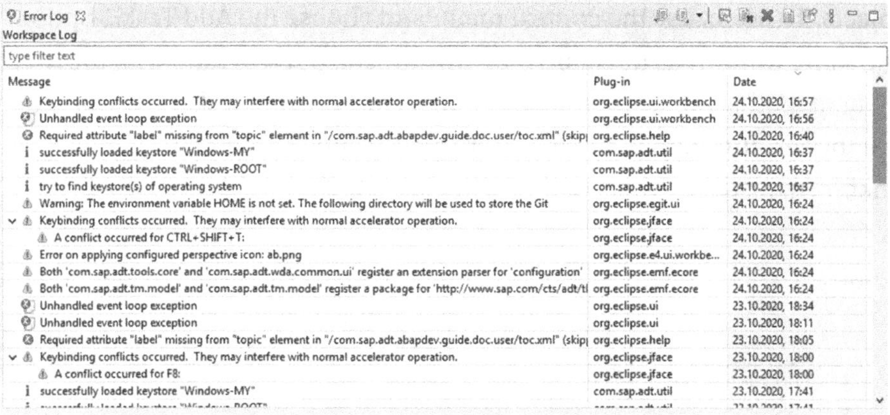

Figure 2-67. *Error log view*

If you want to see the details of the message, just double-click the message text. The details will be shown, including the stack trace and some session data. An example of the details you can find are shown in Figure 2-68.

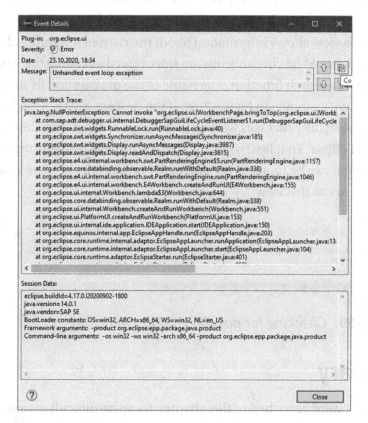

Figure 2-68. *Error details*

You may wonder why you would need to check these details, but the answer is very easy—ADT and Eclipse are frequently updated and some of the functionality can contain bugs after an upgrade. This details view sent to the Eclipse community or SAP support can raise awareness of the issue and can speed up resolution time. It can also be helpful, when you create your own Eclipse plugin, to see where your code is failing.

Progress

Normally, you should not be concerned about the background calls that are happening in Eclipse, but if there are some issues with your IDE or one of its plugins, this view can help you figure out where the error is coming from.

Progress view shows information about the current background jobs in Eclipse. This could be checking update sites as well as calling the where-used list or the search function. The name of the process and its progress will be shown, as shown in Figure 2-69. If the process will take too long or there are too many processes waiting in the queue, it can slow down your work with Eclipse. That is why you can kill the process by using the Stop button, which can be found at the end of the progress bar. I hope you will never have to use this view.

Figure 2-69. *Checking for possible updates to Eclipse*

Summary

Many views were described in this chapter. It can be difficult to remember what all of them do, but you should have an idea about what information you can get in ADT without using the SAP GUI. You can come back to this chapter whenever you see one of the views on your screen and need more information.

The next chapter focuses on the ABAP Editor and the possibilities that it gives every developer to work faster and more efficient with ABAP code.

CHAPTER 3

How to Use ABAP in Eclipse to Accelerate Your Work

In my opinion, using the ABAP Development Tools in Eclipse instead of the ABAP Workbench (SE80) brings lots of efficiency and new possibilities to ABAP developers' lives. Although I know it is not easy to switch to Eclipse if you have used SE80 for many years, I hope that after reading this chapter, you will give it a try and will be happy that you did.

ABAP Source Code Editor View

Before learning how to use Eclipse and ADT, let's take a look at how the ABAP source code editor looks. Figure 3-1 shows the following elements:

- Editor tabs
- Breadcrumbs
- Vertical ruler
- Overview ruler
- Line numbers

© Lukasz Pegiel 2021
Ł. Pęgiel, *ABAP in Eclipse*, https://doi.org/10.1007/978-1-4842-6963-3_3

- Source code

- Internal editor tabs

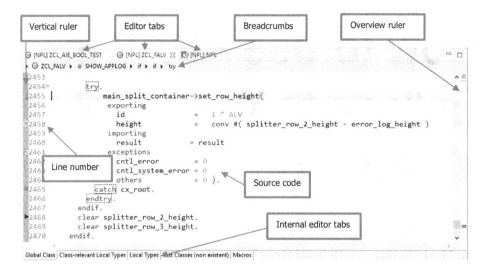

Figure 3-1. *The ABAP Editor with bookmarks, tasks, breakpoints, and logpoints*

Editor Tabs

When you open an object in Eclipse, it is displayed in a separate tab. You can have multiple tabs open at the same time, but the more tabs that are open, the more memory Eclipse takes, which you can compare to the behavior of web browsers.

In the case of ABAP objects, all tabs have the prefix [sytemID] before the name of the object. That is why it is better to give your project a short name if possible.

If you open many tabs, the object's name will be shortened to the maximum number of characters followed by ..., which will tell you that you do not see the full name. Figure 3-2 displays this behavior and shows the window that appears when you click the Show List button. This button is visible only if there are tabs that do not fit in the editor area. When you look at the list of tabs, you will notice that some of them are in bold and a few of them not. The bold ones are currently hidden, and those with normal font are currently visible.

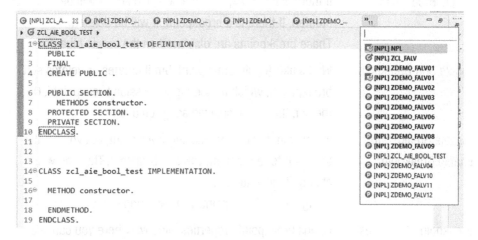

***Figure 3-2.** Eclipse with many opened objects*

Icons of the object types are also visible in the tab. This makes navigation easier if, for whatever reason, you used the same name for a few different object types and you opened them in the same time.

Vertical Ruler

There are a few things that the vertical ruler is used for. First of all, it displays several markers, including breakpoints, syntax errors, ATC findings, current debug locations, and many more. All of the markers have their own unique icon and can display more details when you hover the mouse over them. By double-clicking on one, you can toggle the breakpoint on the selected line.

Secondly, you can use the context menu to create, change, or delete the breakpoints, logpoints, tasks, or bookmarks on a selected line. All these functions are listed in Table 3-1.

Table 3-1. *Vertical Ruler Context Menu Actions*

Action	Use
Toggle Breakpoint	If there is no breakpoint at a selected line, it will be created. If there is a breakpoint, it will be deleted. These breakpoints are displayed on the bar as blue dots.
Toggle Soft Breakpoint	Works like Toggle Breakpoint, but it creates or deletes soft breakpoints, which are debugger session breakpoints. On the bar, they are displayed as green dots.
Disable Breakpoint/ Enable Breakpoint	If you want to keep an existing breakpoint, but you want to omit if for a moment, you can disable it. The icon will change to a white dot. Using Enable Breakpoint, you can bring it back.
Breakpoint Properties	Opens breakpoint properties window, where you can see and change the type of breakpoint and its conditions.
Refresh Breakpoints Activation	Sometimes it happens that a breakpoint stops working. One possible solution is to refresh the activation of the breakpoints.
Debug Properties	Opens the debug properties window for the current project. Among others you can set the user used for debugging.
Add Bookmark	Runs an Add Bookmark wizard for the selected line.
Add Task	Runs an Add Task wizard for the selected line.
Create Logpoint	Runs a Create Logpoint wizard for the selected line.
Show Quick Diff	Enables or disables the Quick Difference comparison.
Show Line Numbers	Shows or hides the line numbers in the editor.

(continued)

Table 3-1. (*continued*)

Action	Use
Folding	This group of functions allows you to manage code folding with the following actions:
	• Enable Folding
	• Expand All
	• Collapse All
Preferences	Opens the editor properties for a current project.

One of the last functionalities of the vertical ruler is highlighting the current code unit (for example, a method or form) with a dotted blue pattern. As an example, Figure 3-3 shows ruler highlights when the cursor is inside the implementation of the SET_BLOB_KEY method. When the code is written correctly, you will probably not use this information, but if the method or form has dozens of lines, it can be useful when scrolling down or up. It is easy then to see where the code unit begins or ends, without reading all the code.

```
293
294⊖  method set_blob_key.|
295      change_setting( iv_value = iv_value iv_setting = 'BLOB_KEY' ).
296      r_layout = me.
297  endmethod.
298
299
300⊖  method set_blob_name.
301      change_setting( iv_value = iv_value iv_setting = 'BLOB_NAME' ).
302      r_layout = me.
303  endmethod.
```

Figure 3-3. *Vertical ruler with highlighted implementation of the SET_BLOB_KEY method*

Markers visible on the ruler can be customized in the preferences.

Overview Ruler

This ruler is strongly connected to the Vertical ruler and it shows the places where the markers occur, but there are a few differences. First of all, the ruler is fixed, which means it does not move when you scroll through the code. The ruler represents the whole source code and the occurrence of the marker will be set on this ruler proportionally to its position in the code.

Occurrences and markers are display as small rectangles that are formatted differently for each type. When you click the occurrence in the ruler, you will be navigated to the source codeline to which the current occurrence is linked. What is shown on this ruler is highly customizable. The next chapter explains how to customize it.

Breadcrumbs

As on many websites, breadcrumbs allow you to quickly identify where you are in the code and navigate through it. This functionality is activated through the button that's available on the main toolbar.

As you can see in Figure 3-4, breadcrumbs show the current unit (method, form) and the block of code (IF, CASE, WHILE, LOOP, etc.). The more complex your code, the more levels will be shown, each of them separated by an ` button. You can use this button for navigation. When you click the object, it will display the current objects or all steps of the block code, depending on what appears after the button. I find this functionality very handy when working with complex CASE or IF statements.

Figure 3-4. *Breadcrumbs of the class source code*

Source Code

Most developers would say that the source code of an object opened in the two different IDEs is exactly the same. I would say the same if I did not work with the ABAP language. There are some slight differences when you work with SE80 compared to what you see in ADT.

I had mentioned that there is no form-base editor for classes in ADT, so you have to write the definitions of methods and attributes manually in the code. Another difference is with the function module, as in SE80 the signature of a function module is shown as a comment in the source code editor and you have to use five additional tabs (Importing, Exporting, Changing, Tables, and Exceptions) to update this signature. As you can see in Figure 3-5, in ADT, you are creating and changing the signature of the function module directly in the code.

```
  ▶ ◉ Z_FALV_ADD_FALV_TO_STACK
  1 ⊖ FUNCTION Z_FALV_ADD_FALV_TO_STACK
  2      IMPORTING
  3        IO_FALV TYPE REF TO ZCL_FALV.|
  4
  5
  6
  7      insert new lcl_output( io_falv ) into table outputs.
  8
  9  endfunction.
```

Figure 3-5. *Source code of the function module in ADT*

The rest looks the same at first sight, as you have line numbers and formatted keywords, literals, numbers, and comments, but you will notice differences when you begin working with the editor.

Internal Editor Tabs

When you edit the classes inside ADT, you will notice that the editor contains five tabs at the bottom:

- Global Class

- Class-Relevant Local Types

- Local Types

- Test Classes

- Macros

They should not be something new if you have developed the classes in SE80. If you are new to ABAP, I'll briefly explain what they can contain.

The Global Class tab always contains the main code of the dictionary class with a public, protected, and private section. ABAP allows you to create local classes inside global classes, which is why you have two additional tabs: Class-Relevant Local Types and Local Types.

Inside Class-Relevant Local Types, you can only put the definition of the class, interface, or type. No implementation is allowed, but the advantage of putting the definitions in this tab is that you can use the declared objects inside the declaration of attributes or method parameters and inside the private section of the global class.

All implementations and additional definitions of classes, interfaces, and types are in the Local Types tab. They cannot be used in the declaration of the attributes or method attributes in any section of the global class definition, but they can be used in any place of global class implementation.

The Test Classes tab creates the unit tests. They are also local classes, but a special type. I will describe unit testing a bit more later in this chapter.

Last but not least, the Macros tab is where you can put all your macros definitions that you want to use in global or local classes. Personally, I have never used this tab, but there are developers who like macros and they use this tab a lot.

Toolbar

Besides the editor itself, you also need to learn about the toolbar and its buttons. Naturally, you can do most actions using the keyboard shortcuts, but the toolbar is helpful as well.

As you may recall, the toolbar depends on the perspective and is customizable. In Figure 3-6, you can see the default toolbar that comes with ABAP perspective.

Figure 3-6. *Default toolbar of ABAP perspective*

When you look at Table 3-2, you can read about the buttons' uses. Some of them are self-explanatory and others need a more detailed explanation, which appear in the next sections of this chapter.

Table 3-2. *Brief Description of the Toolbar Buttons*

Button	Use
□ ▾	New: Opens a new development object wizard.
🖫	Save: Saves changes to the currently active editor tab.
🖫	Save All: Saves changes to all opened and modified editor tabs.
◔	Skip All Breakpoints: Deactivates the breakpoints but keeps them on the breakpoints list.
🗐	Open ABAP Development Object: Opens a window for object selection. After selection, it opens the object in the Eclipse editor.
⚙	Run ABAP Development Object as SAP GUI Application: Opens a window for object selection popup, after selection it runs the selected object in a test environment of the embedded SAP GUI.
🖥	Open SAP GUI: Runs a GUI instance in the new tab.
✔	Check ABAP Development Object: Checks the object for syntax errors.
⚡	Activate: Activates the currently active object.
⚡	Activate inactive ABAP Development objects: Allows activation of many objects at the same time.
⟳	Toggle between active and inactive version: Self explanatory.
🔓	Unlock: Unlocks the object, allowing other developers to go to edit mode.
⟳	Refresh: Reloads the editor content from the database.
⟲	ABAP Where-used list: Launches a usage search of the object or its part.
💭	Toggles the breadcrumb.
▨	Toggles the marked occurrences.

(*continued*)

Table 3-2. (*continued*)

Button	Use
	Debug: Not used in ABAP development, but useful for Eclipse plugin developments.
	Run As: When clicked, shows a popup with the possible run scenarios for an object; for example ATC, ABAP application in console view, etc. When the arrow is expanded, historical runs are visible and run configuration is possible.
	Profile: Runs profiling for the active object. By default, it runs the object as an ABAP application. If you want to run profiling for unit tests or see the history of profiling, use the arrow next to this button.
	External Tool: Allows you to configure and run external tools.
	Search: Runs the search dialog, which allows you to search ABAP objects or ABAP source search.
	Toggle Word Wrap
	Toggle Block Selection Mode
	Show Whitespaces Characters
	Next Annotation: Jumps to the next annotation, You can choose which annotations are supported by using the arrow next to this button.
	Previous Annotation: Similar to the Next Annotation, but sends it back to the previous annotation.
	Previous Edit Location
	Next Edit Location
	Back To: Navigates back, works similarly to the back button of SAP GUI, but for editor tabs.

(*continued*)

Table 3-2. (*continued*)

Button	Use
⇨ ▾	Forward To: When you click the Back To button at least once, this will be activated and you will be able to navigate forward.
⌐	Pin Editor

Writing ABAP Code in Eclipse

Now that you've looked at the ABAP editor, it's time to start to learn how to develop ABAP in Eclipse. Of course, the syntax does not differ between the IDEs, but there are huge differences in Eclipse and the SE80. All the options described here are available in the ADT default settings.

Creating New ABAP Objects

When you want to create a class, program, or any other ABAP object in SAP GUI, you go to SE80, select the object type in the repository browser, type the name of the new object, and press Enter. The system checks if the object exists, and if it doesn't, it asks if you want to create it. If the object does exist, it's opened in the editor. The same process happens in SE11 for the dictionary objects, like table, structures, data elements, and domains.

In Eclipse, objects are created by calling the New action from the Project Explorer's menu bar, toolbar, or context menu. You could observe this when you created your first ABAP project. You simply choose File ➤ New ➤ Other... or use the Ctrl+N shortcut to call a new object wizard, as shown in Figure 3-7. All the ABAP and SAP object types will be listed under the ABAP folder and its subfolders.

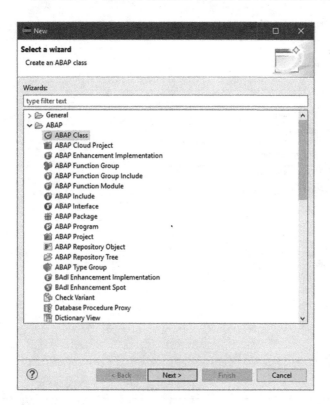

Figure 3-7. *New object wizard*

After selecting the object type, you have to give it a name, description, package, and set up some other attributes, depending on the object type. In my example, I created a class called ZCL_AIE_FIRST_CLASS in the local package $CHAPTER03. As you can see in Figure 3-8, I can also add a superclass and any interfaces I want to implement in my class, but I left this empty for now.

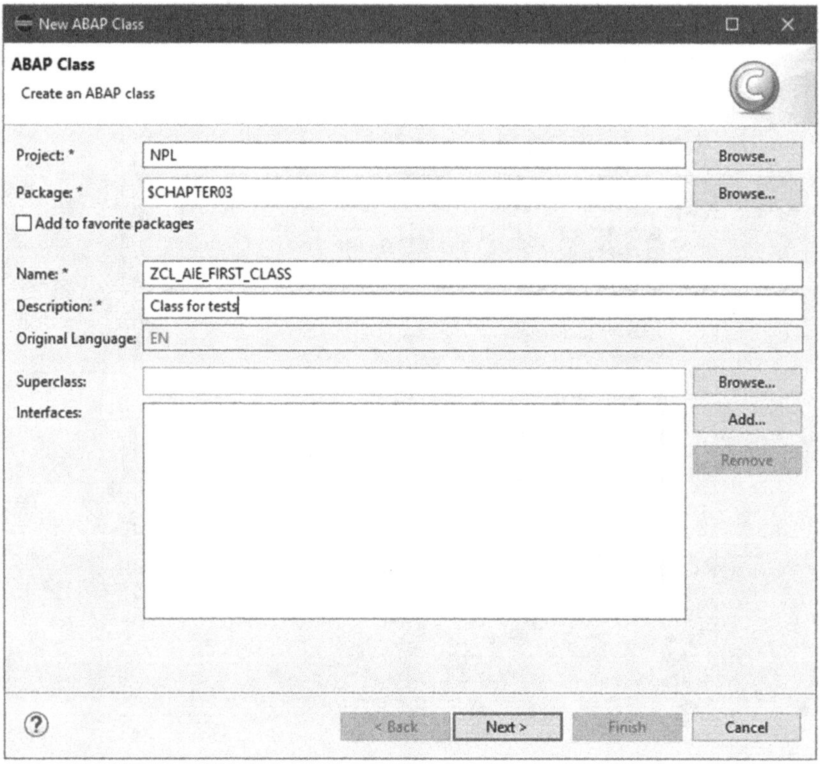

Figure 3-8. *ABAP class creation wizard*

The next window that appears is selecting transport requests. This window will appear whenever you create or modify an object in Eclipse. As you can imagine, you can create a new transport request, use one from a list of requests, or select any other existing modifiable transport request.

I am creating an object that belongs to the local package, so the window shown in Figure 3-9 is informing me that change recording is disabled for the $CHAPTER03 package, which is why all the options for selecting the proper transport request are disabled.

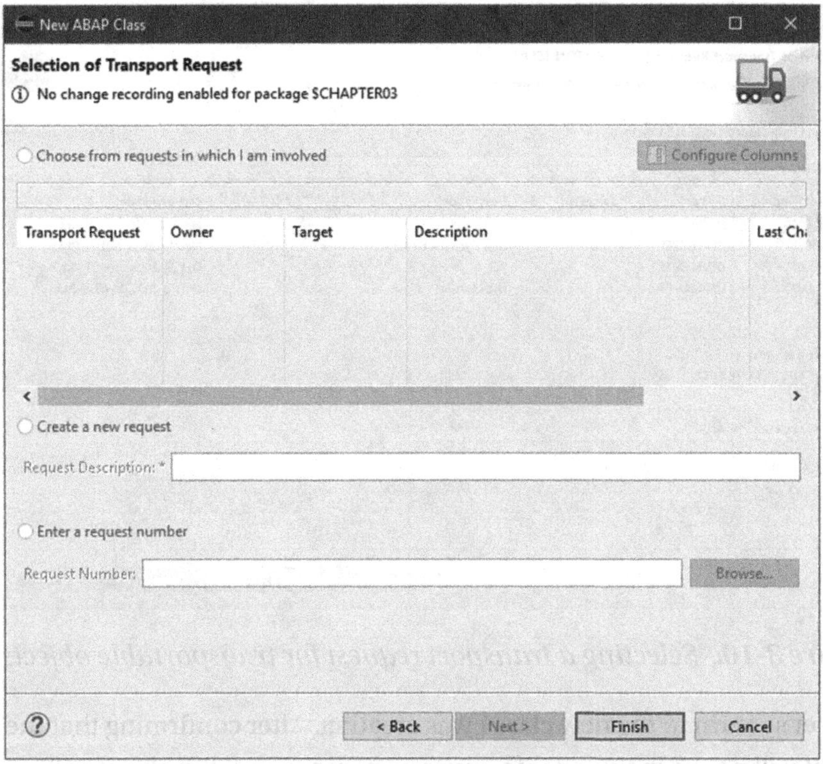

Figure 3-9. *Selecting a transport request for local package objects*

To see how it would look for a transportable object, see Figure 3-10. All the radio buttons are active and you can select transport requests according to your needs.

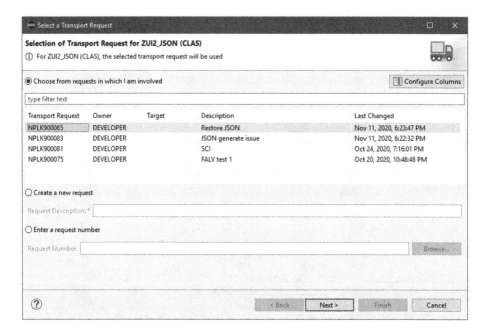

Figure 3-10.   *Selecting a transport request for transportable objects*

Let's return to the new class I was creating. After confirming that the object will not be included into any transport request, the object will be created and opened in the new tab of the ABAP editor. As shown in Figure 3-11, the class will contain empty definition and implementation parts and the fun with ABAP begins here.

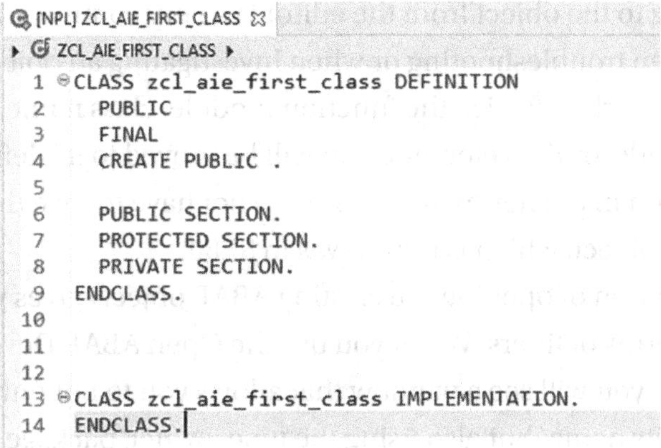

```
 [NPL] ZCL_AIE_FIRST_CLASS 
▸  ZCL_AIE_FIRST_CLASS ▸
 1 ⊖CLASS zcl_aie_first_class DEFINITION
 2     PUBLIC
 3     FINAL
 4     CREATE PUBLIC .
 5
 6     PUBLIC SECTION.
 7     PROTECTED SECTION.
 8     PRIVATE SECTION.
 9  ENDCLASS.
10
11
12
13 ⊖CLASS zcl_aie_first_class IMPLEMENTATION.
14  ENDCLASS.
```

Figure 3-11. *New class with empty definition and implementation parts*

For the other objects, it looks exactly the same. However, if your system doesn't yet support all the ADT features, instead of the ADT editor, you will see SAP GUI opened with the proper transaction that you have used so far to create this particular type of object.

Opening Existing ABAP Objects

There are three ways to open existing objects in ADT:

- Select an object from the Project Explorer and double-click it

- Navigate to the object from another object that is using it (by default, using Ctrl+Left click)

- Select the object using the Open ABAP Development Object button of the ADT toolbar (or its shortcut, Ctrl+Shift+A)

Navigating to the object from the editor is a very common situation, especially when troubleshooting or when investigating an object. Whenever you Ctrl+Left click the function module, class name, program, include, or data element, you will be moved to its definition or implementation in the new window. You do not have to save the changes in the current object, which is how it was in SE80.

The last option of opening the existing ABAP objects gives you flexibility in terms of filters. When you use the Open ABAP Development Object button, you will see a window that allows you to not only search the objects using its name, but also using the type, owner, package and a few other filters. When this option is used and when you have the active editor open, the project will be automatically set to the same project as the object from the active tab. Figure 3-12 displays the initial state of this window.

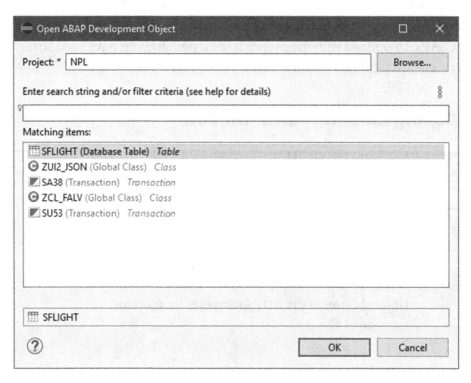

Figure 3-12. *Open the ABAP Development Object window*

You can now place the search string inside the input field. It can be a standard string like ZCL_AAA or you can use patterns with asterisk (*) and question mark (?) signs. As in SAP GUI, an asterisk replaces any number of characters and a question mark replaces exactly one character. Figure 3-13 displays the results of an ABAP search using the Z?L_FA* pattern. The pattern found is in bold so you can see how ADT determined the objects to display.

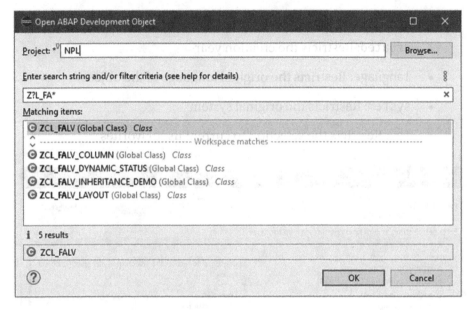

Figure 3-13. *Searching for an object using patterns*

Patterns are sometimes not enough, as we may want to narrow it down more. In such cases, it is reasonable to use filters. Filters can differ between systems, as they are linked to the backend version, but their behavior and use will be the same.

To use filters, you can write code into the search field followed by a colon and add the parameters separated by commas. For example owner: developer,developer2. You can also use the Ctrl+Space shortcut, which calls a completion assistant for the filters, allowing you to select proper entries from the list.

Figure 3-14 shows the possible types of filters on newer systems:

- type: Restricts the type of the searched object

- appl: Restricts the application component of the object

- package: Restricts the search to the selected packages

- owner: Restricts the creator of the objects

- api: Restricts the API state

- created: Restricts the creation year

- language: Restricts the original language of the objects

- system: Restricts the original system

- fav: Restricts the selection to current user favorites

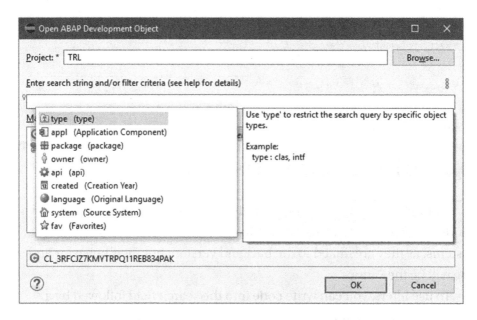

Figure 3-14. *Possible filters for searching objects*

After selecting a filter type, you need to give the parameter or parameters to it, which depend on the type of filter. I recommend you use the completion assistant to get a list of possible entries, as it is hard to remember all the possibilities of each filter. Just look at Figure 3-15, which shows a few possible entries for the Type filter. Without the description in the brackets, it would be hard to imagine what you could use a specific object type. I have noticed that the type names are the same as the object types that are used inside the transport requests, but still there are so many types that I cannot remember them all.

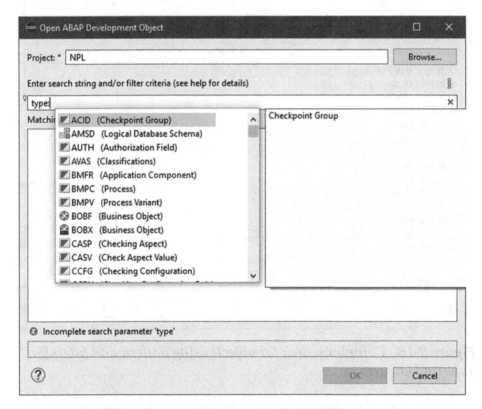

Figure 3-15. Completion assistant for the Type filter

After selecting the proper filter or filters (you can use more than one at a time), you can add a string or pattern to narrow the search results. Figure 3-16 shows the search results for pattern Z*falv used together with the type: prog and owner:developer filters. This represents all programs that were created by user DEVELOPER with a name containing the pattern Z*falv. Notice also that the sequence of the filters does not matter.

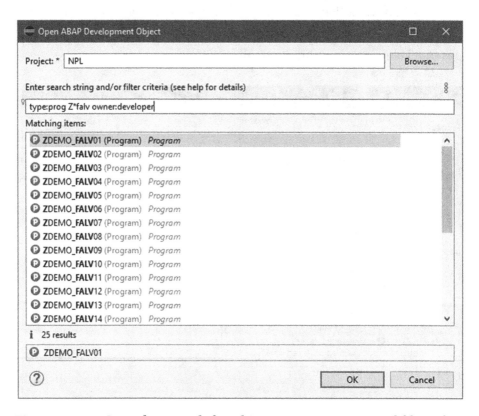

Figure 3-16. *Complex search for objects using pattern and filters for Type and Owner*

After you find the object you are looking for, just double-click it or select a few objects on the list using the Shift or Ctrl key and click the OK button. The selected object will be opened in the editor tab.

Note All objects are opened in display mode, but there is no button to go to edit mode. Simply go to the place of code or definition that you want to adjust and start writing. At the first key stroke, ADT will verify that someone else is not blocking the object at the moment. If not, you will be able to make the modifications. If it is blocked, you will be informed.

Syntax Check

One of the first things you will notice while developing in Eclipse is the constant syntax check. I have been waiting for this functionality for many years, as it is not available in SE80. Of course, you can use Ctrl+F2 to check it manually after writing a line or block of code, but I was used to having direct syntax check in other programming languages. I really think this a basic feature that every IDE should have.

When you make a mistake in ADT, you will be notified directly when you stop writing for a second. The error is underlined with a red zigzag line and an error marker will appear on the vertical ruler close to the line number. Additionally, you will see the error in the Problems view, if it is open. This behavior is shown in Figure 3-17.

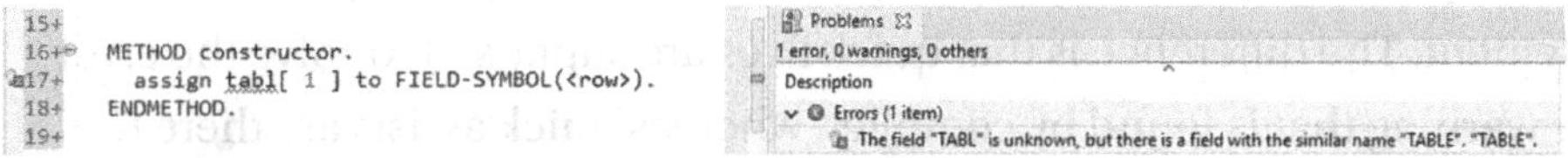

Figure 3-17. *Syntax check during ABAP development*

Closing Brackets and Literals Automatically

Another very simple, but useful, functionality is closing the brackets and literals automatically and allowing you to skip outside of them with the Tab key. Whenever you write a [{ (' " ` | character, they will automatically be closed. The cursor will remain inside, but you can use the Tab key to move the cursor outside.

What is nice here is that it works with complex expressions, so if you are writing a codeline with several brackets and literals, until you are using your keyboard, Eclipse will remember which location to jump to after you press Tab again.

By default, when you open a bracket, Eclipse adds space after it and puts the cursor in that position. If you want to use the old syntax, you can press the Tab key directly and the space will be removed, leaving [ ] in place and taking you outside the closing bracket. With literals, no space is added, and the closing sign is added directly after the opening one. The cursor stays in between them.

Quick Assist and Quick Fixes

I like to use quick fixes and assists in other languages, which is why I was very happy when I could finally do this ABAP developments inside Eclipse. Both options are called using the same shortcut, Ctrl+1, on an object element. The difference is that quick fixes are supposed to solve the error or warning that is found by compiler, whereas quick assists are there to automate or accelerate the writing and refactoring processes.

Quick fixes can be called by clicking the marker icon on the vertical ruler. In such cases, only the quick fixes are displayed and all quick assists will be gone. If you do not like using keyboard shortcuts, you can open Quick Assist view. On each change of the cursor position, the possible assists and fixes are shown in that view.

There are many assists and fixes that you can use in ADT, depending on the backend version, as they are all calculated in your SAP instance. Figure 3-18 shows how assist popup, which consists of the main window where you have all possible assists and fixes, and the description window, which shows the action details for the chosen proposal.

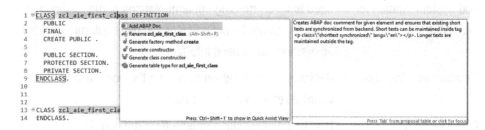

Figure 3-18. *Quick Assist for new ABAP class*

You will get different proposals for different objects, but most of them are linked to development in classes (both local and global), which could be one argument to move to them instead of using old procedural programming. The current proposals of the Quick Assist view are listed in Table 3-3, although I may have missed a few that I have not seen yet.

Table 3-3. *Available Quick Assist Proposals*

Proposal	Description
Add ABAP Doc	Creates an ABAP Doc comment for selected elements. This proposal appears on definitions of methods, classes, and interfaces. In newer NetWeaver releases, it allows the synchronization of the short text.
Rename	Runs the renaming action checking if the selected element is not used outside current object. It replaces the name in all its occurrences.

(continued)

Table 3-3. (*continued*)

Proposal	Description
Rename in Source Unit	Runs the renaming action only in a local source unit, like class. Can be found on older releases of the backend.
Add Implementation for Method(s)	Used to insert missing implementations of the methods in case you created a definition or you have not implemented all methods from used interfaces.
Declare Local Variable	Declares a new local variable from the non-existing variable referred to in your code.
Declare Attribute	Declares a new class attribute from the non-existing variable referred to in your code.
Create Method	Appears when you call code a method in your that does not exist yet.
Create Method Using Wizard	Does exactly what the Create method does, but always shows the wizard to enter the method parameters. Can be found on older NW backends.
Create Function Module	Calls the creation of FM from the CALL FUNCTION statement.
Extract Method	Creates a new method from a selected part of code. One of my favorite proposals. To make it appear, you need to select the code that you want to extract.
Extract Local Constant	Creates a local constant from the selected literal.
Extract Member Constant	Creates a global constant from the selected literal.
Extract Local Variable	Creates a local variable from the selected literal or variable expression.

(*continued*)

Table 3-3. (*continued*)

Proposal	Description
Extract Local Variable (Replace All Occurrences)	Creates a local variable from the selected variable expression and replaces any future occurrences. Known also as Split Variable.
Extract Attribute	Creates a global variable from the selected literal.
Extract Importing Parameter	Converts a selected literal into an importing parameter of the current method.
Create Text … in the Text Pool	Creates a new text with the next free number in the text pool for the selected literal.
Add Literal for Text … from the Text Pool	When used on the text pool (such as `text-001`), this will add a literal in front of the text ID (such as `'My text'(001)`).
Remove Literal for Text …	Will do the exact opposite action of adding literals for text.
Replace Literal by Text … from Text Pool	If the literal is linked with the text pool and the text in the literal is different than the one in the text pool, it will fetch the literal from the text pool and replace the current literal.
Replace Text … in Text Pool with Literal	If the literal is linked to the text pool and the text in the literal is different than the one in the text pool, it will push the literal to the text pool.
Edit Text .. in Text Pool	Opens the edit dialog for text in the text pool.
Add ##NO_TEXT Pragma	Adds pragma for literals.
Generate Getter for …	When used on an attribute inside class, creates a getter method for it.
Generate Setter for ..	When used on an attribute inside class, creates a setter method for it.

(*continued*)

Table 3-3. (*continued*)

Proposal	Description
Generate Getter and Setter for …	Creates a getter and setter for an attribute inside the class.
Make … Private	Moves the selected class element to a private section.
Make … Protected	Moves the selected class element to a protected section.
Make … Public	Moves the selected class element to a public section.
Make Attribute Public (Read-Only)	Moves an attribute to a public section and sets it to read-only.
Pull-Up … to Superclass	Pulls a selected class element to a superclass.
Pull-Up … to Interface	Pulls a selected class element to one of the interfaces that is used in the current class or its superclass.
Delete	Deletes the element.
Generate Constructor	When used on a class name, allows quick creation of constructor.
Generate Class-Constructor	When used on a class name, allows quick creation of class-constructor.
Generate Factory Method Create	When used on a class name, allows quick creation of the factory method for your class.
Generate Table Type for	Generates a table type inside the class.
Convert … to Class Constant	Converts the local constant into a global.
Convert … to Attribute	Converts the local variable into a class attribute.
Convert … to Importing Parameter	Converts the local variable into an importing parameter of the current method.

(*continued*)

Table 3-3. (*continued*)

Proposal	Description
Convert ... to Exporting Parameter	Converts a local variable into an exporting parameter of the current method.
Convert ... to Changing Parameter	Converts a local variable into the changing parameter of a current method.
Convert ... to Returning Parameter	Converts a local variable into a returning parameter of the current method. Available only if there is no returning parameter so far.
Create Include ...	When you try to put a new include in your program, it will allow you to create this include using the wizard.

Code Completion

If you have developed in SE80, you probably know this feature, as it has been available for a long while. The ADT version is very similar, but has some advantages like using wildcards (*).

In ADT, automatic code completion is set as the default, and it appears when you use one of the components selectors -,~, ->,=>. The available components appear shortly after, together with the information about the type of components and their documentation. Figure 3-19 shows this behavior, where automatic code completion appears after using ->.

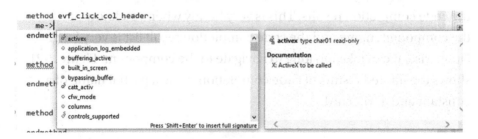

Figure 3-19. *Automatic code completion*

151

By default, when you use this on a method or function module name, it will only put its name in the code when you use the Enter key, but when you use the Shift+Enter combination, it will include the whole signature. That includes all the parameters. You can define which behavior is the default in the preferences.

As in SE80, code completion can also be called on demand using the Ctrl+Space shortcut. You can call it not only to get the components of the object but also to see possible ABAP statements and their additions. For example, as shown in Figure 3-20, code completion shows the other additions that are possible when used on the class definition.

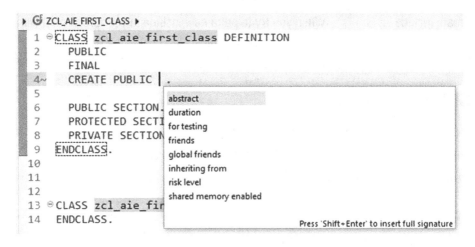

Figure 3-20. *Code completion for syntax*

I mentioned previously that in ADT we can use wildcards (*) to limit the code completion results. This is very handy when you know part of the component name and the code completion result list is very long. Otherwise, it can take too long to navigate to the component. Figure 3-21 shows the filtered results of code completion using a partial name of a constant and a wildcard.

```
method evf_click_col_header.
  data(action) = fc_*page|

endmethod.
                            ⚹ fc_first_page
                            ⚹ fc_last_page
                            ⚹ fc_next_page
                            ⚹ fc_previous_page
```

Figure 3-21. *Code Completion using a wildcard (*)*

One quite hidden function is overriding superclass methods. I normally would expect such a thing in the definition part of the class, not in the implementation part, but for ABAP it works this way. To override a method, press Ctrl+Space on the first line after the class implementation. You will see all the methods that you can redefine. Of course, you can redefine them manually, but code completion is sometimes very helpful. As an example, look at Figure 3-22, where I used code completion to override methods of the class that inherits from CL_GUI_ALV_GRID.

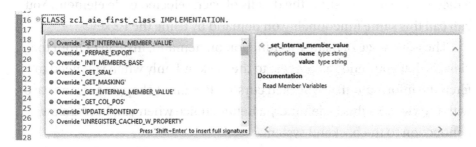

Figure 3-22. *Overriding superclass methods*

Word Completion

This functionality is very limited, but because of that sometimes it can be useful. It called in Eclipse, so it does not wait for the SAP backend to respond, which makes it very fast. You can call it using the Alt+/ shortcut, but only after entering at least one letter.

The benefit and the limitation of word completion is that it will only show the names used inside the current object. That means it will not propose the inherited methods or attributes. It will also not insert the signature of the methods or function modules when used. This completion is strictly linked to words found inside your current editor.

When you have a slow connection, you can still use word completion. Additionally, it is very similar to the Tab key functionality in the system console, so when you use the shortcut a few times, it will show the matching words sequentially as you press Tab. And it will do so very quickly. It prompts keywords and non-keywords for you. Unfortunately, it does not allow you to use wildcards.

Element Info

In a previous chapter, I described the view called ABAP Element Info, which can be used to show the details of each selected code element. You can call this same functionality on demand by using the F2 key.

The advantage of using this function on demand, instead of from the view, is that you send the request to the backend only when you need to fetch the information, not at each cursor placement change, as is the case with the view. So this is definitely a better choice when you have a slow connection to the backend system.

Figure 3-23 displays the Element info popup window for the OFFLINE method of the CL_GUI_ALV_GRID class. You can see that the content is exactly the same as in the case of the ABAP Element Info view. It also allows the same navigation using hyperlinks for types, structures, methods, attributes, and documentation.

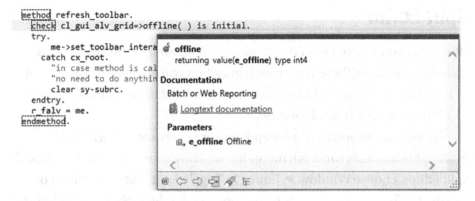

Figure 3-23. Element info of the class method

Word Wrap

This is yet another very simple function that helps some developers work with Eclipse. Many developers use the new ABAP syntax, which can make the work faster, but also sometimes uses more characters on one line. I know this is personal habit, as many developers format their code according to corporate rules, which disallow placing more than 72 characters on a line.

In such cases, when you open the code with lots of characters in one line in SE80, you have to use the scrollbar to see the whole line. When you open the same object in Eclipse, the behavior depends on how much space you give the editor tab, but there is always an option to toggle the word wrap or to maximize the editor.

If you want to stay with your current views, use the Alt+Shift+Y shortcut or choose Window ➤ Editor ➤ Toggle Word Wrap to activate word wrapping in your editor. This will make the hidden code appear in the editor below the line in which it was hidden. What is nice is that Eclipse will show the empty line number, so line numbering is retained.

This might not be a perfect way to read the code, but it helps you avoid having to scroll when working with lower screen resolutions.

Split Editor

Whenever you worked with the classes in SE80, even in the Source Code-Base Class Builder, there were problems when you wanted to create local or test classes, as you had to move to that part of class without being able to adapt or see the base class code.

Eclipse allows you to use the split editor in vertical or horizontal modes. Both modes run from menu bar or using shortcuts. For the vertical split editor, choose Window ➤ Editor ➤ Toggle Split Editor (Vertical) or use the Ctrl+_ shortcut. For the horizontal split editor, choose Window ➤ Editor ➤ Toggle Split Editor (Horizontal) or use the Ctrl+{ shortcut.

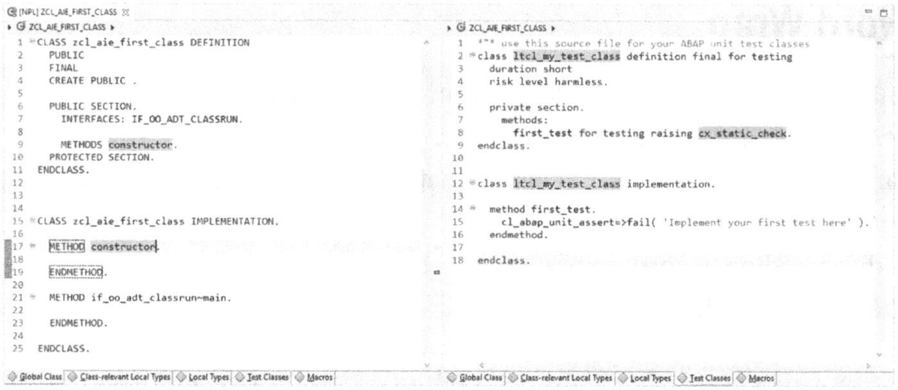

Figure 3-24. *Split editor for a class*

Now you can edit global class implementations and local classes or test classes at the same time, which is very useful if you're using TDD or TAD methodologies.

The split editor is helpful not only during class development, but also with old-style programs where you have all declarations for global variables in the beginning of source code. In such cases, you can set up one of the screens on the declarations and the other on the currently implemented code.

The Clone Function

If the split editor is still not enough, you can call the clone function, which will open the current development object in a second tab. To clone the tab, choose Window ➤ Editor ➤ Clone. The difference between clone and the split editor is that you can open as many clones as you want.

So again, when developing in classes, you can run five separate tabs for each class part and edit all of them at once. You can also open two and use the split editor on each of them to access four at the same time.

As you see, there are many usage combinations, but this functionality is best if you have a monitor with high resolution, as you can afford to put all of the tabs next to each other on the screen, without losing the comfort of programming.

Templates

I described this view in the previous chapter, which is why you might wonder why I come back to this topic here. This section covers usage and some small tricks in this view.

As you may remember, you can double-click the template, or drag and drop it into the source code in order to use it. There is one additional way: using code completion. To use the template, you need to remember its name, or at least the beginning of the name. You type the name into the source code and then press Ctrl+Space to activate code completion. The template will appear on the list. As you can see in Figure 3-24, the template code is visible in the proposal's description.

Figure 3-25. *Code completion for a local class template*

I use built-in templates widely, but only ones connected to building local or test classes, such as `lcl`, `lif`, `testClass`, `textIdExceptionClass`, and `assertEquals`. Additionally, I have some templates that are tailored to my current needs. One of them is an object signature template, which I described earlier. The other templates I use frequently are for creating exception classes, raising exceptions, and creating bool attributes.

Bool attributes templates are very simple, as they consist of one value, which is `ABAP_BOOL`, `ABAP_TRUE`, or `ABAP_FALSE`. I name those templates boolean, true, or false, and they allow me to use the same Boolean type values in every programming language that I use. Of course, I need to use code completion to replace the ABAP constants, but I still prefer to do it this way.

Exception templates are very useful as well. The one in Listing 3-1 is used for the global exception class. When I create a new exception class in Eclipse, I mark the default code and use this template to quickly prepare the exception.

Listing 3-1. Global Exception Class Template

```
CLASS ${enclosing_object} DEFINITION
  PUBLIC
  INHERITING FROM cx_${base}_check
  FINAL
  CREATE PUBLIC.
```

```abap
PUBLIC SECTION.
  CONSTANTS:
    BEGIN OF default_arguments,
      msgid TYPE symsgid VALUE '${messageID}',
      msgno TYPE symsgno VALUE '${messageNumber}',
      attr1 TYPE scx_attrname VALUE '',
      attr2 TYPE scx_attrname VALUE '',
      attr3 TYPE scx_attrname VALUE '',
      attr4 TYPE scx_attrname VALUE '',
    END OF default_arguments.
  INTERFACES:
    if_t100_message.
  METHODS: constructor
    IMPORTING textid    LIKE if_t100_message~t100key OPTIONAL
              previous  LIKE previous OPTIONAL.
  PROTECTED SECTION.
  PRIVATE SECTION.
ENDCLASS.

CLASS ${enclosing_object} IMPLEMENTATION.
  METHOD constructor.
    super->constructor( previous = previous ).

    CLEAR me->textid.
    IF textid IS INITIAL.
      if_t100_message~t100key = default_arguments.
    ELSE.
      if_t100_message~t100key = textid.
    ENDIF.
  ENDMETHOD.
ENDCLASS.
```

When I work with local classes and need to create a local exception, I use the template in Listing 3-2. It is very similar to the global exception class template, but with some changes, such as the fixed prefix for the class name or the lack of DEFINITION PUBLIC addition to the CLASS statement, as it is allowed only in global classes.

Listing 3-2. Local Exception Class Template

```
CLASS lcx_${exception} DEFINITION
  INHERITING FROM cx_${base}_check
  FINAL
  CREATE PUBLIC.

  PUBLIC SECTION.
    CONSTANTS:
      BEGIN OF default_arguments,
        msgid TYPE symsgid VALUE '${messageID}',
        msgno TYPE symsgno VALUE '${messageNumber}',
        attr1 TYPE scx_attrname VALUE '',
        attr2 TYPE scx_attrname VALUE '',
        attr3 TYPE scx_attrname VALUE '',
        attr4 TYPE scx_attrname VALUE '',
      END OF default_arguments.
    INTERFACES:
      if_t100_message.
    METHODS: constructor
      IMPORTING textid   LIKE if_t100_message~t100key OPTIONAL
                previous LIKE previous OPTIONAL.
  PROTECTED SECTION.
  PRIVATE SECTION.
ENDCLASS.
```

```
CLASS lcx_${exception} IMPLEMENTATION.
  METHOD constructor.
    super->constructor( previous = previous ).

    CLEAR me->textid.
    IF textid IS INITIAL.
      if_t100_message~t100key = default_arguments.
    ELSE.
      if_t100_message~t100key = textid.
    ENDIF.
  ENDMETHOD.
ENDCLASS.
```

The last two exception templates I use are prepared to throw the exception. The template shown in Listing 3-3 throws an exception with parameters to specify, and the one in Listing 3-4 simply throws an exception without any parameters.

Listing 3-3. Raise Exception with Parameters Template

```
RAISE EXCEPTION type ${exception_class}
  EXPORTING
    textid   = ${textid}
    previous = ${previous}.
```

Listing 3-4. Raise Exception Without Parameters

```
RAISE EXCEPTION type ${exception_class}.
```

This is what I use, but you are free to create your own templates or modify existing ones to meet your personal preferences.

Block Selection

Another function of Eclipse that might be helpful with types and structure declarations is the ability to toggle block selection from the Eclipse toolbar or by pressing the Alt+Shift+A key combination. When this is enabled, the cursor of the mouse will change from a caret into crossed lines and you can select multiple lines of the code.

You can select lines using mouse or by keeping the Shift key pressed and using the arrow keys. Once you select the code or the empty places in your source code, you can edit multiple lines at the same time. You can also copy the contents of the selection, which is very handy.

To give you an example, I copied a few components of the SFLIGHT table to the clipboard. I did this in Outline view after opening the table in the editor, but if your backend does not support this yet, you can copy the values using an SE11 transaction. Then, as the next step I started to write the declaration of the type T_FLIGHT and after writing TYPES: BEGIN OF T_FLIGHT, I pasted the column names from the clipboard. On the next line, I closed the declaration by typing END OF T_FLIGHT. The result is shown in Figure 3-26.

```
11          TYPES: BEGIN OF t_flight,
12~                    carrid
13~                    connid
14~                    currency
15~                    fldate
16~                    mandt
17~                    paymentsum
18~                    planetype
19~                    price
20                 END OF t_flight.|
```

Figure 3-26. *Block selection: initial state of type declaration*

In the next step, I toggled the block selection and selected all the lines on which I want to continue the type declaration. As you see in Figure 3-27, I selected the lines in the place where I was not touching any pasted column names.

162

```
11          TYPES: BEGIN OF t_flight,
12~                    carrid
13~                    connid
14~                    currency
15~                    fldate
16~                    mandt
17~                    paymentsum
18~                    planetype
19~                    price
20          END OF t_flight.
```

Figure 3-27. *Source code with block selection activated and several selected lines*

Then I added a space and started to write TYPE REF TO SFLIGHT- and pasted the columns again, followed by a colon. Figure 3-28 shows how the declaration looks at this stage. You can see that it was quite quick to create this type.

```
11          TYPES: BEGIN OF t_flight,
12~                    carrid        type ref to sflight-carrid     ,
13~                    connid        type ref to sflight-connid     ,
14~                    currency      type ref to sflight-currency   ,
15~                    fldate        type ref to sflight-fldate     ,
16~                    mandt         type ref to sflight-mandt      ,
17~                    paymentsum    type ref to sflight-paymentsum ,
18~                    planetype     type ref to sflight-planetype  ,
19~                    price         type ref to sflight-price      ,
20          END OF t_flight.
```

Figure 3-28. *Block selection: final view of type declaration*

This can also be used in code implementations. You might wonder why I used the reference types inside the declaration of the T_FLIGHT. I did this on purpose, to show you in Figure 3-29, that using the same approach I could initialize all components of the structure. I did this again using the typed text and pasting the components from the clipboard.

```
flight-carrid       = NEW #( ).
flight-connid       = NEW #( ).
flight-currency     = NEW #( ).
flight-fldate       = NEW #( ).
flight-mandt        = NEW #( ).
flight-paymentsum   = NEW #( ).
flight-planetype    = NEW #( ).
flight-price        = NEW #( ).
```

Figure 3-29. *Initialization of structure fields using block selection*

Even if these examples aren't fancy, they show that functionality exists and is helpful.

Quick Difference

When you start editing code, you will notice that on the vertical ruler, changed lines are highlighted differently than unchanged ones. Additionally, a ~ mark is shown next to the changed line, as shown in Figure 3-30. This is because Quick Difference is activated by default.

```
10
11      TYPES: BEGIN OF t_flight,
12~            carrid        type sflight-carrid    ,
13~            connid        type sflight-connid    ,
```

Figure 3-30. *Quick difference on the vertical ruler*

Whenever you hover over the changed line number, the popup with the previous code version will appear (see Figure 3-31). You can see that the type definitions have changed.

```
11          TYPES: BEGIN OF t_flight,
12~  >              carrid        type ref to sflight-carrid    ,
13~  >              connid        type ref to sflight-connid    ,
14
15                                                      Press 'F2' for focus
16
```

Figure 3-31. *Quick difference: preview of previous code*

Changed lines are highlighted until you save your changes or activate the object.

Compare Local History

Have you ever lost your ABAP code because of a broken connection and automatic closure of SAP GUI? Well, this should not happen anymore in Eclipse, because after reconnecting, the session is reestablished and you can continue your work. But a good old habit of saving your changes every few lines can still be helpful.

Eclipse keeps a version of your code locally, each time you click the Save button. By default, Eclipse keeps the files in local history for seven days and a maximum of the last 50 versions. In most cases, this should be enough to return to one of the previous versions of your code.

This functionality has saved me a lot of time, and I have used it to recreate deleted parts of my code. You could compare your current code to local history, just like with the previous versions that are stored in the SAP backend. You may wonder, why use local history when you have versions in the SAP backend. Keep in mind that versions in SAP are only generated on demand or when transport requests are released. So until you generate the version manually, you cannot see the previous versions of the released code.

To do the comparison, use the context menu of the editor and choose Compare With ➤ Local History. A History view will open, but this time with local revisions, as you can see in Figure 3-32.

165

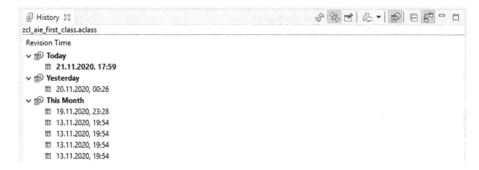

Figure 3-32. *History view with local revisions*

When you double-click the selected version, the comparison tab will open (see Figure 3-33). You can now review the changes and adapt them if necessary.

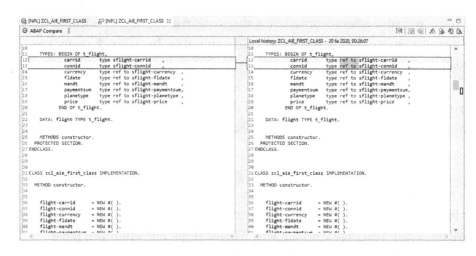

Figure 3-33. *Local revision comparison*

Formatting

Standard formatting does not differ from the way it was done in SE80. You call it by using Shift+F1 or choosing Source Code ➤ Format. When you call the formatting on the system for the first time, you will be notified that there are no formatting settings. Following the link in the popup, you will be moved into the properties window of the current project, where you can set up the formatter according to your preferences (see Figure 3-34).

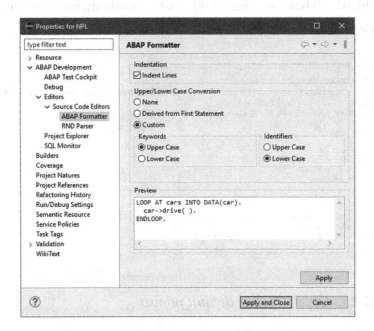

Figure 3-34. ABAP Code Formatter settings

Additionally to standard formatter, which formats whole object, you may want to beatify only a block of code that you have just created. In SE80 that was not possible, but in Eclipse you can achieve that by selecting the code to format and using Ctrl+Shift+F1 or choosing Source Code ➤ Format Block.

Quick Outline

I already described how the outline view works, so what is the purpose of Quick Outline? It is very handy when you work mostly with the keyboard and don't want to touch the mouse to navigate to an element of currently edited object. The Quick Outline is called using Ctrl+O. As you can see in Figure 3-35, it shows the same values as the outline view. The difference is that you can filter visible elements by writing part of their name in the input field, which is active after the Quick Outline is shown. You can use the wildcard character * here as well.

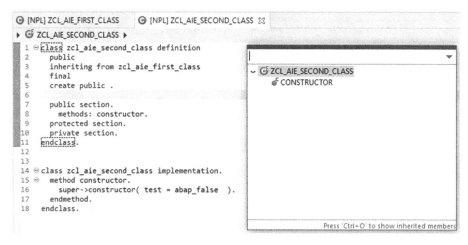

Figure 3-35. *Quick Outline default popup*

Quick Outline also allows you to show inherited members of subclasses. To use it, you need to press Ctrl+O while the Quick Outline is visible. Look at Figure 3-36 to see how the outline has changed, although the object is the same.

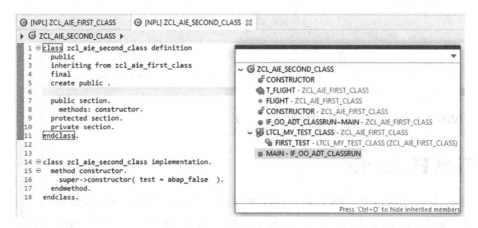

Figure 3-36. *Quick Outline with inherited members*

Many ADT users would like to see the outline with inherited members inside the outline view, but so far this is the only way to quickly navigate through an inherited class structure.

Open in Project

Being able to switch between the systems easily is useful when you are bringing your code from development into a test environment so can test your code with real data. But you may also like to see how the object looks in another system. In both cases, when you are in the editor, you can run this action by:

- Using the context menu and choosing Open in Project

- Using the Alt+Ctrl+P shortcut to select any available project in your workspace (see Figure 3-37)

Either way, after selecting the project, ADT will check if the currently opened object exists in the target system and will open it if that is true. For example, as I have only two projects in my installation NPL and TPL, and as I was editing a class on NPL, Eclipse proposed the TRL as the one in which I could open this class.

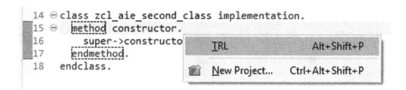

Figure 3-37. *Open in Project action*

Text Elements

Text elements and selection texts are things that ABAP developers have to handle during their work. In SE80, you had to click the Text Elements button or double-click the text element to see what text was behind it. What always bothered me was that you always had to save or activate the object in order to jump to its text elements, as SE80 worked on a single GUI LUW.

In ADT, it is much easier, as you can simply use F2 (ABAP Element Info) to get the popup with the text in a language that you are currently logged on (see Figure 3-38).

Figure 3-38. *ABAP Element Info for text element*

When you want to create the text element, it is enough to write the text into literals and then use Quick Assist (Ctrl+1) to call the Create Text ... in the Text Pool Action. As I described earlier, you can also:

- Edit the text in the text pool

- Replace the text in the text pool from the literal

- Replace the literal with the text from the text pool

- Add a literal for the text

- Remove a literal from the text

All this quick assist allows you to create code without interruption and with limited need to open the Text Elements in SAP GUI. I wrote limited need, because for selection-screen texts, you still have to use the Text Elements editor in SAP GUI. To do this, use context menu of the editor and choose Open Other ➤ Text Elements. You will be moved to embedded SAP GUI, as shown in Figure 3-39.

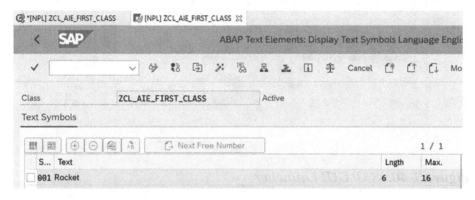

Figure 3-39. *ABAP Text elements editor in embedded SAP GUI*

Embedded SAP GUI

There are a few times when you'll need to jump to SE80 from Eclipse. When it comes to development, such moments are usually connected with enhancement developments, although in the newest versions of SAP NetWeaver, it is already possible to create or edit enhancements and BAdI implementations. This may also be necessary during the learning period, when you cannot find an SE80 equivalent in ADT. The other need to run SAP GUI will be when you're using another SAP transaction or testing your GUI application.

There are a few ways to open an object in embedded SAP GUI. You can use the Ctrl+6 shortcut, choose Navigate ➤ Open SAP GUI, or click the Open SAP GUI button on the Eclipse toolbar. The popup in Figure 3-40 will appear, where you can choose a project for which you want to open GUI. You should also determine whether any development objects supported by Eclipse should be opened in Eclipse or SAP GUI.

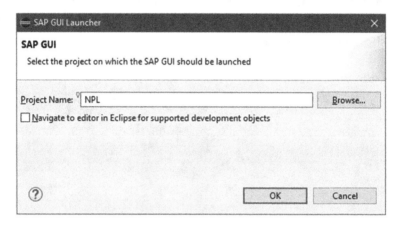

Figure 3-40. *SAP GUI Launcher*

Once you choose your settings and click OK, the embedded GUI will appear in a separate tab in Eclipse. If you were using the SAP Business Client, you will not surprised about the small differences of embedded SAP GUI to the one that you run from the SAP Logon Pad. Otherwise, you will notice that there is no user menu on the screen and there is no menu bar on it, only a More button. As shown in Figure 3-41, the More button contains everything what was visible in the menu bar of the standard SAP GUI.

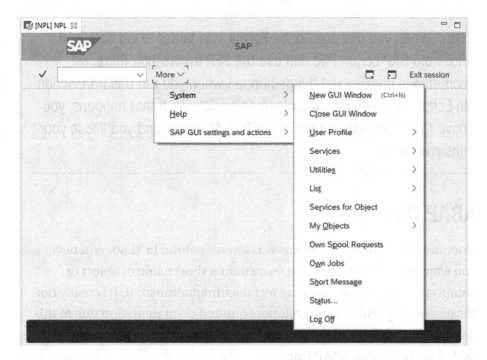

Figure 3-41. Embedded SAP GUI after launching

If you want to open the user menu, you need to manually call transaction SMEN. But do not worry, you will forget about the user menu after you read this book to the end.

The next way to call the SAP GUI is from the context menu of editor, simply choose Open With ➤ SAP GUI on an object you are editing, and it will be opened inside SE80.

When you test your GUI applications you will quickly remember F8, as it will run your current object in SAP GUI. Of course, you can call the same action using the menu bar and the toolbar button, but F8 is always faster.

Tip   When you develop Adobe Forms, it is better to log onto SAP GUI from SAP Logon Pad and use the SFP transaction there, as sometimes unexpected things happen when you run this transaction in Eclipse. Many times, it ends freezing Eclipse. If that happens, you have to kill the Eclipse task in the Task Manager and you'll lose your unsaved work.

ABAP Doc

Documentation of ABAP objects was always painful in SE80. Whenever you wanted to write something more than a short name of object or component, you had to use long text documentation for it. It is really not the easiest way and many developers omitted documentation due to this complexity. When the ADT tools were published, documentation could be added to code using ABAP Doc.

ABAP Doc does not differ much from standard comments, but the comments need to be in the correct place in order to work. To differentiate them from standard ABAP comments, they begin with "! and can be placed before the definition of class, interface, method, function module, attribute, constant, or type.

Depending on the backend version, you may notice that the objects' short text can be synchronized with ABAP Doc, which makes it even more powerful and developer friendly. Figure 3-42 shows that if you use the HTML paragraph tag in ABAP Doc with the class set to "shorttext synchronized", you can set the description of the class to your desired one.

```
2+
3+    "! <p class="shorttext synchronized" lang="en">Class for tests</p>
4 ⊖ CLASS zcl_aie_first_class DEFINITION
5       PUBLIC|
6       FINAL
7       CREATE PUBLIC .
```

Figure 3-42. *Short text synchronization for the short text class*

But text synchronization is just the beginning of the possibilities. The main purpose of ABAP Doc for me is to explain public methods or any other components of the ABAP class, program, or function group that are not correctly named or are unclear. You see in Figure 3-43 that I've added my own text to the description of the construction method, although it was proposed by ADT. Normally, with a properly named method, I remove it. But you can put a warning for developers inside the documentation.

```
32        "! <p class="shorttext synchronized" lang="en"></p>
33        "! Be sure what you are doing with it
34        "! @parameter test | <p class="shorttext synchronized" lang="en">Run in test mode</p>
35        METHODS constructor IMPORTING test TYPE abap_bool.
```

Figure 3-43. *Class ABAP Doc comment*

I added a description for the parameter TEST inside this ABAP Doc. Normally I name it TEST_MODE and I wanted to show how the ABAP Element Info reacts to these kinds of additions. When you look at Figure 3-44, you will notice that, besides the standard method signature, the documentation part shows the comment about the method and its parameter.

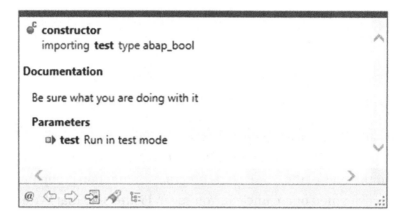

Figure 3-44. *ABAP Element Info for the method with ABAP Doc*

You can also use HTML tags inside the ABAP Doc, such as : <h1>, <h2>, <h3>, <br/>, <em>, <strong>, <ul>, and <ol>. This is partially shown in Figure 3-45.

```
12    TYPES:
13      "! Type with fields references<br/>Second line
14      "! This is still <em>second</em> <strong>line</strong>
15      "! With list <ol><li>One</li><li>Two</li><li>Tree</li></ol>
16      "! </br>This is lin with typo
17      BEGIN OF t_flight,
18        carrid      TYPE REF TO sflight-carrid,
19        connid      TYPE REF TO sflight-connid,
20        currency    TYPE REF TO sflight-currency,
21        fldate      TYPE REF TO sflight-fldate,
22        mandt       TYPE REF TO sflight-mandt,
23        paymentsum  TYPE REF TO sflight-paymentsum,
24        planetype   TYPE REF TO sflight-planetype,
25        price       TYPE REF TO sflight-price,
26      END OF t_flight.
```

Figure 3-45. *ABAP Doc for type with HTML tags*

After using the ABAP Element Info on this type, you will see the documentation, as shown in Figure 3-46. This is definitely much easier than using SAP GUI's long text documentation, at least for people used to HTML, like me.

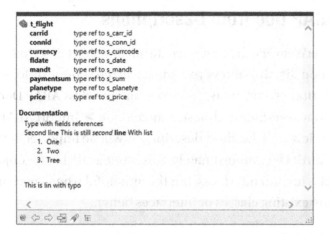

Figure 3-46. *ABAP Element Info for the T_FLIGHT type*

The next Eclipse feature I want to describe is the spell checker. It can be used whenever you create a comment in ABAP. By default, the text in the comment is checked in English, which is the most common used language in programming. Note that in the ABAP Doc for T_FLIGHT I made a typo in the code. It was underlined by the editor. If you use Quick Assistant on this highlighted word, you get word suggestions, as shown in Figure 3-47. You can also add the word to the dictionary, if it is not already there.

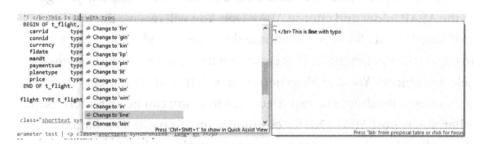

Figure 3-47. *Spell Checker proposals for comments*

Import ABAP Doc from Descriptions

If your SAP NetWeaver can handle synchronizing short descriptions, there is a small functionality that allows you import all the short texts for methods, interfaces, attributes, constants, and types into the class ABAP Doc.

To import a description, choose Source Code ➤ Import ABAP Doc from Descriptions. All the short descriptions will be imported into your class using ABAP Doc. Unfortunately, this is not available for object types other than classes and interfaces, but this is helpful when you want to document the existing classes or interfaces better.

Export ABAP Doc

When there is an import, usually there is also an export. This is the case for ABAP Doc. You can export all of your ABAP Docs into HTML files in Eclipse, which you can then pass to your co-workers or customers.

I am pretty sure that the idea of exporting ABAP Doc comes from the JAVA Doc, but this is not the most important thing. The most important thing is that we can generate the documentation from our ABAP code, which was not possible before without custom development.

To export your ABAP Doc comments, choose File ➤ Export, then go to the ABAP folder and choose ABAP Doc. You will receive the window in Figure 3-48. It allows you to choose the object for which you want to export the documentation. It can be a whole package or just single selected objects. You can also choose for which kind of members the documentation should be exported. This function can be extremely useful when you export ABAP Doc for customers and for partners separately. If the ABAP Doc does not exist, you can determine if the short texts created in SAP GUI should be exported. Of course, you can also select the destination folder, but you should not be scared of overwriting existing documentation, as the subfolders for each export are created automatically.

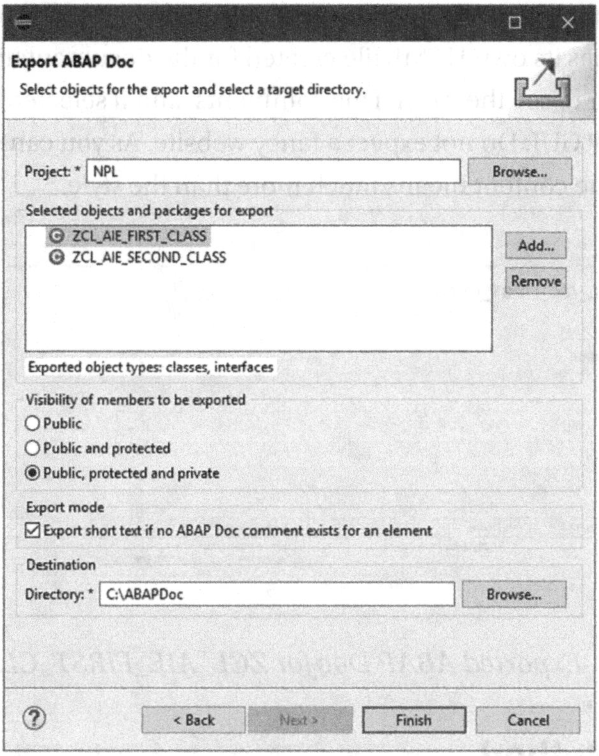

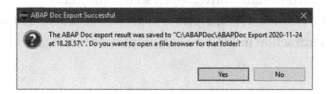

Figure 3-48. *ABAP Doc export settings*

After a successful export, you will be notified by Eclipse and you will be able to open the folder directly, with all the exported documentation (see Figure 3-49).

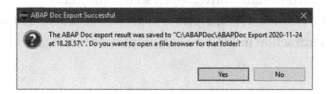

Figure 3-49. *ABAP Doc Export successful message*

When you navigate through the available folders, you will notice that every object has its own HTML file created for the documentation. Just double-click it to see the ABAP Doc comments, and if selected, the short texts from SAP GUI. Do not expect a fancy website. As you can see in Figure 3-50, the content means much more than the style.

Interfaces | Types | Attributes | Methods

Class ZCL_AIE_FIRST_CLASS

public create public

Documentation

Class for tests

Interfaces

if_oo_adt_classrun

Types

Visibility and Level	Name	Documentation
public	t_flight (structured type)	Type with fields references Second line This is still *second* **line** With list 1. One 2. Two 3. Tree

Figure 3-50. *Exported ABAP Doc for ZCL_AIE_FIRST_CLASS*

Extract Method

ABAP developers care about code quality. You can see it inside standard SAP applications as well as in open source projects. SAP employees have even published their own clean code guidelines on GitHub[1]. They allow every developer to discuss each rule and make proposals for changes, so it has became an community driven open source project.

One of the clean code principles is to keep code units small, which is why method extraction in ADT is a very important tool. There are a few

---

[1]Guidelines can be found at https://github.com/SAP/styleguides/blob/master/clean-abap/CleanABAP.md

ways to launch the extraction process, but in each case you need to select
the part of the code that you want to extract. You can:

- Call Quick Assist (Ctrl+1) and select Extract Method or
  Extract Method from Expression Action

- Choose Source Code ➤ Extract Method or use the
  Alt+Shift+M shortcut

In most cases, I use the Quick Assist to extract methods, as it can be
used on whole statements and on expressions. Figure 3-51 shows the
proposal of the method extraction for the selected codelines. To make this
proposal appear in the Quick Assist, you must select full statements. This
means that the selected statements must be selected with the statement
closing character (a dot in ABAP). The same rule applies to the extraction
done using the Alt+Shift+M shortcut.

Figure 3-51. *Extract method Quick Assist proposal*

After activating the extraction, the method definition and
implementation are created automatically and the editor runs the rename
action directly for this newly created method (see Figure 3-52). The
definition will be created in the private section of the class. If the selected
code contains parameters of the method from which you were extracting,
they will also be added automatically to the method's definition. The type
of the parameter is also properly copied.

```
38+        METHODS new_method.
39  ENDCLASS.
40
41
42
43 ⊝ CLASS zcl_aie_first_class IMPLEMENTATION.
44
45 ⊝   METHOD constructor.
46
47
48+ |    new_method( ).
49+
50+
51+
52+     ENDMETHOD.
53+
54+⊝   METHOD new_method.
55+
56       flight-carrid     = NEW #( ).
57       flight-connid     = NEW #( ).
58       flight-currency   = NEW #( ).
59       flight-fldate     = NEW #( ).
60       flight-mandt      = NEW #( ).
61       flight-paymentsum = NEW #( ).
62       flight-planetype  = NEW #( ).
63       flight-price      = NEW #( ).
64
65+     ENDMETHOD.
```

Figure 3-52. *Method extracted using Quick Assist*

I mentioned that Quick Assist also allows extraction of methods from expressions. This can be done in any statement that allows the usage of methods as arguments. For example, in IF or a method call. To use it, select the full expression and call Quick Assist. Choose Extract Method from Expression, as shown in Figure 3-53. If the extraction is done inside the IF or CHECK statement, the returning parameter of the newly created method will be set to ABAP_BOOL.

```
"if XLSX is possible then we create it,  if not then MHTML excel file
salv_intf_descr ?= cl_abap_intfdescr=>describe_by_name( exporting p_name = 'IF_SALV_BS_XML' ).
if salv_intf_descr is not initial and line_exists( salv_intf_descr->attributes[ name = 'C_TYPE_XLSX' ] ).
    file_type = 10.                                                                  Creates a
else.                           ⊕ Extract local variable (Alt+Shift+L)               expressic
    file_type = 02.            ▣ Extract method from expression                       call to th
endif.                                                                               Further o
```

Figure 3-53. *Extract method from expression proposal*

If you launch the extraction by using Alt+Shift+M, you will always receive a window in which you have to set up the name of the method and its visibility. You can also change the default parameters' names and directions (see Figure 3-54).

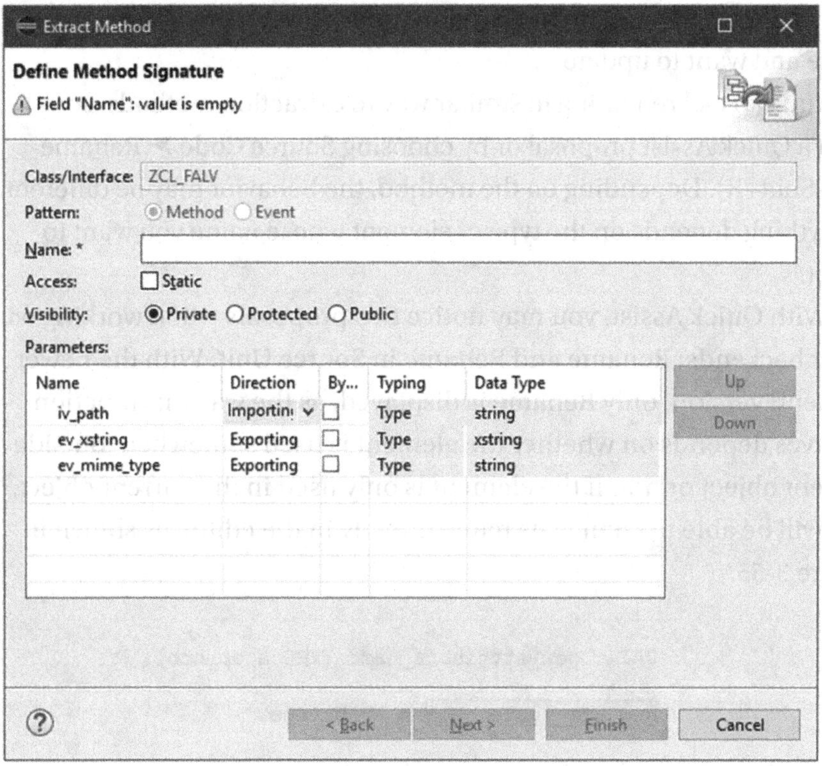

Figure 3-54. Extracting a method using Alt+Shift+M

The advantage of using Alt+Shift+M, in comparison to Quick Assist, is that it directly calls the extraction process. With Quick Assist, all proposals need to be calculated and displayed in the popup, and then you need to select the proposal to apply. It can be helpful when you have a slow connection to the backend.

Renaming

Adapting the names of objects and their components is one of the most common tasks of the development process. Developers change the names because the content of the internal table has changed, or when they adjusted what the method does. Sometimes, developers just find a better name and want to update it.

You can call renaming in similar way to extraction methods, so from a Quick Assist proposal or by choosing Source Code ➤ Rename (Alt+Shift+R). Depending on the method, the behavior may be different. Everything depends on the type of element whose name you want to adapt. s

With Quick Assist, you may notice two proposals when working with older backends: Rename and Rename in Source Unit. With the newer backend version, only Rename is displayed, as the way this function behaves depends on whether the element is used somewhere outside current object or not. If the element is only used in the current object, you will be able to change its name directly in the editor, as shown in Figure 3-55.

```
DATA: new_attribute_name TYPE abap_bool.

new attribute name = abap_true.
```

Figure 3-55. *Renaming an attribute in the editor*

The same editor behavior will take place on projects connected to older systems, after using Rename in the source unit proposal. The difference here is that it doesn't check if the element is used elsewhere and you may create syntax errors in another object because of that.

When you use the Rename Quick Assist proposal in a project linked to an older backend, or on one linked to a newer one but the element is used somewhere outside of that object, you will see the rename wizard window on your screen. The same wizard will appear if you use the menu bar or the Alt+Shift+R shortcut.

Figure 3-56 shows the first screen of the renaming wizard. It requires you to rename the element. You could click the Finish button straight away, but you then can't see which other objects will be refactored. That is why I suggest you click the Next button.

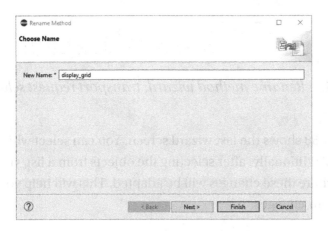

Figure 3-56. *Rename method wizard: set up a new name*

When you move to the next screen of the wizard, you can choose the transport request and see the list of affected objects. You may also decide if you want to ignore syntax errors while refactoring, which in most cases I suggest you not do. One very important setting visible is the ability to activate all changes during the refactoring objects. As you can see in Figure 3-57, by default it is not selected. After choosing your settings, again I suggest you use the Next button to see the detailed changes in the code.

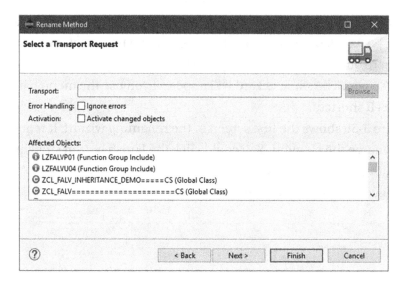

Figure 3-57. *Rename method wizard: transport request selection and settings*

Figure 3-58 shows the last wizard screen. You can select which objects to refactor. Additionally, after selecting the objects from a list, you will see what and where these changes will be adapted. This will help you see the impact of your changes.

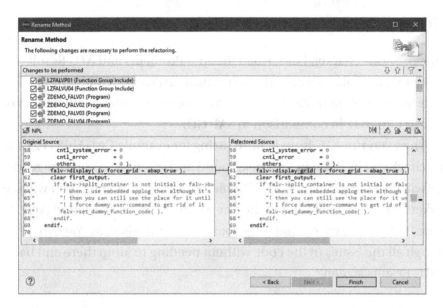

Figure 3-58. *Rename method wizard: list of necessary refactorings*

Deleting Unused Variables

Some developers hate to clean code from unused variables, especially when they are modifying somebody else's code. Maybe if they used Eclipse, they would stop complaining about this action, because there are two very nice ways to get rid of unused variables.

Both functions can be found in the Source Code section of the menu bar. The first is called Delete Unused Variables (All) and the second is Delete Unused Variables (Selection). Both can be called using the Alt+U and Alt+Shift+U shortcuts. The second function works only with selected code, while the first function works with whole object code.

When you run these functions, you'll notice that if there are programs, function groups, and function modules, it will delete both the global and local unused variables. It will delete only private and local classes. Do not be surprised if an unused variable from the public or protected section remains untouched.

ATC

In the previous chapter, I described the ATC Problems and ATC Result Browser views. I also described how to run an ATC check and how to create an exemption request. That is why I focus here on the differences of using ATC in ADT in comparison to SAP GUI.

When you run ATC from Eclipse (using for example Ctrl+Shift+F2), the ATC check will be done in the background and when the results are ready they will be displayed in the ATC Problems view. Additionally, you will see markers on the vertical ruler in the line where the issue was found (see Figure 3-59). Code correction is less painful than in SE80, as you can go through all the issues in the code without needing to jump there and back to ATC Results screen.

```
46 ⊖    METHOD constructor.
```

Figure 3-59. *ATC Error marker on vertical ruler*

Unit Tests

Unit test views were also described in Chapter 2, but it is worth mentioning again that after running unit tests (Ctrl+Shift+F10), information about the run will be displayed in the ABAP Unit view. This view will allow you to navigate to the code of the unit test, which is useful especially if it fails.

Highlighting unit tests in the editor after using Ctrl+Shift+F11 is another advantage of working with ADT. In SAP GUI, you could get the coverage statistics on the screen and then manually click each method to get the highlighted coverage.

Troubleshooting

Besides the day-to-day programming, developers are also responsible for troubleshooting. This can involve finding an error in an application, or just addressing the low performance of your code. Since profiling views were clearly described in Chapter 2, I focus on debugging and using logpoints in this chapter.

Debugging

I hear a lot of bad things about debugging in ADT. About how slow it is to debug here, or that not all the GUI Debugger functionalities are available. I think that half the ABAP developers love it (or at least don't mind it), and the other half hates it. I understand both groups, but I am definitely one that loves to debug in ADT, especially if I am debugging custom code.

I know that it's not possible to debug scripts in ADT. Watchpoints are available on newer NetWeaver versions, but there is one huge advantage to debugging in Eclipse—you can change the code directly when you find the problem. Unfortunately, it does not work in Java, where after changing and saving, you have to restart debugging with the changed code at the beginning of the changed unit. At least you do not have to manually navigate to the error.

When ADT switches to debugging mode, you will notice that there is a special debugging toolbar (see Figure 3-60). When you finish debugging, these tools become inactive.

Figure 3-60. *Debugging toolbar*

For ease of switching from the GUI Debugger to the ADT Debugger, all the shortcuts remained the same. If you had no chance to work with the GUI debugger or you want to assign the icons to the functions, Table 3-4 lists and explains the buttons.

Table 3-4. *Debugging Buttons*

Button	Usage	Shortcut
▷	Resume: Goes to the next breakpoint statement.	F8
▣	Terminate: Closes both the editor and the process.	
⋈	Disconnect: Ends debugging, but let process run till the end.	
⋑	Step Into: Executes the next step. If it's a procedure call, it goes inside.	F5
⋒	Step Over: Executes the next step. Does not jump inside the procedure call.	F6
⋒	Step Return: Ends debugging of current procedure and stops right after it.	F7
⋈	Run to Line: Jumps forward to the cursor position executing all statements between the current line and the cursor position.	Shift+F8
⋈	Jump to Line: Jumps forward or backward to the cursor position without executing any statement between the current position and the cursor position.	Shift+F12

Setting breakpoints, their conditions, and explanations of the Debug, Breakpoints, Variables, ABAP Exception and ABAP Internal Table views took place in a previous chapter, but there are still a few things about the debugging process in ADT that I want to share with you.

One of them is the ability to preview the value inside the variable, structure table, or object when you hover your cursor over it. You then don't have to place every possible variable into Variables view in order to see how the variable has changed. This preview allows navigation to all components of the object, internal table lines, or structure. An example of this behavior is presented in Figure 3-61. If you have trouble during navigation through this value preview, use the F2 button to put focus on it. This will surely help.

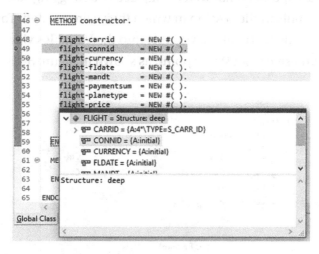

***Figure 3-61.** Data preview when debugging*

The next functionality of the ADT debugger is the ability to debug screen flow logic. To do so, you need to stop the debugger at the CALL SCREEN statement and use F5 or the Step Into button. You will move into screen flow logic, as shown in Figure 3-62. You can set up soft breakpoints inside it, which as you may remember, are valid only during a particular debugging session.

[NPL] 0100 (SAPLZFALV) [SCREEN] ⌗
```
1  process before output.
2  | module pbo.
3  *
4  process after input.
5      module pai.
```

Figure 3-62. *Screen debugging in ADT*

Setting watchpoints is allowed during active debugging sessions; they are active only in the session in which they were created. To set a watchpoint, you need to put the variable into the Variables view and then right-click it and select Set Watchpoint, as shown in Figure 3-63.

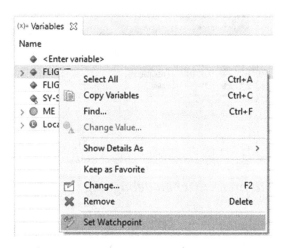

Figure 3-63. *Setting watchpoints*

A new entry will appear in Variables view, called Watchpoint xxx Values, where *xxx* represents your variable name. When you expand it, you will see two subnodes: Recent Value and Current Value (see Figure 3-64). Each time the variable is updated, the debugger will stop and update the values in Variables view.

(x)= Variables ⊠	
Name	Value
∨ 🔍 Watchpoint FLIGHT Values	
∨ ◆ Recent Value	Structure: deep
> 🔲 CARRID	{A:10"\TYPE=S_CARR_ID}
> 🔲 CONNID	{A:6"\TYPE=S_CONN_ID}
🔲 CURRENCY	{A:initial}
🔲 FLDATE	{A:initial}
🔲 MANDT	{A:initial}
🔲 PAYMENTSUM	{A:initial}
🔲 PLANETYPE	{A:initial}
🔲 PRICE	{A:initial}
∨ ◆ Current Value	Structure: deep
> 🔲 CARRID	{A:10"\TYPE=S_CARR_ID}
> 🔲 CONNID	{A:6"\TYPE=S_CONN_ID}
> 🔲 CURRENCY	{A:9"\TYPE=S_CURRCODE}
🔲 FLDATE	{A:initial}
🔲 MANDT	{A:initial}
🔲 PAYMENTSUM	{A:initial}
🔲 PLANETYPE	{A:initial}
🔲 PRICE	{A:initial}

Figure 3-64. *Watchpoints in Variables view*

When you no longer need a watchpoint in your debugging session, you can delete it only when the debugger stops on the change in the watched variable. At that time, right-click the vertical ruler and select Delete Watchpoint.

You have to decide for yourself if you like the ADT debugger or not. Note that when you are working on on-premise systems, as when you use ABAP in Cloud systems, you have no other choice.

Logpoints

If you want to set up watchpoints for another user or if are collecting information when you are not debugging, dynamic logpoints are the answer for you. They can be created in the ABAP editor's using vertical ruler by choosing Create Logpoint or by using the Ctrl+Alt+L shortcut.

When you're creating dynamic logpoints, you can set up how long they should be active, how many times for one internal sessions the values should be kept, and how long the data should be stored in the system. Additionally, as shown in Figure 3-65, you can choose the activity to log (variable, call stack, SQL trace, table buffer trace, or user defined logging).

Figure 3-65. *Creating logpoints*

In each case, you can set up simple logical conditions when to store the logs. Conditions can use syntax similar to ABAP and its operators, such as: EQ, =, NE, <>, ><, <, LT, >, GT, <=, =<, LE, >=, =<, GE, CO, CN, CA, NA, CS, NS, CP, NP, NOT, AND, OR, IS INITIAL, IS BOUND, IS ASSIGNED. It is almost the same as the breakpoint conditions.

Where you place the logpoint is very important. As you may imagine, when you set it up in the line, where the variable has the value assignment, you will not be able to catch its current value. That is why you should always create a logpoint in the next line after the watched variable. If your code unit has only one line, choose the end of the unit as place for the logpoints, just like in Figure 3-66, where I put it near the ENDMETHOD statement in line 22.

```
13      private section.
14         data: value_to_watch type sy-uzeit.
15
16   ENDCLASS.
17
18 ⊝ CLASS zcl_aie_first_class IMPLEMENTATION.
19
20 ⊝   METHOD constructor.
21         value_to_watch = sy-uzeit.
22      ENDMETHOD.
23
24 ⊝   METHOD if_oo_adt_classrun~main.
25         out->write( 'Run successfull' ).
26      ENDMETHOD.
27
28   ENDCLASS.
```

Figure 3-66. *Positioning logpoints*

When your logpoint is created and the logs are collected, you can see them in Logpoints view. After double-clicking the logpoint line, you can see the collected values, visible in Figure 3-67.

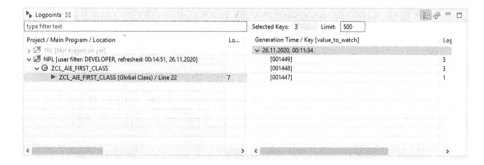

Figure 3-67. *Logpoints view with collected keys*

Other Editors

ABAP Source editor is not the only editor in ADT. There are also Table, Structure, and CDS view editors. They all looks mainly the same and I assume the base for all of them is the same. There are also form base editors for data elements and domains, which you can use in newer NetWeaver systems. Let's take a brief look at these editors.

CDS, Table, and Structure Editor

With newer SAP NetWeaver releases, structures, and tables by default are displayed in the text editor, just like CDS views. If you've only used SE11 transactions to create dictionary objects, it can be a shock to see a table definition like the one shown in Figure 3-69, but when you start working with it, you'll quickly get used to it. There is always an option to open the definition in SAP GUI, but with CDS views or in cloud environment, you will not have a such possibility, so the sooner you start using the text editor for structures and tables, the better off you'll be.

```
⊞ [NPL] SAIRPORT ⊠
⚠ 1    @EndUserText.label : 'Flughäfen'
  2    @AbapCatalog.enhancementCategory : #EXTENSIBLE_CHARACTER_NUMERIC
  3    @AbapCatalog.tableCategory : #TRANSPARENT
  4    @AbapCatalog.deliveryClass : #A
  5    @AbapCatalog.dataMaintenance : #ALLOWED
  6    define table sairport {
  7      @AbapCatalog.foreignKey.label : 'Mandant'
  8      @AbapCatalog.foreignKey.keyType : #KEY
  9      @AbapCatalog.foreignKey.screenCheck : true
 10      key mandt : s_mandt not null
 11        with foreign key [0..*,1] t000
 12          where mandt = sairport.mandt;
 13      key id    : s_airport not null;
 14      name      : s_airpname not null;
 15      @AbapCatalog.foreignKey.screenCheck : true
 16      time_zone : s_tzone not null
 17        with foreign key ttzz
 18          where client = sairport.mandt
 19            and tzone = sairport.time_zone;
 20
 21    }
```

Figure 3-68. *Editor with SAIRPORT table definition*

Notice that lots of settings are displayed in the editor as annotations. This was taken over from CDS views. When you compare this to the CDS view found in Figure 3-69, you may notice the similarities directly.

```
 ⓘ [TRL] CDS_WITH_EXTENDEDVIEW_1 ⌘
  1 ⊖@AbapCatalog.sqlViewName: 'CdsFrwk_DEMO_9A'
  2  @ClientDependent: true
  3  @AbapCatalog.compiler.compareFilter: true
  4  @AccessControl.authorizationCheck: #CHECK
  5  @EndUserText.label: 'Base View which is extended'
  6  define view CdsFrwk_Sales_Orders
  7    as select from snwd_so
  8  {
  9    key snwd_so.so_id,
 10        snwd_so.buyer_guid,
 11        snwd_so.created_at,
 12        snwd_so.currency_code,
 13        snwd_so.delivery_status,
 14        snwd_so.lifecycle_status,
 15        snwd_so.gross_amount,
 16        snwd_so.net_amount,
 17        snwd_so.tax_amount
 18  }
 19
```

Figure 3-69. *CDS Editor with CDS_WITH_EXTENDEDVIEW_1*

Both editors allow completion assistant and quick assist, but the real description for creation and usage of CDS views, structures, and tables is worth a separate book.

Data Elements and Domains

Creating domains and data elements are one of the fundamentals of the ABAP Developers. As in the case of dictionary tables, we used to create them in SE11, but since the NetWeaver versions, we also have form base editors for domains and data elements inside ADT.

You will not find anything special in them, as in my opinion, they are the Eclipse representation of the SE11 forms.

Summary

I hope after reading this chapter you know what can be done faster in ADT in comparison to SE80. You should also be getting used to the new user interface of Eclipse and understand how ABAP Source Code editor works in ADT. There were many shortcuts mentioned in this chapter and many more not mentioned, which is why the most important ones are listed in Appendix A.

This chapter provides tons of information, but this is just beginning. Head to the next chapter to learn how to use Eclipse and ADT preferences to get even more from your Eclipse installation.

CHAPTER 4

Eclipse and ADT Preferences

The last chapter explained what you can do with Eclipse out of the box, but there are many more possibilities if you dig a bit into the preferences, which are the settings kept for your workspace or project. This chapter covers the most important Eclipse and ADT preferences.

Before you get started, it is important to remember that almost all of the preferences in Eclipse can be found using Window ➤ Preferences. Figure 4-1 shows you the Preferences window, which will follow us through most of this chapter.

© Lukasz Pegiel 2021
Ł. Pęgiel, *ABAP in Eclipse*, https://doi.org/10.1007/978-1-4842-6963-3_4

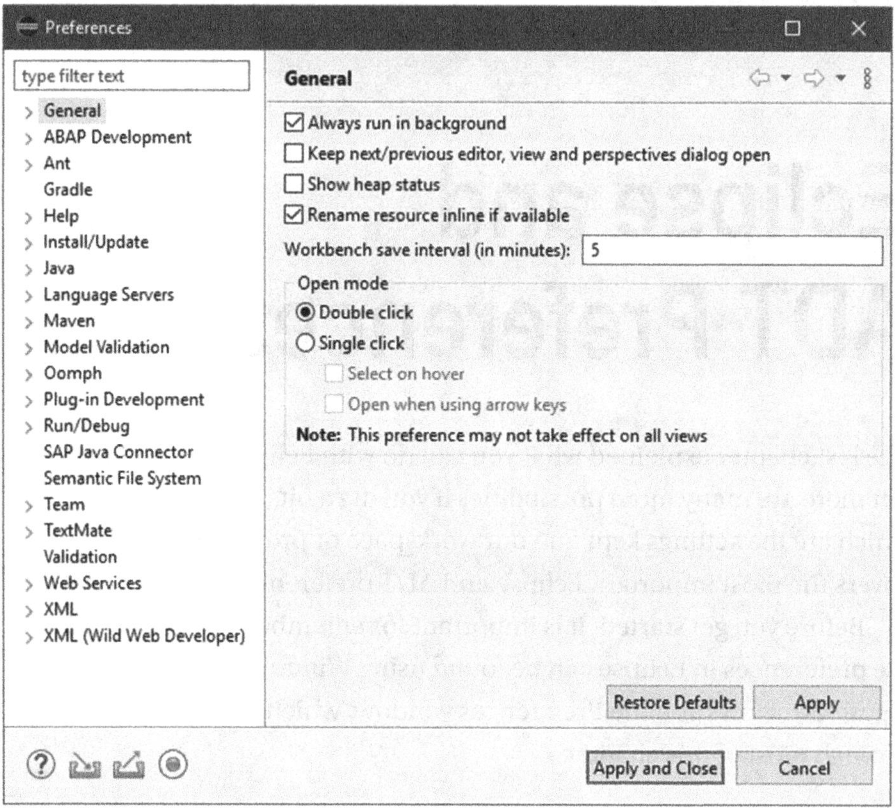

Figure 4-1. *Preferences window in Eclipse*

As you can see, there are many kinds of preferences, but I will focus on the three most important to ABAP: General, ABAP Development, and Install/Update. I also explain some additional parameters that you can put into an `eclipse.ini` file, which in some circumstances can boost your Eclipse installation.

When you look at the preferences tree, you may be a bit astonished to see how many settings there are. But do not worry, not all of these settings affect ABAP development. Most of them are related to Java or the collaboration tools, which unfortunately are not useful in our work.

Each of the main nodes has settings at the top level, as well as on the child levels. In some cases the preferences tree can be very deep, but as there is a filter on top of it, you do not have to remember the whole path, just the setting's name, or part of it.

General

In each program you have some global settings. Eclipse does not differ from them. You can set up Eclipse to work in a similar way regardless of the programming language you use. Those settings are available from the General node of the Eclipse preferences.

There are two important preferences directly on this level that you may want to remember. One is Workbench Save Internal, which sets how often the settings, such as the layout of your perspectives and open editor settings, are saved to your workbench. By default, this is set to 5 minutes and normally you will not need to change it. But there are times when this setting may be useful, such as when you are setting up your new Eclipse workspace or when are installing a release candidate of the newest version. It's better to set it to a lower value at those times, in case of crashes.

The second important setting on the Global node is Always Run in Background, which by default is selected. This setting is responsible for sending long-lasting jobs to the background so you can still use Eclipse while waiting for results. In the ABAP world, this could be waiting for ATC or unit testing, for example.

Appearance

In Poland, where I come from, we have a proverb: "How they see you, that is how they perceive you," which I think is close to the English saying, "Fine feathers make fine birds". I think you may understand why I have used these proverbs. We will be now dealing with the look of Eclipse and our code. For many developers, it is very important to customize themes and colors. Here you will find information about how to do this in Eclipse.

First of all, the theme settings. Currently when you install Eclipse, it comes with the default Light theme, but using the Appearance node, you can change it to Dark or Classic. You can also adapt the color and fonts theme to Default, Reduced Palette, or Classic Theme. As shown in Figure 4-2, if you change an appearance theme, you have to restart Eclipse to see the changes applied.

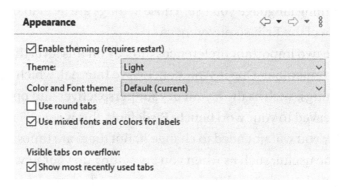

Figure 4-2. *Appearance: main preferences page*

Additionally, you can determine if the tabs should be rounded or if you want to use mixed fonts and colors for label decorations. Using mixed fonts and colors is set by default to true and it is better to leave it like this, as you can easily read the contents of the tree viewers. As an example, Figure 4-3 shows the difference between having this option on and off.

```
∨ 🗁 Classes                                    ∨ 🗁 Classes
  > ⓖ ZCL_FALV  Fast ALV                          > ⓖ ZCL_FALV  Fast ALV
  > ⓖ ZCL_FALV_COLUMN  FALV column                > ⓖ ZCL_FALV_COLUMN  FALV column
  > ⓖ ZCL_FALV_DYNAMIC_STATUS  FALV Dynamic Status > ⓖ ZCL_FALV_DYNAMIC_STATUS  FALV Dynamic Status
  > ⓖ ZCL_FALV_INHERITANCE_DEMO  Test             > ⓖ ZCL_FALV_INHERITANCE_DEMO  Test
  > ⓖ ZCL_FALV_LAYOUT  FALV layout                > ⓖ ZCL_FALV_LAYOUT  FALV layout
```

Figure 4-3. *Project Explorer with (left side) and without (right side) mixed fonts and colors enabled*

The Show Most Recently Used Tabs setting allows you to decide whether you want multiple editor tabs in the sequence of recently used or in the sequence that they were opened.

Colors and Fonts

When you expand the Appearance node, you will find another option: Colors and Fonts. You can manually update most of the settings for your editor, as well as for the popup windows. All the settings are categorized, but the most interesting ones for you should be contained in the ABAP and Basic nodes.

Font settings contain a font icon before the setting name, whereas color settings have always a square icon that is filled with the current color. When you select one of the settings and click the Edit button, depending on the type of setting, you will receive the Font Selection dialog or the Color Selection dialog.

The Font dialog setting can be seen in Figure 4-4 and it is very simple. You can choose the font, style, and size. It also shows a short example of how the font and style look, as the name of the font is displayed in the font.

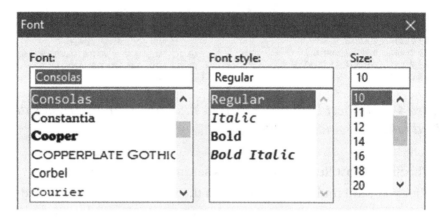

Figure 4-4. *Font selection dialog*

Many of you will probably stick to adjusting the size of the font, but I recommend you also try other fonts. My favorite is Cascadia Code,[1] by Microsoft. I find it clearer than Consolas and it has very nice feature called code ligature. Code ligature joins several code symbols into one. For example, the GE operator >= will be shown as ≥, and the static method call => will be displayed as ⇒. You can see a small example of different code displays in Figure 4-5. The choice is yours, but I recommend you at least try this feature.

```
2010 ⊟  method refresh_toolbar.
2011       check cl_gui_alv_grid->offline( ) is initial.
2012 ⊟     try.
2013           me->set_toolbar_interactive( ).
2014       catch cx_root.
2015           "in case method is called before the display of grid
2016           "no need to do anything with that
2017           clear sy-subrc.
2018       endtry.
2019       r_falv = me.
2020   endmethod.
```

```
2010 ⊟  method refresh_toolbar.
2011       check cl_gui_alv_grid⇒offline( ) is initial.
2012 ⊟     try.
2013           me→set_toolbar_interactive( ).
2014       catch cx_root.
2015           "in case method is called before the display of grid
2016           "no need to do anything with that
2017           clear sy-subrc.
2018       endtry.
2019       r_falv = me.
2020   endmethod.
```

Figure 4-5. *Comparison of code with Consolas (left) and Cascadia Code (right) fonts*

---

[1]The Cascadia Code font can be downloaded free of charge from https://github.com/microsoft/cascadia-code/.

Color settings are also very easy to change. When you edit colors, you get the standard Windows color selection popup that you may know from Paint (Figure 4-6). You can select one of the basic colors or click the Define Custom Colors button and choose one from the RGB palette.

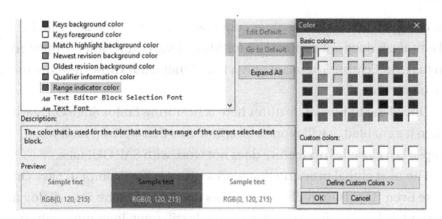

Figure 4-6. *Color selection dialog*

Label Decorations

Normally I would not describe label decorations, as disabling them does not add value. But it happened to me, when I was looking one day at the Eclipse preferences, that I disabled the project label decoration. When I did that, I was not able to see the client, user, and language information of the project in Project Explorer. It was shown as in the left part of Figure 4-7. After some investigation, I found out that I had disabled a ADT-Project Label Decorator.

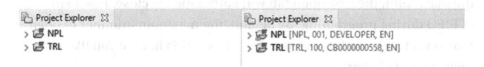

Figure 4-7. *Project Explorer without (left) and with (right) Project Decoration enabled*

I guess there is no need to cover the others, but it is good to know such preferences exist, especially if you have issues like I had.

Editors

This node of the General settings contains preferences that are valid for all editors. It does not matter if it's for ABAP, Java, or any other supported language in Eclipse. There are only a few of them, but knowing about them can be very helpful.

One of the important features here is Restoring Editor State On Startup. When it's enabled, it will reopen all editor tabs that were opened when Eclipse last closed. This feature does not work with SAP GUI tabs.

The next global property that works with ADT is Prompt to Save On Close Even If Still Open Elsewhere. This option forces the Save dialog to appear for the modified object, even if it is still open in another tab. Such behavior can be seen when you clone the tab or use the standard ABAP editor and ABAP Compare view. Maybe this is not a game changer, but my experience tells me that the more often we save, the more secure our code.

The last property worth mentioning is Automatic Closing of Editors. Normally it should not be an issue to have many tabs open. If you are working on old machine, however, you must watch the memory consumption in order to work comfortably. In this case, I assume having 20 tabs open at time is enough. I also cannot imagine that you work on all of them at the same time. That is why you can set how many active tabs can be visible at once. When you open a tab that exceeds the maximum, the first open tab will automatically close. It is a kind of FIFO during programing. By default, the maximum number of open tabs is set to 99, but I recommend you lower this in case you like to open a lot of objects.

Autosave

This is one of my favorite features of Eclipse. When you select the Autosave node from General ➤ Editors, you will see only one checkbox—Enable Autosave for Dirty Editors—and one input field for the autosave interval in seconds.

You may remember in a previous chapter I described the local history, which is created each time you use the Save button. With the autosave functionality, you can forget about saving manually. Each time you are inactive for a defined interval, changes are saved and a local history is created. I set the autosave interval to 120 seconds to secure my work when I leave my office or am thinking about a solution. If you leave your PC unblocked by accident, it may save you from colleagues' bad pranks as well.

Text Editors

One of the more important preference nodes of General ➤ Editors is Text Editors. This node has a few children which I will describe later, but there are many settings (Figure 4-8) that can help you customize your IDE directly on that level. As with parent nodes, these settings are valid for all text editors, so choose wisely if you are using Eclipse in several areas. Or you could have two separate workspaces for each language, so you wouldn't have to mix the settings.

Again, I will not go through every setting; I focus on the ones applicable to the ABAP developer.

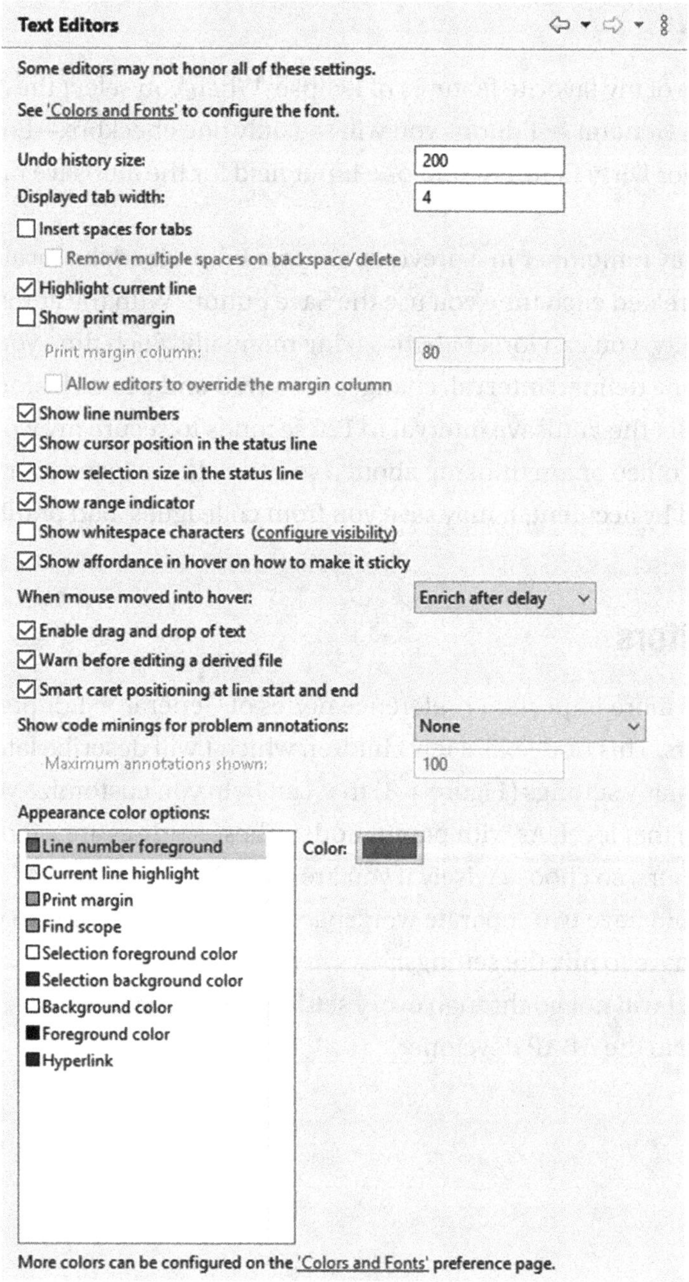

Text Editors   ⇦ ▼ ⇨ ▼ ⦂

Some editors may not honor all of these settings.

See 'Colors and Fonts' to configure the font.

Undo history size: `200`

Displayed tab width: `4`

☐ Insert spaces for tabs

☐ Remove multiple spaces on backspace/delete

☑ Highlight current line

☐ Show print margin

Print margin column: `80`

☐ Allow editors to override the margin column

☑ Show line numbers

☑ Show cursor position in the status line

☑ Show selection size in the status line

☑ Show range indicator

☐ Show whitespace characters (configure visibility)

☑ Show affordance in hover on how to make it sticky

When mouse moved into hover: Enrich after delay ∨

☑ Enable drag and drop of text

☑ Warn before editing a derived file

☑ Smart caret positioning at line start and end

Show code minings for problem annotations: None   ∨

Maximum annotations shown: `100`

Appearance color options:

◼ Line number foreground
☐ Current line highlight
◼ Print margin
◼ Find scope
☐ Selection foreground color
◼ Selection background color
☐ Background color
◼ Foreground color
◼ Hyperlink

Color: ▮

More colors can be configured on the 'Colors and Fonts' preference page.

Figure 4-8. *Text Editors preferences page*

Undo History Size allows you to set how many steps can be undone with Ctrl+Z. The default value is 200, and in most cases, this is sufficient. When you are using block selection a lot, increasing this value can help you. That's because, when you undoing the block selection changes, each character in each line that was changed is one step in history.

The Displayed Tab Width setting is useful for people who want to show indents in the code differently than the standard. By default, the tab takes four spaces, but you can increase or decrease that value. This setting only changes the display. It doesn't impact how others see your code.

Another setting linked to Text Editors is Insert Spaces Instead for Tabs. In this case, when you are using the Tab key, the spaces in quantity set in the Displayed tab width are inserted into the code. This will impact how others see the code, as each space is saved separately in the source code. Additionally, when you replace tabs with spaces, the next option will became active: Remove Multiple Spaces On Backspace/Delete. When you press the Delete or Backspace button, you will remove the trailing or concurring spaces in a number set by the tab width. In other words, it will work exactly like standard tabs work.

Highlight Current Line is enabled by default. It can be useful when you are scrolling up or down to check something and you want to come back to the selected line without remembering the line number. Figure 4-9 shows how the highlighting works in line 1369.

```
1366 ⊝   method evf_before_ucommand_internal.
1367        field-symbols: <outtab> type standard table.
1368 ⊝     case e_ucomm.
1369          when me->mc_fc_select_all.
1370 ⊝            if layout->mark_field is not initial and
1371               line_exists( fcat[ fieldname = layout->mark_field checkbox = abap_true ] ).
1372                 assign outtab->* to <outtab>.
```

Figure 4-9. *The Highlight Current Line option turned on*

In SE80, it was common to restrict the width of the codeline using the workbench settings. By default, it was set to 72 characters. In the past, this was supposed to allow the codeline to fit in the monitor and to allow easy printing. Nowadays, I do not know anyone who would print the code (besides in programming books), which is why in most cases you won't find this option useful. But, if your internal policies and guidelines force you to limit the width of the codeline, you can use the Show Print Margin setting. Setting the print margin will not block you from using more characters in the line, but at least it will show you where the border is. Figure 4-10 shows the print margin, which is just a vertical line in the editor.

```
⊙ ZCL_FALV ▸
  1    "! <p class="shorttext synchronized" lang="en">Fast ALV</p>
  2  ⊝class zcl_falv definition
  3      public
  4      inheriting from cl_gui_alv_grid
  5      create public
  6
  7      global friends zcl_falv_layout .
  8
  9      public section.
 10
 11        interfaces if_alv_rm_grid_friend .
 12
 13        types:
 14          begin of t_subcl_call,
 15            progname type progname,
 16            line     type i,
 17            column   type i,
 18            class    type string,
 19          end of t_subcl_call .
 20        types:
 21          tt_subcl_call type sorted table of t_subcl_call with unique key progname line column .|
 22        types:
```

Figure 4-10. *Print margin set to 72 characters*

You probably won't need the Show Line Numbers and Show Range Indicator options. If you are annoyed by line numbers in the editor, you can switch this off. The same is true for range indicators, which may not be clear. The range indicator is the vertical bar shown on a vertical ruler, which with ABAP, marks the current code unit. For example, it's the method, form, or class if you put the cursor between the method's implementations. Figure 4-11 shows an example of a range indicator from line 1214 to 1223.

```
1211      endmethod.
1212
1213
1214 ⊖   method disable_button.
1215 ⊖       try.|
1216           toolbar_added[ function = iv_function ]-disabled = abap_true.
1217         catch cx_sy_itab_line_not_found.
1218           clear sy-subrc.
1219       endtry.
1220       insert value #( function = iv_function ) into table toolbar_disabled.
1221       me->refresh_toolbar( ).
1222       r_falv = me.
1223      endmethod.
1224
1225
1226 ⊖   method display.
```

Figure 4-11. *Range indicator for the DISABLE_BUTTON method*

The Show Whitespace Characters functionality can be useful when you work with the strings in ABAP. Some developers also use this for better code formatting. You can switch the display of whitespace characters as well as decide which of them should be displayed and in which region of the line. Figure 4-12 shows the possible configurations of the whitespace characters.

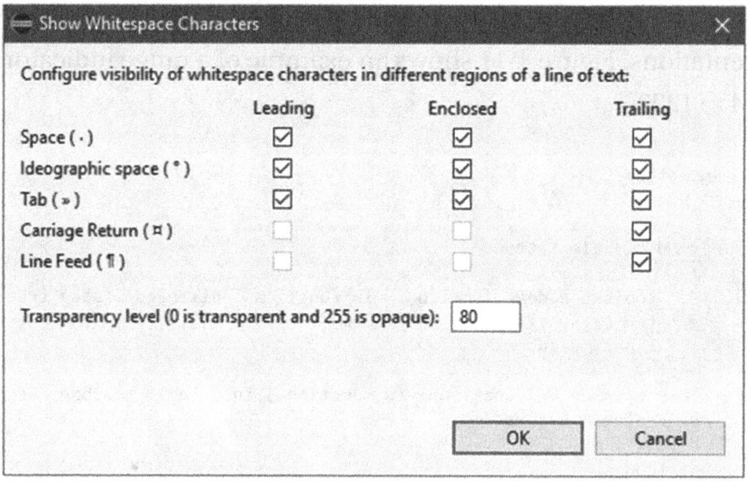
Show Whitespace Characters
Configure visibility of whitespace characters in different regions of a line of text:
Leading
Enclosed
Trailing
Space (·)
Ideographic space (°)
Tab (»)
Carriage Return (¤)
Line Feed (¶)
Transparency level (0 is transparent and 255 is opaque):
80
OK
Cancel

Figure 4-12. *Whitespace characters display settings*

When you are reviewing your code, you may want to turn on the Show Code Minings for Problem Annotations option. You can do this by selecting one of the problem types from the drop-down menu: Errors, Errors and Warnings, Errors, Warnings, and Infos. The details will be then displayed before the occurrence, as shown in Figure 4-13. Besides limiting the type of annotations, you can also adjust the maximum number of shown annotations for performance reasons.

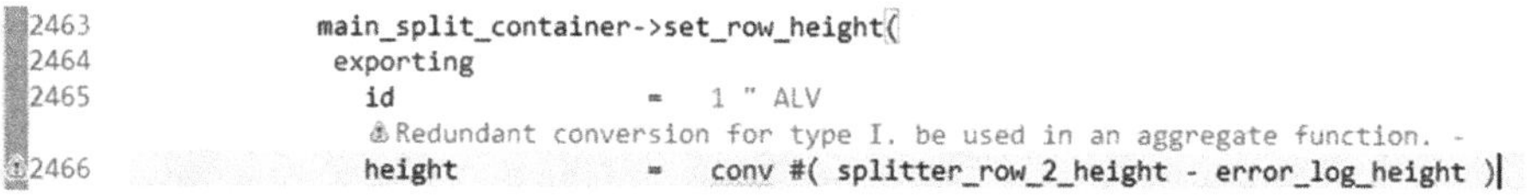
2463 main_split_container->set_row_height(
2464 exporting
2465 id = 1 " ALV
Redundant conversion for type I. be used in an aggregate function. -
2466 height = conv #(splitter_row_2_height - error_log_height)

Figure 4-13. *Code mining for problem annotations turned on*

Although I like this code mining option during the code review process, I switch it off during development. When you write code and you have instant check of the syntax, the syntax errors often appear before you finish writing the statements. This issue pops up until you finish the statement, at which point it disappears. This behavior can make it hard to follow the code on the screen, as the line will go up and down so often.

Annotations

There are many types of standard annotations in Eclipse, and ADT adds a whole pack of its own. Too much information can lead to losing readability, especially on the overview ruler. That is why it is good to know that you can customize the appearance of the annotations and decide if they should be displayed on a vertical ruler or an overview ruler. You can also determine if the annotation source should be highlighted in the code, and if yes, then how.

Notice in Figure 4-14 that some of the annotations don't have icons displayed before their names. In such cases, there is no point in switching on the visibility of the annotation on the vertical ruler, because only annotations with icons are displayed there.

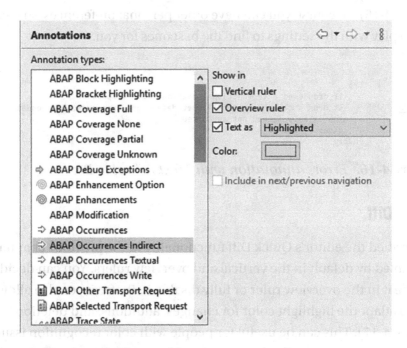

Figure 4-14. Annotations settings

Just to give you an example of how customizing the annotation display can change readability, let's update one of the most common annotations, which is Errors. The default setting for Texts As is Native Problem Underline. In my opinion, it is not that easy to catch the error in two shakes of a lamb's tail (Figure 4-15).

```
1695 ⊖     try.
1696           lr_dropdowns = lr_functional_settings→get_dropdowns( ).
1697           lt_drdn = cl_salv_controller_metadata⇒ get_dropdowns( lr_dropdowns ).
1698         catch cx_salv_method_not_supported.
1699           clear sy-subrc.
1700       endtry.
```

Figure 4-15. *Errors annotated with the standard "Text As" setting*

Changing Text As to Box will make it more visible and cleaner (Figure 4-16). Of course you can have other personal preferences, so feel free to play with the settings to find the best ones for you.

```
1695 ⊖     try.
1696           lr_dropdowns = lr_functional_settings→get_dropdowns( ).
1697~          lt_drdn = cl_salv_controller_metadata⇒ get_dropdowns( lr_dropdowns ).
1698         catch cx_salv_method_not_supported.
1699           clear sy-subrc.
1700       endtry.
```

Figure 4-16. *Errors annotation with "Text As" set to Box*

Quick Diff

I described the editor's Quick Diff functionality in the previous chapter. It is enabled by default in the vertical and overview rulers. You can decide to hide it in the overview ruler or fully disable it. Preferences also allows you to adapt the highlight color for changes, additions, and deletion (Figure 4-17). This can be useful for people with color recognition issues or when you are manually changing the colors of the line numbers and editor background.

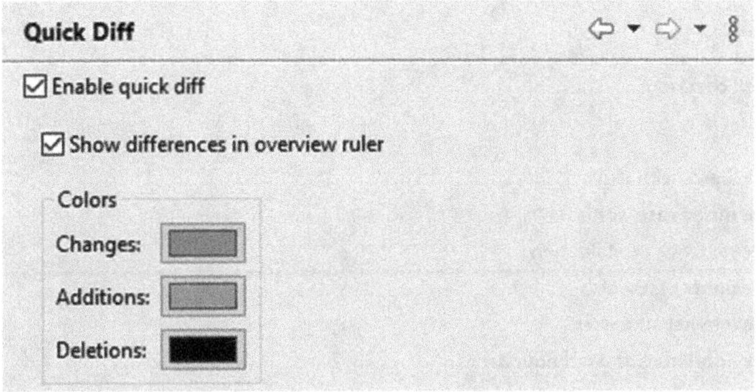

Figure 4-17. Quick Diff properties

Spelling

Spell checking in English is also enabled by default. Although I recommend you use it, you may be forced to use other languages for object descriptions and comments. In such cases, you can disable spell checking here, or you can download the appropriate word list from the Internet and use it as a dictionary. If you want to use an external file, it is important that the text file contain one word per line. You may also need to adapt the encoding of the file for the spell checker to work correctly.

Besides choosing the dictionary, you can change some minor settings, like ignoring single letters or words with digits (Figure 4-18).

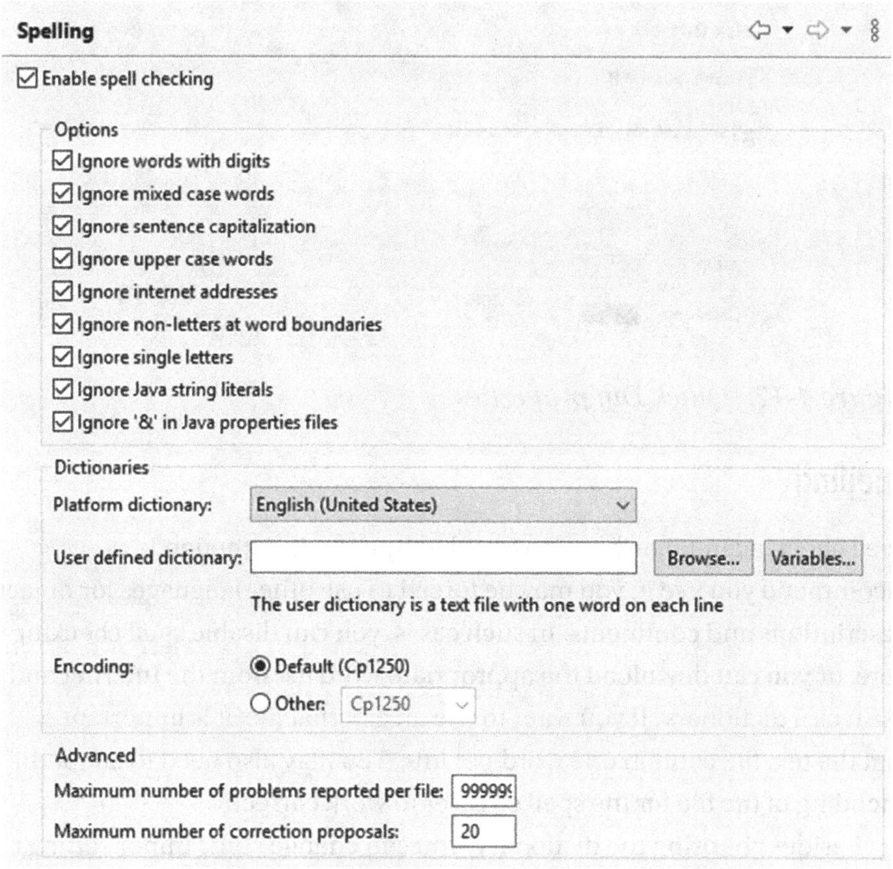

Spelling

☑ Enable spell checking

Options
☑ Ignore words with digits
☑ Ignore mixed case words
☑ Ignore sentence capitalization
☑ Ignore upper case words
☑ Ignore internet addresses
☑ Ignore non-letters at word boundaries
☑ Ignore single letters
☑ Ignore Java string literals
☑ Ignore '&' in Java properties files

Dictionaries

Platform dictionary: English (United States)

User defined dictionary: [   ] Browse... Variables...

The user dictionary is a text file with one word on each line

Encoding: ● Default (Cp1250)
           ○ Other: Cp1250

Advanced

Maximum number of problems reported per file: 999999

Maximum number of correction proposals: 20

Figure 4-18. Spelling preferences page

Keys

To write code more quickly, you need to avoid using the mouse as much as possible. To do so, you need to know the key bindings for the most common commands. For developers who tend to use the mouse often, this is not easy at the beginning, especially when they are switching from SE80 to Eclipse. ADT provides many more key bindings in comparison to SE80. Sometimes they are also a bit different. That is why you will like the Keys preferences page (Figure 4-19).

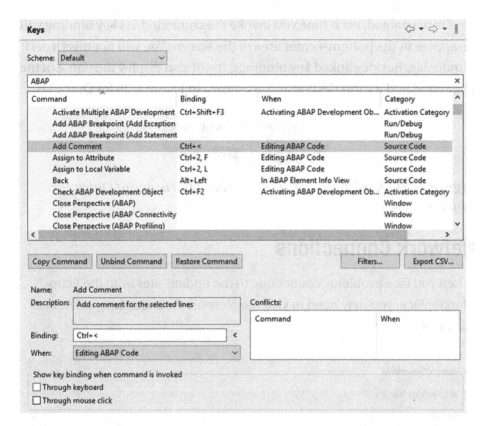

Figure 4-19. *Shortcuts settings screen*

Besides the ability to check and change the key bindings, you can also turn on a very powerful functionality—showing key bindings when a command is invoked (see the bottom of Figure 4-19). You can allow this when using mouse clicks or when calling commands using the keyboard.

Showing the key bindings after you used menu bar, toolbar, or context menu helps you memorize what key combinations you have to use to call a command. Many people find it helpful when they are switching from SE80 to Eclipse, or when they are new to ABAP.

Showing the key binding after using it through the keyboard finds its usage on trainings and presentations. People who are watching you code can more easily follow your actions.

Once enabled, each time you invoke the command, its key binding will be appear in the bottom-center area of the screen. You will not miss it, as it is quite big. Besides linked key bindings, it will also display the name of the command and a short description, as shown in Figure 4-20 for Quick Fix.

Figure 4-20. *Key binding displayed about the usage of Quick Fix function*

Network Connections

When you face problems connecting to the update sites or to the Eclipse Marketplace, you may need to visit the Network Connections preferences (Figure 4-21).

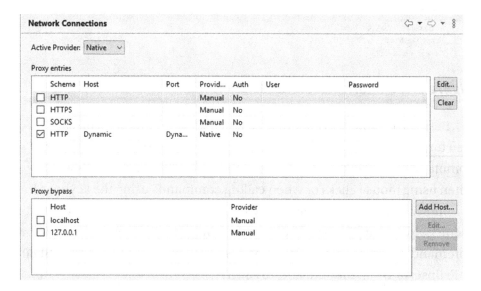

Figure 4-21. *Proxy preferences for Eclipse*

By default, Active Provider is set to Native, which corresponds to the operating system settings. If this does not work, you need to change the provider to Manual and edit the HTTP, HTTPS, and SOCKS schemes. You need to provide the proxy host and port and the credentials if authorization is required by the proxy. You can also use Direct provider, which forces Eclipse to not use a proxy.

When you are using the Manual provider, you may also want to set up some exceptions. You can add hosts to the proxy bypass list, if they can be accessed directly.

Workspaces

When you run Eclipse the first time, you have to indicate which workspace to use. When you select the Use This As a Default And Do Not Ask Again option, you will need to switch workspaces after the default one is fully loaded. To change this option, go to preferences and choose General ➤ Startup and Shutdown ➤ Workspaces. Select Prompt for Workspace on Startup (Figure 4-22).

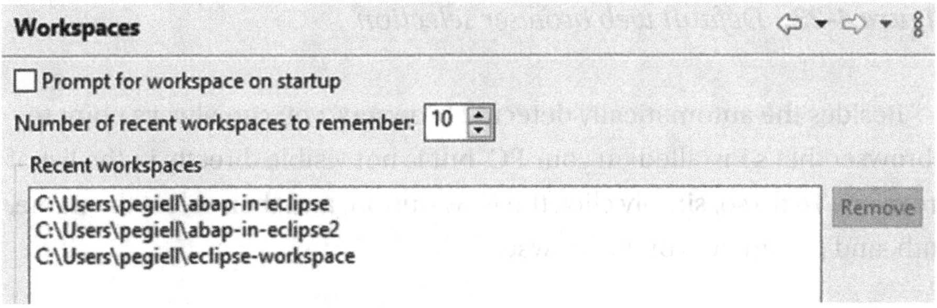

Figure 4-22. *Workspace preferences*

You can also set the number of recent workspaces to remember and remove unnecessary workspaces from the recent workspaces list.

Web Browser

Eclipse has its own web browser, which is set by default. This web browser runs in a tab, just like another editor window. If you want the URLs to open in a different browser, you can change this from the Web Browser preferences page (Figure 4-23).

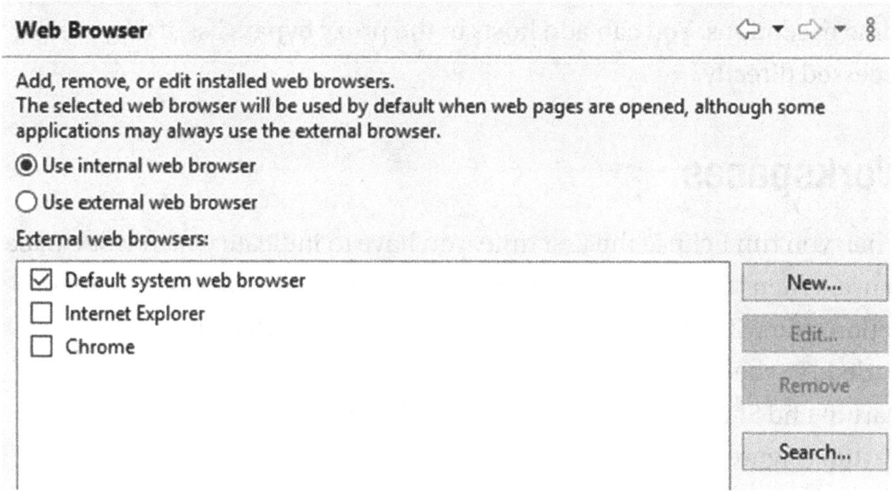

Figure 4-23. *Default web browser selection*

Besides the automatically detected browsers, you can always point to a browser that's installed on your PC, but is not visible directly in the list of browsers. To do so, simply click the New button, and then select the name, path, and parameters of the browser.

ABAP Development

All the previous settings were linked to global Eclipse settings. Plugins and ABAP Development Tools can have their own settings. This section of the chapter focuses on the ADT preferences pages and their impact on the IDE.

Activation

The first important node in the ABAP Development preferences is
Activation, although there are only two settings in here (Figure 4-24).

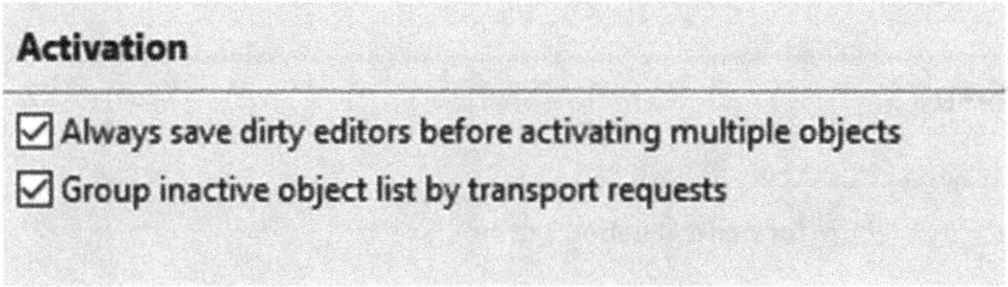

Activation

☑ Always save dirty editors before activating multiple objects
☑ Group inactive object list by transport requests

Figure 4-24. *Activation preferences for ATD*

The Always Save Dirty Editors Before Activating Multiple Objects
option is enabled by default. It can be sometimes a problem, especially
if you work in parallel with a few minor changes from several projects. In
general, I find it useful to have it enabled, especially with bigger scope
developments.

The second option, Group Inactive Object List By Transport Request, is
also enabled by default. It can be annoying when your changes have been
split into several transport requests, because of a previous lock on part of
the object. In this case, it is better to see it on object level, not as a transport
request. So at that time it may be useful to disable this setting for a while.

Debug

The Debug preferences have two levels of settings, a global one for all
workspace projects and one that's project specific. Let's see what you can
set at the global level.

When you look at these settings (Figure 4-25), they might be not always easy to understand. In the case of Enable Debugging of System Programs, it should be clear that if the program status is SYSTEM and the setting is enabled, you can debug it. In other cases, it will be omitted, even if the breakpoints are set.

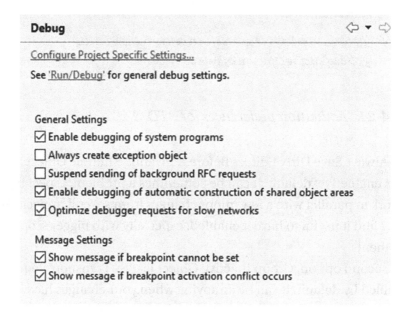

Figure 4-25. *Debug preferences are valid for all projects*

Enabling the Always Create Exception Object option is highly recommended when you deal with object-oriented ABAP, and I really do hope you all do. This function creates an exception object during the debugging process, even if the developer hasn't used INTO with a CATCH statement. Let's look at a short example. You are debugging a call of a method that is wrapped in a TRY statement, but when the CATCH of the exception takes place, you see that there is no exception object (Figure 4-26).

```
706 ⊖     TRY.
707           lo_converter->convert(
708             EXPORTING
709               io_alv         = io_alv
710               it_table       = it_table
711               i_row_int      = i_top
712               i_column_int   = i_left
713               i_table        = i_table
714               i_style_table  = table_style
715               io_worksheet   = me
716             CHANGING
717               co_excel       = excel ).
718         CATCH zcx_excel .
719     ENDTRY.
```

Figure 4-26. *Code with a TRY CATCH block, but without an INTO statement*

After enabling the creation of the Exception Objects Always setting, you can right-click the Vertical ruler, where we should see the exclamation mark icon and choose Show Exception Variable and then select the exception to show (Figure 4-27).

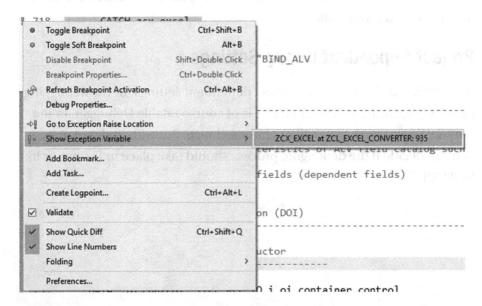

Figure 4-27. *The context menu of the Vertical ruler for an exception*

Now you should see the exception object in the Variables view (Figure 4-28). This should help you investigate the exception messages, as well as any other exception variable, regardless of the way it was caught.

Name	Value	Actual Type	Technical Type	Length
● <Enter variable>				0
∨ ● {O:407\CLASS=ZCX_EXCEL}	OBJECT	ZCX_EXCEL		0
○ TEXTID	028C0ED2B5601ED78EB6F3368B1E4F9B	SOTR_CONC	C	32
○ PREVIOUS	{O:INITIAL}	{O:initial}	Ref to CX_ROOT	0
○ KERNEL_ERRID		S380ERRID	C	30
○ IS_RESUMABLE		ABAP_BOOL	C	1
○ ERROR		STRING	CString	0
> ○ SYST_AT_RAISE	Structure: flat, not charlike...	SYST	Structure: flat, no...	4612
> □ INTERNAL_SOURCE_POS	Structure: flat, not charlike	SCX_SRCPOS	Structure: flat, no...	8

Figure 4-28. *Exception object in the Variables view*

The next global debugger option we discuss is Suspend Sending of Background RFC Requests. When you work with bgRFC or tRFC, this can be your lifesaver when troubleshooting, as is the case of bgRFC. You can debug later with the transaction SBGRFCMON, and in the case of tRFC this would be SM58. If this option is disabled, you cannot follow the code inside these RFC requests.

Project Dependent Debug Settings

As mentioned, there are also project dependent settings for the debugging process (Figure 4-29). The main one is of course Enable Debugger. In the old NetWeaver stack, you will not have a choice. But with updated ones, you can decide if the debugging process should take place in Eclipse or in SAP GUI.

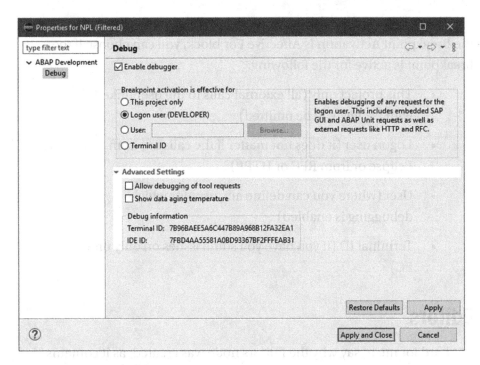

Figure 4-29. *Project debug preferences*

Many people using Eclipse are still disabling the debug option so that they can work with the GUI debugger. I can understand that; when I started using Eclipse, I did the same. But I have learned that it makes no difference as long as you are not using debugger scripts, which are not available in Eclipse (so far). As I have stated, the ability to edit code directly when you find an issue makes it more useful than the GUI debugger. Of course, you have a choice, but imagine that your company is going to use ABAP in the cloud, where you no longer have a choice. I think it is better to step out from GUI and learn to live without it.

The next part of the debugger settings invoke the debugger. In the Breakpoint Activation Is Affective For block, you can choose if the breakpoint is active for the following:

- This project only (all external calls to the user linked with project will be omitted)

- Logon user (it does not matter if the calls are from Eclipse or from RFC or HTPP)

- User (where you can define any user for which debugging is enabled)

- Terminal ID (if you have you some issues on only one PC)

Editors

It is hard for me to say why the Editors node was created, as it contains only one child, called Source Code Editors. Maybe SAP wanted to use Eclipse and ADT for other editor types, or the idea was that each editor type would have a separate node.

Anyway, there is still a very important setting that you can change on that preferences level: Automatic Syntax Check on Active ABAP Editor (Figure 4-30). In most cases, you will want to leave it active, but I have had to deactivate it a few times. This happened when I was working on slow connections with huge sources (more than 10,000 lines). I was refactoring or splitting the source into several classes or includes before activating the automatic syntax.

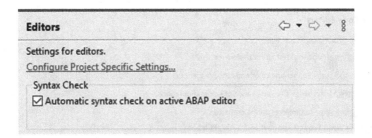

Figure 4-30. *ADT Editors global setting*

When you use the Configure Project Specific Settings hyperlink and you choose the proper project, you can also choose if you want to do a package check during the syntax check. Personally, I have used this option only for tests a few times, but I understand this can be useful sometimes, especially when you're creating your own addon to SAP.

Source Code Editors

As mentioned, Source Code Editors is the only child of the Editors node. As you can see in Figure 4-31, at this level, it contains links to the global Eclipse settings and to the ABAP Formatter, which I briefly described in the previous chapter. There are also two important preferences: Show Transport Request Information for ABAP Classes and Wrap and Escape Text When Pasting into String Literals.

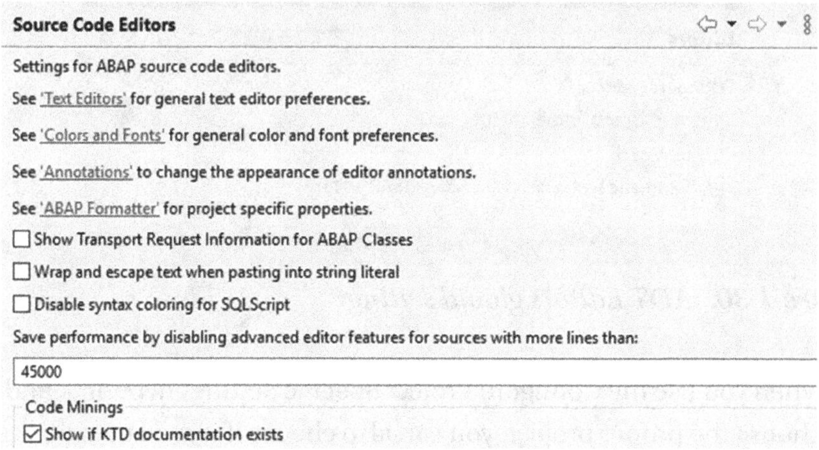

Figure 4-31. *Source Code Editors preferences page*

The Show Transport Request Information for ABAP Classes option is useful when a few people are editing the same class. This is especially true when they are doing this for two totally different tasks or projects, and they are blocking different parts of the same class in different transport requests. It can even happen with one developer; the changes are stored in two separate not released transport requests. In such a case, you will notice a new annotation in the vertical ruler (Figure 4-32) close to the blocked part source codeline. When you hover over this annotation, you'll see the detailed information about the transport request and the user.

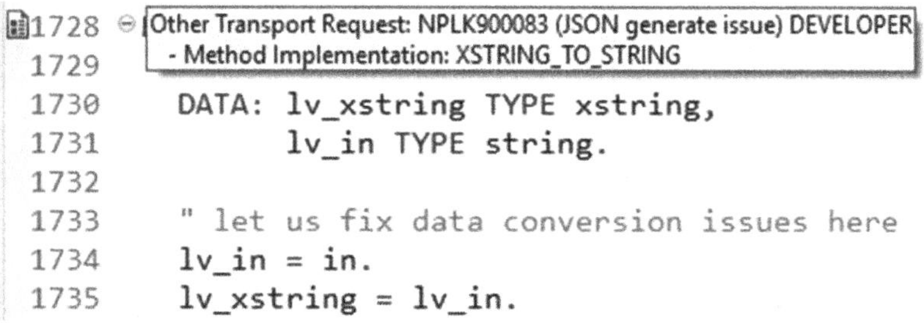

Figure 4-32. *Transport request annotation for classes*

Wrap and Escape Text When Pasting into String Literals is one of my favorite options. It's disabled by default. It's powerful when you need to create long, multiline literals like HTML or mockups for long text. This is usually HTML code or long text that you prepare outside of Eclipse and want to paste it into the ADT. When you do so using the standard settings, you will get poor results, as you can see in Figure 4-33.

```
⊗473    data(html) = '<html>
  474   <body>
  475   <a href="CALLTO:test@test.corp">Teams call</a></br>
  476   <a href="TEL:+48800900100">Telephone call</a></br>
  477   <a href="IM:test@test.corp">Teams chat</a></br>
  478   </body>
  479   </html>'
```

Figure 4-33. *HTML pasted into a string literal with the default settings*

When you enable wrapping and escaping of pasted text, you directly see the difference. Just look at Figure 4-34; each line of the pasted text is escaped with literals and a carriage return is added at the end of each line to keep the source formatting. Fast and easy.

```
473  data(html) = '<html>' && |\r\n|  &&
474               '<body>' && |\r\n|  &&
475               '<a href="CALLTO:test@test.corp">Teams call</a></br>' && |\r\n|  &&
476               '<a href="TEL:+48800900100">Telephone call</a></br>' && |\r\n|  &&
477               '<a href="IM:test@test.corp">Teams chat</a></br>' && |\r\n|  &&
478               '</body>' && |\r\n|  &&
479               '</html>'.
```

Figure 4-34. *Text pasted after enabling text wrapping and escaping*

ABAP Keyword Colors

The next option that I suggest you check is ABAP Keyword Colors. By default, coloring is disabled (Figure 4-35), but you can enable it by selecting the checkbox next to ABAP Keyword. You can also edit how the default keywords are displayed or add keywords to the list.

Figure 4-35. *ABAP Keyword Colors default preferences*

Personally I like this option very much and I often add keywords for different colors. It helps me catch important statements while scrolling through the source code, especially when I work with old, big reports. Some may say that after activation of additional colors, your code looks like a Christmas tree (Figure 4-36), but I really enjoy having it enabled. Maybe it is because, when I work with other programming languages, such coloring is enabled by default for distinction of static attributes and methods or for interfaces.

```
707 ⊖  method add_button.
708 ⊖    if not line_exists( toolbar_added[ function = iv_function ] ).
709        insert value #( function = iv_function
710                        icon = conv #( iv_icon )
711                        quickinfo = iv_quickinfo
712                        butn_type = iv_butn_type
713                        disabled = iv_disabled
714                        text = iv_text
715                        checked = iv_checked
716                          ) into table toolbar_added .
717
718        delete toolbar_deleted where function = iv_function.
719        me->refresh_toolbar( ).
720      endif.
721      r_falv = me.
722    endmethod.
```

Figure 4-36. *Display of source code with activated ABAP Keyword Colors*

Templates

In previous chapters, I showed you how to use ABAP Templates. One of ways to edit them is from the proper Preferences page, where you do exactly the same thing as in the Templates view.

You can also adjust the templates for the following:

- Access controls

- Annotation definitions

- Behavior definitions

- Data definitions

- Dictionary structures

- JSON

- Metadata extensions

- Service definitions

- Transformations

233

Each has its own preferences subnode inside the Source Code Editors (Figure 4-37). You can edit the existing templates or create your own custom ones. I am sure you will find it useful at least for CDS views (Data Definition Templates), and with time, you will also adjust all the others. You just need some practice in order to figure out what kind of templates will be useful.

```
∨ Source Code Editors
      ABAP Keyword Colors
      ABAP Templates
      Access Control Templates
      Annotation Definition Templates
      Behavior Definition Templates
   > CDS
      Code Completion
      Data Definition Templates
      DDL Formatter
      Dictionary Structure Templates
      Dynamic Cache Templates
      JSON Templates
      Mark Occurrences
      Metadata Extension Templates
      Quick Assist
      Service Definition Templates
      Transformation Templates
```

Figure 4-37. *Children of Source Code Editors preferences*

Code Completion

I really like the code completion option that ADT provides. It includes automatic closing brackets and literals, adding additional whitespace inside the brackets, and automatic triggering code completion in the case of typing proper characters. It should, in my opinion, always be enabled in order to code efficiently. But there are some more settings that you might also like (Figure 4-38).

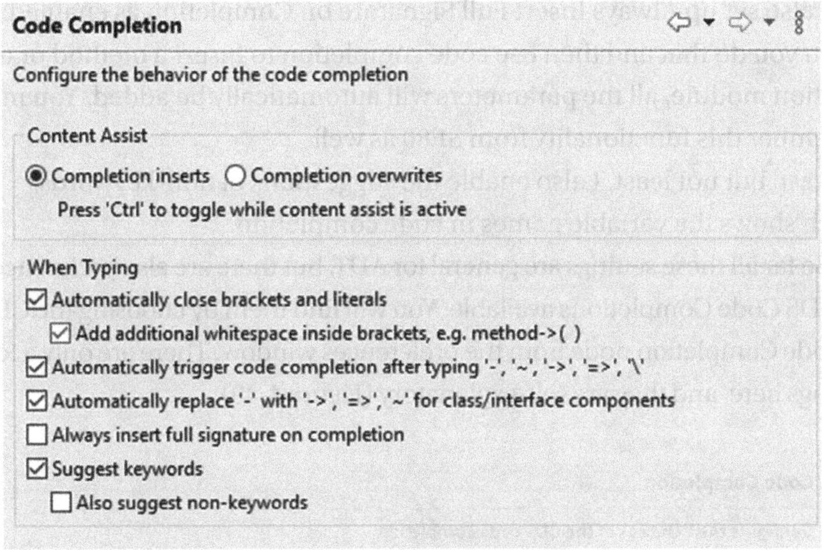

Code Completion   ⇦ ▾ ⇨ ▾ ⁝

Configure the behavior of the code completion

Content Assist

◉ Completion inserts   ○ Completion overwrites

    Press 'Ctrl' to toggle while content assist is active

When Typing

☑ Automatically close brackets and literals

    ☑ Add additional whitespace inside brackets, e.g. method->( )

☑ Automatically trigger code completion after typing '-', '~', '->', '=>', '\'

☑ Automatically replace '-' with '->', '=>', '~' for class/interface components

☐ Always insert full signature on completion

☑ Suggest keywords

    ☐ Also suggest non-keywords

Figure 4-38. *ABAP Code Completion settings*

For example, you can switch the default code completion behavior,
which inserts the code completion at the cursor place instead of
overwriting the following code. If you want the code to be overwritten in
most cases, but you want to use this functionality from time to time, you
can simply press the Ctrl key while code completion is active. In this case,
as shown in Figure 4-39, the part of the code that will be overwritten is
highlighted.

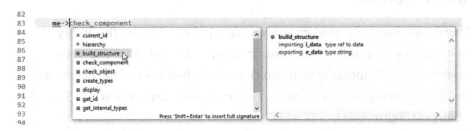

Figure 4-39. *Highlighted method CHECK_COMPONENT as the one
to be overwritten*

I also set up Always Insert Full Signature on Completion as enabled. When you do that and then use code completion to insert a method or a function module, all the parameters will automatically be added. You may remember this functionality from SE80 as well.

Last, but not least, I also enable the suggestions of non-keywords, which shows the variable names in code completion.

So far all these settings are general for ADT, but there are also preferences for CDS Code Completions available. You will find them by choosing the CDS ➤ Code Completion node from the preferences window. There are only a few settings here, and they are self-explanatory (Figure 4-40).

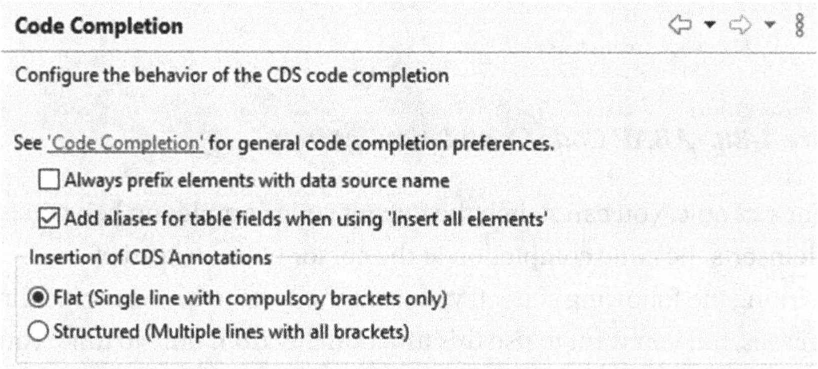

Figure 4-40. *CDS Views Code Completion settings*

Mark Occurrence

I have mentioned the occurrence markers before. Besides the ability to switch them off from the toolbar button, you can do this also in the preferences. Additionally, you can change the behavior of the occurrence markers, which by default is set to Determine Occurrences When Selection Changes (Figure 4-41).

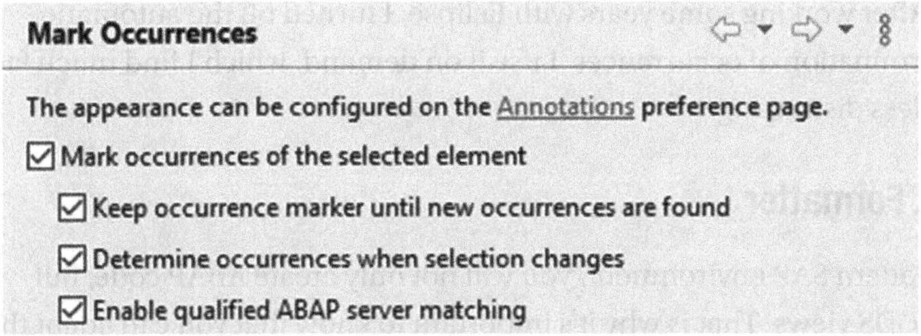

Mark Occurrences   ⇦ ▾ ⇨ ▾ ⣿

The appearance can be configured on the <u>Annotations</u> preference page.

☑ Mark occurrences of the selected element

   ☑ Keep occurrence marker until new occurrences are found

   ☑ Determine occurrences when selection changes

   ☑ Enable qualified ABAP server matching

Figure 4-41. *Mark Occurrences preferences page*

The added value of disabling automatic determination of occurrences at a selection is helpful when you click the source code with the mouse. In such cases, the previous occurrences will not be lost. But each time you want to find the occurrences of the element, you need to use the Ctrl+Shift+U combination to force it.

Whatever way you choose, occurrence markers can replace where-used lists for the current source code editor and will highlight the occurrences directly in the editor (Figure 4-42), as well as in the occurrence bar.

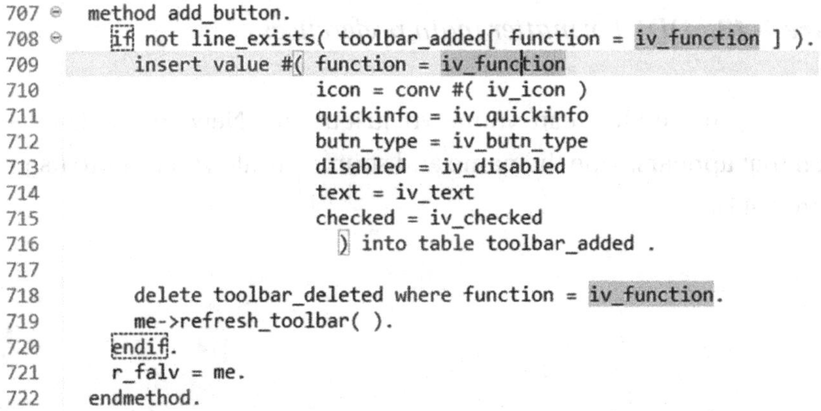

```
707 ⊖  method add_button.
708 ⊖    if not line_exists( toolbar_added[ function = iv_function ] ).
709        insert value #( function = iv_function
710                        icon = conv #( iv_icon )
711                        quickinfo = iv_quickinfo
712                        butn_type = iv_butn_type
713                        disabled = iv_disabled
714                        text = iv_text
715                        checked = iv_checked
716                          ) into table toolbar_added .
717
718        delete toolbar_deleted where function = iv_function.
719        me->refresh_toolbar( ).
720      endif.
721      r_falv = me.
722    endmethod.
```

Figure 4-42. *ABAP code with occurrence markers enabled and chosen for the IV_FUNCTION variable*

After working some years with Eclipse, I turned off the automatic determination of occurrences. I use it on demand, which I find much faster and less distracting.

DDL Formatter

In modern SAP environment, you will not only create ABAP code, but also CDS views. That is why it's important to know that you can adapt the formatting of the CDS views using DDL Formatter.

By default, SAP set up the formatter of CDS views. You can also create own formatting preferences for the CDS view. To do so, go to DDL Formatter preferences (Figure 4-43) to select, edit, create, or import a profile. You can also choose to always format DDLs at save, which I find very convenient.

Figure 4-43. *DDL Formatter main preferences*

When you want to create your own, just use the New button. On the screen that appears, type the name and source profile you want to use (Figure 4-44).

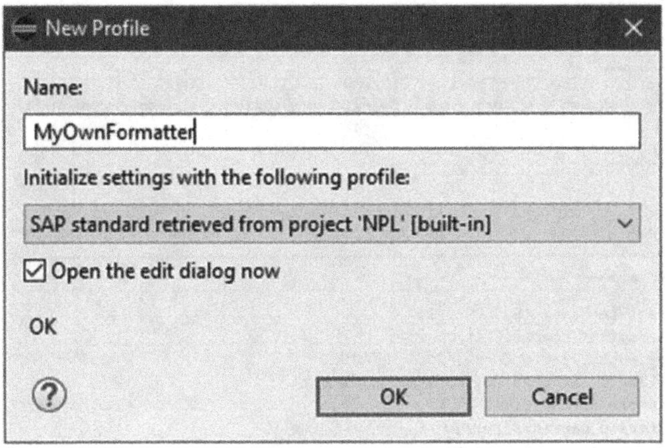

Figure 4-44. *New DDL Formatter profile*

The next screen that appears (Figure 4-45) contains a lot of tabs. On each of them, you can set different settings. You can indent most the elements, add breaks inside the blocks, and determine the alignment.

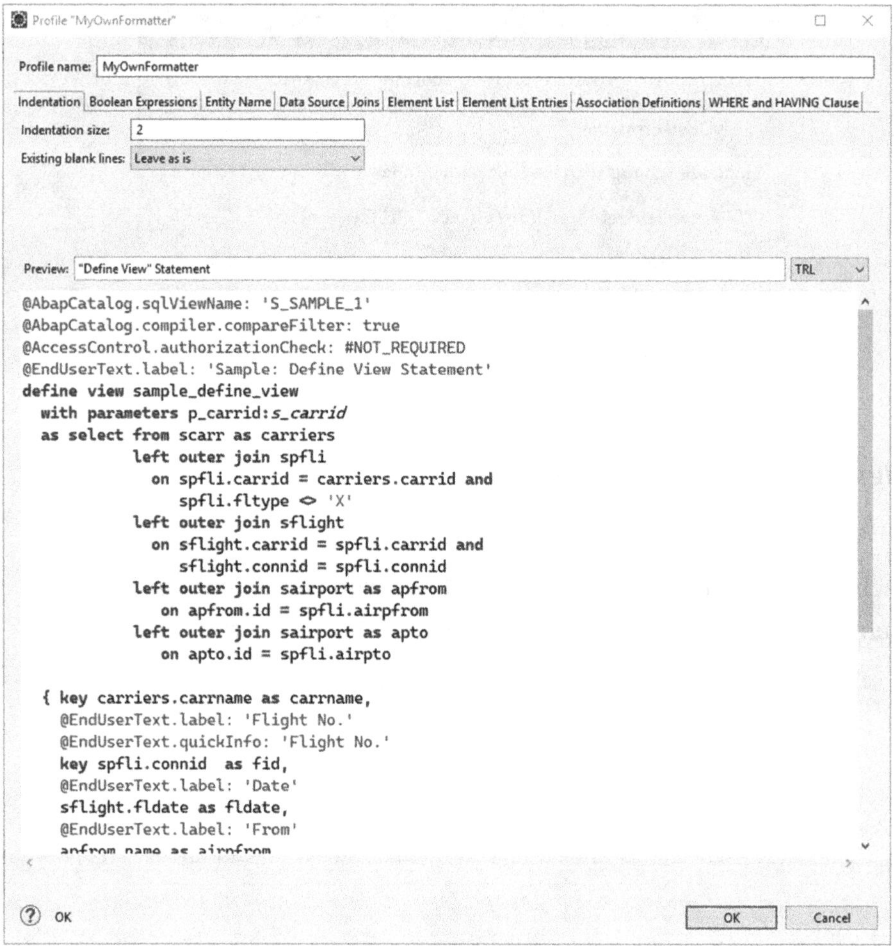

Figure 4-45. *DDL Formatter profile edit screen*

You will immediately see all the changes on the preview, so you do not need to imagine what effect your changes will have. Play with the formatter and adjust it to your screen resolution and personal preferences.

Profiling

While you create the trace requests, you may have your favorite settings predefined. In order to set them, use Profiling preferences (Figure 4-46). You can prepare your own defaults for each new trace request.

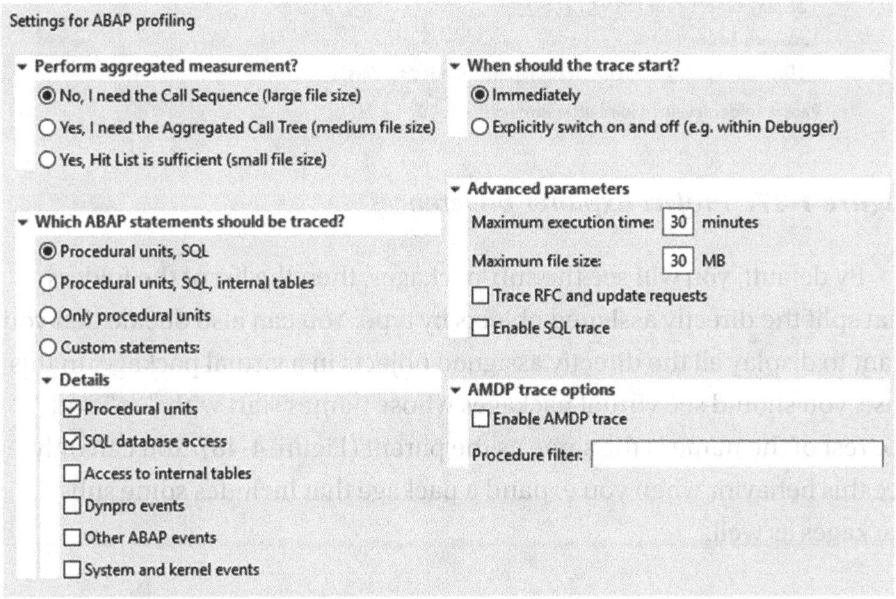

Settings for ABAP profiling

▾ Perform aggregated measurement?
- ◉ No, I need the Call Sequence (large file size)
- ○ Yes, I need the Aggregated Call Tree (medium file size)
- ○ Yes, Hit List is sufficient (small file size)

▾ Which ABAP statements should be traced?
- ◉ Procedural units, SQL
- ○ Procedural units, SQL, internal tables
- ○ Only procedural units
- ○ Custom statements:
  - ▾ Details
    - ☑ Procedural units
    - ☑ SQL database access
    - ☐ Access to internal tables
    - ☐ Dynpro events
    - ☐ Other ABAP events
    - ☐ System and kernel events

▾ When should the trace start?
- ◉ Immediately
- ○ Explicitly switch on and off (e.g. within Debugger)

▾ Advanced parameters
- Maximum execution time: `30` minutes
- Maximum file size: `30` MB
- ☐ Trace RFC and update requests
- ☐ Enable SQL trace

▾ AMDP trace options
- ☐ Enable AMDP trace
- Procedure filter:

Figure 4-46. *Default ABAP Profiling settings*

Project Explorer

When I described the label decorations, I mentioned that I have disabled project information by mistake one time. But there are also some other decorators and settings for ABAP projects.

When you look at Figure 4-47, you can see that you can choose whether you want to see short descriptions of the objects in Project Explorer, as well as use a decorator for inactive objects. You can adjust the color of the object descriptions as well.

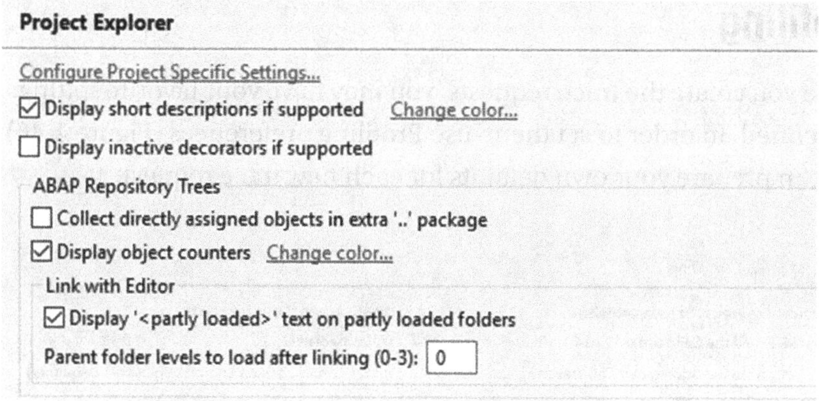

Figure 4-47. *Project Explorer preferences*

By default, you will see the sub-packages, then the list of the folders that split the directly assigned objects by type. You can also decide that you want to display all the directly assigned objects in a virtual package. In this case, you should see virtual packages whose names start with "**..**" and the rest of the name is the same as the parent (Figure 4-48). You can only see this behavior when you expand a package that includes some sub-packages as well.

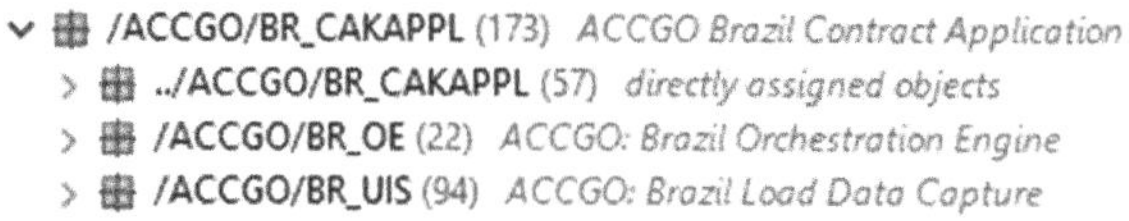

Figure 4-48. *Virtual package ../ACCGO/BR_CAKAPPL*

Additionally, you can decide if you want to see the object counters inside the packages and how liking with the editor will influence Project Explorer. Both of these settings make Project Explorer perform differently, so adjust them according to your system's needs.

SAP GUI Integration

Although we are inside Eclipse, we should not forget about SAP GUI, which in the case of on-premise systems, is still in use. So far there are only three settings for the integration of ADT with SAP GUI (Figure 4-49), but they can change the way you perceive this integration.

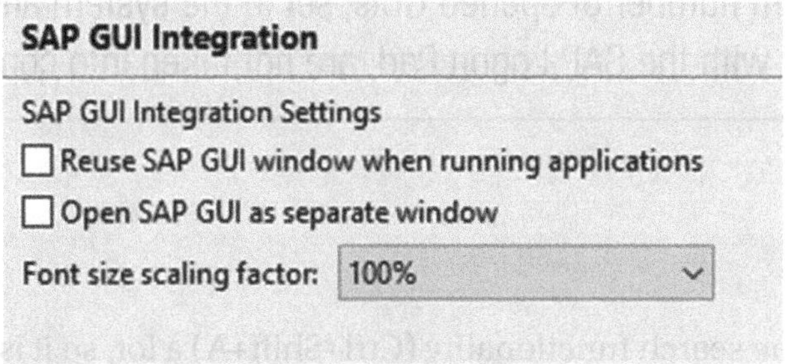

SAP GUI Integration

SAP GUI Integration Settings
☐ Reuse SAP GUI window when running applications
☐ Open SAP GUI as separate window

Font size scaling factor: 100% ⌄

Figure 4-49. *SAP GUI Integration preferences*

Normally, each time you run the program or class inside ADT, a new tab with the embedded GUI is opened. This can be messy when you run the same program many times for tests. That is why I was very happy when the Reuse SAP GUI Window When Running Application setting was introduced in ADT. It helps you keep the number of opened tabs in check and reduces the amount of manual closing you need to do.

The option to Open SAP GUI as a Separate Window is good for people who like to keep only the code in Eclipse and use SAP Logon Pad for testing. You won't see the embedded SAP GUI in the Eclipse tab, instead it will be always opened as a separate instance of SAP GUI.

The Font Size Scaling Factor option can be useful on smaller monitors and when you are using the embedded GUI inside Eclipse, where usually you have less space for SAP GUI, as you would run it from the logon pad. In such cases, you can lower the font scaling factor and all the controls on the

GUI will become smaller. This can of course work the other way around. If you have high resolution screens, you can increase the font scaling for better readability.

Tip   When you are using Eclipse to run the SAP GUI, it always creates a new logon to your backend. This means that limitations to the maximum number of opened GUIs, set in the system and visible during work with the SAP Logon Pad, are not taken into consideration.

Search

You will use the search functionality (Ctrl+Shift+A) a lot, so it is good to know that you can customize it as well. All the settings are visible in Figure 4-50. In some cases, they can really save you some time while searching through your objects.

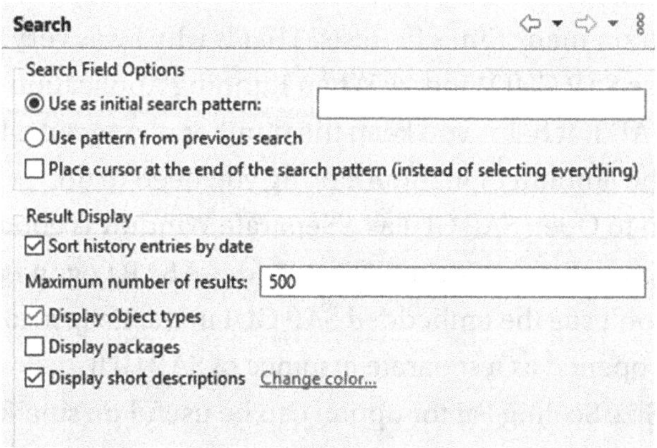

Figure 4-50. *Search preferences*

The first important option is to use a default pattern when launching the search. Most of us deal with Z or Y objects, so you can put that here as a default start of a search string. When you are working with custom namespaces, you can also put them here and forget about the nasty prefix.

You can also decide to always use a pattern from a previous search, which is especially useful when you are working on a project in which the naming convention for all objects is the same.

The last search field is the option to place the cursor at the end of search pattern (instead of selecting everything). By default, the initial pattern will be selected and you need to click the right arrow key in order to restrict the pattern more. However, you can change this so it will appear at the end of the pattern, allowing you to directly add more characters to the filter (Figure 4-51).

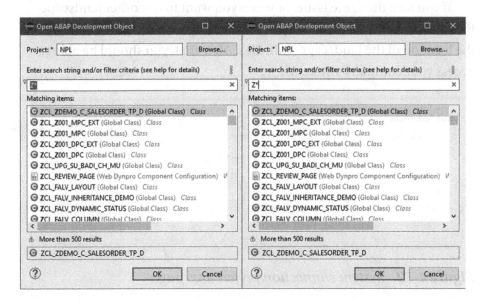

Figure 4-51. *Searching using Z* pattern with the default selection behavior (left) and the cursor placed at the end of pattern (right)*

When you run a search for the first time, you'll notice that the number of results is limited to 50. You can adapt this setting, taking into consideration that the more results are fetched, the more time it takes.

Additionally, information about the packages, object type, and a short description of the objects can be enabled on the object result list. You can also decide if recently used objects that fit the pattern should be visible on top of the list (using the Sort History Entries By Date option).

System Connections

Usually you do not have to worry about the system connections list that's used while creating new ABAP projects. But I had a situation in which somehow they were not detected automatically, which made it impossible to create projects.

If you face the same issue, or when you want to test other landscape files, go to system connections preferences (Figure 4-52) and manually set the location of the landscape XML files. After that, you should be able to access your company's systems.

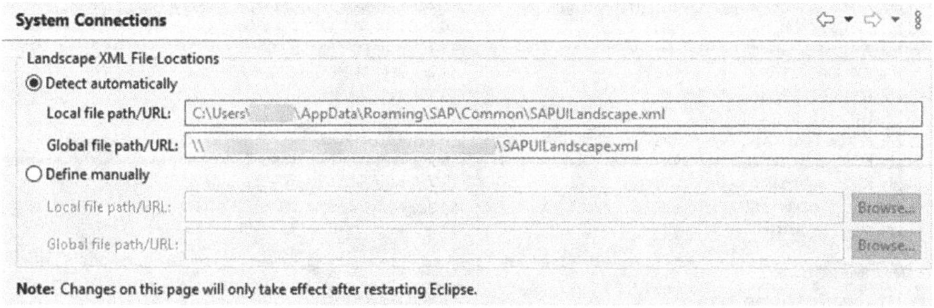

Figure 4-52. *System connection preferences page*

Install/Update

The last group of preferences that I want to describe is Install/Update. These settings allow you to choose the way installation will be handled by Eclipse (Figure 4-53).

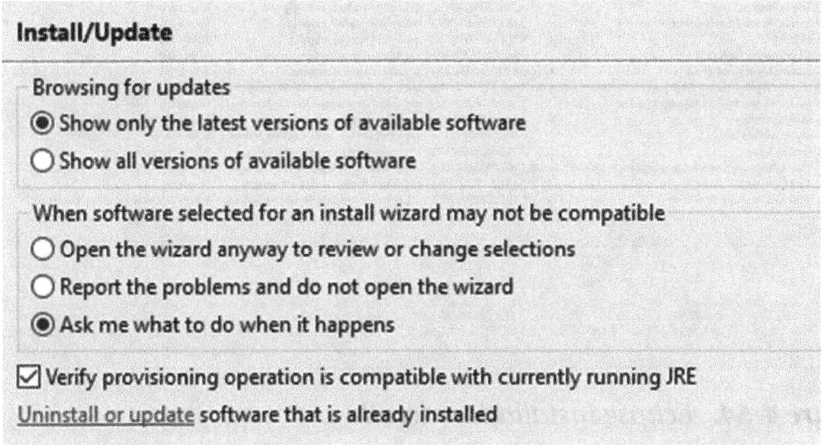

Figure 4-53. Basic installation and update preferences

Two groups of radio buttons are responsible for selecting update browsing and the behavior of the installer. You can determine whether the provisioning operation should verify the compatibility with the current Java runtime environment.

The hyperlink called Uninstall or Update Software That Is Already Installed will take you to the Eclipse IDE installation details (Figure 4-54). This is an important place that you should commit to memory. It will come in handy when your installation is growing and is visibly slower, as you can find the plugins you are not using and get rid of them. Additionally, in the Installation History tab, you can view the installations and update history, which you can use to revert to the state of Eclipse at a specific point of time.

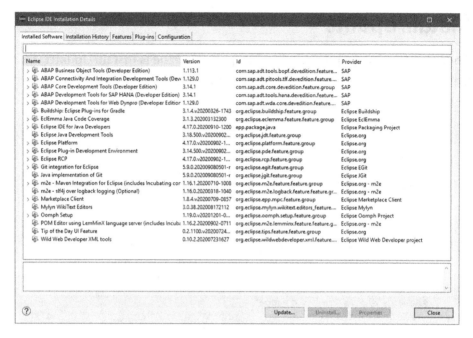

Figure 4-54. Eclipse installation details

Automatic Updates

Current deployment of updates for Eclipse, ADT, and other plugins is very frequent. New major Eclipse versions are released every three months. ADT not only follows the frequency of updates of Eclipse, but according to my observations, deployment of major and minor releases happens at least once every three weeks. This is why you should have the automatic updates activated.

The automatic updates settings (Figure 4-55) are very easy to understand. You can set when to check for updates. Personally I have this option set to check for new updates each time Eclipse IDE is started, but weekly or daily updates are also quite okay.

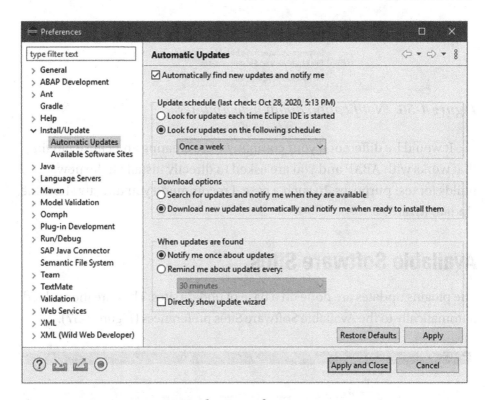

Figure 4-55. *Automatic Updates preferences page*

You can also determine whether the updates should be downloaded directly or on demand. I have no personal preference, but consider the average bandwidth of your network connection.

The last possible option to choose is what to do when new updates are available. I think the standard option (to notify developers about updates) is the best for the ABAP environment. A notification about new updates (Figure 4-56) is displayed in bottom-left corner of Eclipse, in the same place where ABAP dump information appears.

Figure 4-56. *Notification about new updates*

It would be different if your company were creating an Eclipse plugin that works with ABAP and you are asked to directly install all the new builds for test purposes. In such a case, I recommend you directly show the Update wizard.

Available Software Sites

The plugins updates are done on a base of update sites. They are then added automatically to the Available Software Sites preferences (Figure 4-57).

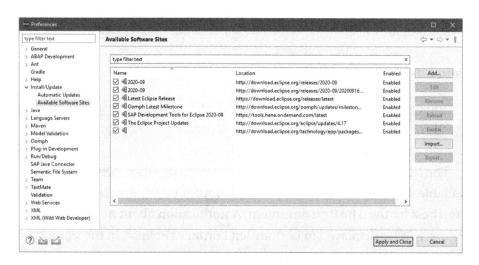

Figure 4-57. *Available Software Sites preferences page*

There are a few scenarios whereby you will want to disable, add, or remove update sites. Let's go through them.

The first scenario is very simple. Something is happening to the plugin update site; for example, it changed its location or the plugin has been discontinued. In such a case, you would get an error message with the information that site is unavailable. You can remove it or update to get rid of this message.

The second scenario is connected to company rules. Sometimes, you do not have access to the Internet from Eclipse. You are given the preinstalled IDE with no option to use the Eclipse Marketplace to install new plugins. In such a case, if the developer of the plugin provides a ZIP file with the updates, you can click the Add button to create a new update site from the local archive.

The third scenario is very similar to the second one. Because of company rules or bandwidth issues, your company decides that the updates should be fetched to a local network share and then spread to all machines using an internal network. You would probably get then a link to them from your admin or those links would be inserted automatically during installation.

The fourth scenario is plugin development. When you are creating your own plugins for Eclipse, and you want to test the installation on a few Eclipse versions, you can create the entry for a local update site (a place on the hard drive) (Figure 4-58). I must admit that since I create my own plugins, I use this option for tests very frequently.

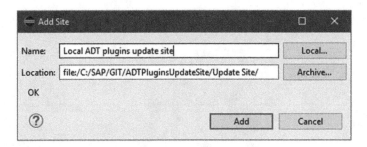

Figure 4-58. *Local update site configuration*

Summary

This chapter focused on the Eclipse preferences that you can access by choosing Window ➤ Preferences and that are helpful for ABAP development. Yes, there are still a lot of preferences yet to discover. In most cases, those settings will be linked to development in Java, which is why there is no reason to mention them here.

The next chapter focuses on Eclipse plugins that come in handy during ABAP development. Some of them are really strict ABAP plugins, and some are global ones that serve any language or whose functionality is not directly linked to development.

CHAPTER 5

Eclipse Extensions That Will Make the Difference

The previous chapters described everything that's available in Eclipse and ADT by default. ADT is a plugin for Eclipse itself, without which the ABAP development in Eclipse would not be possible.

Now it is time to look at other plugins that can help you in your daily work. I present a few plugins in this chapter that will help you enjoy developing in ADT even more. Some of these plugins work independently of the programming language you use; others are useful only in ABAP.

The Eclipse Marketplace

Let's begin the journey through the Eclipse plugins from the Eclipse Marketplace (Figure 5-1), which you can find by choosing Help ➤ Eclipse Marketplace. You can search for, install, update, or uninstall plugins that are listed on the official plugin list. Of course, as with ADT, there are many more plugins that are not available on the marketplace. When they are listed there, they are easier to find and their compatibility with new releases of Eclipse is automatically checked.

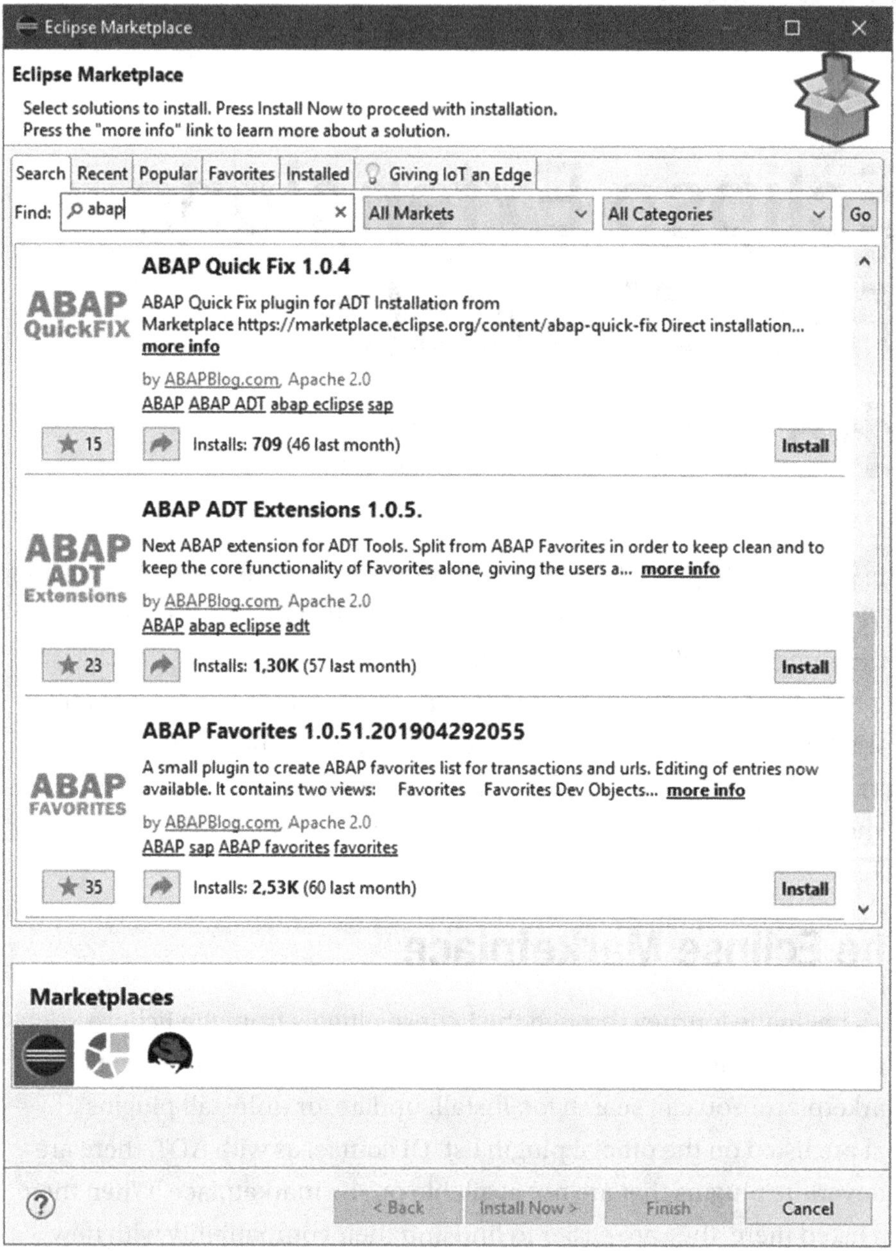

Figure 5-1. Eclipse Marketplace: ABAP plugins search

Besides the names and short descriptions of the plugins, you can also see the following attributes in the Eclipse Marketplace:

- How many people have the plugin in their favorites

- How many total installations were completed through the Marketplace

- Home many installations happened last month through the Marketplace

- The publisher of the plugin

- License under which the plugin is published

The Eclipse Marketplace allows you to set up your own favorite plugins, which you can do from the Favorites tab. In order to do this, you need to create a marketplace account. Once you create an account, at each new installation of Eclipse, you can easily go to the Favorites tab and install all the previously bookmarked plugins, without needing to search for them again.

If you search for the ABAP word, you will find at the moment eight plugins:

- ABAP Continues Integration

- ABAP Code Insight

- ABAP Search and Analysis Tools

- ABAP Tags

- Task Scanner for ABAP in Eclipse

- ABAP Favorites

- ABAP Quick Fixes

- ABAP Extensions

This chapter discusses each of these plugins, and I will start by describing the one that can be used in Eclipse with all programming languages.

AnyEdit Tools

One of the first plugins that I installed in Eclipse was AnyEdit Tools. I think it is with me from the beginning of the journey with Eclipse. As you can see in Figure 5-2, it is very popular. Almost 150,000 installations is impressive, especially for a small, yet powerful, tool.

AnyEdit Tools 2.7.2.202006062100

AnyEdit plugin adds several new tools to the context menu of text- based Eclipse editors, to output consoles, to Eclipse main menu and editor toolbar. AnyEdit... **more info**

by Andrey Loskutov, EPL
convert white space tabs compare clipboard

★ 870   Installs: **149K** (973 last month)   Install

Figure 5-2. *AnyEdit Tools on the Eclipse Marketplace*

Let's go through the options of this small plugin, starting from string conversion and continuing with sorting, code comparison, and saving the console output.

String Conversion

One of the best functionalities of this plugin is string conversion. You can run it using shortcuts, or after selecting a string in the editor, you can use Convert from the editor context menu (Figure 5-3) to select the action you want to do.

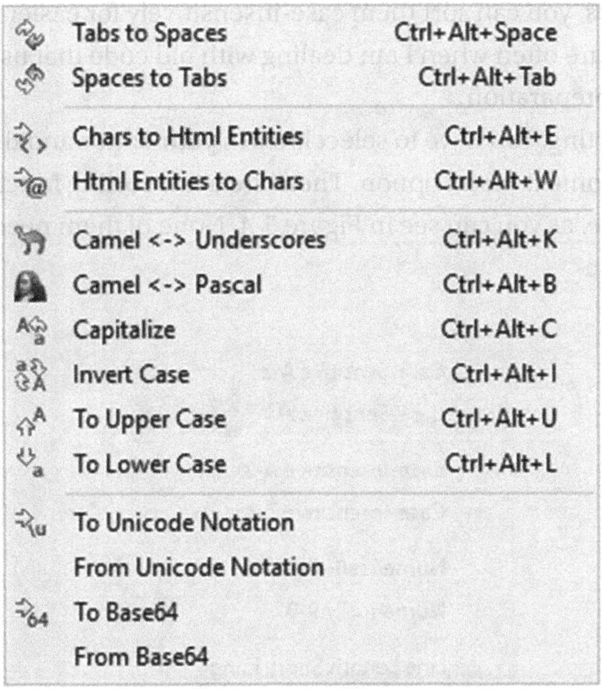

🖋	Tabs to Spaces	Ctrl+Alt+Space
🖋	Spaces to Tabs	Ctrl+Alt+Tab
🖋	Chars to Html Entities	Ctrl+Alt+E
🖋	Html Entities to Chars	Ctrl+Alt+W
🐫	Camel <-> Underscores	Ctrl+Alt+K
🖋	Camel <-> Pascal	Ctrl+Alt+B
A🖋	Capitalize	Ctrl+Alt+C
🖋	Invert Case	Ctrl+Alt+I
🖋	To Upper Case	Ctrl+Alt+U
🖋	To Lower Case	Ctrl+Alt+L
🖋	To Unicode Notation	
	From Unicode Notation	
🖋	To Base64	
	From Base64	

Figure 5-3. *Convert context menu content*

I use To Upper Case, To Lower Case, and Chars to Html Entities the most, but the all the others can be useful as well.

When you are using the newest NetWeaver version, you can use the Capitalize function or you can choose to keep CamelCase formatting on such backends.

Sorting

The next function that comes with the AnyEdit Tools is sorting selected text. You may wonder what you need such a function for, but when you are preparing mockups, it can be very handy. Additionally, when you deal with old code and the assignment of the structure values is spread through dozens of lines, you can sort them case-insensitively for easier readability. I use this feature often when I am dealing with old code that uses the ALV field catalog preparation.

To call sorting, you have to select lines in your editor and then use the Sort context menu option. There are a few sorting functions available there, as you can see in Figure 5-4. None of them needs a deeper explanation.

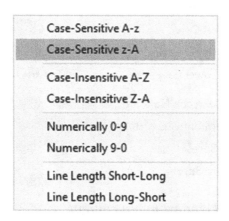

Figure 5-4. *Sort menu context*

Comparison

Normally you use the Compare With editor context menu to compare current code with the code available on another SAP system, revision, or local history. But AnyEdit Tools introduces another four possibilities: Clipboard, Workspace File, External File, and Opened Editor. In ABAP development, I use the comparison with other opened editor (Figure 5-5).

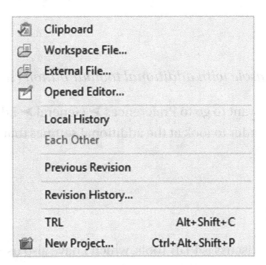

Figure 5-5. *New Compare With menu entries*

There are two scenarios in which I use this option. First, when I am dealing with one of the dozens of versions of print programs, which are in fact copies of standard SAP print programs with some adaptations. If I want to combine some of them, I use this comparison to see the places in which they differ.

The second scenario is when I am asked to do some performance improvements in legacy program. I create a copy of the existing program with the new name, then start the adaptations. When I do a lot of refactoring, I sometimes need to check what I have changed in order to be sure that I have done things correctly. Comparing two programs opened in two different tabs is very useful at that moment.

Save Console Output

The next nice function that comes with this plugin is a new button in the Console view—the Save to File button (Figure 5-6). It allows you to quickly store the output of the console in a .log or .txt file. It is most useful for ABAP cloud developers, as they use the console output a lot.

Figure 5-6. *Console with additional toolbar button (save)*

You may also want to go to Preferences ➤ General ➤ Editors ➤ AnyEdit Tools in order to look at the additional settings that come with this plugin.

PDE Tools

The next plugin I discuss is PDE Tools, which I have also used for a long time. It is not as popular, but that doesn't mean it is not good. This plugin contains several views and functionalities, as listed in Figure 5-7, but I mainly use one of them: Clipboard History.

Figure 5-7. *PDE Tools on the Eclipse Marketplace*

Clipboard History

Having a clipboard that keeps a long history can be a huge timesaver. When you do not have such a tool installed on your OS, you can use the one from PDE Tools. It only works inside Eclipse, but isn't that where you spend most of your time?

To call the extended clipboard, you have to use Ctrl+Shift+V. When you do so, the list of previous clipboard entries will appear (Figure 5-8). By default, the first five lines of copied text are shown in the preview. To look at the full content of the clipboard, you need to select an entry using the arrow key and look at the right popup, which will show you not only the full contents of the clipboard, but also indicate where it was captured.

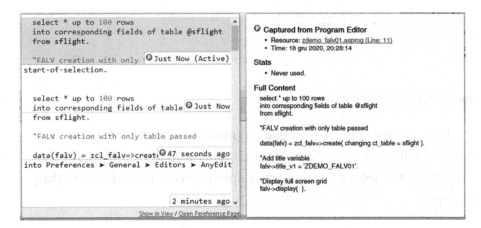

Figure 5-8. *Preview of the Ctrl+Shift+V Clipboard*

You can use a link found in the source of the capture to navigate to the code if it was copied from the Eclipse editor. The nice thing here is that the code is copied with its formatting, so it is easy to read.

Besides the key shortcut, which you can use to call the clipboard history, you can also open a view called Clipboard (Figure 5-9). It contains the same data.

Figure 5-9. Clipboard view

If you want to change the default number of clipboards kept, or the number of lines in the preview of the clipboard, go to Preferences ➤ PDE-Tools ➤ Clipboard in order to adapt the preferences of this plugin function.

Darkest Dark (DevStyle)

When some people hear about Darkest Dark, they think only about the dark Eclipse theme that was created by the Genuitec company and given free of charge to the Eclipse community. But besides the theme itself, there are two additional functionalities that you will hopefully like as much: Icon Designer and CodeTogether.

Darkest Dark is very popular, as you can see in Figure 5-10. One and a half million installs is something extraordinary, and in my opinion it is very worth it.

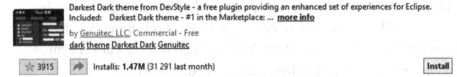

Darkest Dark Theme with DevStyle 2020.12.11

Darkest Dark theme from DevStyle - a free plugin providing an enhanced set of experiences for Eclipse. Included: Darkest Dark theme - #1 in the Marketplace: ... **more info**

by Genuitec, LLC. Commercial - Free

dark theme Darkest Dark Genuitec

⭐ 3915   ➤   Installs: **1.47M** (31 291 last month)   Install

Figure 5-10. *Darkest Dark on the Eclipse Marketplace*

When you click the Install button, you have to choose if you want to install only the core of the plugin, which is the Darkest Dark theme, or Icon Designer and CodeTogether. I recommend you install all of the features and check out the functionality they give.

After installing and restarting the environment, you should see the DevStyle welcome screen (new name of the bundle of features), which will guide you through the plugin's basic information (Figure 5-11).

Figure 5-11. *DevStyle welcome screen*

In the next step, you can choose which theme you want to use in Eclipse. There will be three possibilities on the screen (Figure 5-12), but when you will click the Advanced link, you can access more possibilities. Personally, I use the Darkest Dark Theme, but if you are a fan of light themes, select Fresh Light Theme to see the difference.

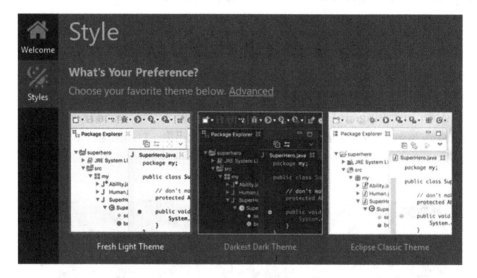

Figure 5-12. Style selection screen of DevStyle

The last step is to fine-tune the workbench, where you will be able to choose the editor theme (Figure 5-13). The editor theme determines the way the syntax is colored. You can also choose from a few embedded settings, such as Notepad++, VS2010, IntelliJ, and a few more. I always use Eclipse Standard.

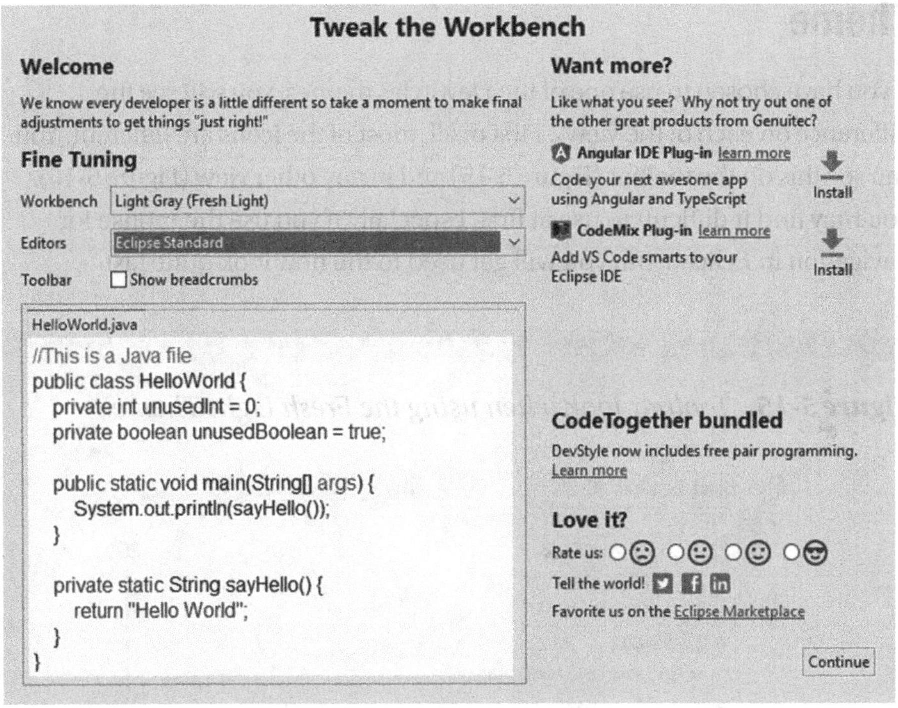

Tweak the Workbench

Welcome

We know every developer is a little different so take a moment to make final adjustments to get things "just right!"

Fine Tuning

Workbench	Light Gray (Fresh Light)
Editors	Eclipse Standard
Toolbar	☐ Show breadcrumbs

```
HelloWorld.java

//This is a Java file
public class HelloWorld {
    private int unusedInt = 0;
    private boolean unusedBoolean = true;

    public static void main(String[] args) {
        System.out.println(sayHello());
    }

    private static String sayHello() {
        return "Hello World";
    }
}
```

Want more?

Like what you see? Why not try out one of the other great products from Genuitec?

🅰 **Angular IDE Plug-in** learn more
Code your next awesome app using Angular and TypeScript   Install

▓ **CodeMix Plug-in** learn more
Add VS Code smarts to your Eclipse IDE   Install

CodeTogether bundled

DevStyle now includes free pair programming. Learn more

Love it?

Rate us: ○😦 ○😐 ○🙂 ○😄

Tell the world! 🐦 📘 in

Favorite us on the Eclipse Marketplace

Continue

Figure 5-13. Tweaking the workbench

After you set up all the settings, you will finally be able to use the nice-looking Eclipse. What you can also see during startup is that, instead of the standard progress bar, you will see the one from DevStyle (Figure 5-14). I really like it because of the IT jokes that appear randomly on that bar.

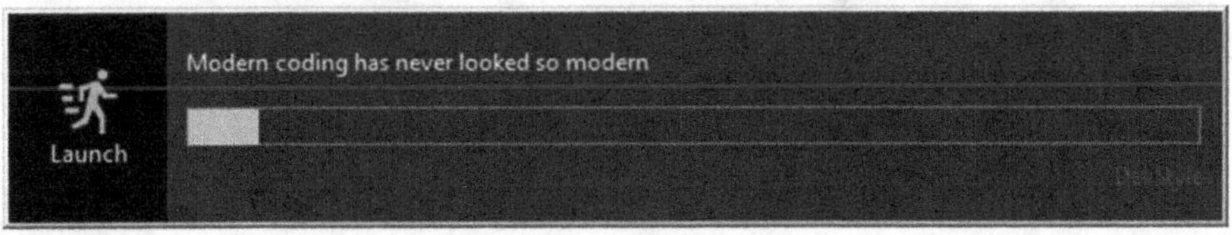

Modern coding has never looked so modern

Launch

Figure 5-14. DevStyle startup progress bar

Theme

If you have chosen to use one of the DevStyles themes, you will see the difference on each of the views. First of all, most of the icons are different. You can see this on the toolbar (Figure 5-15) and in any other view (Figure 5-16). You may find it difficult to use at first, especially if you use the mouse for navigation in Eclipse, but you will get used to the new look quite fast.

Figure 5-15. *Toolbar look when using the Fresh Light Theme*

Figure 5-16. *Project Explorer look when using the Fresh Light Theme*

I found these new icons more readable and clearer, but of course this is only my personal opinion. What is more important for me is that whenever I want to switch between the dark and the light themes, I do not need to set the colors of the ABAP Editor again to fit the new theme settings. DevStyle makes the changes automatically, so it saves lots of time.

Just to explain myself, since I claim to be an ambassador of using dark themes, I have to switch from time to time to a light theme. In most cases, it is due to presentations done on projectors in the conferences rooms with bad lightning. In such cases, the light theme is a better option.

Icon Designer

You can adjust and create the new icons that come with the DevStyle yourself. In the past, I made a lot of adaptations to the ADT icons, but you can always adapt the icons so that they fit your preferences.

To do so, you need to call the Icon Designer view. Each time you run it, it will check your Eclipse installation and gather all the used icons. They will be listed in a table (Figure 5-17), where besides the name, origin, and preview, you will see if the icon has been replaced by the DevStyle icon (column Replacement) and if the icon is official DevStyle (status live). If you create your own icons, the status will change to custom.

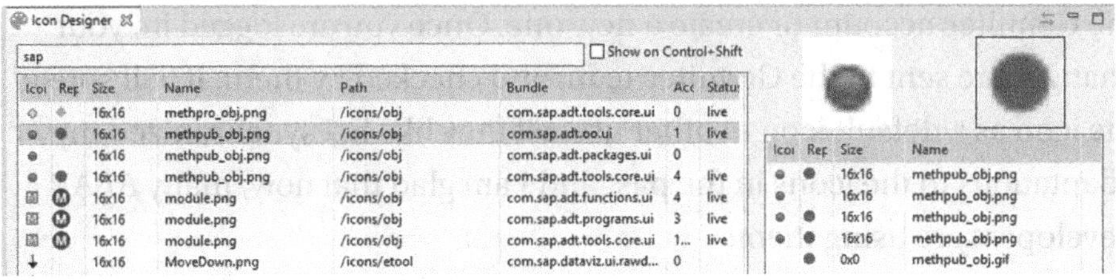

Figure 5-17. *Icon Designer view*

To create or edit an icon, simply double-click to open the Icon Editor (Figure 5-18). You will not be able to manually draw an icon, but you can select one from the list of icons and characters. You can also use two icons at the same time, by setting the icon layout to overlay. For each icon, you can also choose a primary color, scale, and fill color.

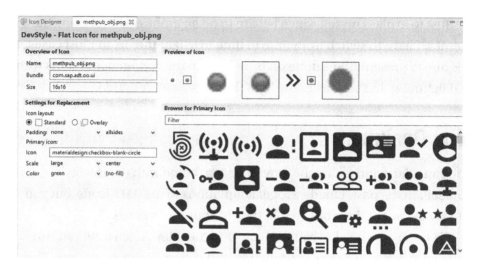

Figure 5-18. *DevStyle Icon Editor*

If you are happy with your changes, you can share the icon with the Genuitec team by using the Sync option in the Icon Designer view. When you click the Sync button, you need to pass your credentials to the Genuitec account or create a new one. Once you are logged in, your changes are sent to the Genuitec team and checked by them. If will spread the icon as a default icon to other users if they like it. I synchronized my adaptations to the icons in the past and I am glad that now, many ABAP developers are using them.

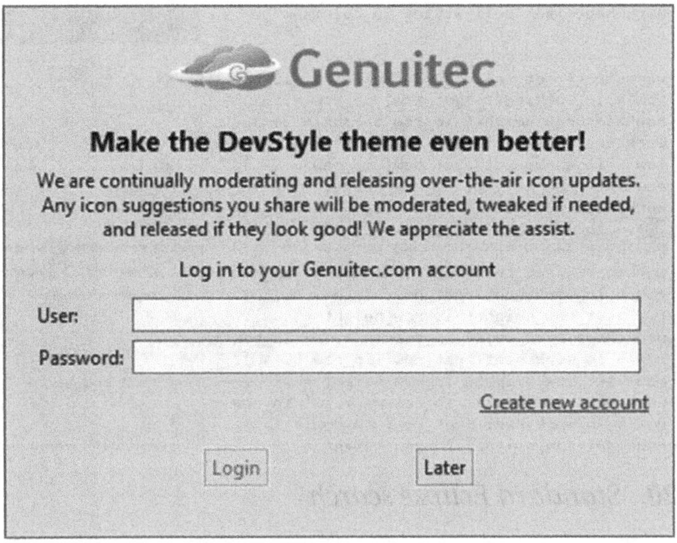

Figure 5-19. *Genuitec logon screen for icon synchronization*

Inline Search

Inline Search is a small yet useful function that replaces the standard find/replace dialog of Eclipse (Figure 5-20). It is activated by default on installation of Darkest Dark. If you have worked with other IDEs, such as Visual Studio, you will be really happy with it.

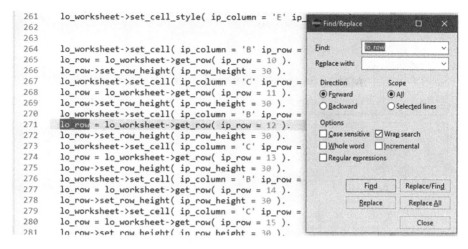

Figure 5-20. *Standard Eclipse search*

Besides the minimal view of the inline search (Figure 5-21), it also adds the hits counter, highlights all of the results in the editor, and adds markers to the vertical and overview rulers.

```
  ▶ ℗ ZDEMO_EXCEL2 ▶
  260        nttps://coae.san.sap
  261        lo_worksheet->set_cell         lo_row                    Aa A̅b̅ .* 0 of 29 ∨ ∧ ⊠  tic
  262                                        Replace with                      ⤒ ⤓      ⓘ   sty
  263
  264        lo_worksheet->set_cell( ip_column = 'B' ip_row = 10  ip_style =
→ 265        lo_row = lo_worksheet->get_row( ip_row = 10 ).
→ 266        lo_row->set_row_height( ip_row_height = 30 ).
  267        lo_worksheet->set_cell( ip_column = 'C' ip_row = 11  ip_style =
→ 268        lo_row = lo_worksheet->get_row( ip_row = 11 ).
→ 269        lo_row->set_row_height( ip_row_height = 30 ).
  270        lo_worksheet->set_cell( ip_column = 'B' ip_row = 12  ip_style =
→ 271        lo_row = lo_worksheet->get_row( ip_row = 12 ).
```

Figure 5-21. *Inline search*

CodeTogether

In the initial versions of Darkest Dark, CodeTogether was not available. When it was published I gave it a try, as I like to discover new software. I was pleasantly surprised with the ease of code sharing with other people around the globe.

Unfortunately, in the first releases, I was not able to share the ABAP code, but for Java files it worked perfectly. I kept it in my Eclipse installation, hoping that someday I would be able to share my ABAP code. And now it is possible, allowing developers to do pair programming or solving issues with other developers without sitting next to each other.

To start or join a session, you need to open CodeTogether view (Figure 5-22) and use the links.

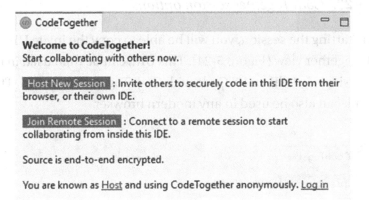

Figure 5-22. *CodeTogether view*

When you choose to start a session, you will be asked to set up the parameters of that session (Figure 5-23). You can choose how you want to allow participants to join, who can lead the navigation through the code, and who can edit.

271

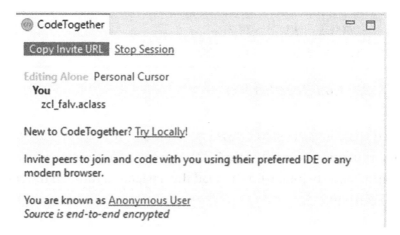

Figure 5-23. *CodeTogether session options*

After starting the session, you will be able to copy the invite URL from the CodeTogether view (Figure 5-24). This URL can be then used in other Eclipse versions, IntelliJ, or VS Code with CodeTogether installed. The session link can also be used in any modern browser.

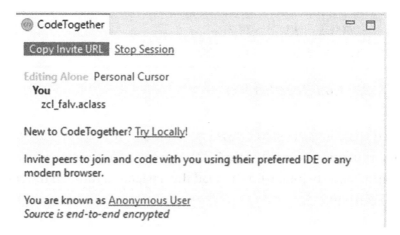

Figure 5-24. *CodeTogether view with an active session*

If the people you invited to the session want to join from Eclipse, they need to paste the invite URL and their name into the Join Session window, which is called by clicking the Join Remote Session button of the CodeTogether view.

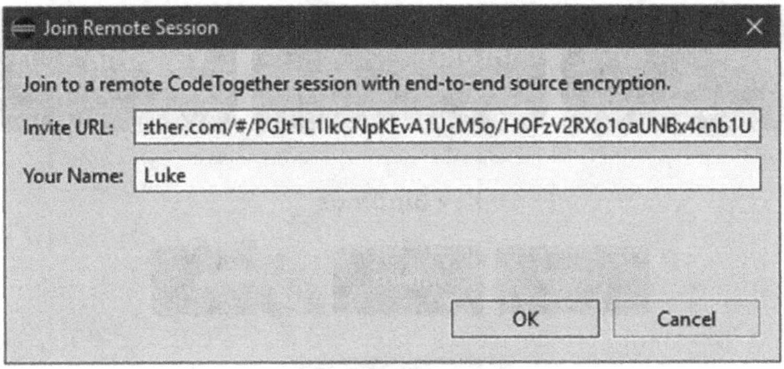

Figure 5-25. Joining a remote session from Eclipse

Once this is done, you as a host will receive an authorization request with the name of participant (Figure 5-26).

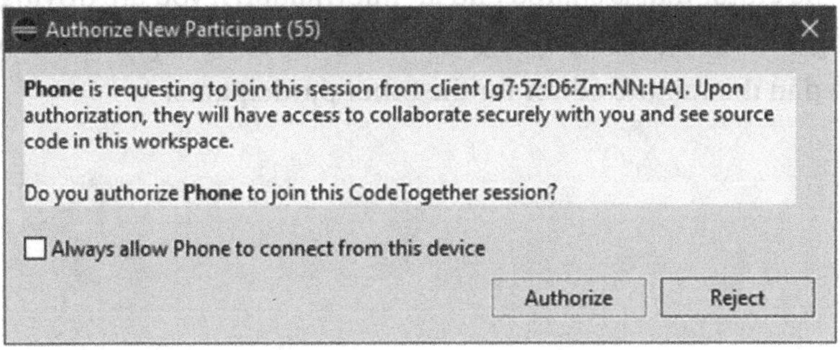

Figure 5-26. Authorization of session participant

If your peers want to join using a web browser, they will be asked not only for their name, but also for the IDE theme and key bindings that they want to use in the remote editor (Figure 5-27).

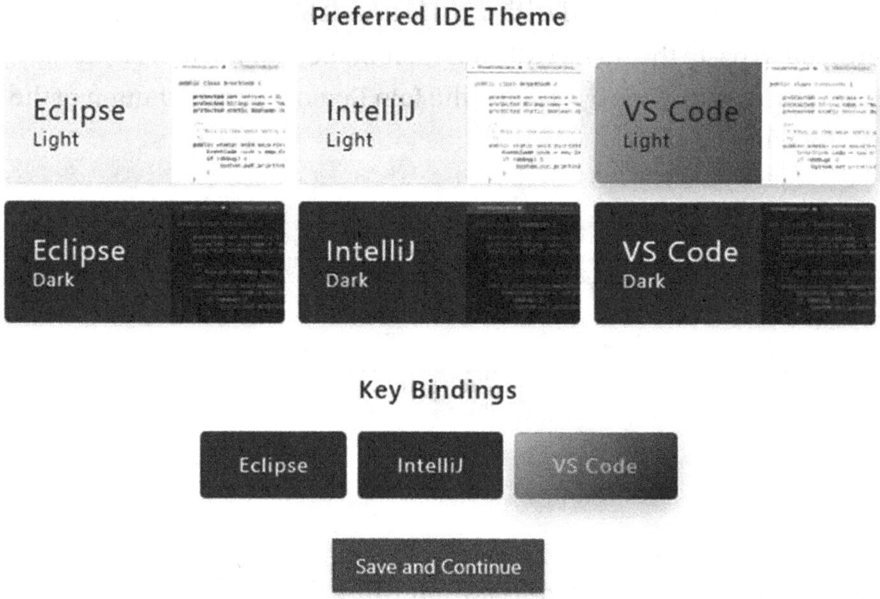

Figure 5-27. Joining session from web browser

After starting the session in Eclipse, you will notice a green frame around the editor that is shared and an information if you are driving or following others (Figure 5-28). If you are driving, each step you take will be replicated in the remote editor for the other participants.

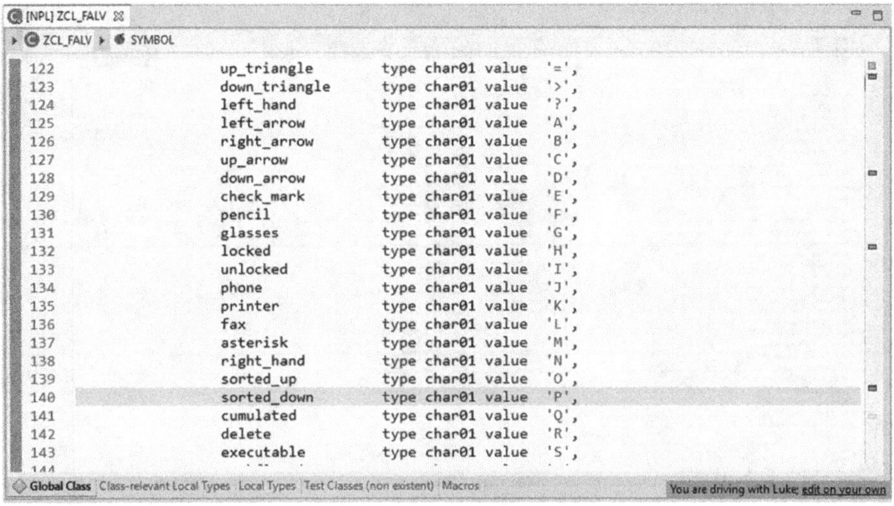

Figure 5-28. *Eclipse: host view of a CodeTogether session*

The participant view is a bit different than the host view. This is because ABAP syntax highlighting is not yet available in CodeTogether. For problem solving, this should not be an issue, but I am waiting for the day when ABAP syntax highlighting is available. As you can see in Figure 5-29, besides the shared code, the participant will have access to the Project Explorer of the host. With ABAP projects, which are virtual folders, only previously opened objects will be available, but it is still something.

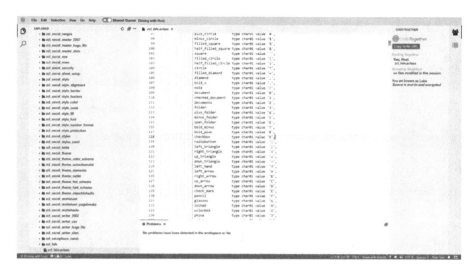

Figure 5-29. *Web browser view of the session participant*

As I wrote before, all changes are synchronized between the host and participants, as well as the Problems view, selection of code, and cursor position (Figure 5-30). It is easy to see who is changing the code and where, as the full name or initials of the person who is editing the code is displayed next to the cursor position.

```
20    METHOD constructor2.
21      value_to_watch = 8-uzeit.
22    ENDMETHOD.
23
24    METHOD if_oo_adt_classrun~main.
25      out->write( 'Run successfull' ).
26    ENDMETHOD.
27
28
29
30    ENDCLASS.
31
```

● Problems ×   ↗ Output

▸ ▓ zcl_aie_first_class.aclass ①

   ● [eclipse] Method "CONSTRUCTOR2" does not exist. There is, however, a method with the similar name "CONSTRUCTOR". (20, 10)

Figure 5-30. *Problems highlighting in the remote editor*

Code completion is not synchronized on-screen, but you can still use it on the remote editor and get the code completion results that are calculated in the session host IDE.

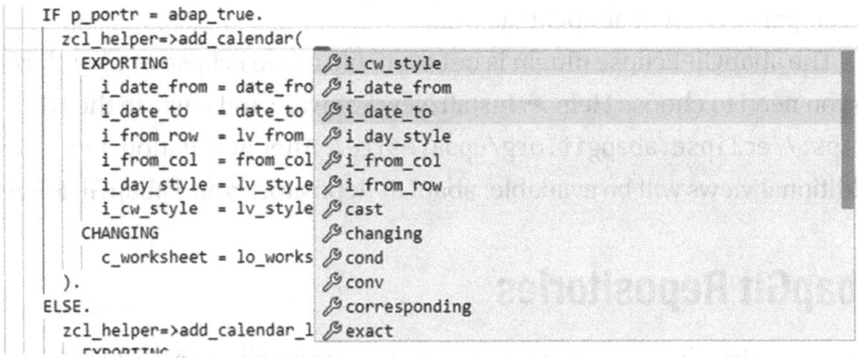

```
IF p_portr = abap_true.
    zcl_helper=>add_calendar(
        EXPORTING              🔑 i_cw_style
            i_date_from = date_fro  🔑 i_date_from
            i_date_to   = date_to   🔑 i_date_to
            i_from_row  = lv_from_   🔑 i_day_style
            i_from_col  = from_col   🔑 i_from_col
            i_day_style = lv_style   🔑 i_from_row
            i_cw_style  = lv_style   🔑 cast
        CHANGING               🔑 changing
            c_worksheet = lo_works   🔑 cond
    ).                         🔑 conv
ELSE.                          🔑 corresponding
    zcl_helper=>add_calendar_l 🔑 exact
      ┌──────────────
```

Figure 5-31. *Code completion in a web browser*

You can achieve the same using any online meeting software. But this works very fast, much faster than screen sharing, as you are exchanging code, not images. This could be extremely useful when working remotely and when the network connection is not fast.

abapGit

If you have been following the ABAP news for some years, then abapGit is not something new. But in case it is a new term to you, abapGit is a tool built by SAP Mentor Lars Hvam Petersen[1] and the SAP Community, which helps share the code using Git repositories. It is widely used for open source ABAP projects and makes collaboration very easy.

---

[1]You can find more information about Lars Hvam Petersen at https://people. sap.com/lars.hvam

I could write a separate book about abapGit, but as I am focusing on Eclipse plugins, let me introduce you to only that part of the abapGit project. Now, if you are using the ABAP in cloud, you need to install the plugin only. If you are using on-premise systems, you need to install the developer version of abapGit[2] as well.

The abapGit Eclipse plugin is not available in the Eclipse Marketplace, so you need to choose Help ➤ Install New Software and paste in the URL https://eclipse.abapgit.org/updatesite/. After installation, two additional views will be available: abapGit Repositories and abapGit Staging.

abapGit Repositories

If you are already using abapGit in your backend using the ZABAPGIT transaction, all your repositories will be listed in this view (Figure 5-32), but you will not have all the functionality of the GUI transaction yet.

Package	URL	Branch	User	Last Changed (UTC)	Status
$FALV	https://github.com/fidley/falv.git	refs/heads/master	DEVELOPER	2020-09-21 17:39:45	
ZJSON2ABAPTYPE	https://github.com/fidley/JSON2ABAPType	refs/heads/newBranch	DEVELOPER	2020-10-20 21:03:47	
$ABAP2XLSX	https://github.com/sapmentors/abap2xlsx.git	refs/heads/master	DEVELOPER	2020-10-24 16:21:09	
$AOC	https://github.com/larshp/abapOpenChecks.git	refs/heads/master	DEVELOPER	2020-10-24 17:12:59	
ZABAPGITADT	https://github.com/abapGit/ADT_Backend.git	refs/heads/master	DEVELOPER	2020-12-14 21:15:51	
$ABAPGIT	https://github.com/abapGit/abapGit.git	refs/heads/master	DEVELOPER	2020-12-14 21:14:58	
$ABAPTAGS	https://github.com/stockbal/abap-tags-backend.git	refs/heads/master	DEVELOPER	2020-12-15 21:42:07	
$ABAP_SEARCH	https://github.com/stockbal/abap-search-tools.git	refs/heads/nw-752	DEVELOPER	2020-12-18 14:07:30	

Figure 5-32. *List of abapGit repositories*

I hope that with the next updates, we will get more functionality, but so far we can do following actions:

- Add new repositories using the ✚ button

- Pull, to update the local version with remote

---

[2]The installation steps for the developer version of abapGit can be found at https://docs.abapgit.org/guide-install.html

- Stage and Push, to commit your local changes to a remote repository

- Open Package, which opens a package linked with the repository

- Open the repository in a web browser

- Unlink, which will keep the objects in the system, but the link to repository will be deleted

These sets of functions are suitable for the basic actions with the Git repositories. Especially when you are only installing the repositories of others, you will not have to switch to a GUI transaction anymore. With ABAP in the cloud, you will not have GUI, so this plugin is the only way to bring ABAP repositories to your system.

Let's now go through the process of linking a new abapGit repository to your system. First of all, you need to select the repository you want to bring into your system and copy its clone URL. If you do not have a project in mind, but you would like to try the plugin, simply go to https://dotabap. org (Figure 5-33). This is a list of ABAP open source projects with short descriptions and clone URLs.

Figure 5-33. *dotabap.org is a list of ABAP open source projects*

When you have the clone URL, you need to click the Link New abapGit Repository button from the view. On the first screen, you need to paste in the clone URL, just like I did in Figure 5-34.

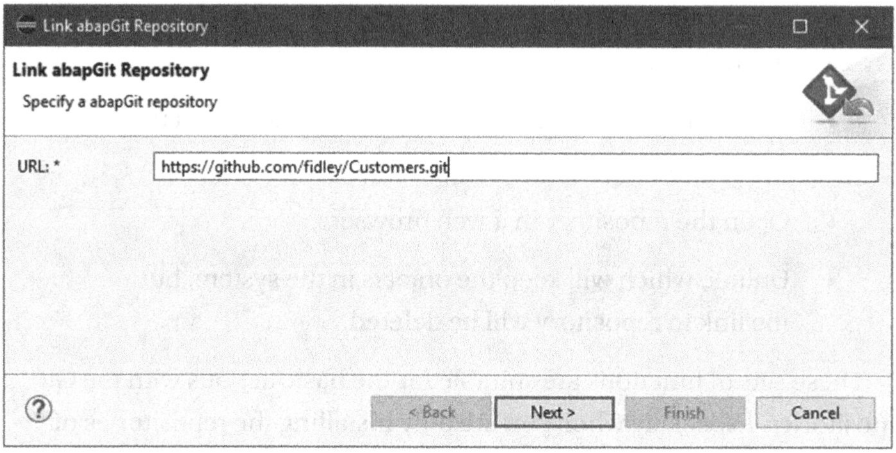

Figure 5-34. Linking a new abapGit repository: clone URL

The second step is to select the branch and package (Figure 5-35). The changes of the linked branch are not possible in the Eclipse plugin, so pay attention to which branch you are linking your package to. If you make a mistake, you will need to unlink and recreate the link to the package. During this step, you can also decide if pulling (installing) the repository should happen directly after creating the link.

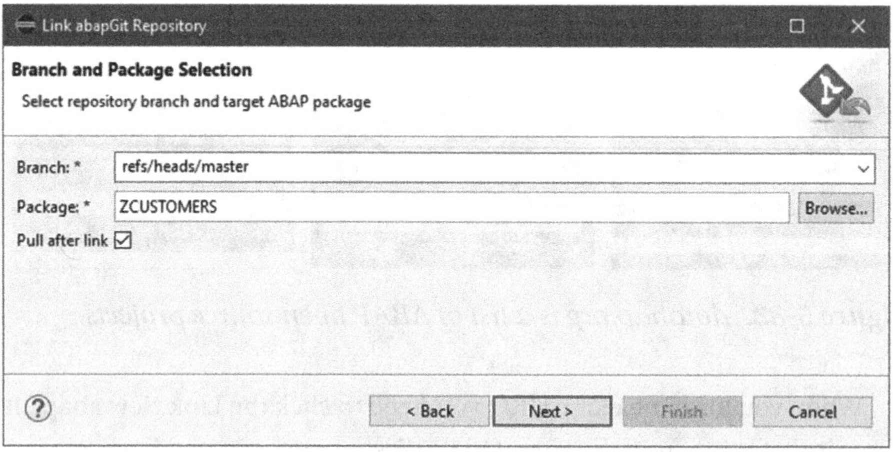

Figure 5-35. Linking a new abapGit repository: branch and package selection

The next screen that will appear is the Transport Request Selection dialog, which you should have seen a dozen times. When you click the Finish button, you should see the linked repository on your list, just like in Figure 5-36.

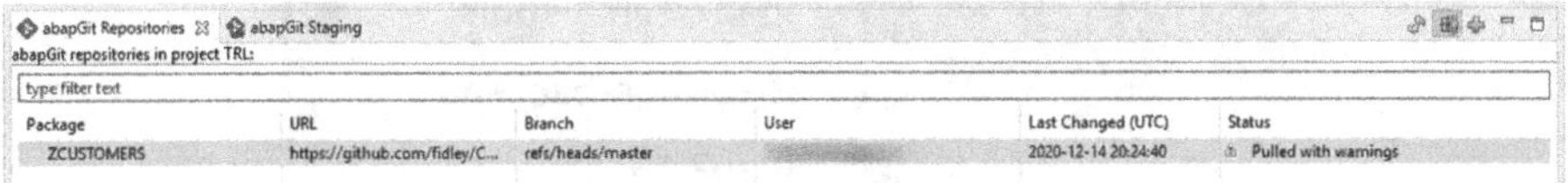

Figure 5-36. *Linking a new abapGit repository: pulling status*

Note in Figure 5-36 that there were some warnings during the installation of the repository in the backend system. You can double-click the Status column to get the details. For example, in my case, it was a message that programs are not allowed in the cloud environment, that is why they were not imported. The rest of the objects were imported and are available in the selected package.

abapGit Staging

When you want to contribute to the open source projects or create your own versions, abapGit Staging view can be useful. It is a very simple view that shows which local objects differ from the one stored in the remote repository. It allows you to commit and push the changes into a remote repository.

Despite the project type (your own or a community one), it is recommended to have your own branch for any adaptations. If you want to contribute to somebody else's project, first fork it to your own Git repository, then link to your backend using abapGit and start the changes in code.

To commit and push the changes, you need to jump to abapGit Staging view and select the repository to check using the Switch Repository button on the view toolbar (Figure 5-37).

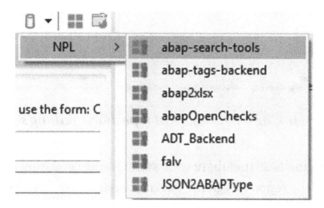

Figure 5-37. *Switching the repository in abapGit Staging view*

If there are any changes, you will see them as Unstaged Changes (Figure 5-38). Now you have to select the object you want to stage. You can do that by selecting the objects on the list and using the Stage button or choosing Stage Objects from the context menu. They will be moved to the Staged Changes tree. The last fields you need to fill in are Commit Message, Author, and Committer. At that stage, the Commit and Push button will became active.

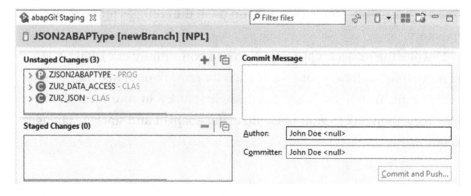

Figure 5-38. *Unstaged changes of local objects*

282

When you commit your changes, you will be asked for the remote repository credentials. Your changes will then appear in the remote repository. There is also one additional function available here. When you use the context menu on staged or unstaged objects, you can run a comparison of the local object version with the one in the remote repository.

ABAP Continuous Integration

The next plugin from the ABAP world that I want to present is ABAP Continuous Integration. This plugin was created by SAP Champion Andreas Gautsch.[3] It is available on the marketplace and, as you can see in Figure 5-39, it has already around 2500 installations, which is quite a big number for an ABAP plugin.

ABAP Continuous Integration 0.5.5.2

AbapCI is an Open Source Eclipse plugin which provides various Continuous Integration (CI) tools for the ABAP development with Eclipse. The plugin is based on the... **more info**

by Andreas Gautsch, Apache 2.0
ABAP continuous integration ci

★ 32   ↱ Installs: **2,47K** (85 last month)   Install Pending

Figure 5-39. *ABAP Continuous Integration on the Eclipse Marketplace*

The plugin gives you four additional views: ABAP CI Dashboard, ABAP CI Suppressions, ABAP Continuous Integration, and ABAP Colored Projects. The last view is linked to a small functionality: coloring the IDE depending on the active project.

---

[3]Andreas Gautsch SAP Community's profile is found at https://people.sap.com/ andreas.gautsch

Coloring Projects

After installing the ABAP CI and restarting Eclipse, you will see the first of the popup windows that comes with the plugin. It's a screen with the color assignment selection for the project (Figure 5-40). Color changing may be useful for quick recognition of the development, integration, or production systems. You can of course decide not to color the project. On this screen, you can also decide if it should appear when you switch to the project.

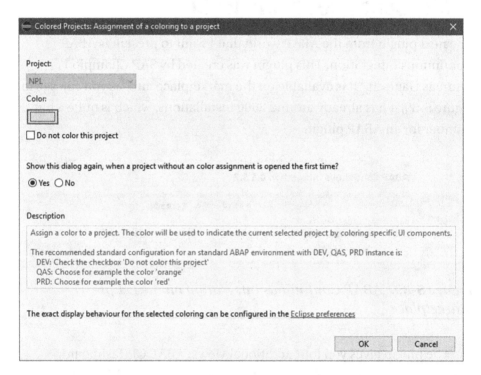

Figure 5-40. *Assigning color to a project*

The basic settings are set to update the status color only, as it is presented in Figure 5-41, but you can make more adaptations. My personal feeling is that when you decide to color the project, status coloring is enough.

Figure 5-41. *Colored status bar*

All assigned coloring projects will be listed on the ABAP Colored Projects view (Figure 5-42). From that view, you can add, edit, or delete the assignments using either the view toolbar or the context menu.

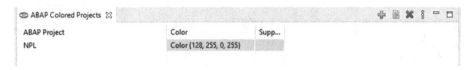

Figure 5-42. *ABAP Colored Projects view*

Continuous Integration

When you activate the first object after the installation of ABAP CI, you will see another screen from that plugin (Figure 5-43). This time it will be configuration of CI jobs for the package containing the object you just activated. CI jobs are done in the background after objects are activated, when you select from this screen that the package should be included in the automatic Unit Test run or the automatic ATC run.

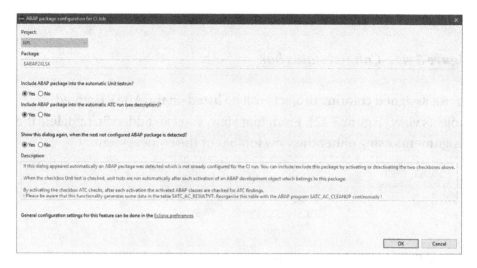

Figure 5-43. *CI job configuration screen for a package*

Once you set up the package to be included in the CI jobs, you will see this package listed in the ABAP Continuous Integration view together with the last state of the Unit Tests and ATC run (Figure 5-44). From the view toolbar and context menu, you will also be able to add new packages to the list, or edit or delete the package from the CI jobs. You can also call Unit Tests and ATC Check on demand from here.

Figure 5-44. *ABAP Continuous Integration view after running the CI job*

The ABAP Continuous Integration view is helpful if you are activating objects from several packages, as in other case you will be also notified about the result of the last CI run in the status bar. The widget shown in the bottom-left corner of Eclipse will show you the status of the CI job, the number tests passed and failed, and the number of the ATC results

(Figure 5-45). By default, when the job is be successful, the color of the widget will remain white. With failed Unit Tests, it changes to pink. With ATC issues, it becomes purple.

Figure 5-45. *Source code state widget on the status bar*

If you have some ATC results, they will also be listed when you hover over the widget. A sample list can be found in Figure 5-46. It can be used to look quickly at any errors you made.

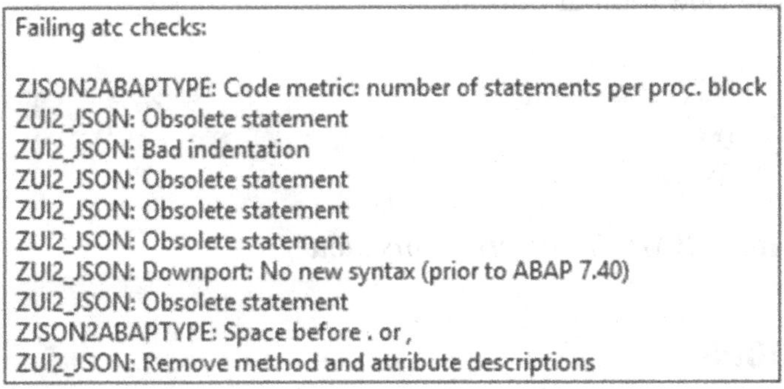

Figure 5-46. *Detailed info about failed ATC checks*

When you do not want to use the status bar widget to display the last CI job details, you can deactivate this in the plugin's preferences. In this case, you can still follow the last calls of the job using the ABAP CI Dashboard view (Figure 5-47), which displays the same information as the status bar widget.

Figure 5-47. *ABAP CI Dashboard after running a CI job*

You may want to you want omit some classes from the CI jobs, but still want to check the other contents of the package. In such cases, you can use the ABAP CI Suppressions view (Figure 5-48) to exclude classes from the CI jobs run. Of course, at any stage, you can clear the list or add new objects to it using the view toolbar buttons.

Figure 5-48. *ABAP CI Suppressions view*

Preferences

You should be used to the fact that not everything is available directly, but after making changes in the preferences, you can get much more. The same is true with the ABAP CI plugin. When you go to Window ➤ Preferences ➤ ABAP Development ➤ Continuous Integration, you will notice that there are some nice functionalities available and you can also adjust the ones I have described.

First of all, you can choose to run a Unit Test not for whole package, but only for activated object. This should speed up the visibility of the results on the status bar widget.

You can also set up a variant for ATC. It does not need to correspond to the default variant available in your system.

The third group of settings is the visualization of the source code state in the UI, where in addition to the color customization for failed Unit Tests and ATC results, you can decide if the widget for the source code state should be shown in the status bar. Additionally, you can decide if the popup for the unconfigured CI jobs packages should appear.

If you are using the TDD approach, you may like also to activate the Show TDD Labels for Source Code State Output option (Figure 5-49). Choosing this option, instead of the test results, means the status bar widget will guide you if you should now write test, write code, or refactor. The last step appears when your unit tests pass the checks and ATC has no result. Once you achieve that, the refactor state will remain visible for the time specified in the Minimal Time The TDD Cycle Will Remain in the Refactor State option.

Figure 5-49. *TDD labels configuration*

The next nice possibility of the ABAP CI configuration is to allow automatic source code formatting when you activate or save an object. By default, the mandatory prefix in the source code is set to #autoformat. You would need to put this in each object you are changing in the first line in order for this function to be triggered. I guess this is something most of us would not do, but instead if you fill the mandatory prefix with <NO_ FILTER> (Figure 5-50), each activated or saved object will be automatically formatted. You can also decide to clean up unused variables.

> 4. Automatic source code formatting
> ☑ Automatic sourcecode formatting enabled
> Mandatory prefix in source code to enable formatter   `<NO_FILTER>`
> ☐ Automatically cleanup not used variabels (when formatting enabled)

Figure 5-50. *Formatting options of the ABAP CI plugin*

ABAP Code Insight

The next plugin of Andreas Gautsch available on the marketplace is called ABAP Code Insight (Figure 5-51). Version 0.4.0.0 shows this is maybe not yet the final version of the plugin, but it already can bring added value, which is the inline information about ABAP code elements.

ABAP Code Insight 0.4.0.0

ABAP Code Insight is an Open Source Plugin which enabled inline code information for ABAP code in Eclipse. The only prerequisite to use this plugin for developing... **more info**

by Andreas Gautsch, MIT

★ 18   Installs: **1,27K** (51 last month)   Install

Figure 5-51. *ABAP Code Insight in the Eclipse Marketplace*

If you are using non-HANA releases of SAP, this plugin may look slow to you, especially if you are opening a class that contains a huge number of methods and attributes. This is because the time needed to gather the information from the backend and the amount of selected information to fetch in the preferences. When you are using it on S/4HANA or C/4HANA systems, the code insight information appears quickly.

This information can be useful to you, for example the signature of the method shown before the implementation (to avoid using F2) or the reference counter including tests (Figure 5-52). The reference counters are the hyperlinks as well, so when you click them, you move to the where-used list of the given element. For me, the most important information here is whether the method is used in the test classes.

```
     3 references (1 test) | public [] ()
72 ⊖ METHOD constructor.
73     screen_helper = NEW #( ).
74     screen_handler = NEW #( me ).
75   ENDMETHOD.
76

     4 references (1 test) | public [ok:ABAP_BOOL] ()
77 ⊖ METHOD check.
78     CHECK: check_statement( ),
79            check_plant( ),
80            check_year( ),
81            check_edit_mode( ),
82            check_status( ),
83            check_storage_location( ),
84            check_stock_type( ),
85            check_material( ).
86     ok = abap_true.
87   ENDMETHOD.
```

Figure 5-52. *Inline ABAP code information*

Personally, I use the preferences of Code Insight, which you can find in Figure 5-53. To set up your own preferences, just go to Window ➤ Preferences ➤ ABAP Development ➤ Code Insight. I recommend you also look at the Show Values of Variables in the Debug View parameter to get a surprise during debugging from time to time.

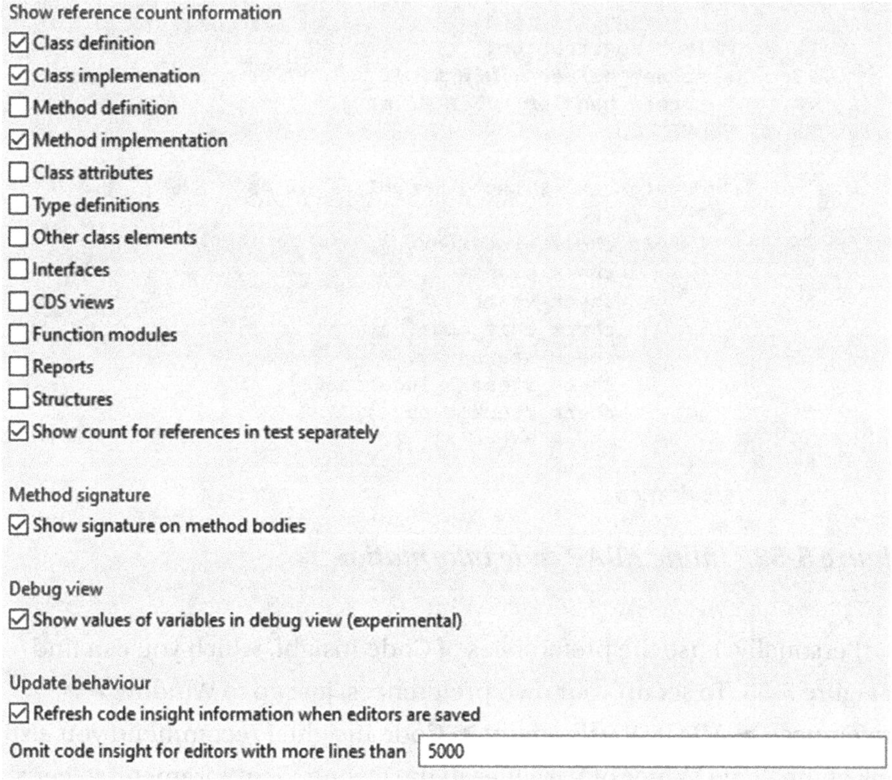

Show reference count information
- ☑ Class definition
- ☑ Class implemenation
- ☐ Method definition
- ☑ Method implementation
- ☐ Class attributes
- ☐ Type definitions
- ☐ Other class elements
- ☐ Interfaces
- ☐ CDS views
- ☐ Function modules
- ☐ Reports
- ☐ Structures
- ☑ Show count for references in test separately

Method signature
- ☑ Show signature on method bodies

Debug view
- ☑ Show values of variables in debug view (experimental)

Update behaviour
- ☑ Refresh code insight information when editors are saved

Omit code insight for editors with more lines than | 5000 |

Figure 5-53. My ABAP Code Insight plugin settings

ABAP Search and Analysis Tools

This is the first of two plugins published by Ludwig Stockbauer-Muhr.[4] It has been available on the marketplace since November 2019. So far, it has only a bit more than 400 downloads (Figure 5-54), but I hope after reading about the possibilities of this plugin, it will become more popular.

---

[4]Ludwig Stockbauer-Muhr profile's on the SAP Community is found at https:// people.sap.com/ludwig.stockbauer-muhr

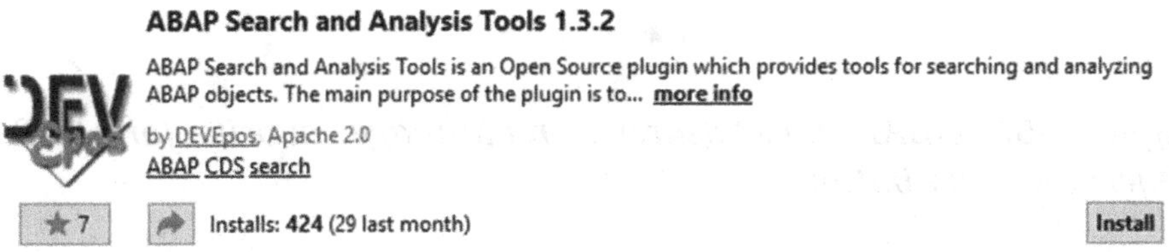

ABAP Search and Analysis Tools 1.3.2

ABAP Search and Analysis Tools is an Open Source plugin which provides tools for searching and analyzing ABAP objects. The main purpose of the plugin is to... **more info**

by DEVEpos, Apache 2.0
ABAP CDS search

★ 7   Installs: **424** (29 last month)   Install

Figure 5-54. *ABAP Search and Analysis Tools on the Eclipse Marketplace*

In order to use this plugin, besides installing it from the Eclipse Marketplace, you also need to install the backend components using abapGit and one of the branches from `https://github.com/stockbal/ abap-search-tools`. When you enter the GitHub page of the plugin, you will see that there are separate branches for versions 7.40, 7.50, 7.51, 7.52, and newer. Remember to install the version that fits your backend.

I am sure that I cannot fully describe all the features of this plugin, that is why I encourage you to take a look at the F1 help that Ludwig has prepared whenever you think you need clarification.

Search Tools

Search Tools is a part of the plugin that extends the search capabilities for the following:

- CDS Views

- Database tables/views

- Classes/interfaces

You can use it directly, using two new buttons on the Eclipse toolbar (Figure 5-55), or you can just run a standard Eclipse search (Ctrl+H) and switch the tab to ABAP Objects Search+.

Figure 5-55. *ABAP Object Search+ and Manage Favorites for ABAP Objects Search+ buttons*

The standard ADT ABAP Object Search is very limited. It only allows you to search the objects by name. ABAP Object Search+ brings the searching functionality to another level. It is limited to CDS Views, Database tables and views, classes and interfaces. It covers most of the needs of the developers. This is because it contains search filters that you will love to use.

You should remember search filters from many other ADT places, such as from the ABAP Repository Trees or the Open ABAP Development Object dialog (Ctrl+Shift+A). There are quite a few more of them in this plugin (Figure 5-56).

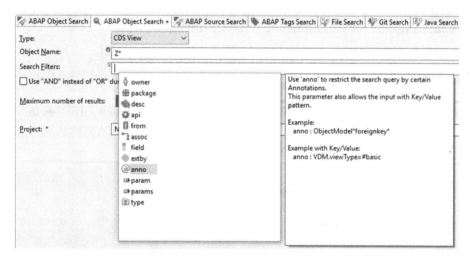

Figure 5-56. *Search Filters for CDS Views*

You can use the Owner, Package, Desc (Description), and Type filters. For CDS Views and database tables/views, you can also use the Field filter, which searches each of these objects that contain a specified field name. For classes and CDS Views, you can use the API state filter. The rest of the filters are unique:

- CDS View

  - From: Restricts the selection to CDS Views that in its `SELECT` statement uses the given Tables/Views/CDS Views.

  - Assoc: Restricts the selection to CDS Views that have associations to givenTables/Views/CDS Views.

  - Extby: Restricts the selection to CDS Views that are extended by given CDS Views.

  - Anno: Restricts the selection to CDS Views that contain the given annotations.

  - Param: Restricts the selection to CDS Views that have the given parameters.

  - Params: Restricts the selection to CDS Views that either contain or do not contain the parameters (`params:true`: contains parameters, `params:false`: have no parameters)

- Class/Interfaces

  - Cat: Selects the category of class from General, Exit, Persistent, Persistent Factory, Exception, WD Runtime, Area Class, or Test Class.

  - Flag: Selects the classes that have flags, such as Abstract, Final, Test, Fixpoint, or Shared Memory.

- Lang: Selects classes with the chosen ABAP Language version.

- Friend: Selects classes that have a specified friend.

- Supe: Selects classes that inherit from a specified class.

- Intf: Selects classes that implement specified interfaces.

- Meth: Selects classes or interfaces that contain methods with a specified name.

- Attr: Selects classes or interfaces that contain attributes with a specified name.

A great feature of some of the search filters is code completion. For example, for Anno or From (Figure 5-57). A few of them allow you not only to select the filter criteria, but also to enter a strict value of the filter criteria. For example, CDS View search filter `anno: accesscontrol. authorizationcheck=#NOT_ALLOWED` will search for only CDS Views with the annotation `@Accesscontrol.authorizationCheck` set to `#NOT_ALLOWED`.

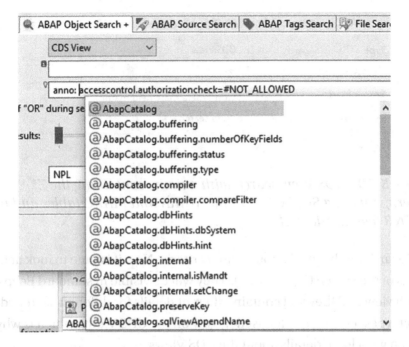

Figure 5-57. *ABAP Object Search+ with annotation code completion*

You can put several search filters together and use more than one value for each filter. By default, when you put several values into one filter, they work as if they were part of an OR clause. If you want to change that behavior, click the Use "AND" instead of "OR" during search checkbox; the search results will then be more accurate. In Figure 5-58 there is an example of search of CDS Views that are having SELECTs from MARA AND MARC tables and the field called MATNR.

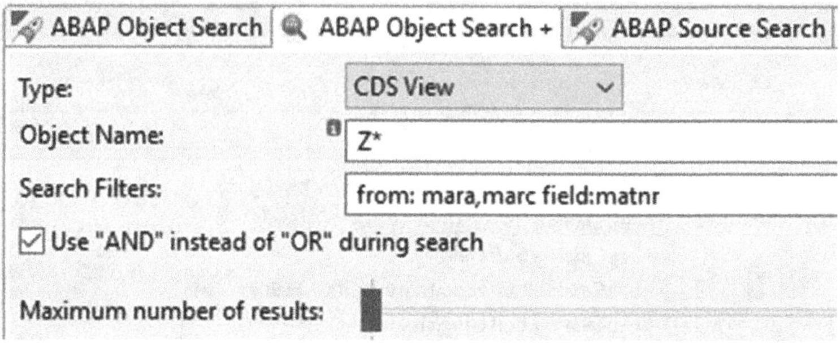

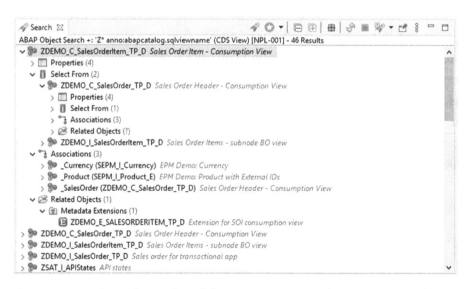

Figure 5-58. *CDS View search with a name containing the Z* pattern, having a SELECT from the MARA and MARC tables and the MATNR field inside itself*

So far, it has been all about search criteria. Now it is time to look at the results of the search (Figure 5-59). They will be visible in standard Eclipse Search view and they will contain different details for different searched object types. Ludwig has focused mostly on the CDS Views, which is why you can get a lot of details about the CDS Views.

Figure 5-59. *Search results of the CDS Views with Z* name and abapCatalog.sqlviewname annotation*

You can also mark the search as a favorite. To do that, just use the Favorite button on the Search view toolbar and select Create Favorite from Current Query (Figure 5-60). With repeatable searches, this can save you some time. Of course, this comes mostly in hand when you search for the same objects, as the standard history also saves your queries.

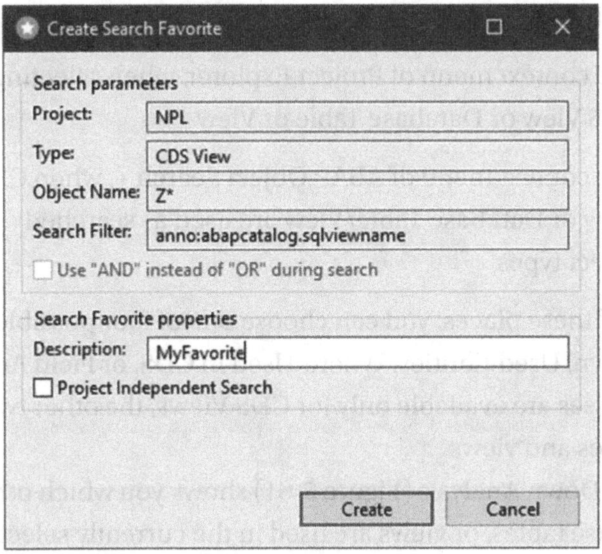

Figure 5-60. *Creating a Search Favorite*

Besides creating favorites, from the context menu of ABAP Object Search + results, you can also call the favorites organizer, the data preview, and the analysis tools that are the second part of this plugin.

Analysis Tools

With this part of the plugin, we receive the additional view called CDS Analyzer. The view itself will not work until you call the analyzer from one of three possible places:

- The context menu of CDS View or Database Table Editor

- The context menu of Project Explorer, when selecting CDS View or Database Table or View

- The context menu of ABAP Object Search +, when CDS View or Database Table/View are used as searched object types

In each of these places, you can choose one of four possible analyses: CDS Top-Down, Used Entities, Where-Used in CDS, or Field Analysis. The first two analyses are available only for CDS Views, the other two work with database tables and views.

CDS Top-Down Analysis (Figure 5-61) shows you which other CDS Views, database tables, or views are used in the currently selected CDS. It drills down the usage to the last level, so you can see all types of CDS Views and the database tables used at each CDS level. This analysis can be extremely helpful when you're working with complex, multilevel CDS Views. In the view menu, you can also enable the display of used associations.

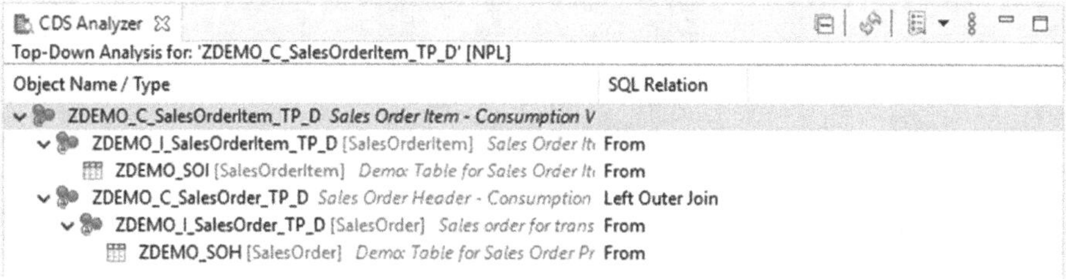

Figure 5-61. *Top-down analysis of CDS Analyzer*

Used Entities Analysis (Figure 5-62) gives you an aggregated view of the data from the Dependency Analyzer and usage information of the CDS View. This view can be useful to determine if you need to reduce the number of used entities or transform the CDS. This view can also give you an overview about the importance of the CDS View.

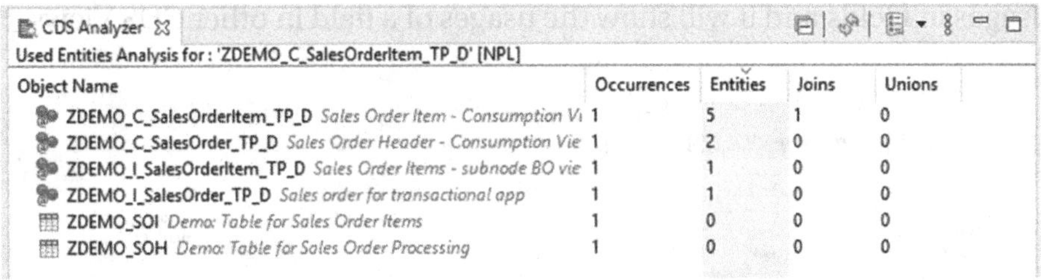

Figure 5-62. *Used entities analysis of CDS Analyzer*

Where-used in CDS Views analysis can show you if the analyzed object is used in a SELECT or the association part of CDS Views (Figure 5-63). Using the view menu, you can choose to see only usage in CDS Views for whom the API state is set to Released. Viewing only locally defined associations can also be set in the same place.

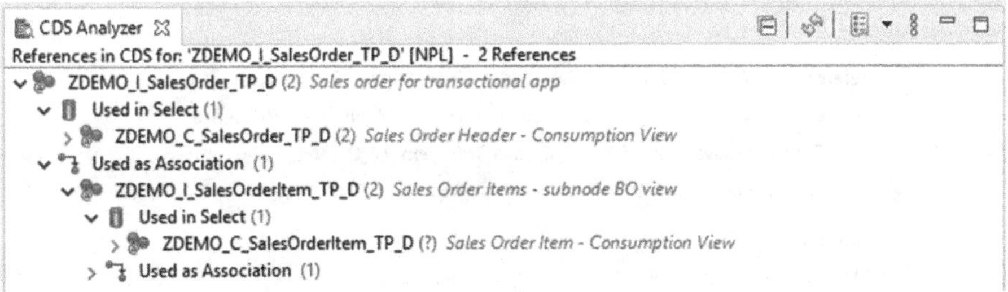

Figure 5-63. *Where-used in CDS views analysis*

The last of the analysis tools is Field Analysis (Figure 5-64). It is very useful for quickly checking the origin of a CDS View field. The view for this analysis is split into two parts: Field list and Field details. The Field detail area has two modes. The Field origin mode uses a top-down approach to display the origin of field down to the database layer. It also shows the name of the field at each level in the field hierarchy. The other mode is Usages in Fields and it will show the usages of a field in other CDS Views.

Figure 5-64. *Field analysis of CDS Analyzer*

CDS Analyzer also collects the history of the analysis. Using the Show Previous Analyses button, you can return to the cached results of the previous analysis (Figure 5-65). Its behavior is exactly the same as the history on the Search view.

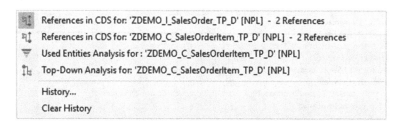

Figure 5-65. *Drop-down menu of CDS Analyzer history*

ABAP Tags

The second plugin by Ludwig Stockbauer-Muhr is called ABAP Tags. It is quite a new plugin, published on July 2020, which is why it is not that popular yet (Figure 5-66). You need to install the backend component using the abapGit repository, which can be found at `https://github.com/stockbal/abap-tags-backend`.

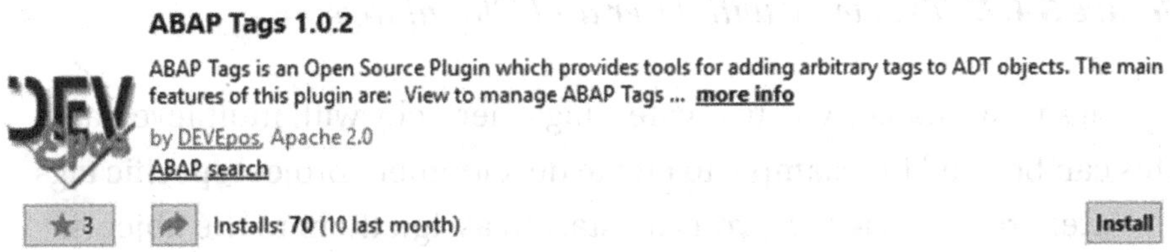

ABAP Tags 1.0.2

 ABAP Tags is an Open Source Plugin which provides tools for adding arbitrary tags to ADT objects. The main features of this plugin are: View to manage ABAP Tags ... **more info**

by DEVEpos, Apache 2.0
ABAP <u>search</u>

 ★ 3   Installs: **70** (10 last month)   Install

Figure 5-66. ABAP Tags plugin on the Eclipse Marketplace

After I installing the plugin and backend components, you can use the two new views (Tags, Tag Explorer) and the new search tab (ABAP Tag Search).

Tags

In order to tag the objects in ADT, you need to create them inside the Tags view (Figure 5-67). You can create user and global tags. As you can foresee, user tags are visible only for you and global tags are visible for every developer, that is using your system. Each of the tags is stored in the backend, so they are system specific.

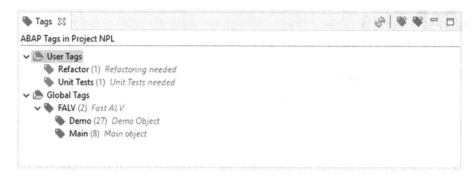

Figure 5-67. *Tags view with User and Global tags*

Tags view enables you to create a tags hierarchy with multilevel tags. This can be used for example to create development project specific tags.

After creating the tags, you can start to assign them to the objects. You can do that from the Assign Tags To Object button that is found on the Eclipse toolbar, or using the context menu of the Project Explorer and ABAP Editor. You can do this also from the Tag Explorer view. In each case, a wizard for adding tags to your object is displayed (Figure 5-68). If you try to assign a sub-tag, you will also have to select the parent object of the tag. The parent object is one of the objects that is assigned to the parent tag. Using my example, if I want to assign an object to the Demo tag of the FALV node, then the FALV tag would need to be assigned to any of the objects.

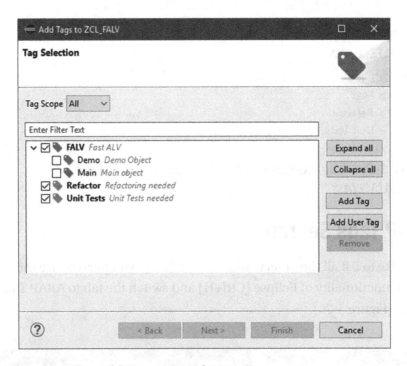

Figure 5-68. *The Add Tags wizard*

You can find several uses for the tags. They can be useful for onboarding new developers, describing the tasks that need to be done with the object or for highlighting of the object's purpose.

Tag Explorer

The second view that is installed with the ABAP Tags plugin is Tag Explorer (Figure 5-69). By default, it is linked with the active editor and shows all the tags that are assigned to edited objects. You can also manually select other objects to be used by clicking the Other Object button on the view toolbar. You can also assign new tags or delete linked tags from this view.

Figure 5-69. Tag Explorer with the tags assigned to the ZCL_FALV class

ABAP Tags Search

If you like to list all the objects with a specific tag, you need to use the search functionality of Eclipse (Ctrl+H) and switch the tab to ABAP Tags Search (Figure 5-70).

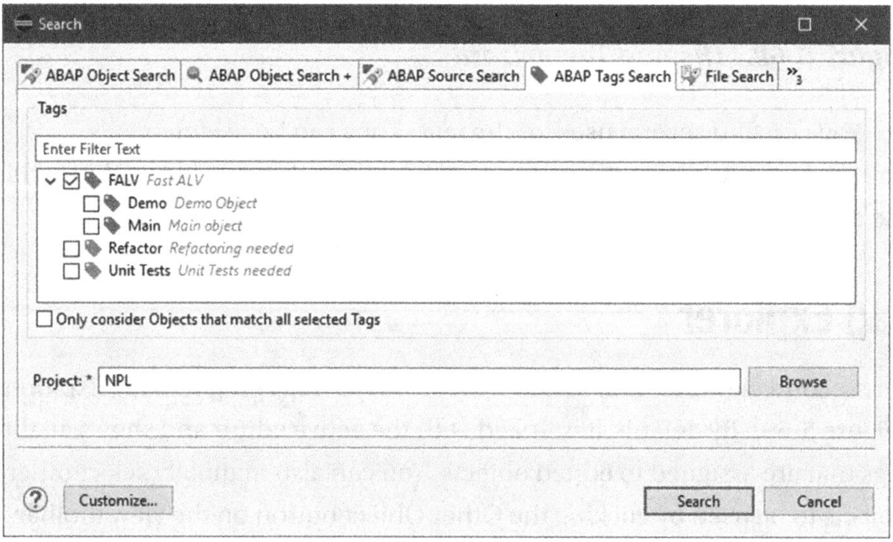

Figure 5-70. ABAP Tags Search tab

You can select one or more tags here and then choose if the search should only consider objects that match all the SELECT tags. After you click the Search button, the result will appear in the standard Search view. If the object is a parent of other objects, the list of liked sub-tags and the objects assigned to them will be visible after you expand the object node, as shown in Figure 5-71.

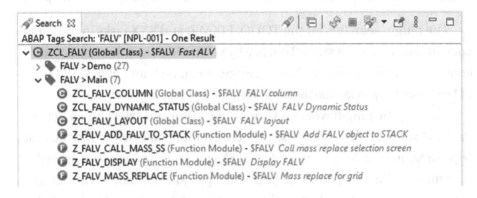

Figure 5-71. *Results of a FALV tag search*

The maximum number of results is set to 50 by default, but you can use the ABAP Tags preferences (Window ➤ Preferences ➤ ABAP Tags ➤ Search) to adjust this value to your needs. You will be able to adapt a few more minor options as well.

Task Scanner for ABAP in Eclipse

Akysh Baymuhammedov[5] published another plugin for ADT in July 2020 called Task Scanner for ABAP in Eclipse. As this is also a new plugin, the number of downloads from the marketplace is not large yet (Figure 5-72), but as with any other plugins, it will definitely grow in time.

---

[5]Akysh Baymuhammedov's profile on the SAP Community can be found at
https://people.sap.com/akysh96

Task Scanner for ABAP in Eclipse 1.0.2.202007182104

ABAP
TO**DO**

ABAP Task Scanner is an Open Source Eclipse plugin which provides the possibility to scan for TODOs, FIXMEs and XXXs in the source code of ABAP Objects such as... **more info**

by Akysh Baymuhammedov, Apache 2.0
ABAP ADT ABAP code search todos tasks

★ 5   Installs: **77** (15 last month)   Install

Figure 5-72. *Task Scanner for ABAP in Eclipse in Eclipse Marketplace*

The plugin searches for the TODO, FIXME, and XXX tasks in the source code in the backend system. That is why you need to install its backend component using abapGit. This component can be found at `https://github.com/AkyshBaymuhammedov/ADT_TODO_Plugin_ABAP`.

The way the plugin works is very simple. After you select an object in Project Explorer, you have to use the context menu and select Task Scanner ➤ Scan Source Code. You can select packages for the check scan as well.

Once you're done, the background Eclipse job will run. It will extract the source code of the selected object and check for selected tasks. All the work is done in the backend system and the results are collected in the similar way as in the standard transaction `CODE_SCANNER`.

When the results are ready, they will be displayed in the Problems view as an information (Figure 5-73), together with any accompanying comments.

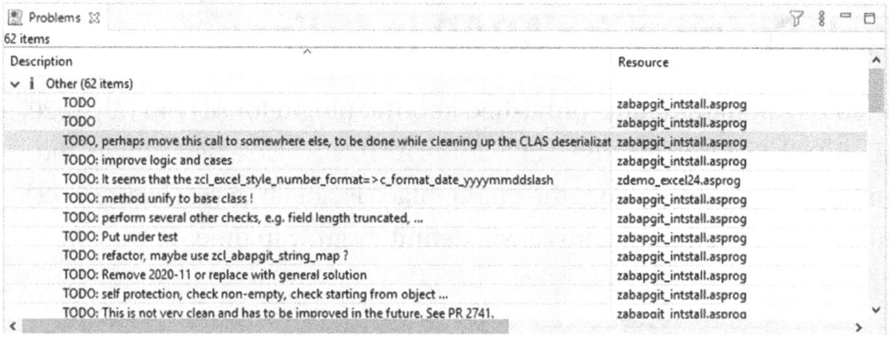

Figure 5-73. *TODOs findings for all temporary objects*

As it is with standard results in the Problems view, when you double-click one of the results, you will be navigated to the place where the task was found (Figure 5-74). An information marker will be added to the vertical ruler.

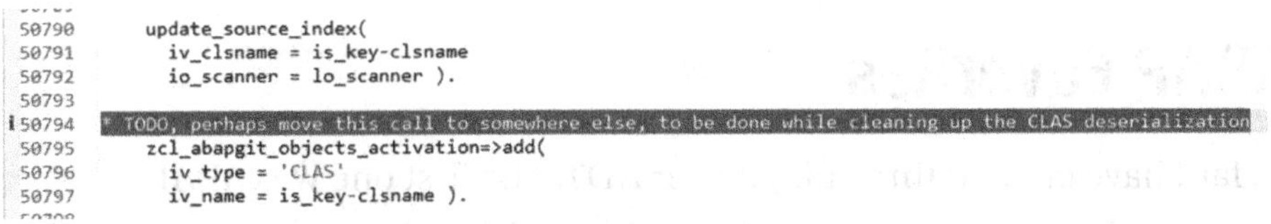

```
50790        update_source_index(
50791           iv_clsname = is_key-clsname
50792           io_scanner = lo_scanner ).
50793
50794    * TODO, perhaps move this call to somewhere else, to be done while cleaning up the CLAS deserialization
50795        zcl_abapgit_objects_activation=>add(
50796           iv_type = 'CLAS'
50797           iv_name = is_key-clsname ).
```

Figure 5-74. *TODO finding with the marker on the source code*

If you use custom markers in your ABAP code, you can add them to the preferences page of the ABAP Task Scanner, using the field Custom Text. You need to select the option Scan the Source Code for Custom text. If you want to scan several objects and keep the results in the Problems view, you need to unselect the Clean Previously Created Markers Before Scanning option.

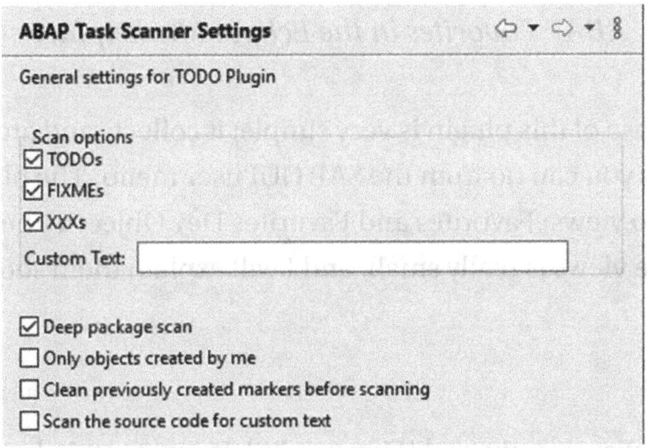

ABAP Task Scanner Settings

General settings for TODO Plugin

Scan options
☑ TODOs
☑ FIXMEs
☑ XXXs

Custom Text: [   ]

☑ Deep package scan
☐ Only objects created by me
☐ Clean previously created markers before scanning
☐ Scan the source code for custom text

Figure 5-75. *ABAP Task Scanner preferences page*

As this is the first plugin from Akysh and its initial version, I believe there are more functionalities that will be added to it. I think it is very good alternative to using ##TODO pragmas and ATC (SLIN) checks and I hope you will enjoy it also.

ABAP Favorites

So far I have created three plugins for ADT. The first one was ABAP Favorites. I am very happy that according to the Eclipse Marketplace, it has 2530 installations so far (Figure 5-76). I know that the plugin could be written better, but as for the first touch with Java and Eclipse plugins, it is not too bad.

ABAP Favorites 1.0.51.201904292055

A small plugin to create ABAP favorites list for transactions and urls. Editing of entries now available. It contains two views: Favorites   Favorites Dev Objects... **more info**

by ABAPBlog.com, Apache 2.0
ABAP sap ABAP favorites favorites

⭐ 35   ➡   Installs: **2,53K** (60 last month)   `Install`

Figure 5-76. ABAP Favorites in the Eclipse Marketplace

The purpose of this plugin is very simple: it collects and groups favorite objects just as you can do from the SAP GUI user menu. The plugin consists of two views: Favorites and Favorites Dev Objects. The difference between these views is really small, and I will explain them soon.

Favorites

The Favorites view is universal (Figure 5-76). It can contain both standard and Development Objects folders. Both types of folders can contain different object types and act a bit differently.

Standard folders work exactly like the user favorites menu from SAP GUI, which means when you store a program or transaction, you can double-click it to run it.

The Development Objects folders work similarly to the Favorites Objects ABAP Repository Tree that I described in previous chapters. So when you double-click one of the favorite objects, it will open in the editor. Additionally, Development Objects folders have a different icon than the standard one, for faster recognition.

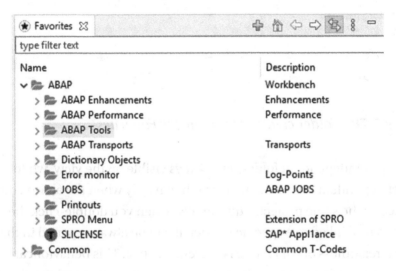

Figure 5-77. *Favorites view*

In order to assign an object to favorites, you first need to create a folder using the view toolbar or its context menu. When you create a folder (Figure 5-78), besides the name and descriptions, you can choose if the folder is project independent and the folder type. Using proper names and descriptions can help you filter the view entries.

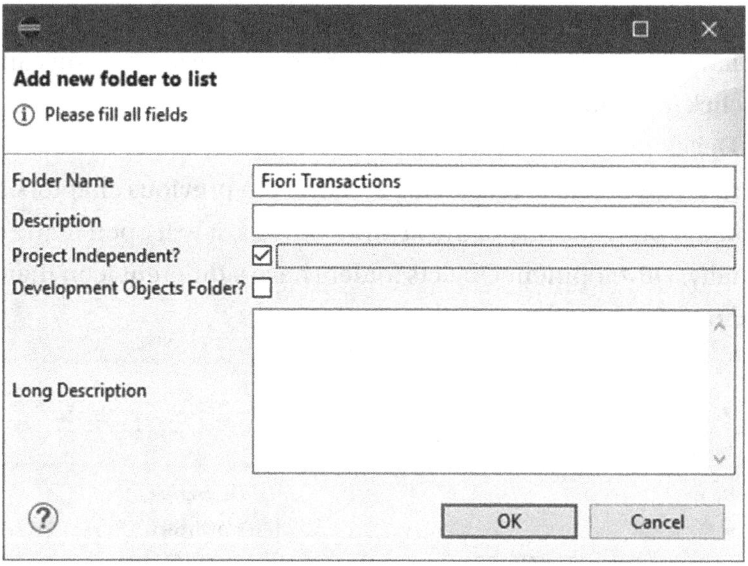

Figure 5-78. *Folder creation window for Favorites*

Project independent folders are always visible on the view, while project dependent ones by default are shown only when the active editor is linked to the same project. Additionally, when you double-click the object that is linked to a specific project, it will be always opened in that project, regardless of which one is currently active. This behavior can be helpful when you work with several customer systems and they have totally different sets of transactions or when you work with different types of ABAP systems (CRM, HR, etc.) that have their own specific transaction codes. Currently there is no way to manually select the linked project; it is always currently the active project.

After creating the folder, you can start assigning objects to it. The basic option to do this is to use the context menu on the created folder and choose the selected type of object to create. After that, you will see a favorite object creation window (Figure 5-79). In all cases, besides URLs and ADT links, the name used should correspond to the real object name. For the two other kinds of objects, the name can be anything, as there is another input field to enter the whole URL or ADT link.

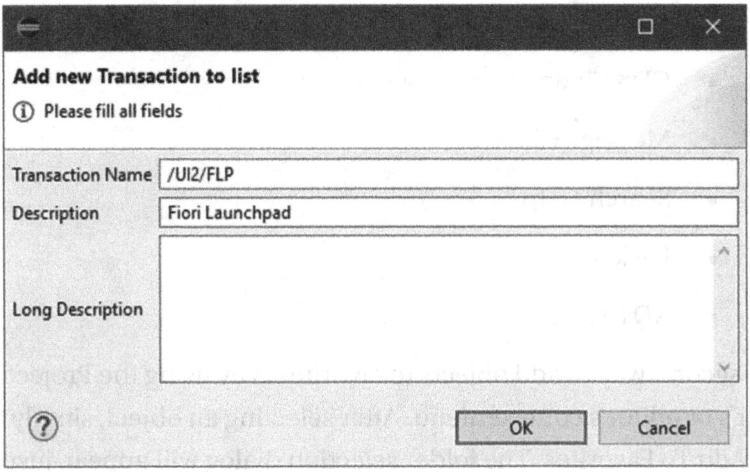

Figure 5-79. *Popup window for entering new favorite object details*

As I mentioned, you can assign specific favorites objects to different folder types. The currently supported objects are as follows:

- Standard folder
    - Transaction
    - Program
    - URL
- Development Objects Folder
    - Program
    - Class
    - Interface

- Function Group

- Function Module

- Database View

- Database Table

- CDS View

- Message Class

- Search Help

- Package

- ADT Link

The second way to add objects to favorites is by using the Project Explorer's or editor's context menu. After selecting an object, simply choose Add To Favorites. The folder selection dialog will appear, just like in Figure 5-80.

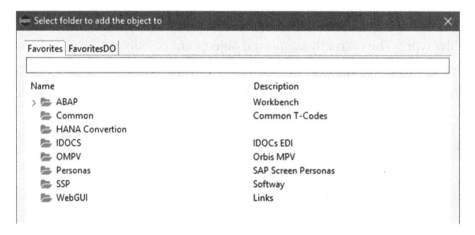

Figure 5-80. *Target folder selection for adding objects to Favorites from the context menu*

Once you have your favorite object list, you can also open or run the elements in each of the projects that are available in your workspace. To do this, use the context menu on the object and choose Open in Project. The second possibility is to press the Ctrl button while double-clicking the object. In such cases, you will get a popup window, where you can select the project to which the objects should be opened. This functionality was added by Ludwig Stockbauer-Muhr and it is extremely helpful when you have a long list of projects in your workspace.

If you create the object in the wrong folder, you can drag and drop the favorite to the correct place.

Favorites Dev Objects

The second view of the plugin is Favorites Dev Objects (Figure 5-81). It has the same behavior as the Favorites, but with one difference—you can only create Development Objects folders here. This split for two different views was done to enable developers to choose their own way, with one view containing both types of folders or using two views with separation of the folder types. Personally, I use the second approach.

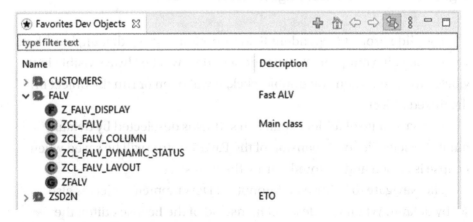

Figure 5-81. *Favorites Dev Objects view*

315

Preferences

For flexibility of usage, I've created a preferences page for Favorites. It can be found in ABAP Development ➤ Favorites (Figure 5-82) and consists of five settings so far.

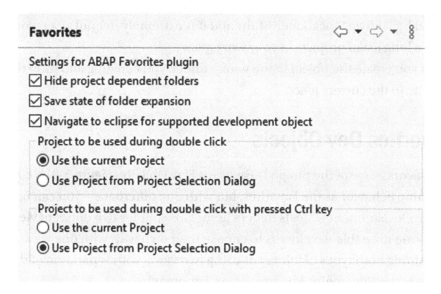

Figure 5-82. *Preferences page for ABAP Favorites*

The Hide Project Dependent Folders option is set by default, but when you deselect it, your project-dependent folders will be always visible in the views. However, when you double-click, it will open or run the object in the linked object.

The Save state of folder expansion setting is deselected by default, but if you select it, the expansion of the Favorites tree will be saved when Eclipse is closed and restored during the next start.

The Navigate to Eclipse for Supported Development object is also set by default. When you deselect it, instead of the Eclipse editor, the development objects will be opened in the SAP GUI transactions.

The last two radio buttons groups are responsible for the behavior of double-click and double-click with the Ctrl key pressed. You can decide which behaviors should be the defaults.

ABAP ADT Extensions

The second of my plugins is called ABAP ADT Extensions (Figure 5-83). At the beginning, it was part of the ABAP Favorites plugin, but after a suggestion, I moved it to a separate plugin in order to keep the Favorites plugin linked to its name.

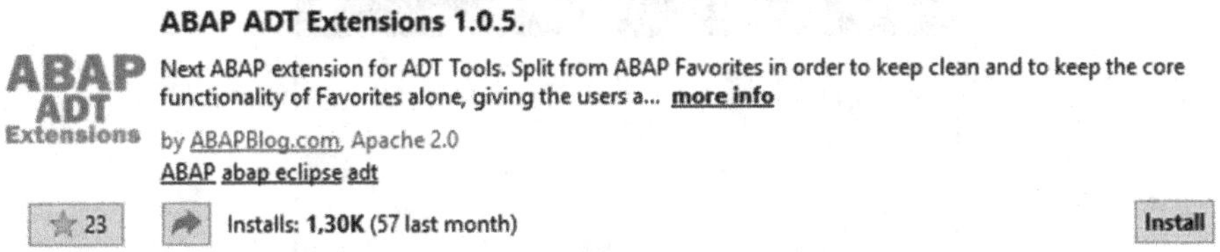

ABAP ADT Extensions 1.0.5.

 Next ABAP extension for ADT Tools. Split from ABAP Favorites in order to keep clean and to keep the core functionality of Favorites alone, giving the users a... **more info**

by ABAPBlog.com, Apache 2.0
ABAP abap eclipse adt

☆ 23   ➔   Installs: 1,30K (57 last month)   Install

Figure 5-83. *ABAP Extensions on the Eclipse Marketplace*

The plugin has two functionalities: changing the project settings and automatic logon (without SSO). Both are described next.

Project Settings

When you create an ABAP project in Eclipse, you are not able to change the client, language, or user. That is the standard behavior of the ADT. If you install ABAP ADT Extensions, you can however update each of these preferences using the Project Explorer's context menu (Figure 5-84).

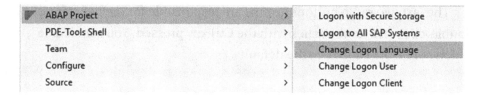

Figure 5-84. *ABAP Project on the context menu of Project Explorer*

When you choose a change action, a proper window will appear, where you can enter a new value for the changed parameter. So far there is no completion of the possible entries, so you need to be sure you are entering them correctly.

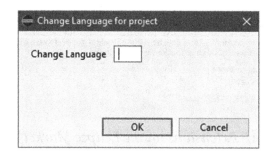

Figure 5-85. *Logon language change*

To change the settings, all currently opened objects from the changed project will be closed. So make sure that you have saved your work before adopting those settings.

Personally, I like the Change of Language option the best, and sometimes I also change the user on the integration systems. This is because I do not like to have several systems as different projects in Eclipse. I keep one project for one system and adjust the logon settings when necessary.

Automatic Logon

When your company does not have single sign-on (SSO) enabled for your SAP systems, starting Eclipse might be boring. Especially if you have dozens of systems to which you need to log in, or maybe you have to remember the passwords to many customer systems. In such cases, I think you will like this part of the ABAP ADT Extensions plugin.

You can now use the Passwords view (Figure 5-86) to store the passwords of each of your projects. When you install the plugin, it will read the workspace's configuration and add all the projects, clients, and users to the Passwords view.

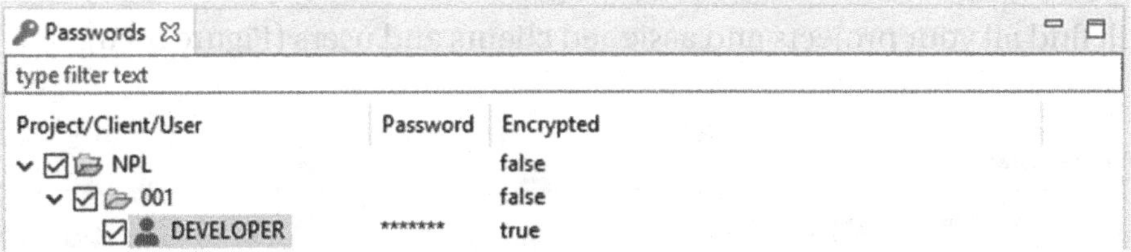

Figure 5-86. *Passwords view*

You can then find the system, client, and user for which you want to use automatic logon. You double-click the username and enter a password (Figure 5-87). If your instance is not the developer edition of SAP with the default password for the DEVELOPER user, I recommend you use the Encrypt Password option. That way, no one will be able to read it.

319

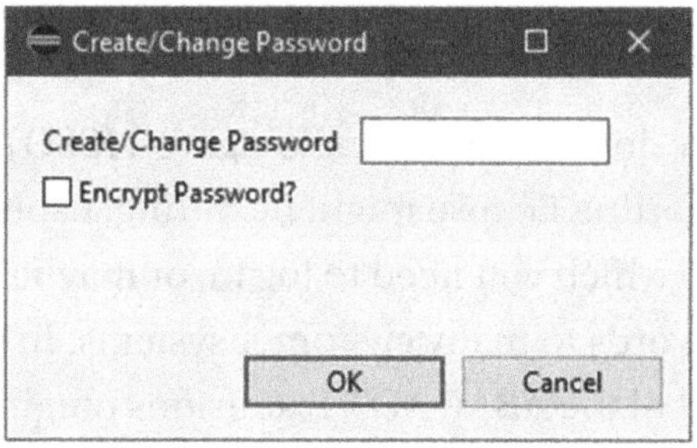

Figure 5-87. *Create/Change Password window*

The passwords are stored in Secure Storage. You can check this by going to Window ➤ Preferences ➤ General ➤ Security ➤ Secure Storage. Under the storage called com.abapblog.adt.extension.passwords, you will find all your projects and assigned clients and users (Figure 5-88).

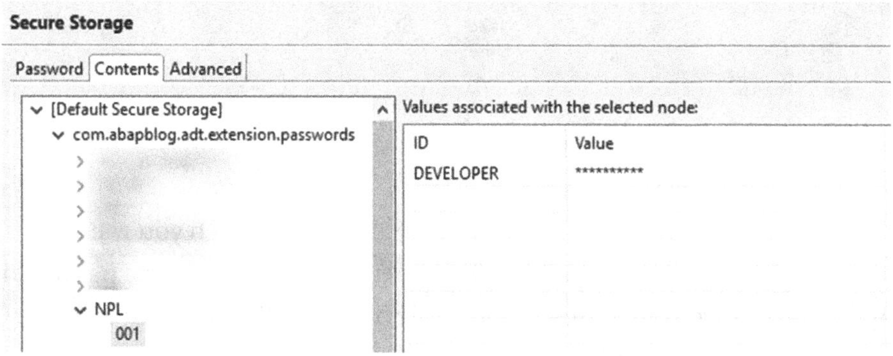

Figure 5-88. *Secure storage entries of Passwords view*

Now each time you start your Eclipse workspace, you will automatically be logged in to these systems. All the logon is happening in the background job, so you might have to wait a bit if you have dozens of system to log on, to. This behavior is visible if you have a slow connection to the backend systems.

This standard behavior of this plugin can be configured using the preference page of Automatic Logon, which can be found in the ABAP Development preferences node (Figure 5-89). You can resign from automatic logon at start or by raising a save password popup for each new created ABAP project. You can also decide if you want to log on to all ABAP systems, not only to those for which you have a password saved. In such a case, if the plugin finds a system that has no password stored, it will raise the standard ADT logon widget.

The Logon Automatically For All Stored Users setting can be useful if you want to restrict the automatic logon at start for only some of the system\client\user combinations. In this case, the checkboxes found on the Passwords view will tell the plugin which system\client\user it should log on to automatically.

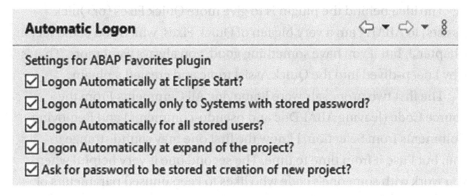

Figure 5-89. Automatic Logon preferences page

When you disable automatic logon at the start of Eclipse, I suggest you keep the Logon Automatically at Expand of the Project Setting enabled. In this case, whenever you need to log on to a system and save your credentials, it is enough to expand the project folder on Project Explorer. The other option for logging on is to use the same context menu as for project settings, but then select the Logon with Secure Storage (logon only to selected system) or Logon to All SAP Systems option.

ABAP Quick Fix

The last of my plugins that was published so far is called ABAP Quick Fix. It is the youngest of my plugins, but it is doing quite well so far, as you can see in Figure 5-90.

ABAP Quick Fix 1.0.4

ABAP Quick Fix plugin for ADT Installation from Marketplace https://marketplace.eclipse.org/content/abap-quick-fix Direct installation... **more info**

by ABAPBlog.com, Apache 2.0
ABAP ABAP ADT abap eclipse sap

☆ 15   ➡   Installs: **709** (46 last month)   Install

Figure 5-90. *ABAP Quick Fix on the Eclipse Marketplace*

The idea behind the plugin is to give more Quick Fixes (or Quick Assists) to ABAP. I am a very big fan of Quick Fixes, which you could feel in Chapter 3, but if you have something good, you always want more. That is why I deep-dived into the Quick Assist topic and created a plugin.

The first two proposals were Removing All Comments From the Source Code (leaving ABAPDoc and pseudo-comments) and Removing Comments from Selection. I know the first one may sound strange to you, but I use it from time to time. The second one is very helpful when you work with someone's code who likes to keep unused parameters of function modules or methods as a comment, or when you just want to get rid of unnecessary comments from a block of code.

The next proposal for selected comments is Translate Selection into English (Figure 5-91). This proposal works only if you have an Internet connection, as it calls an external API to do the translation. What is nice here is that the source language does not matter; it is recognized automatically. When you hover over the proposal, on the right side you will see the translated text. You can use this popup for translation help when investigating programs on integration or productive systems.

Figure 5-91. *Translate selection to English*

Besides the proposals for comments, you can find a number of code change proposals. All of them were built on regex patterns, but so far I have not noticed any issues with them.

The list of all included Quick Assists is as follows:

- Remove all comments (do not delete pseudo-comments and ADT comments)

- Remove all comments in a selection (do not delete pseudo-comments and ADT comments)

- Replace icon literals with constants

- Translate comments into English

- Replace READ TABLE with ASSIGN

- Replace READ TABLE with REF #( )

- Replace READ TABLE with Table Expression

- Replace READ TABLE TRANSPORTING NO FIELDS with LINE_EXISTS

- Replace CALL METHOD with a direct call

- Replace MOVE with a direct assignment

- Combine statements: DATA, TYPES, CONSTANTS, FIELD-SYMBOLS, CHECK, CLEAR, REFRESH, FREE, PARAMETERS, SELECT-OPTIONS, METHODS, CLASS-METHODS

- Change APPEND TO to APPEND VALUE #( ) TO

- Change `APPEND TO` to `INSERT VALUE #( ) INTO`

- Change `INSERT INTO` to `INSERT VALUE #( ) INTO`

- Split combined (chained) statements

- Remove the line break at end of statement

- Replace `CREATE OBJECT` with `NEW`

- Omit `EXPORTING` in a method call

- Omit `RECEIVING` in a method call

- Replace `GET REFERENCE` with `REF #`

- Remove full-line comments from a statement

- Omit the self-reference `ME->`

When you face problems with the Translate Selection into English proposal, for example because of a slow Internet connection, you can switch to Quick Fix from the Preferences page. You can also decide to hide the Remove All Comments proposal if it bothers you. These settings can be again found as a sub-node of the ABAP Development preferences (Figure 5-92).

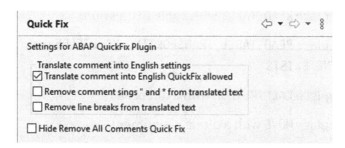

Figure 5-92. *Quick Fix preferences page*

Summary

There are quite a few nice plugins that you can use right now. You learned that most of them were created by SAP Community members as open source projects to which you can contribute, raise issues, or improve requests. It would be nice if you would leave feedback for the creators on the Eclipse Marketplace or the Git repository, so they feel that their work is not in vein.

The next chapter covers basic information about creating own plugins for Eclipse. After reading it, you'll understand how to create the plugins, what you can extend them, how to test them, and what to do to publish your plugins, so other developers can use them.

CHAPTER 6

Extending Eclipse

After reading about the Eclipse plugins and seeing how many of them are listed in the Eclipse Marketplace, you might be curious if it is hard to create an Eclipse plugin. This chapter should give you some insights about this process, so at the end of it, you will have your own opinion about the effort needed to create an extension. What is important to underline is that Eclipse plugins are developed in Java. You can of course call the SAP backend when you use ABAP (we cover that in next chapter), but even then, the UI part will be done in Java.

Extension Possibilities

The Eclipse IDE is an extensible framework that allows you to add, remove, and customize functionalities. You may remember that during installation of the Eclipse, you were able to choose from many different versions of the IDE. Each of the version is in fact an Eclipse IDE with different sets of plugins, created and published by the Eclipse Foundation. In order to extend Eclipse, you need to create a plugin.

The nice thing is that you create the plugins inside Eclipse itself. All you need to have is the Eclipse PDE (Plug-in Development Environment) installed. To check if it is available in your IDE, simply search for *Eclipse PDE* in the marketplace (Figure 6-1). You can then install it if it is missing.

© Lukasz Pegiel 2021
Ł. Pęgiel, *ABAP in Eclipse*, https://doi.org/10.1007/978-1-4842-6963-3_6

Eclipse PDE (Plug-in Development Environment) latest

The Plug-in Development Environment (PDE) provides tools to create, develop, test, debug, build and deploy Eclipse plug-ins, fragments, features, update sites and... **more info**

by Eclipse, EPL

PDE plugin-dev RCP eclipse-rcp

★ 92   Installs: **27,9K** (351 last month)   *Installed*

Figure 6-1. *Eclipse PDE in the Eclipse Marketplace*

You can create stand-alone plugins that don't use any existing functionalities. Buts in most cases, you will like at least to add a preferences page or menu and toolbar entries. To do that, you need to use *extension points*.

Extension points are APIs that are defined inside plugins. Besides the definition of the extension point, defining a plugin should also evaluate the plugins that use the extension points and call them. Extending plugins can at this point contribute to the extension point by creating a handler class. Contribution can mean either execution of code or providing data. The scheme of the interaction between the plugins defining and calling extension points is shown in Figure 6-2.

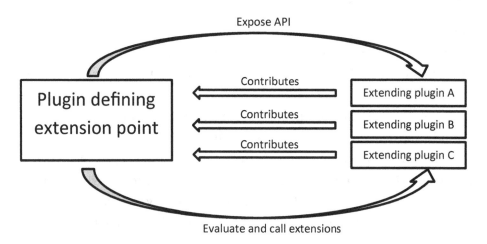

Figure 6-2. *Using extension points and extension plugins*

One plugin can provide several extension points. At the same time, it can use several extension points from other plugins. Creating and using extension points is covered later in this chapter.

Plugin Development Projects

To create a plugin, you need to create separate project for it. As you learned when creating ABAP projects, you have to use the Eclipse menu File ➤ New ➤ Project, but this time you need to expand the Plug-in Development folder to select one of the available project types (Figure 6-3).

Figure 6-3. *Plugin development projects on the New Project wizard*

There are three project types to focus on at the beginning: the plug-in project, feature project, and update site project. These three projects types are sufficient to create, group, and publish your plugins.

The plug-in project is the first one you should create. It contains the plugin itself. If you want to share your plugin with others, you need to create a feature project and then an update site project. Feature projects allow you to put one or several plugins into a group called a *feature*. A feature is a single logical unit or set of connected plugins of yours that serve one purpose. The update site project is used for building and publishing features. You can put one or more features into one update site.

I understand that the little information about project types I have given you so far may not be sufficient to fully understand their purpose, but you will learn about them more in the next parts of this chapter.

Plugin Development

The most important part of this whole process is creating the plugins. If you are new to Java development it is good to start with something simple. I did that as well. When you learn what is possible to do and how, you can take on something more complex.

Creating Your First Plugin

Let's start with a simple example. You need to create the plug-in project. The first screen of the Project Creation wizard is very simple; you need to select the name and location of the plugin project (Figure 6-4). I also added this project to the working set ADT book, so it is not mixed with the ABAP projects. You can leave the rest of the settings at their defaults.

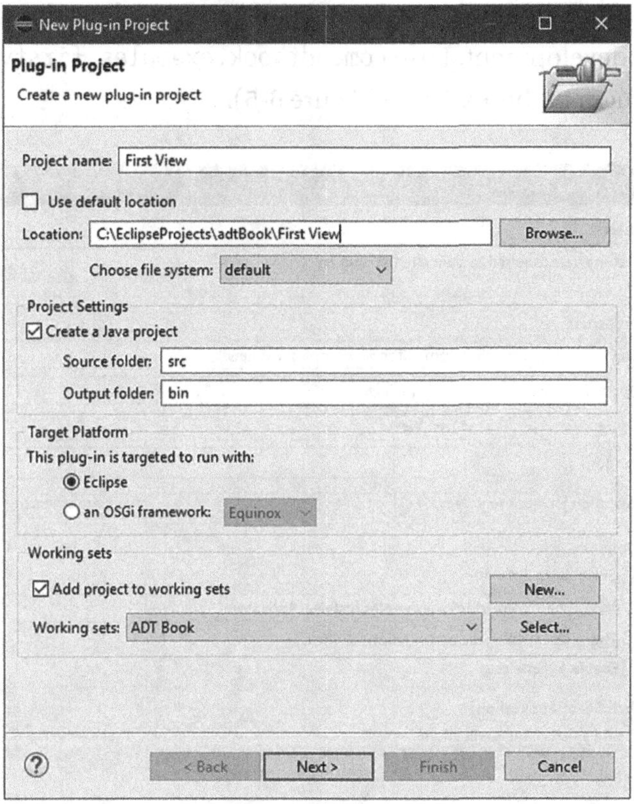

Figure 6-4. *The first screen of the plug-in project wizard*

In the next step, you provide an ID, name, and version for your plugin. You can also choose the execution environment and select if the activator for your plugin should be automatically generated.

With community plugins, the ID usually starts with COM. Generally it should look like this com.<yourName>.<project>.<component>, where <yourName> would be your nickname or company name, <project> would be the solution you are working on, and <component> would be its part. Of course, you can go deeper in details. Everything depends how complex your solution will be. You can read more about the package-naming conventions for Eclipse on its wiki site[1] and you can follow the same rules in your own development. I use `com.adtbook.examples.firstview` as an ID for the plugin in this example (Figure 6-5).

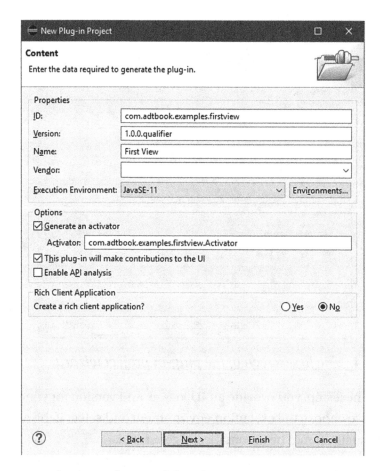

Figure 6-5. *The second step of the plug-in project wizard*

Version management is very important in Eclipse, and you will need to update it whenever you make changes to your code. By default, it is

---

[1]Naming conventions for Java Packages in Eclipse are found at `https://wiki.eclipse.org/Naming_Conventions#Java_Packages`

set to `1.0.0.`*`qualifier`*, where the first segment may be understood as the main release version, the second as a major release, and the third as a minor release or bug fixing. The word *qualifier* at the end is set to the timestamp of build time by default and in my opinion there is no point in changing it, but I will come back to this during the description of the update site project.

In my example, the Vendor field is not filled in, but it can be used to provide the full name of the company or the person who created the plugin. It will be visible in the detailed information about your Eclipse IDE and during the plugin installation process.

The Execution environment is optional, but it is good to set it to the recommended minimum version of Java. With Eclipse versions 2020-09 and above, that is Java 11.

The Generation of an Activator is an optional, but usually necessary, step. The Activator class is called when your plugin is used the first time and when Eclipse is closed.

On the next wizard screen (Figure 6-6), you can choose the template for your plugin. Choose View Contribution Using 3.x API and again click the Next button. If you are wondering why I do not ask you to use a version newer than 4.x API, most of the views, menus, and toolbars used in ADT and Eclipse are still built using 3.x API, and it is easier to interact with them using the same version.

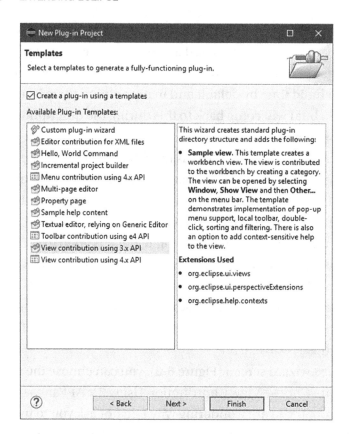

Figure 6-6. *Plug-in project wizard: template selection*

On the last wizard screen (Figure 6-7), you may adjust the names of the class, view, category ID, and category name. You can also choose the type of viewer that will be hosted inside the view created by the wizard. Leave the Table Viewer selected here and click the Finish button.

Tip   Use the same IDs and names that I do. This will make it much easier to find an error if something is not working as I describe it in this chapter.

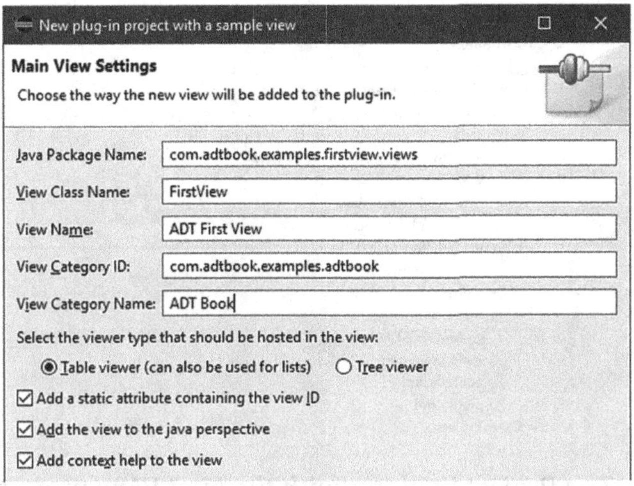

Figure 6-7. *The final screen of the plug-in project wizard*

After all these steps, you should see the First View project on the Project Explorer view (Figure 6-8). When you expand it, you will see a few folders, including SRC, where the whole source code is kept. When you expand this folder, you should see the Activator.java and FirstView.java files. Activator is directly shown in the com.adtbook.examples.firstview package, while FirstView is contained in the sub-package called views. If your view of the packages is different, go to Project Explorer view menu and choose Package Presentation ➤ Hierarchical.

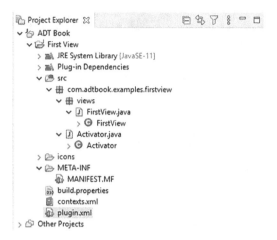

Figure 6-8. *The Project Explorer with the First View project*

Testing and Debugging

The plugin has been created, so let's test it before we jump into the plugin code and preferences. It will be easier for you to understand the parts of code that I describe later.

Configurations

To test or debug, we need to create a run and debug configuration. This configuration will allow you to choose the way Eclipse runtime environment is called. You can create one configuration that you will use for running and debugging. To do this, select the arrow next to the Debug or Run button and select Debug Configurations (Figure 6-9) or Run Configurations, respectively.

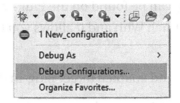

Figure 6-9. *Debug and Launch toolbar*

From the configuration types visible on the left side of the window, select Eclipse Application and click the New button. This will create a new configuration for you (Figure 6-10). You can use it as it is by default, but there are a few settings you might want to consider too.

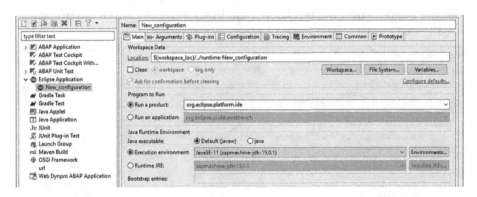

Figure 6-10. *Main tab of the Debug and Run configuration*

The Clear checkbox is on the Main tab. When it's selected, each time you use this configuration, Eclipse runtime will be called in a fresh mode. That means all settings that were done during the previous run of this configuration will be reverted to their initial states. This can be very useful when you are programming the behavior of your plugin after it is used the first time.

Another nice feature can be found on the Plug-ins tab (Figure 6-11). It is a dropdown called Launch With and it allows you to select three launch modes:

- All workspace and enabled target plug-ins (default)

- Plug-ins selected below only

- Features selected below

When you have lots of plugins installed in Eclipse, the booting time can be long. It is not good when you are debugging your own plugins and you have to restart the Eclipse runtime many times. That is why, with the Launch With setting, you can get rid of some of the plugins (or features) from the Eclipse runtime, but keep them in your development environment.

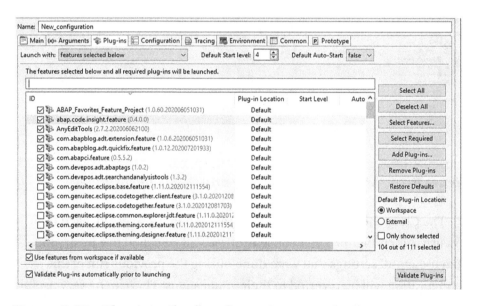

Figure 6-11. *Plug-ins tab of configurations*

Of course, there are many more tabs and settings here, but the default settings plus these two should be enough to start. Use the Close button so you can start testing the plugin.

Testing

Now choose the arrow next to the Run button and select the newly created configuration. You should notice a second Eclipse instance booting on your PC. This is the Eclipse runtime that we just configured.

Once it is running, go to Window ➤ Show View ➤ Other, expand the ADT Book category that we have created together with the plugin, and double-click ADT First View.

Figure 6-12. *ADT Book category and ADT First View on Show View popup*

The view will appear and it will contain the table viewer control, a view toolbar, and menu (Figure 6-13). Additionally, you can call the context menu on it and use the F1 help. Double-clicking the table entries should also work. Play a bit with this view to figure out what is possible.

Figure 6-13. *ADT First View with table viewer, view toolbar, and view menu*

Debugging

Since we were just running the plugin, even if you put a breakpoint in one of the plugin classes, it would not stop for debugging. You need to run the debugging process explicitly by selecting the arrow next to the Debug button and choosing the configuration.

You will like debugging in Java. When you make changes to the code without adding new `imports`, your changes will be directly applied after saving the code. When this happens, the debugger will return to the first statement of the current method and you can check the behavior of the class with the new code.

Plugin Preferences

Before going to the code part, note that you should also see an editor called `com.adtbook.examples.firstview`. This is a graphical editor of the plugin settings that can be lunched by double-clicking the `plugin.xml` file. This editor has several pages (tabs) that are placed on the bottom, just like in the case of ABAP classes tabs. On the Overview tab (Figure 6-14), besides the information that you added from the wizard screen, you will see the links to the other parts of the settings and the links to run or debug the application.

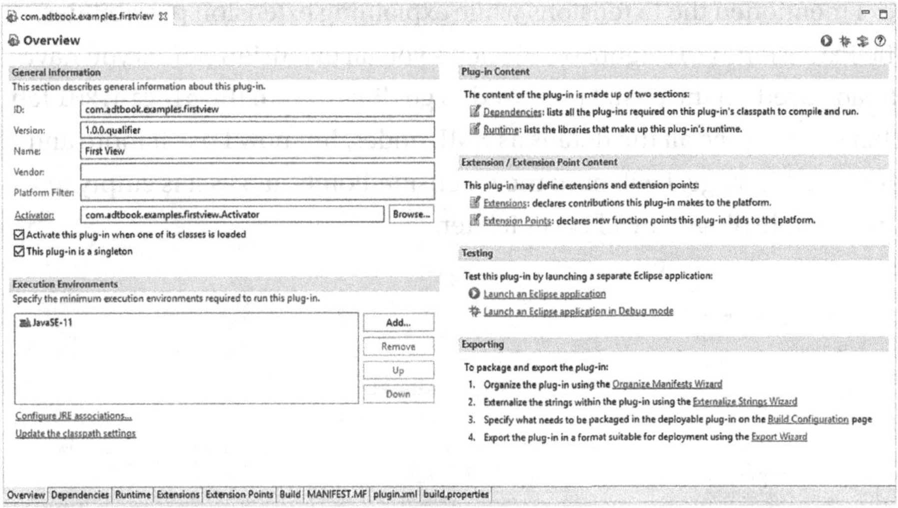

Figure 6-14. *Overview tab of plugin.xml*

The next important tab is Dependencies (Figure 6-15). It is responsible for setting up plugins that are required in order for your plugin to work correctly. The wizard added two standard Eclipse plugins directly, but when you create your own fancy plugin, you have to add the plugins manually by using the Add button. You will use that whenever you need to use a class that is outside your own plugin.

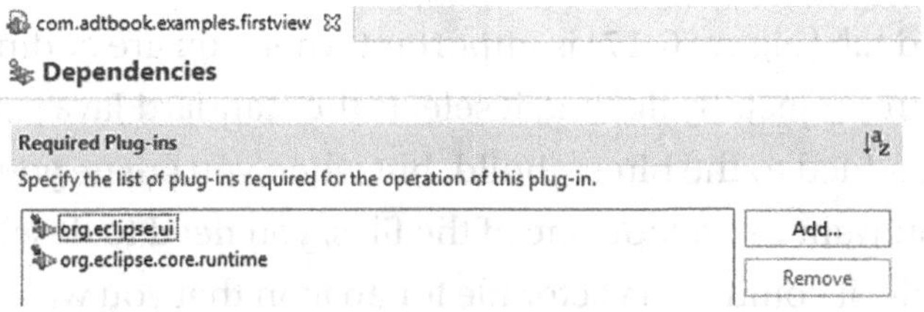

Figure 6-15. *Dependencies screen of plugin.xml*

I mentioned the Extensions while explaining extension possibilities. The Extensions tab (Figure 6-16) shows you all extension points you have already used. In the past, I preferred to go directly into the `plugin.xml` tab, where I could see all the details as XML nodes, but now I use it more and more. At this stage, I will omit the Extension Points, tab as it is empty in this example plugin. I will cover it later.

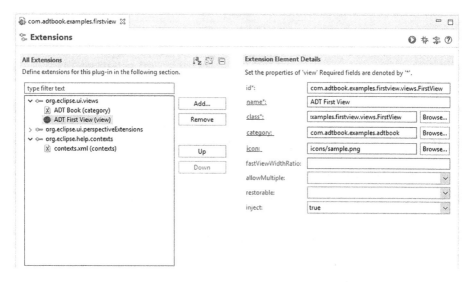

Figure 6-16. *Extensions used in the current plugin*

The Build tab (Figure 6-17) is important when you are adding resource folders to your project. By default, it selects the standard Java project folders to be added to the binary build, but when you create your own folders or you want to exclude one of the files, you need to deselect it here. As an example, it could be a vector file for an icon that you want to put in your project and commit to your Git repository. You might not want to put it into the plugin, as it is unnecessary and will only make the plugin binary files larger.

Binary Build	
Select the folders and files to include in the binary build.	

```
☐ ☒ .classpath
☐ 🗋 .gitignore
☐ ☒ .project
> ☐ 🗁 .settings
> ☑ 🗁 META-INF
> ☐ 🗁 bin
☐ 🗃 build.properties
☑ 🗋 contexts.xml
> ☑ 🗁 icons
☑ 🗋 plugin.xml
> ☐ 🗁 src
```

Source Build	
Select the folders and files to include in the source build.	

```
☐ ☒ .classpath
☐ 🗋 .gitignore
☐ ☒ .project
> ☐ 🗁 .settings
> ☐ 🗁 META-INF
> ☐ 🗁 bin
☐ 🗃 build.properties
☐ 🗋 contexts.xml
> ☐ 🗁 icons
☐ 🗋 plugin.xml
> ☐ 🗁 src
```

Figure 6-17. *Build configuration of the plugin*

The plugin.xml tab will contain an XML version of the plugin configuration (Listing 6-1). It contains information about the target eclipse version as well as all the used extension points. It can also contain the extension point definition, but in this example plugin, we do not have any. We can say that this tab is an XML representation of the Extensions and Extension Points tabs.

Listing 6-1. Plugin.xml code Visible in the plugin.xml Tab

```xml
<?xml version="1.0" encoding="UTF-8"?>
<?eclipse version="3.4"?>
<plugin>
<extension point="org.eclipse.ui.views">
  <category name="ADT Book"
            id="com.adtbook.examples.adtbook">
  </category>
  <view id="com.adtbook.examples.firstview.views.FirstView"
        name="ADT First View"
        icon="icons/sample.png"
        class="com.adtbook.examples.firstview.views.FirstView"
        category="com.adtbook.examples.adtbook"
        inject="true">
  </view>
</extension>
```

```
<extension point="org.eclipse.ui.perspectiveExtensions">
  <perspectiveExtension
            targetID="org.eclipse.jdt.ui.JavaPerspective">
  <view id="com.adtbook.examples.firstview.views.FirstView"
      relative="org.eclipse.ui.views.ProblemView"
      relationship="right"
      ratio="0.5">
  </view>
  </perspectiveExtension>
</extension>
<extension point="org.eclipse.help.contexts">
   <contexts file="contexts.xml"></contexts>
</extension>
</plugin>
```

Plugin Code

Now it is time to go through the generated plugin code in order to get an idea about how it works. Let's start with the `Activator.java` file, which is responsible for the lifecycle of the plugin. As I mentioned before, is called when your plugin is used the first time and when Eclipse closes.

When you double-click the file, it will be opened in the editor, just like with the ABAP objects, but this time it will be in the Java editor. In principal, most functions that you learned in ABAP editor will work in the Java editor as well. That includes, among others, code completion, quick fixes, and setting up breakpoints. You need to learn to read the Java code if you do not know it yet, but you will see that learning another programming language is not difficult when you already know one.

Activator.java

The first few lines of the `Activator.java` file contain package information and imported types (Listing 6-2). You will see this in all Java files. The `import` statement is like the `TYPE-POOLS` in ABAP. When you want to use a certain type, you need to declare it, like it was for `TYPE-POOLS` in older releases. The only difference is that in Java, you are allowed to import only certain types, for example `AbstractUIPlugin`, or you can import all types from a package. To import all types from a package, you need to use the * wildcard instead of a specific name.

Listing 6-2. Package Information and Imported Types of the Activator Class

```
package com.adtbook.examples.firstview;

import org.eclipse.ui.plugin.AbstractUIPlugin;
import org.osgi.framework.BundleContext;
```

Declaration and implementation of the class in Java is not separated like in ABAP. When you look at Listing 6-3, you can see that besides the name of the class, there is information about the `AbstractUIPlugin` superclass that Activator is extending (inheriting from).

Listing 6-3. Activator Class Definition

```
public class Activator extends AbstractUIPlugin
```

Below the class definition, you will find some constants and methods definition and implementations. As with case of a class, method definition and implementation is done in the same place. Listing 6-4 shows the constructor of the class (a method called exactly the same as a class) and two methods, `start` and `stop`. The `start` method runs when any part of the plugin is called the first time, a maximum of one time per Eclipse session. The `stop` method is called when you close Eclipse.

Listing 6-4. Constructor, Start, and Stop Methods of Activator

```
public Activator() { }

@Override
public void start(BundleContext context)
          throws Exception {
    super.start(context);
    plugin = this; }

@Override
public void stop(BundleContext context)
          throws Exception {
    plugin = null;
    super.stop(context); }
```

FirstView.java

The second and the last Java file created by the wizard is `FirstView.java`. It contains the code for the *ADT* First View. This code is not fully created according to the clean code rules, but it will show you the main steps that need to be done to create a view. It contains fewer than 200 lines, which should make it easy to understand, but let me go through the most important parts of this class.

One of the two public methods of the `FirstView` class is `createPartControl`, which is overridden (redefined) from the `ViewPart` class. This method is responsible for implementing a view specific presentation (look). This means you can define:

- Which Standard Widget Toolkit (SWT) controls are visible on the view as well as their listeners (event handlers), content, selection, and label providers

- The View toolbar and its actions

- The View menu and its actions

- The Context menu and its actions

You will use this method when you create a new view for your plugin, so it is good to know its possibilities. Even if the plugin you create is not fancy one, it presents lots of the capabilities of the views. In our example (Listing 6-5), the first thing we do is create TableViewer, which can be compared to ALV grid in ABAP.

Listing 6-5. The createPartControl Method of the FirstView Class

```
@Override
public void createPartControl(Composite parent) {
    viewer = new TableViewer(parent,
            SWT.MULTI | SWT.H_SCROLL | SWT.V_SCROLL);

    viewer.setContentProvider(
                ArrayContentProvider.getInstance());
    viewer.setInput(
                new String[] { "One", "Two", "Three" });
    viewer.setLabelProvider(new ViewLabelProvider());
    // Create the help context id for the viewer's
    // control
    workbench.getHelpSystem().setHelp(
            viewer.getControl(),
            "com.adtbook.examples.firstview.viewer");
    getSite().setSelectionProvider(viewer);
    makeActions();
    hookContextMenu();
    hookDoubleClickAction();
    contributeToActionBars(); }
```

After creating the TableViewer, you can see that Content Provider is assigned to the viewer object. Content Provider is responsible for assigning and updating the source data of your controls. You will use it in many places when you are using SWT controls, but most probably more complex than the one in the example, where the input values are hardcoded. But we will cover this later.

The second action done with TableViewer is assigning the Label Provider, which is responsible for the way the content provider entries are displayed on the viewer. For example, by assigning proper icon and text.

Next, the ID of the help context is assigned to the control. This ID com. adtbook.examples.firstview.viewer consists of the plugin ID and the unique ID in that package. In our case, it will be com.adtbook.examples. firstview and viewer, respectively. You can find the definition of the help context extension in the Extensions tab of the plugin.xml file editor, where you should see a link to the contexts.xml file. Locate that file in the main folder of your plugin (in Project Explorer) and double-click it. The context help editor will be opened (Figure 6-18) and the ID will be specified there.

Caution   It does not matter which package of the plugin you store your help context files. You always need to assign them in the code using the plugin ID and context ID.

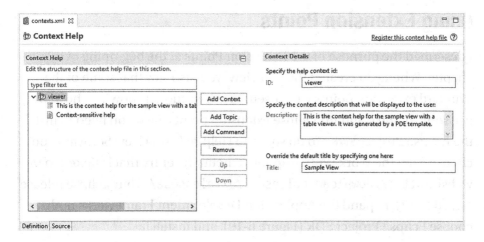

Figure 6-18. *Contexts.xml file editor for the context help*

On the next line, the code points the TableViewer object as the object responsible for giving information about the current selection on a view. Such an object function is called Selection Provider. In our example, the whole view is taken by the table viewer, that is why it is so easy. However, if you have two table viewers on the screen, you would need to switch the selection provider each time the focus changes between the two viewers.

The last four lines of the createPartControl method are strongly linked. The makeActions method creates all actions that will be used in the context menu, view menu, toolbar, and at double-click. When you go inside this method, you will notice that three actions are created with their specific action code. Two of them will simply call a message on the screen, while the doubleClickAction object will additionally read the selection from the viewer. Those three action objects are then later used in hookContextMenu, hookDoubleClickAction, and contributeToActionBars methods.

Before moving on, I recommend that you set up a few breakpoints and follow the initialization process of the plugin as well as call the actions. This will definitely clarify some points for you. You can set up breakpoints exactly the same way as in the ABAP editor.

Using Extension Points

I described the purpose of the Extension Points at the beginning of this chapter. When you created the first view, you also saw that some of the standard extension points were used. In this section, I show you how to use some of the standard Eclipse extension points. First you need to install the Eclipse Project SDK. To do so, go to Help ➤ Install New Software and choose from the Work With dropdown menu the entry that is linked to the website http://download.eclipse.org/releasese/ (your Eclipse release e.g. 2020-12). Expand the Application Development Frameworks node, choose Eclipse Project SDK (Figure 6-19), and install it.

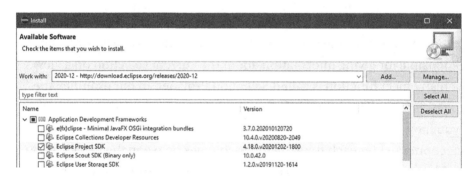

Figure 6-19. *Installing the Eclipse Project SDK*

Although this step is officially not mandatory to extend Eclipse, it will be extremely helpful. I will explain why when you're creating the view.

Views

When we created the plugin using the wizard, the view was created for us using the extension point org.eclipse.ui.views. Let me now guide you through the process of creating the views and handlers manually.

First of all, create a new plugin project called ExtPointView and add it to the same working set as the FirstView plugin. This time, use

the following ID for your plugin: `com.adtbook.examples.extpointview`
(Figure 6-20). You can also adapt the path for the activator class or
disable its generation. Then click the Finish button, as we will not use the
templates this time.

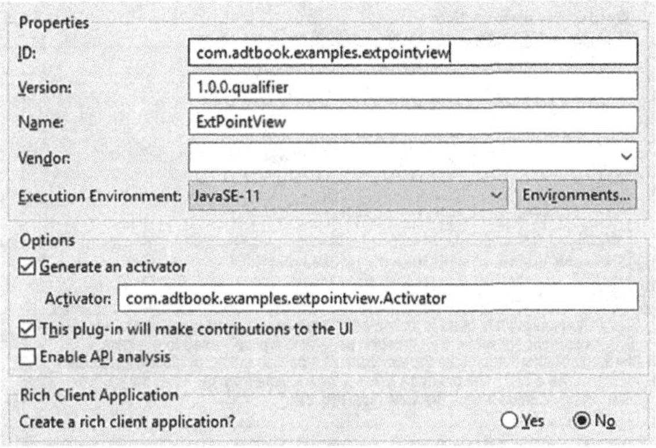

Figure 6-20. *ExtPointView plugin settings*

Now go to the Extensions tab of the plugin editor and click the Add
button to select the extension point. In the Extension Point Filter field, type
`view`, select `org.eclipse.ui.views`, and click the Finish button (Figure 6-21).

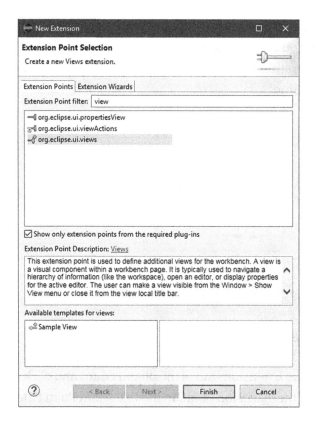

Figure 6-21. *Extension Point selection wizard*

Now the extension is added to the list. When you select it from the Extension Details area, you will notice the input fields ID and Name (both optional), as well as three very important links: Show Extension Point Description, Open Extension Point Schema, and Find Declaring Extension Point (Figure 6-22).

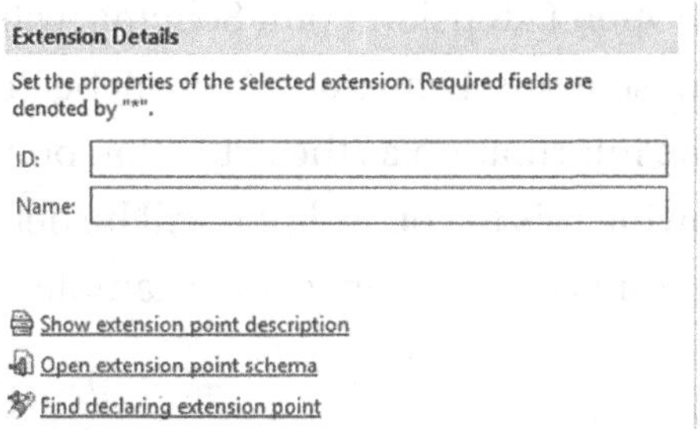

Figure 6-22. *Extension details area*

If you do not install the Eclipse Plugin SDK, after using the Show Extension Point Description and Open Extension Point Schema links, you would get a message that the Extension Point Description and Schema is not available.

If the SDK is installed, after using the Show Extension Point Description link, a new browser tab with an HTML description of the extension point will be shown (Figure 6-23). It should contain information about the elements of the extension, as well as a description of the parameters and examples of usage.

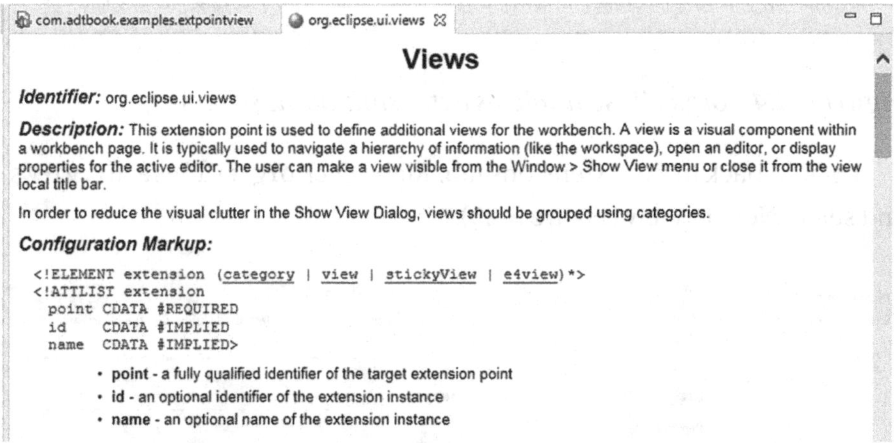

Figure 6-23. *org.eclipse.ui.views extension point description*

The second link, Open Extension Point Schema, will open an editor of the extension point scheme (Figure 6-24). It will be in read-only mode and will give the same information as the extension point description. The reason that I am showing this to you is that it will be helpful when creating your own extension points as a reference and example.

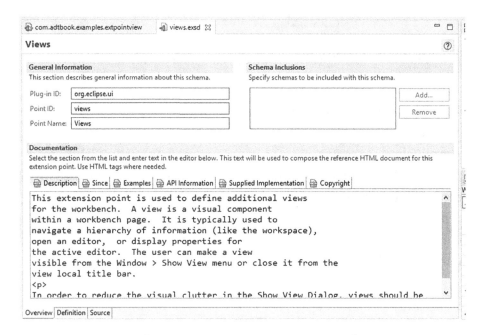

Figure 6-24. *org.eclipse.ui.views extension point scheme*

Let's go back to the Extensions tab. Right-click `org.eclipse.ui.views` and select New ➤ View (Figure 6-25).

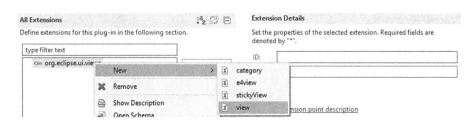

Figure 6-25. *Adding a new view*

The ID of the view, name, and class will be set to default values, which you should adapt and set as shown in Figure 6-26. To select the icon, simply open the Plug-in Image Browser view, which I have shown in the first chapter, pick any icon that you like, and paste the reference to it into the Icon field. In the Category field, I put the ID of the category that I created when creating the FirstView plugin. If you chose a different name at that stage, browse and select the proper category ID.

Extension Element Details

Set the properties of 'view' Required fields are denoted by '*'.

id*:	com.adtbook.examples.extpointview.view1
name*:	View 1 of ExtPointView plugin
class*:	com.adtbook.examples.extpointview.views.View1 [Browse...]
category:	com.adtbook.examples.adtbook [Browse...]
icon:	platform:/plugin/org.eclipse.wst.xsd.ui/org/eclipse/wst/xsd/ui/internal/editor/icons/XSDInclude.gif [Browse...]
fastViewWidthRatio:	
allowMultiple:	false ∨
restorable:	true ∨
inject:	true ∨

Figure 6-26. *View extension details*

Although we provided a name for the view class, it does not exist yet. We can easily create it by clicking the class*: link to call the wizard that will create a class that inherits from org.eclipse.ui.part.ViewPart (Figure 6-27). Now it is enough to click the Finish button. The View1.java file will be opened in the editor. Close it, as we will not add code in this example.

Source folder:	ExtPointView/src	Browse...
Package:	com.adtbook.examples.extpointview.views	Browse...
☐ Enclosing type:		Browse...
Name:	View1	
Modifiers:	⦿ public ○ package ○ private ○ protected	
	☐ abstract ☐ final ☐ static	
Superclass:	org.eclipse.ui.part.ViewPart	Browse...
Interfaces:		Add...
		Remove

Figure 6-27. *View class generation wizard*

Go back to the Extension tab, select the view node, and then right-click and select New ➤ Description. In the Body Text field in the Extension Element Details, add a description of the view (Figure 6-28).

Figure 6-28. *Description of the view*

Now select the `org.eclipse.ui.views` node and repeat the steps for creating a new view again, adapting the ID, name, class, and icon for it. After this is done, simply use the Eclipse run configuration that you created in the previous steps. When the test environment starts, go to Window ➤ Show View ➤ Others and search for the `ADT  Book` folder. After expanding it, the two additional views will be visible (Figure 6-29). If you hover over one of the two new views, a tooltip with its description will appear on the screen.

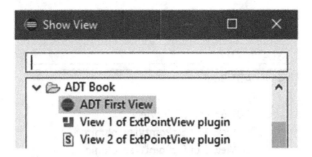

Figure 6-29. *Two additional views in the ADT Book category*

Now close the test environment and go back to the Extensions tab again. Select the `org.eclipse.ui.views` node and right-click it, but this time select New ➤ Category. In the details area, replace the default ID of the category with `com.adtbook.examples.extpointview.category` and the default name with the ADT Book ExtPointView (Figure 6-30). Now put this new category ID in both views of your plugin. Save your changes and run the test environment again.

Extension Element Details

Set the properties of 'category' Required fields are denoted by '*'.

id*:	com.adtbook.examples.extpointview.category	
name*:	ADT Book ExtPointView	
parentCategory:		Browse...

Figure 6-30. *ADT Book ExtPointView category details*

When you open the Show View window, both of the views will be placed in the new folder ADT Book ExtPointView (Figure 6-31).

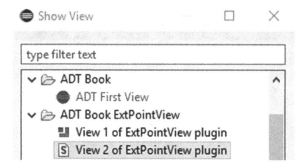

Figure 6-31. *New category ADT Book ExtPointView with two views*

Menus, Toolbars, Commands, and Handlers

If you come back to the FirstView plugin, you will notice that to create the toolbar and the menu on the view, the wizard used the view class for that. It is one of the ways to create them, but with complex developments, it will be easier to create and maintain the menus and toolbars using the extension point org.eclipse.ui.menus.

This extension point can be used not only to adapt your own view toolbar and menus, but also to add entries on:

- Main Eclipse menu

- Main Eclipse toolbars

- Other views menus

- Other views toolbars

Own View Toolbar

Let's start with our own view toolbar. Open the Extensions tab of the ExtPointView plugin and click the Add button to add org.eclipse. ui.menus to the extension list. Right-click the new entry and select New ➤ menuContribution. Replace the value found in the locationURI field with the ID of the View1. If you used the same naming system as me, it is called `toolbar:com.adtbook.examples.extpointview.view1` (Figure 6-32).

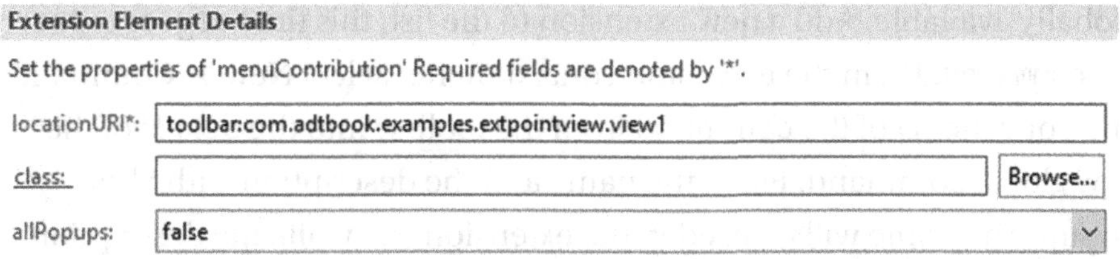

Extension Element Details

Set the properties of 'menuContribution' Required fields are denoted by '*'.

locationURI*:	toolbar:com.adtbook.examples.extpointview.view1
class:	[ ] Browse...
allPopups:	false

Figure 6-32. *Toolbar location URI for your own view*

Now select the toolbar entry on the extension list, right-click and select New ➤ Command. Fill the Label field with Show Popup Message, the commandId field with `com.adtbook.examples.extpointview.commands.ShowPopup`, and the Style field with Push (Figure 6-33). Leave the other fields empty, as we will define them in another extension soon as global settings for this command ID.

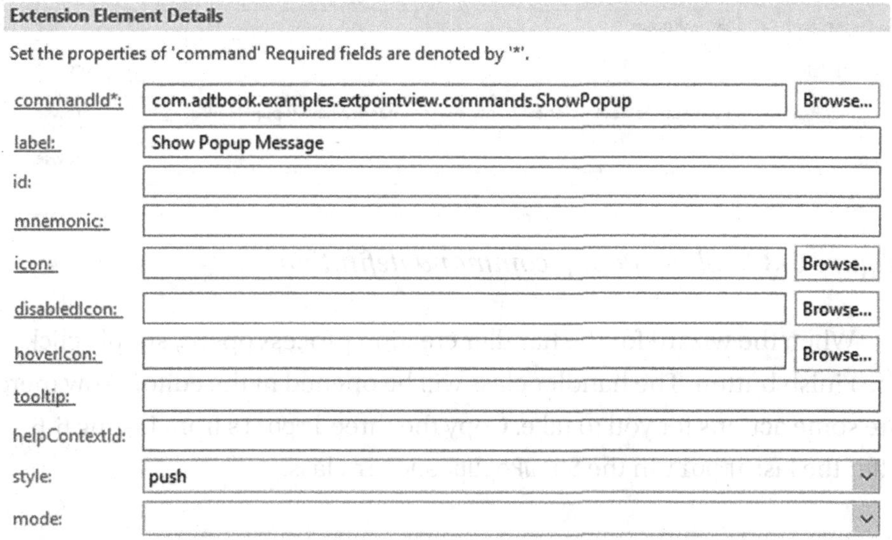

Extension Element Details

Set the properties of 'command' Required fields are denoted by '*'.

commandId*:	com.adtbook.examples.extpointview.commands.ShowPopup Browse...
label:	Show Popup Message
id:	
mnemonic:	
icon:	Browse...
disabledIcon:	Browse...
hoverIcon:	Browse...
tooltip:	
helpContextId:	
style:	push
mode:	

Figure 6-33. *Toolbar command details for ShowPopup*

If you run the test environment now, your command would be visible on the view toolbar, but disabled. This is because this command has no handler defined. Before defining the handler, let's create our command as globally available. Add a new extension to the list, this time `org.eclipse.ui.commands`. From the extension context menu, select New ➤ Command and copy the ID of the command from the toolbar into the details of the new global command. Fill in the name and the description with Show Popup. The name will be used in the extension list, while the description will serve as a tooltip for our command.

Copy the `com.adtbook.examples.extpointview.commands.ShowPopupHandler` value to the `defaultHandler` field (Figure 6-34) and click its label to create the handler class.

Extension Element Details

Set the properties of 'command'. Required fields are denoted by '*'. Deprecated fields are denoted by '(!)'.

id*:	com.adtbook.examples.extpointview.commands.ShowPopup	
name*:	Show Popup	
category(!):		
description:	Show Popup	
categoryId:		Browse...
defaultHandler:	com.adtbook.examples.extpointview.commands.ShowPopupHandler	Browse...
returnTypeId:		Browse...
helpContextId:		

Figure 6-34. *Show Popup command definition*

When the wizard for the handler creation process opens, simply click the Finish button. The handler class will be opened in the editor. Now there are some actions for you to take. Copy the three `imports` from Listing 6-6 after the last `import` in the `ShowPopupHandler` class.

Listing 6-6. Imports to Be Added to the ShowPopupHandler Class

```
import org.eclipse.swt.SWT;
import org.eclipse.swt.widgets.MessageBox;
import org.eclipse.ui.handlers.HandlerUtil;
```

In the next step, replace the code of the execute, isEnabled, and isHandled methods with the code from Listing 6-7 and save the file.

Listing 6-7. Code of the Execute, isEnabled, and isHandled Methods

```
@Override
public Object execute(ExecutionEvent event)
            throws ExecutionException {
    MessageBox popup = new MessageBox(
            HandlerUtil.getActiveShellChecked(event),
                        SWT.OK);
    popup.setText("This is a title");
    popup.setMessage("Show popup command was triggered");
    popup.open();
    return null;
}

@Override
public boolean isEnabled() {
    return true;
}

@Override
public boolean isHandled() {
    return true;
}
```

Come back to the Extensions tab and add one more extension, this time to decorate the command with an icon: `org.eclipse.ui.commandImages`. Use the context menu on it to add an image node (New ➤ Image). Now select an icon from the Plug-in Image Browser view and paste it into the Icon field (Figure 6-35).

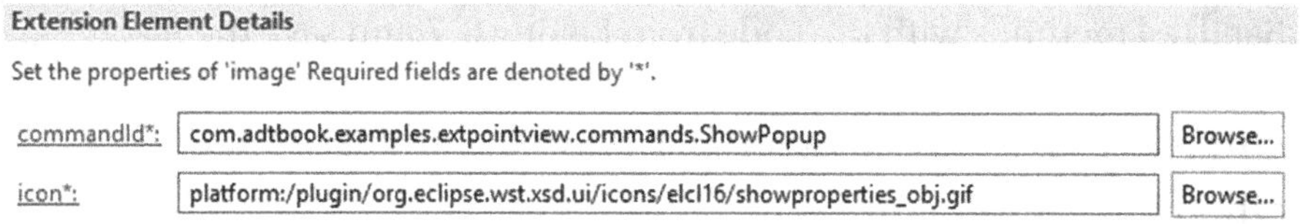

Figure 6-35. *The org.eclipse.ui.commandImages extension details for the Show Popup command*

Save the changes and run the test environment. When you open the view called View1 of ExtPointView plugin, you will see the icon you selected on the view toolbar (Figure 6-36).

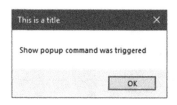

Figure 6-36. *The Show Popup command on the toolbar of the View1 of ExtPointView plugin*

After clicking the button, a popup message from the `ShowPopupHandler` class will appear on the screen (Figure 6-37).

Figure 6-37. *Popup message from the ShowPopupHandler class*

Third Party View Toolbar

When we added a command to our view, we had to pass the full ID of the view to the locationURI field. We need to determine the ID of the view we want to extend.

Open the Feed Reader view and place a cursor in it. Now call Plug-in Selection Spy by using the key combination Alt+Shift+F1. You will receive a popup screen with the active view details, including the active view identifier, which you should copy (Figure 6-38).

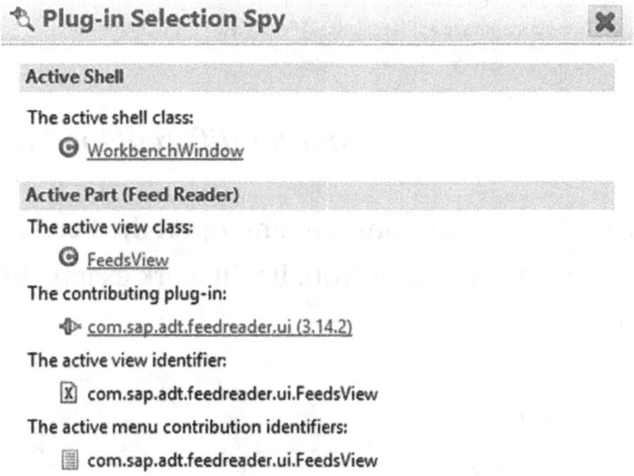

Figure 6-38. *Plug-in Selection Spy on the Feed Reader of ADT*

Now go to the Extensions tab and create new entry for `org.eclipse.ui.menus`. This time, add the ID of the Feed Reader to the locationURI field (this is `toolbar:com.sap.adt.feedreader.ui.FeedsView`). See Figure 6-39.

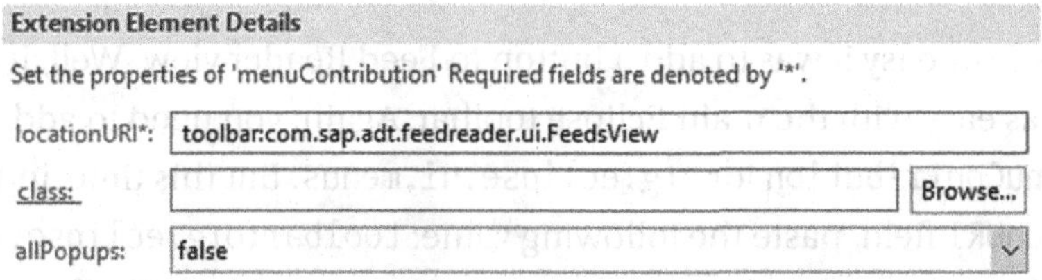

Figure 6-39. *Extension details for Feed Reader view*

Once this is done, copy the Show Popup Message command from the toolbar for your own view and paste it into the toolbar for Feed Reader (Figure 6-40).

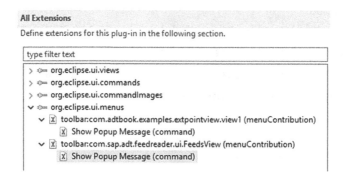

Figure 6-40. *Duplicated commands for different toolbar extensions*

When you run the test environment and open the Feed Reader view, you will notice the Show Popup button. It will work exactly like our own view (Figure 6-41).

Figure 6-41. *Feed Reader view of ADT with the Show Popup button*

Main Eclipse Toolbar

You saw how easy it was to add a button to Feed Reader view. Well, it is almost as easy with the main Eclipse toolbar. Again, you need to add a new `menuContribution` for `org.eclipse.ui.menus`. But this time, in the `locationURI` field, paste the following value: `toolbar:org.eclipse.ui.main.toolbar`. Now use the context menu on it, add the Toolbar node, and give the `com.adtbook.examples.ExtPointView.toolbar` ID to it. The last step is to copy the Show Popup Message command and paste it as a child. Your extensions list should have the hierarchy shown in Figure 6-42.

> ∨ ⬦ org.eclipse.ui.menus
>   ∨ [x] toolbar:com.adtbook.examples.extpointview.view1 (menuContribution)
>   [x] Show Popup Message (command)
>   ∨ [x] toolbar:com.sap.adt.feedreader.ui.FeedsView (menuContribution)
>   [x] Show Popup Message (command)
>   ∨ [x] toolbar:org.eclipse.ui.main.toolbar (menuContribution)
>   ∨ [x] com.adtbook.examples.ExtPointView.toolbar (toolbar)
>   [x] Show Popup Message (command)

Figure 6-42. *Main toolbar extension on the extensions list*

After running the test environment, you will see the Show Popup button on the main Eclipse toolbar (Figure 6-43).

Figure 6-43. *Main Eclipse toolbar with the Show Popup button*

View Menu

If you want to add the command to the View menu, the difference is really small. It is enough to put `menu:` instead of `toolbar:` before the view ID in the `locationURI` field of the `menuContribution` element.

As you already have the extensions for your own view and the Feed Reader view, you simply copy and paste it and update the `locationURI` values for the new entries. Save your changes and check these two views in the test environment. This simple command will be added to the menu of both views (Figure 6-44).

Figure 6-44. *Feed Reader view with the Show Popup command in the view menu*

Main Eclipse Menu

Extending the main Eclipse menu is very similar to extending the main toolbar. Create the menuContribution entry next, but this time in the locationURI, paste the menu:org.eclipse.ui.main.menu value. Select this entry and use the context menu to select New ➤ Menu. Set the value of *Label* to ADT Book and add the following path to the Icon field: platform:/plugin/org.eclipse.help.ui/icons/obj16/bookmarks_view.png. Now copy the Show Popup Message to the newly created menu as a child and then save and run it. The menu is very catchy to the eyes (Figure 6-45).

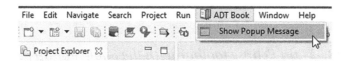

Figure 6-45. *Extended main menu of the Eclipse: New menu*

If you want to put the command into an existing menu, you need to find the menu ID and the name of the command. Choose Plug-in Menu Spy using the Alt+Shift+F2 key combination. Do not be surprised if, after pressing this combination, nothing appears on the screen, only mouse pointer icon changes. Navigate to the Help menu and click the Welcome option (Figure 6-46).

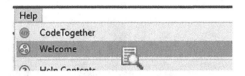

Figure 6-46. *Plug-in Menu Spy command selection*

As a result, you will get the popup screen similar to the one you saw when using Plug-in Selection Spy. Again you should copy the active contribution location URI (Figure 6-47). Notice that, besides the menu ID (help), there is an ?after=intro, which is responsible for placing your own command after the intro (the command ID of Welcome).

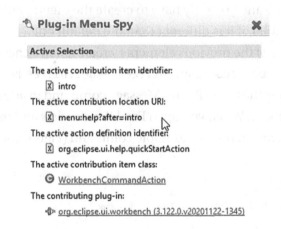

Figure 6-47. *Plug-in Menu Spy details of the Help ➤ Welcome command*

Now that you have the locationURI, create a menuContribution using it. Once you're done, copy the Show Popup Message command to it, then choose ADT Book menu and run the test environment. When you expand the Help menu, you will see the Show Popup Message button and the ADT Book menu placed after the Welcome button (Figure 6-48).

Figure 6-48. *Help menu with the new button and submenu*

Context / Popup Menu

The last thing that you can do with the ***org.eclipse.ui.menus*** extension point is create and adapt the context menus, either for you own or for third-party plugins. With third-party plugins, it will be easier, as the menu is already in place and you only have to create the menu contribution and a command handler, if it is different than the default one.

As in the case of the previous elements, create a new `menuContribution`, but this time use `popup:com.sap.adt.feedreader.ui.FeedsView` as the locationURI. Copy the Show Popup Message command inside it and run the test environment. When you open Feed Reader view and use the context menu, you can see and use our example command (Figure 6-49).

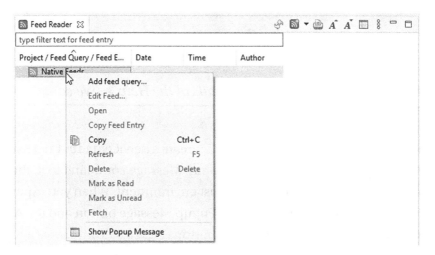

Figure 6-49. *Feed Reader view with the Show Popup Message on the context menu*

Now we need to deal with more a complex scenario, as we will not only create a context menu for our own view, but will also create a second handler for our Show Popup Message command that will be used only when the focus is set on our view.

As a first step, copy the menuContribution from Feed Reader, paste it as a new entry, and replace the existing locationURI with the ***popup:com.adtbook.examples.extpointview.view1*** value.

Open the View1 class and replace its code with the contents of Listing 6-8. In the new code, you will see two main things. One is the createTreeViewer method, where the TableViewer control with two columns inside and three rows is created.

The second important method is createAndRegisterMenu. This method is responsible for creating MenuManager and Menu, assigning the menu to our control, registering the context menu, and setting the table viewer as the selection provider. This may seem awful to you, but you need to get used to the Java way of development if you want to create plugins in Eclipse.

Listing 6-8. View1 with TableViewer Control and Context Menu Manager

```
package com.adtbook.examples.extpointview.views;

import org.eclipse.jface.action.MenuManager;
import org.eclipse.jface.viewers.ArrayContentProvider;
import org.eclipse.jface.viewers.ColumnLabelProvider;
import org.eclipse.jface.viewers.TableViewer;
import org.eclipse.jface.viewers.TableViewerColumn;
import org.eclipse.swt.SWT;
import org.eclipse.swt.widgets.Composite;
import org.eclipse.swt.widgets.Menu;
import org.eclipse.swt.widgets.Table;
import org.eclipse.ui.part.ViewPart;
```

```java
public class View1 extends ViewPart {
 private TableViewer tableViewer;

 public class TableRow {
   public int id;
   public String name;

   public TableRow(int id, String name) {
      this.id = id;
      this.name = name; }
      }

@Override
public void createPartControl(Composite parent) {
 createTreeViewerAndItsMenu(parent); }

 private void createTreeViewerAndItsMenu(Composite parent) {
 createTreeViewer(parent);
 createAndRegisterMenu(getTable()); }

 private void createAndRegisterMenu(Table table) {
 MenuManager menuManager = new MenuManager();
 Menu menu = menuManager.createContextMenu(table);
 table.setMenu(menu);

 getSite().registerContextMenu(menuManager, tableViewer);
 getSite().setSelectionProvider(tableViewer); }

 private void createColumns() {
 createIdColumn();
 createNameColumn(); }

 private Table getTable() {
 Table table = tableViewer.getTable();
 table.setHeaderVisible(true);
```

```
table.setLinesVisible(true);
return table; }

private void createTreeViewer(Composite parent) {
  tableViewer = new TableViewer(parent, SWT.MULTI
      | SWT.FULL_SELECTION | SWT.H_SCROLL | SWT.V_SCROLL);
  tableViewer.setContentProvider(ArrayContentProvider
                    .getInstance());
  createColumns();
  tableViewer.setInput(getContent()); }

private void createNameColumn() {
  TableViewerColumn nameColumn = new TableViewerColumn(
                    tableViewer, SWT.NONE);
  nameColumn.getColumn().setText("Name");
  nameColumn.getColumn().setWidth(200);
  nameColumn.getColumn().setMoveable(true);
  nameColumn.setLabelProvider(new ColumnLabelProvider() {
      @Override
      public String getText(Object element) {
              return ((TableRow) element).name;}
        });
    }

private void createIdColumn() {
  TableViewerColumn idColumn = new TableViewerColumn(
                    tableViewer, SWT.NONE);
  idColumn.getColumn().setText("ID");
  idColumn.getColumn().setWidth(50);
  idColumn.getColumn().setMoveable(true);
  idColumn.setLabelProvider(new ColumnLabelProvider() {
          @Override
```

```
    public String getText(Object element) {
        return String.valueOf(((TableRow) element).id);}
    });
}

@Override
public void setFocus() {
 tableViewer.getControl().setFocus(); }

private TableRow[] getContent() {
 return new TableRow[] { new TableRow(1, "First row"),
                         new TableRow(2, "Second row"),
                         new TableRow(3, "Third row"), };
                                }
}
```

If you the test environment now, you would see a table viewer in View1, as shown in Figure 6-50. After using the context menu, the simple popup will appear, as in all the previous cases.

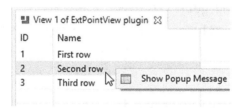

Figure 6-50. *View1 with the TableViewer control*

Second Command Handler

In most cases, when you run a command from the context menu, you want to take a specific action on a selection. To do so, the command handler needs to fetch the selected item and cast it to a proper type in order to be able to get information from it.

I now want you to create a command handler extension in the project. This time, switch the tab from Extensions to plugin.xml and paste the contents of Listing 6-9 before the </plugin> tag. In the pasted XML, you can see a new tag called <activeWhen>, which is used to tell Eclipse when the command handler specified in the <handler> tag needs to be used. In our example it will only be active when View1 has focus of the screen.

Listing 6-9. org.eclipse.ui.handlers Extension Point Details in the XML Version

```
<extension point="org.eclipse.ui.handlers">
<handler             class="com.adtbook.examples.extpointview.
commands.ShowPopupMen➥uHandler"
commandId="com.adtbook.examples.extpointview.commands.
ShowPop➥up">
<activeWhen>
 <with variable="activePartId">
  <equals value="com.adtbook.examples.extpointview.view1">
  </equals>
 </with>
</activeWhen>
</handler>
</extension>
```

Caution   Only one handler can be active at a time in Eclipse. When you have more than one handler for a command, you must use the <activeWhen> node of the handler settings in order to achieve planned functionality. Otherwise, you will get a message about conflicting handlers and the default handler will be always called.

As with the plugin.xml tab, we defined a new handler class, so we need to create it. You can come back to the Extensions tab to see if the changes applied in the XML are replicated in that tab and use the handler creation wizard from the extension details, or you can simply create a new ShowPopupMenuHandler class in the com.adtbook.examples. extpointview.commands package. When you're done, replace the code of the class with the one from Listing 6-10. In the execute method, you will find the static method call getCurrentStructuredSelection of the HandlerUtil class. This method is responsible for getting the structure selection object from any selection providers that are linked to the context menu that raise the command. As our table viewer allows multiple line selection, iteration over the selected entries is done in the next step. During this iteration, the casting to a View1.TableRow object type is done, so we can read the id and name attributes of our selected line.

Listing 6-10. The ShowPopupMenuHandler Class Code

```
package com.adtbook.examples.extpointview.commands;

import java.util.Iterator;

import org.eclipse.core.commands.AbstractHandler;
import org.eclipse.core.commands.ExecutionEvent;
import org.eclipse.core.commands.ExecutionException;
import org.eclipse.jface.viewers.IStructuredSelection;
import org.eclipse.swt.SWT;
import org.eclipse.swt.widgets.MessageBox;
import org.eclipse.ui.handlers.HandlerUtil;

import com.adtbook.examples.extpointview.views.View1;

public class ShowPopupMenuHandler extends AbstractHandler {

    @SuppressWarnings("unchecked")
    @Override
```

```
public Object execute(ExecutionEvent event)
                throws ExecutionException {
  IStructuredSelection structuredSelection = HandlerUtil
                    .getCurrentStructuredSelection(event);
    if (structuredSelection != null) {
      for (Iterator<Object> iterator = structuredSelection
            .iterator(); iterator.hasNext();) {
        View1.TableRow row = (View1.TableRow) iterator.next();
        showMessageBox(event, row);
                }
            }
    return null;
}

private void showMessageBox(ExecutionEvent event,
            View1.TableRow row) throws ExecutionException {

        MessageBox popup = new MessageBox(HandlerUtil
                    .getActiveShellChecked(event), SWT.OK);
        popup.setMessage("Row " + row.id + " " + row.name);
        popup.open(); }
}
```

To test the behavior of the two handlers (the default and the one defined just now), run the test environment and call the Show Popup Message command from the Feed Reader view and then from View1. In the case of Feed Reader, it will look same as before. In the case of View1, it will look like Figure 6-51. The logic that is contained in the second command handler will be used often.

Figure 6-51. *Popup message with information about the selected line*

Key Bindings

So far all the commands that we created were run from toolbars or menus, but you can also call some of them using key combinations. You can define the key combination that will call your command using the org.eclipse. ui.bindings extension point. Add this extension point to the extension lists and use its context menu to create a child node key.

In the details of the extension, set the Sequence to M1+M2+M3+}. M1 represents the Ctrl key in Windows/Linux or the Command key on the Mac. M2 is the Shift key and M3 is the Alt key on Windows/Linux or the Option key on the Mac.

Place org.eclipse.ui.defaultAcceleratorConfiguration into schemeId and com.adtbook.examples.extpointview.commands. ShowPopup into commandID. The given schemeId is the default scheme for the whole workbench and, as we left the contextID field empty, the key combination will work regardless of the active view or field (Figure 6-52). Run the test environment again and try the Ctrl+Alt+Shift+} key combination.

Extension Element Details

Set the properties of 'key' Required fields are denoted by '*'.

sequence*:	M1+M2+M3+}
schemeId*:	org.eclipse.ui.defaultAcceleratorConfiguration	Browse...
contextId:		Browse...
commandId:	com.adtbook.examples.extpointview.commands.ShowPopup	Browse...
platform:	
locale:	

Figure 6-52. *Details of the key node of org.eclipse.ui.bindings*

If you want the key binding to work only when your view is active, you need to add contextId, let it be com.adtbook.examples.extpointview. context. To use it, you need to open the View1.java file and add the import from Listing 6-11.

Listing 6-11. IContextService Import for View1.java

import org.eclipse.ui.contexts.IContextService;

Paste the method from Listing 6-12 into the View1 class and add the call of the method setKeyBindingContext to the createPartControl method.

Listing 6-12. Method for Activating the Key Binding Context in View1

```
private void setKeyBindingContext() {
 String id = "com.adtbook.examples.extpointview.context";
 IContextService contextService = (IContextService) getSite()
                    .getService(IContextService.class);
 contextService.activateContext(id);
}
```

Now run the test environment and use Ctrl+Alt+Shift+} again. This time it will only work if your active view is View1 of the ExtPointView Plugin.

Help

There are two ways to provide help to your users. One is contextual help, called with the F1 button, and the second is help table of contents. Contextual help, as the name says, is linked and updated when the screen focus changes. It can be linked either to the whole view or to a specific control on it. Help table of contents is used for browsing and searching.

Contextual Help

You saw an example of contextual help in the FirstView plugin, where the help was linked to a table viewer that was included in the view. You'll now learn how to create your own contextual help step by step.

We need to use the org.eclipse.help.context extension point and add a contexts child to it, for which we will set the filename to contexts.xml.

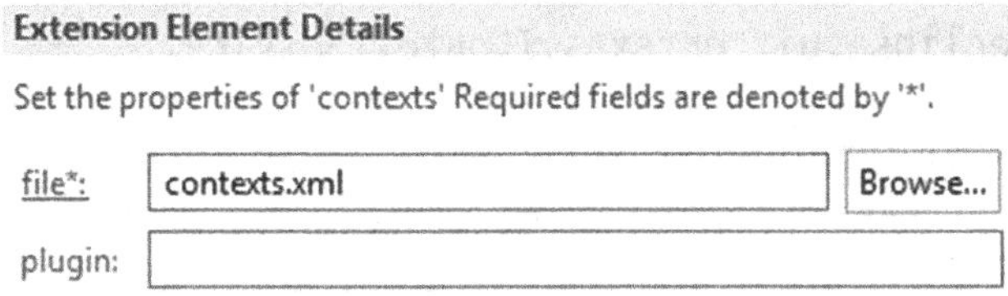

Extension Element Details

Set the properties of 'contexts' Required fields are denoted by '*'.

file*: [contexts.xml   ] [Browse...]
plugin: [   ]

Figure 6-53.   *Details of the org.eclipse.help.context extension*

Unfortunately, you cannot use the File Creation wizard directly from here; you need to go to Project Explorer, right-click the ExtPointView project, and select New ➤ Other from the context menu. Now find the User Assistance folder and select Context Help. Click Next (Figure 6-54).

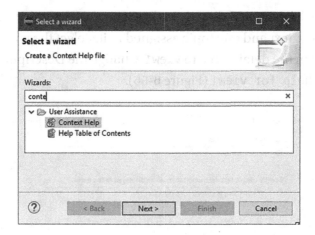

Figure 6-54. *File creation selection wizard: Context Help*

In the next wizard window, add `contexts.xml` as the filename and click the Finish button (Figure 6-55).

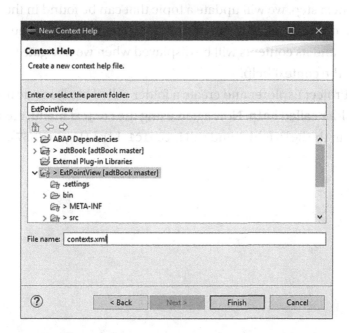

Figure 6-55. *Context Help wizard: filename and path selection*

The file will be opened directly in the Context Help Editor and it will contain one context and one topic assigned to it. Select the context and change its ID in the details area to View1. Change the Description to This is context help for view1 (Figure 6-56).

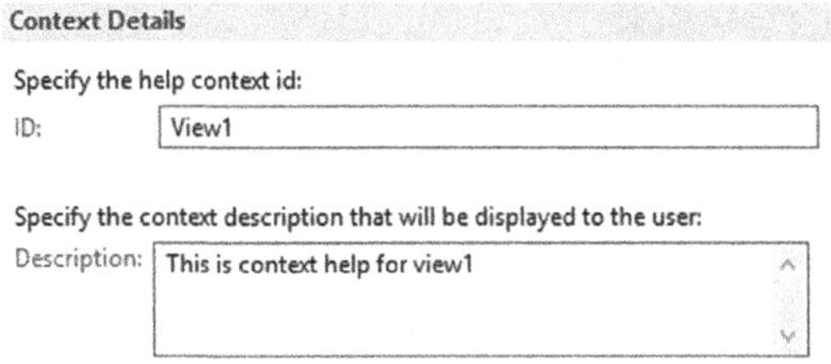

Context Details

Specify the help context id:

ID: `View1`

Specify the context description that will be displayed to the user:

Description: `This is context help for view1`

Figure 6-56. *Context details for View1*

Click the Add Context button and create a new context with the ID View2 and the description This is context help for view2.

In the next step, we will update a topic that can be found in the View1 context. To do so, we need to create an HTML file. This file will be assigned to the topic and its contents will be displayed when we navigate to the topic from the context help.

Go to Project Explorer and create a folder called html. Inside it, create another folder called help. Now again using the context menu, create an HTML file in the help folder and call it topic1.html (Figure 6-57).

Figure 6-57. *Creating the HTML file inside the help folder*

When the file opens in the editor, copy the code from Listing 6-13 and replace the code that was included in the file by the File Creation wizard. After that action, save and close the file.

Listing 6-13. HTML Code of the topic1.html File

```html
<!DOCTYPE html>
<html>
<head>
<meta charset="UTF-8">
<title>Insert title here</title>
</head>
<body>
<h1>Topic 1</h1>
<p>This is the first paragraph</p>
</body>
</html>
```

Come back to the `contexts.xml` file, select the existing topic inside the View1 context, and change it label to Topic 1 of the Help. As the next step, click the Browse button to select the location of the `topic1.html` file (Figure 6-58).

Figure 6-58. *Final version of the contexts.xml file*

The last step needed to make the context help available is to assign the context IDs to the controls. We can do this only in the code. As we were already adapting the View1 class a lot, now open the `View2.java` file and paste into it the code from Listing 6-14, replacing the existing code. In the `setHelpContext` method, you will see an assignment of the `parent` control to the context ID `com.adtbook.examples.extpointview.View2`. Now open the `View1.java` file and copy the `setHelpContext` method from View1, adapting the end of the context help ID to `View1`.

Listing 6-14. The View2.java File with the Context Help Assigned to the Whole View

```
package com.adtbook.examples.extpointview.views;

import org.eclipse.swt.widgets.Composite;
import org.eclipse.ui.PlatformUI;
import org.eclipse.ui.part.ViewPart;
```

```
public class View2 extends ViewPart {
 private Composite parent;

 @Override
 public void createPartControl(Composite parent) {
  this.parent = parent;
  setHelpContext(parent); }

 private void setHelpContext(Composite parent) {
  PlatformUI.getWorkbench().getHelpSystem().setHelp(parent,
     "com.adtbook.examples.extpointview.View2"); }

 @Override
 public void setFocus() {
  parent.setFocus(); }
}
```

You can now run the test environment to see what you have just done. When the test environment starts, open both views and use the F1 button on one of the views. If the selected view is View1, then besides the short description, you will also see the See Also area, where Topic 1 of the Help will be linked (Figure 6-59). If you select View2, then after focusing on View1, the context help will be directly updated.

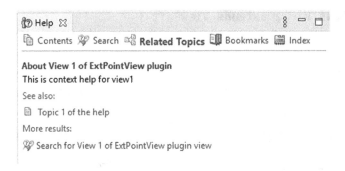

Figure 6-59. *Context help for View1*

Of course, if you click the Topic 1 of the help link, the simple HTML file you created will be displayed in the same window, as you can see in Figure 6-60.

Figure 6-60. *Topic1.html file displayed on the help view*

Help Table of Contents

The type of help is the Help Table of Contents. It is used mostly as plugin documentation and can be called from the main menu using Help ➤ Help Contents. To create your own table of contents, you need to use the `org.eclipse.help.toc` extension point, so add it to the plugin. Using the context menu, create the child element `toc`, set the filename to `defaultToc.xml`, and set Primary to true (Figure 6-61).

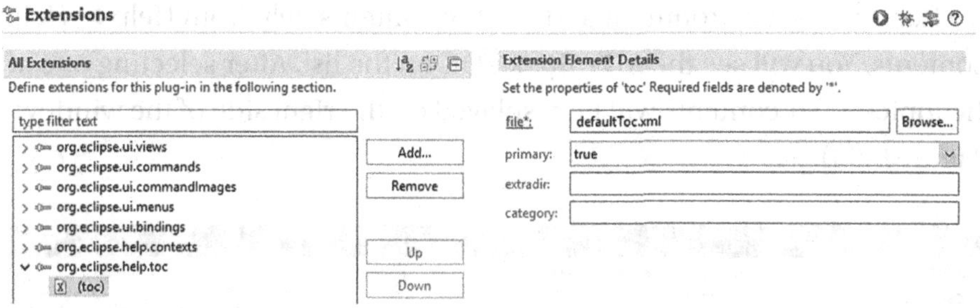

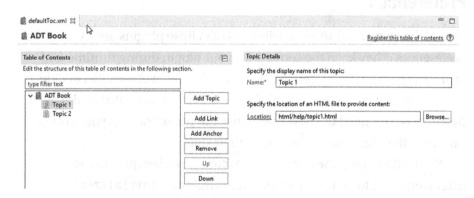

Figure 6-61. *Help Table of Contents extension*

Again you need to create a file from Project Explorer. This time, select the Help Table of Contents file type in the wizard, name it defaultToc.xml, and place it in the main folder of the plugin. After creating the file, it will be opened in the Table of Contents editor, which will look very similar to the Context Help editor. This time instead of the context ID, we will have name of the TOC, which you should set to ADT Book. Now add two topics, the first one linked to the topic1.html file we created for the context help. The second topic should be linked to the topic2.html file, which you should create based on the existing one.

Figure 6-62. *Table of Contents editor for the defaultToc.xml file*

Run the test environment and call the contents help from Help ➤ Help Contents. You will see the ADT Book TOC on the list. After selecting one of the topics, their contents will be displayed on the right side of the window (Figure 6-63).

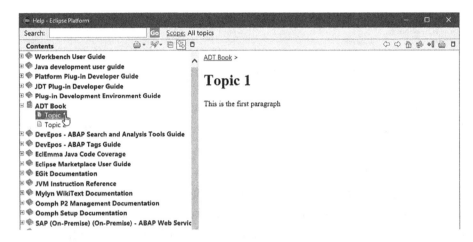

Figure 6-63. *ADT Book Table of Contents*

Preferences

One of the commonly used possibilities of Eclipse plugins are its preferences. They keep the settings for your plugin during runtime and to store them in the preferences files. As a plugin developer, you decide if the settings are maintainable only by the plugin code, or also by the users. Regardless, you need to know how to use the preferences in your code, how to define them, and how to save their state.

Start with adding the `org.eclipse.core.runtime.preferences` extension point to your project and then adding an `initializer` child for it. Then, add `com.adtbook.examples.extpointview.preferenceInitializer` to the Class field (Figure 6-64) and click the class link to create a new file with the handler of the preference initializer.

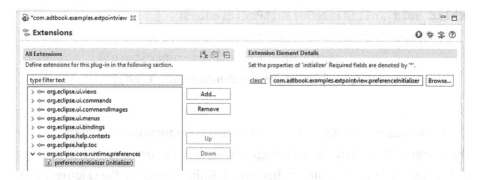

Figure 6-64. *Preference initializer extension definition*

The file will contain single method that you need to override, called initializeDefaultPreferences. This method is executed when your plugin wants to read the preferences the first time and its purpose is to save the default values for each of your preferences. These default values can then be restored when needed.

Preferences have a name and value, where the name is a string and value can take one of the types: Boolean, Int, Double, Long, Float, or String. These types should be enough to store your preferences.

Let's create our first preference. Go to the preferenceInitializer class and replace the existing method with the code from Listing 6-15. In this code, the definition of the ShowPopupWhenOpened preference name is a public constant, so we can reuse it afterwards. When initializing the default parameters, the preferences store object is created and the default value of the preference is set to true.

Listing 6-15. The Body of the preferenceInitializer Class

```
public static final String
    ShowPopupWhenOpened = "ShowPopupWhenOpened";
@Override
```

```
public void initializeDefaultPreferences() {
    final IPreferenceStore store = Activator
                    .getDefault().getPreferenceStore();
    store.setDefault(ShowPopupWhenOpened, true);
}
```

At this stage, the Java compiler may give you information that the IPreferenceStore type is not recognizable. Place a cursor on it and use Ctrl+1 (Quick Assist) to import this type definition into the file (Figure 6-65). The compiler will not show any errors anymore and the code can be used.

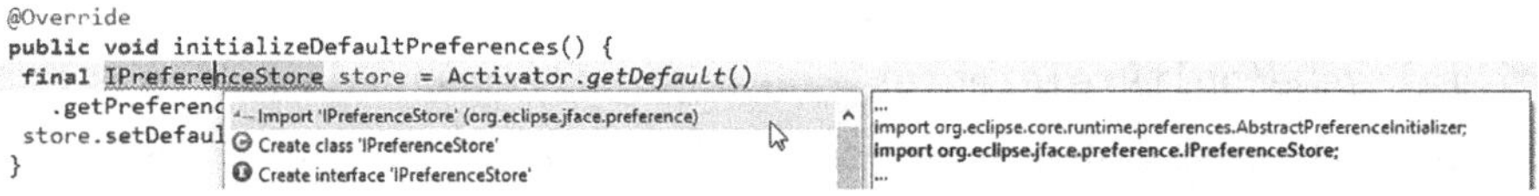

Figure 6-65. *Quick Assist for importing the needed references*

Now open the Activator file. We will use it to read the preferences when opening one of our views and running our ShowPopup command. Once the file's code is loaded to the editor, paste the imports from Listing 6-16 into the file.

Listing 6-16. Imports Needed to Use Preferences and to Call a Command

```
import org.eclipse.jface.preference.IPreferenceStore;
import org.eclipse.ui.PlatformUI;
import org.eclipse.ui.handlers.IHandlerService;
import org.eclipse.ui.services.IServiceLocator;
```

Now paste the two private methods from Listing 6-17 into the implementation of the Activator class. The shouldShowPopup method is used to read the value of the ShowPopupWhenOpened preference, whereas executeCommand gets and uses the handler service that is needed to launch the ShowPopup command.

Listing 6-17. Two New Methods for the Activator Class

```
private boolean shouldShowPopup() {
     IPreferenceStore store = getDefault()
                         .getPreferenceStore();
     Boolean shouldShow = store.getBoolean(
                 preferenceInitializer.ShowPopupWhenOpened);
     return shouldShow;
     }
private void executeCommmand() {
 IHandlerService handlerService = (IHandlerService)
((IServiceLocator) PlatformUI.getWorkbench())   .getService(
IHandlerService.class);
          try {
                 handlerService.executeCommand( "com.adtbook.
                 examples.extpointview.commands.ShowPopup",
                        null);
          } catch (Exception e) {
               // TODO error handling
          }
     }
```

As a last step, replace the code of the start method with the code in Listing 6-18.

Listing 6-18. New Content of the Start Method

```
public void start(BundleContext context) throws Exception {
     super.start(context);
     plugin = this;
     if (shouldShowPopup())
          executeCommmand();
}
```

Now execute the plugin using the test environment. The popup message will appear when Eclipse opens if at least one of the plugin views is visible on the screen. If not, you should open one of the views to activate the code.

Since we set the ShowPopupWhenOpened parameter to true and based displaying the popup message on it, we caused a situation that the popup is now appearing at each usage of a plugin. We could instead set the parameter value to false after the first use, so that the popup appears only once. To do this, we need to use a setValue method of the preferences store. You can try to adapt the code by yourself to achieve this action, or you can go to the next section, where I explain preferences pages.

Preferences Pages

When you want to allow users to set the preferences, you can create your own dialog or view or use the standard Eclipse settings: the preference pages. Each screen in the Window Preferences is a separate preference page, which is created using the org.eclipse.ui.preferencePages extension point. Add this extension point to the plugin and create a page as a child. Now fill in the page details by using com.adtbook.examples.extpointview.preferencePage in the id and class fields. Call it ADT Book (Figure 6-66).

Extension Element Details

Set the properties of 'page' Required fields are denoted by '*'.

id*:	com.adtbook.examples.extpointview.preferencePage
name*:	ADT Book
class*:	com.adtbook.examples.extpointview.preferencePage
category:	

Figure 6-66. *Preferences page extension details*

Now use the class link to call the class creation wizard and replace the superclass with `org.eclipse.jface.preference.FieldEditorPreferencePage` (Figure 6-67). If you used the default setting, you would need to create all the controls and handlers on the screen from scratch, while `FieldEditorPreferencePage` allows you to use predefined and easy-to-use input controls, which are sufficient in most cases[2].

Source folder:	ExtPointView/src	Browse...
Package:	com.adtbook.examples.extpointview	Browse...
☐ Enclosing type:		Browse...
Name:	preferencePage	
Modifiers:	⦿ public ◯ package ◯ private ◯ protected	
	☐ abstract ☐ final ☐ static	
Superclass:	org.eclipse.jface.preference.FieldEditorPreferencePage	Browse...

Figure 6-67. *Class creation wizard for preference page*

Now replace the default class code with the code in Listing 6-19. In the constructor of the preference page, notice that the layout of the preference page is set to `GRID` and the preference store is set to the default one (the same that we used in previous examples). In the `createFieldEditors` method, a checkbox is added to the preferences page. This checkbox is linked to the `ShowPopupWhenOpened` preference. As you can see, there is no code to handle the preference state; it is all done internally by the field editor.

---

[2]You can find more about field editors and when to use them (and when not to) at `https://www.eclipse.org/articles/Article-Field-Editors/field_editors.html`

Listing 6-19. Example Preference Page Class Implementation

```
package com.adtbook.examples.extpointview;

import org.eclipse.jface.preference.BooleanFieldEditor;
import org.eclipse.jface.preference.FieldEditorPreferencePage;
import org.eclipse.jface.preference.IPreferenceStore;
import org.eclipse.ui.IWorkbench;
import org.eclipse.ui.IWorkbenchPreferencePage;

public class preferencePage extends
          FieldEditorPreferencePage implements
          IWorkbenchPreferencePage {

    public preferencePage() {
        super(GRID);
        setPreferenceStore(Activator.getDefault()
                    .getPreferenceStore());
        setDescription("Settings for ADT Book plugin");}
    @Override
    public void init(IWorkbench workbench) { }

    @Override
    protected void createFieldEditors() {
        addField(new BooleanFieldEditor(
            preferenceInitializer.ShowPopupWhenOpened,
            "Show Popup at Start",
            getFieldEditorParent())); }
}
```

Now test the ADT Book preferences page using the test environment. When you open the preferences window, you will see the ADT Book category and, after selecting it, you will see the checkbox that is defined in the handler class (Figure 6-68). Unmark the checkbox, click the Apply and Close buttons, and close the test environment. When you run it again, the checkbox will still be unmarked.

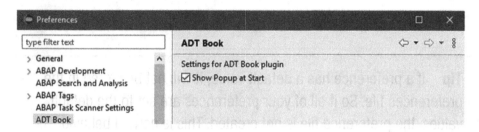

Figure 6-68. *ADT Book Preferences page*

It is also important to know where your preferences are stored. Open your run configuration setting and use the link on the Location field label to open the parent folder of this run configuration (Figure 6-69).

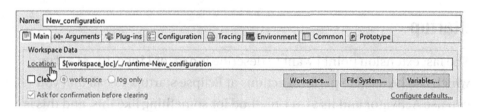

Figure 6-69. *Run configuration settings*

Now navigate to .metadata\.plugins\org.eclipse.core. runtime\.settings\. You will find a file called com.adtbook.examples. extpointview.prefs, which stores the plugin's preferences. Open it in a text editor. For example, in Notepad, you will see the preference ID and its value (Figure 6-70).

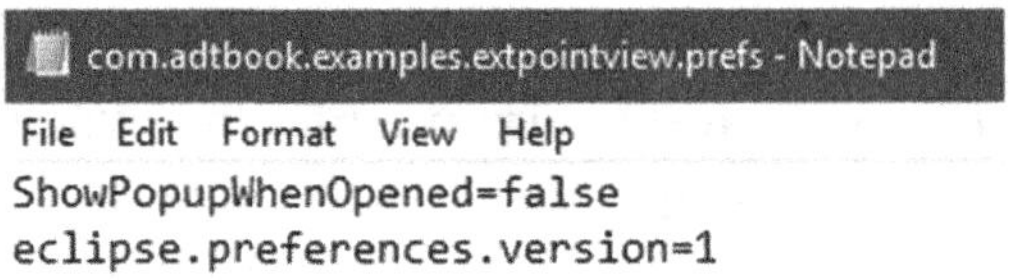

Figure 6-70. Contents of the preference file

Tip   If a preference has a default value, it will not be stored in the preferences file. So if all of your preferences are set to the default values, the preference file is not created. This is normal behavior. Additionally, preferences are saved in the file when Eclipse is closed properly, which means that you may lose any changes to your settings if you close your instance by killing an OS process, or if your Eclipse instance crashes and is not closed properly.

Startup

The last extension point I want to describe is `org.eclipse.ui.startup`, which can be used to perform actions at Eclipse startup. Recall that you can use Activator and its `start` method for something like this, and this is true, but only if your plugin was activated at startup. Since you can create plugins that have no contribution to toolbars, menus, or visible views, you may not be sure that the code from the Activator will be run at Eclipse start. By using the startup extension, you can be sure the code will run.

Create an extension for `org.eclipse.ui.startup` using the following class name: *com*`.adtbook.examples.extpointview.Startup`. Use the wizard to create a class with the default settings and then paste the code in Listing 6-20.

Listing 6-20. Example Startup Handler

```
package com.adtbook.examples.extpointview;

import org.eclipse.ui.IStartup;

public class Startup implements IStartup {

    @Override
    public void earlyStartup() {
        System.err.println("ADT Book plugin startup");
        System.out.println("Standard Console text");
        System.out.println(); }
}
```

There is nothing special in this example, just a simple display of the
text in the Console so you can see without debugging that the code was
called at startup. I used the err and out objects to print the text in the
console, in order to show you the difference in the output (Figure 6-71).
Just a small tip—you will see this text in the console of your main instance,
not in the console of the test environment.

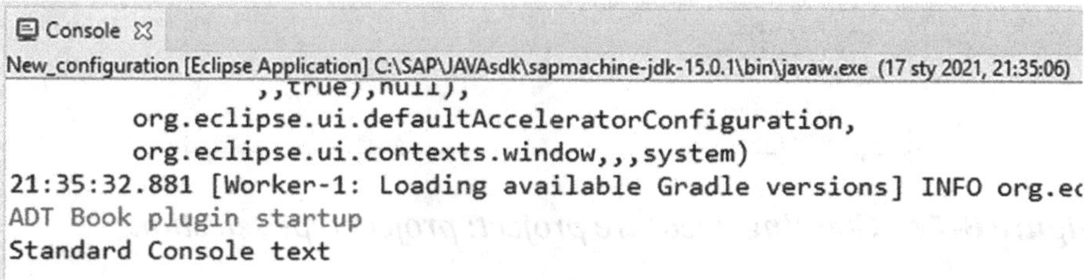

Figure 6-71. *Console output during the test environment startup*

Feature Project

So far you have seen how to create your own plugin and how to test it, but if you want to share your work with others, you need to create a feature project and use Update Site. Let's start with a feature project.

Feature is a pack of linked plugins that are meant to work together or be deployed together. It can also contain only one plugin. In most cases, the license information is attached to the feature.

To create a feature, you need to create a new project. This time, when selecting the project type, choose Feature Project and click the Next button (Figure 6-72).

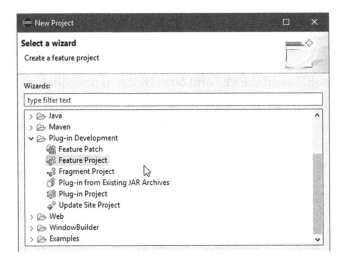

Figure 6-72. *Creating a feature project: project type selection*

On the next screen, set up the project name (for example, Sample Feature Project) and choose the location for it. You also need to set up the feature properties. Use com.adtbook.examples.feature for ID and ADT Book Sample Feature Project for Feature Name (Figure 6-73). Click the Next button.

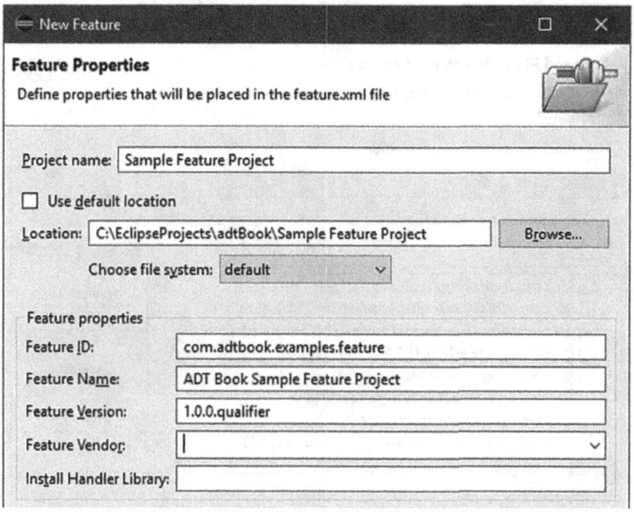

Figure 6-73. *Creating the feature project: properties*

Now select the two plugins created in this chapter (Figure 6-74) and click the Finish button to end the feature project.

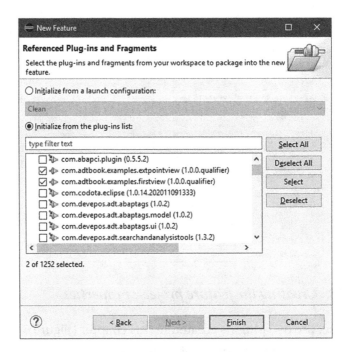

Figure 6-74. *Creating the feature project: plugin selection*

After creating the project, the details will be opened (Figure 6-75), just like with the plugins. If you closed this feature editor, simply double-click the feature.xml file to open it. On the Overview tab, you will see all the settings for the feature as well as the fields for environment combination in which the feature can work. I think that in most cases you will not need these fields, but it's good to know they are there.

General Information

This section describes general information about this feature.

ID:	com.adtbook.examples.feature
Version:	1.0.0.qualifier
Name:	ADT Book Sample Feature Project
Vendor:	
Branding Plug-in:	[_____] Browse...
Update Site URL:	[_____]
Update Site Name:	[_____]

Supported Environments

Specify environment combinations in which this feature can be installed. Leave blank if the feature does not contain platform-specific code.

Operating Systems:	[_____] Browse ...
Window Systems:	[_____] Browse ...
Languages:	[_____] Browse ...
Architecture:	[_____] Browse ...

Feature Content

The content of the feature is made up of five sections:

- Information: holds information about this feature, such as description and license.
- Plug-ins: lists the plug-ins that make up this feature.
- Included Features: lists the features that are included in this feature.
- Dependencies: lists other features and plug-ins required by this feature when installed.

Exporting

To export the feature:

1. Synchronize versions of contained plug-ins and fragments with their version in the workspace
2. Specify what needs to be packaged in the feature archive on the Build Configuration page
3. Export the feature in a format suitable for deployment using the Export Wizard

Publishing

To publish the feature on an update site:

1. Create an Update Site Project
2. Use the site editor to add the feature to the site, and build the site

Figure 6-75. *Feature overview*

The next tab of the feature details is Information (Figure 6-76). It allows you to fill in the feature description, copyright notice, and license agreement and share the links for the sites related to the feature or its publisher. When you create your real plugins and features, it is good to spend some time filling in all of these fields. This is a good place to tell users the rules of using your plugins and exactly what they do. These fields can also bring attention to your websites.

Information

Enter description, license and copyright information. Optionally, provide links to update sites for installing additional features.

| Feature Description | Copyright Notice | License Agreement | Sites to Visit |

Optional URL:	http://www.example.com/description
Text:	[Enter Feature Description here.]

Figure 6-76. *Feature description, copyright notice, license agreement, and sites to visit*

The Included Plug-Ins tab allows you to add plugins to the feature. It also allows you to set up which versions of the plugins are used.

Plug-ins and Fragments

Plug-ins and Fragments		Plug-in Details
Select plug-ins and fragments that should be packaged in this feature.		Specify installation details for the selected plug-in.

com.adtbook.examples.extpointview (0.0.0)
com.adtbook.examples.firstview (0.0.0)

Add...
Remove
Versions...

Name: ExtPointView
Version: 0.0.0
Download Size (kB):   0
Installation Size (kB):   0
☐ Unpack the plug-in archive after the installation

Figure 6-77. *Included plugins and version selection*

By default, synchronizing the version during build is active, which is why you see (0.0.0) after the plugin name. When you click the Versions button, you can adapt the way the feature assigns the version of the plugins (Figure 6-78). But I suggest you keep the default settings until you need them to work differently.

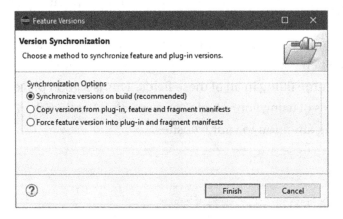

Figure 6-78. *Feature synchronization options*

The Dependencies tab allows you to set up which other plugins are required for your feature to work correctly (Figure 6-79). You can set this up manually or you can use one of the two available functionalities. The Compute button will check all plugins included in your feature and will put any dependencies inside. But this is manual action that needs to be done during each plugin update. That's why you can also select the

Recompute When Feature Plug-Ins Change checkbox. This will make an automatic determination of the dependencies during each build of the feature.

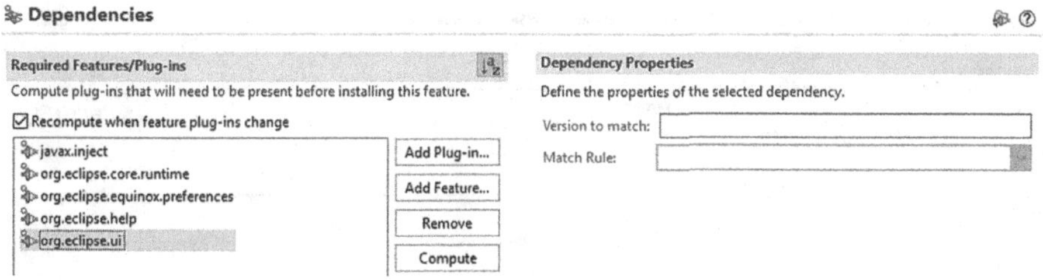

Figure 6-79. Feature dependencies

At this stage, you can use the created feature project to adapt the run configurations, but you cannot share it with other peers yet.

Update Site

In order to share your plugins and features easily, you need to create an update site that contains information about features and plugins. There are two ways to create update sites, one is to use the Export function and the other is to create the update site project. Both have advantages and disadvantages, which we cover shortly.

Deployable Features

If you are testing the plugin yourself or rarely update your plugins, you may think about using the File Export ➤ Plug-in Developments ➤ Deployable Features option. But before using that function, I recommend you create a Category Definition file, which allows you to group the features and plugins into categories. When there is no category and the Group Items by Category Option is selected on the installation screen (default setting), you

401

will get information that there are no categorized items (Figure 6-80). For most users, this message would mean that there is nothing to install from the update site. That is why it is better to create one.

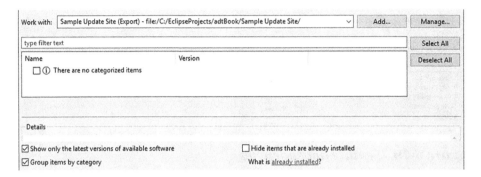

Figure 6-80. *Update site without category on plugin installation screen*

After selecting Feature Project from the Project Explorer, use the context menu to create a new file. Select the Category Definition file type, which can be found in the Plug-in Development folder (Figure 6-81).

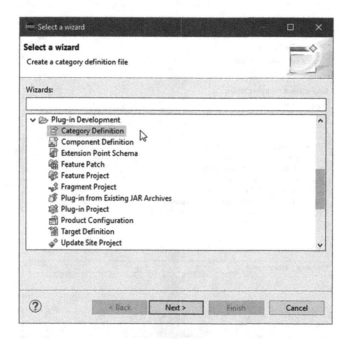

Figure 6-81. *Category definition creation wizard*

On the next screen of the wizard, make sure that the sample feature project is selected (Figure 6-82). You can adapt the filename or leave it as the default value: `category.xml`. Then click the Finish button.

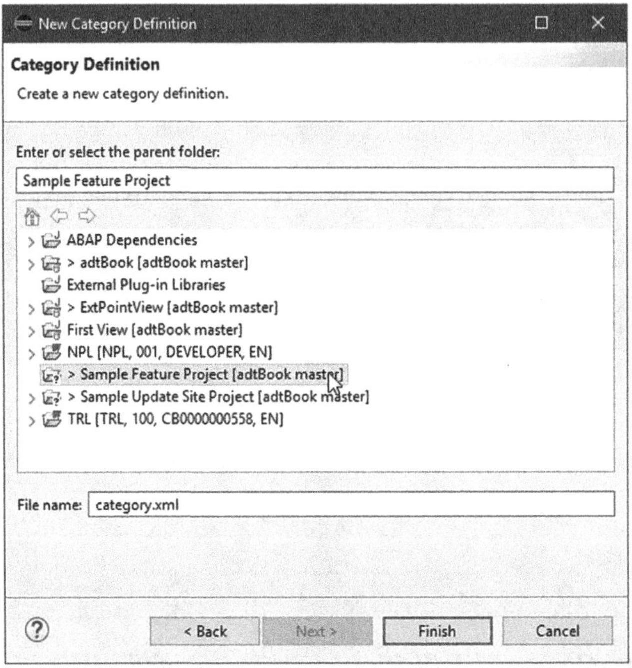

Figure 6-82. *Category definition creation wizard: name and path*

The Category Definition editor will open in a separate tab. Click the New Category button. Set the ID to `SampleFeatureCategory` and the Name to `Sample Category` (Figure 6-83).

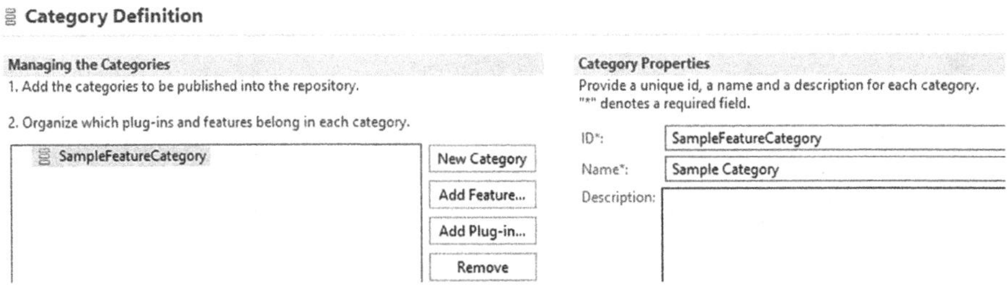

Figure 6-83. *Category definition editor*

Now select the created category and click the Add Feature button. A popup screen will appear on which you'll find the feature created in the previous steps. You can use the Filter field for quicker selection (Figure 6-84).

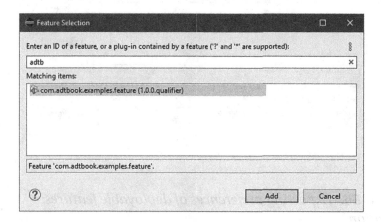

Figure 6-84. *Feature selection screen*

Once you add the feature, make sure it is added as a child of the category. Your screen should look like Figure 6-85.

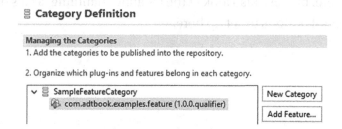

Figure 6-85. *Sample Feature Category with the feature included*

Now it is time to create the update site. Go to the Eclipse menu and choose File ➤ Export ➤ Plug-in Developments ➤ Deployable Features. On the first wizard screen, you will see all of the features that are available in your workspace. Select com.adtbook.examples.feature and set up the destination directory using, for example, Sample Update Site as a final folder name (Figure 6-87). Do not click the Finish button yet.

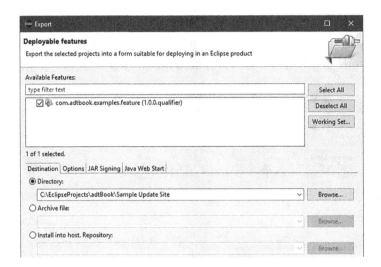

Figure 6-86. *Exporting preferences of deployable features: destination*

Change the tab to option and click the Browse button next to the Categorize Repository field. Choose the `category.xml` file you created in the previous step (Figure 6-88). These options would be sufficient to create the update site, but let's also look at the Qualifier handling, as it's one of the most useful options to set up here.

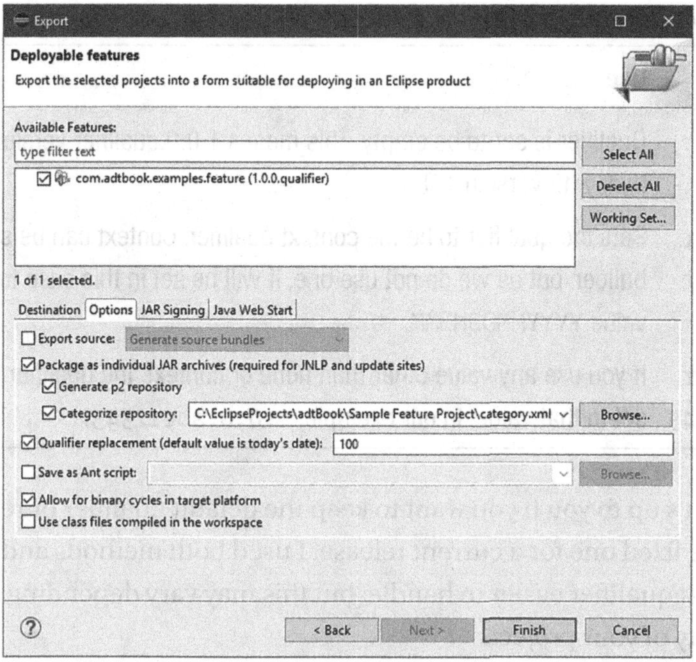

Figure 6-87. *Exporting preferences of deployable features: options*

You may remember that I mentioned Qualifier already. It was available for the plugin as well as for the feature. When you do not specify otherwise, the Qualifier is set to a timestamp in the YYYYMMDDHHMM format. When you are using the export function to create an update site, you can select Qualifier Replacement and set it to any value. It will be used when creating the update site.

You can also manipulate the Qualifier directly by using the build. properties tab in the plugin or feature editor. To do this, you need to add a line with a proper qualifier. Possible qualifier entries are listed in Table 6-1.

Table 6-1. *Possible Qualifier Settings*

Action	Use
`qualifier` `= none`	Qualifier is set to be empty. This means 1.0.0.qualifier version will be built with version 1.0.0.
`qualifier` `= context`	Sets the qualifier to be the context qualifier. Context can be set in builder, but as we do not use one, it will be set in this case to default value YYYYMMDDHHMM.
`qualifier` `= abc12345`	If you use any value other than none or context, the qualifier will be set to that value. In our example, `1.0.0.abc12345`.

Now it's up to you if you want to keep the default qualifier or replace it with the fixed one for a current release. I used both methods and found the default qualifier easier to handle, but this may vary depending on the complexity of your project.

Click the Finish button when you're done. The update site will be created and you can follow the status in the progress bar. After the job is finished, it is time to test the update site. Go to Help ➤ Install New Software and click the Add button to create a new local repository. Use the Local button to search for a folder with the created update site and give the repository a name, such as `Sample Update Site (Export)`, as shown in Figure 6-89.

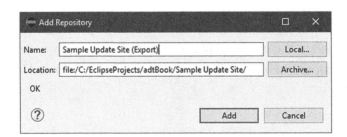

Figure 6-88. *New local repository from the sample update site*

After clicking the Add button, you should see the Sample Category and the ADT Book Sample Feature Project on the screen (Figure 6-90). Quit the installation process by clicking the Cancel button, as we will now create the update site for the same feature in a different way.

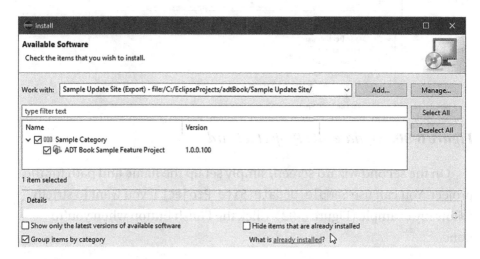

Figure 6-89. *Previewing the items to install for the sample update site*

Update Site Project

The second way to create an update site is by creating the update site project. As with the previous projects, you need to use the project wizard. This time, select File ➤ New ➤ Project ➤ Plug-in Development ➤ Update Site Project (Figure 6-91) and click the Next button.

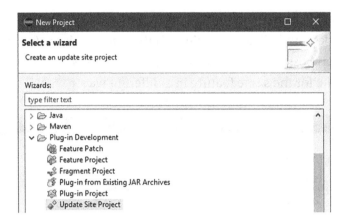

Figure 6-90. *Update Site Project wizard*

On the second wizard screen, simply set up the name and path for the project. You can use `Sample Update Site Project` if you want to strictly follow my example (Figure 6-92). Click the Finish button when you're done.

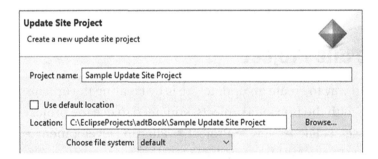

Figure 6-91. *Update Site Project wizard: path selection*

Once the project is created, the Update Site Map editor will open in a new tab. It looks very similar to the Category Definition editor, but it is lacking the Add Plugin button and has three additional buttons: Synchronize, Build, and Build All.

Repeat the steps you followed in the Category Definition editor to create a category and add the feature to it. It should look like Figure 6-92. Now select the feature on the screen and click the Build button, which will became active after selection. After the build is finished, the feature's qualifier will be replaced with the current timestamp. Click the Build button again and go to the Project Explorer view.

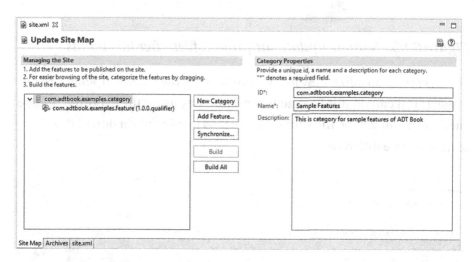

Figure 6-92. *Update Site Map*

Two new folders were created in the update site project: features and plugins. When you expand them, you will see that the features and the plugin's JAR files were created twice with the different qualifier at the end (Figure 6-93).

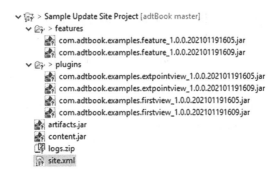

Figure 6-93. *Sample update site project: files after two builds*

Now you can add a new local repository for the sample update site project. You can do this in exactly the same way as for the exported update site. The result will be the same (Figure 6-94), only the version of the feature will be different.

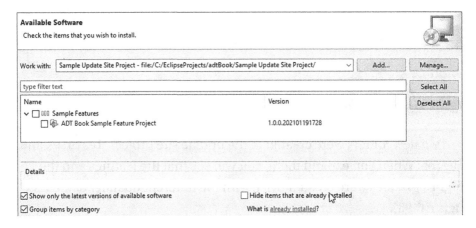

Figure 6-94. *Preview of the items to install for the sample update site project*

I prefer to use the update site project instead of the Export of Deployable Features option because I can update the update site with two clicks: one click opens the site.xml file, the other click is on the Build or Build All buttons. Additionally, when you use the update site project, you keep the category structure of your features away from the features itself. For me, this is more transparent.

Tip   If you want your update site to be available over HTTP(s), you need to upload its content to any web server accessible to the public.

Summary

Extending Eclipse is very large topic. In fact, it could be covered in several books and there would still be a lot information that would be omitted. The idea of this chapter was to explain the basics. I hope that, with the exercises you did here, you are starting to feel comfortable creating your own plugins.

In the next chapter, I guide you through the process of creating a plugin that works with ADT and uses its components. I also explain how to fetch data from the backend system into your plugin.

CHAPTER 7

Extending ABAP Development Tools

This chapter focuses on the ways to make your plugin work with ADT and how to fetch data from the backend using built-in ADT functionalities. This is presented as a separate chapter so you gain basic knowledge about creating an Eclipse plugin. Otherwise, it could be too much to understand at once. It is also the last chapter of this book. I hope you enjoyed reading it, as I enjoyed writing it!

This is a different chapter from the previous one. It's not a tutorial step-by-step on how to create a plugin that fetches data from SAP backend, but it does show you what functionality to use to achieve it. I also describe how to get the ADT SDK and how to read the code of ADT objects.

Basic Information

When I started writing my first plugin for ADT, I had trouble understanding how exactly it worked. There were a few sources that described the extensibility of Eclipse, but the process of extending ADT was barely described in two or three blog posts on the SAP Community. I was also not aware of the decompiling tools for Java, which would make my work with the plugins easier and the SDK for ADT was far from useable. You'll have more luck than me, as I explain how to start, what the basic functionalities that you need to use are, and how to call the backend.

© Lukasz Pegiel 2021
Ł. Pęgiel, *ABAP in Eclipse*, https://doi.org/10.1007/978-1-4842-6963-3_7

SDK for ABAP Development Tools

In the past, the 2015 version of SDK for ADT was only available in the SAP Community, but now it is available and updated frequently in the ADT tools website at `https://tools.hana.ondemand.com/#abap`, in the part called *Software Development Kit (SDK)*, as seen in Figure 7-1. This ZIP file contains several files and folders, which I assume are extractions of JavaDoc for ADT APIs.

ADT APIs are no more than functionalities that SAP gives as a kind of contract to everyone who is creating software or plugins based on it. It explains that they cannot disappear from version to version, but they need to be depreciated before and left for a while, so the developers can adjust their code.

Figure 7-1. *Download page of Software Development Kit for ADT*

Download the SDK, extract it to a folder, and then run the `index.html` file from it. Your default system browser will show you a list of ADT packages that are described in this SDK (Figure 7-2).

OVERVIEW PACKAGE CLASS USE TREE DEPRECATED INDEX HELP

ALL CLASSES

ADT Framework Common Infrastructure 3.16.1 API

Packages

Package	Description
com.sap.adt.communication.content	Content handling in ADT communication framework.
com.sap.adt.communication.content.asx	ADT content handling functionality for the canonical ABAP-XML data format.
com.sap.adt.communication.content.plaintext	ADT content handling functionality for the "text/plain" data format.
com.sap.adt.communication.destinations	Gives access to the destination registry.
com.sap.adt.communication.exceptions	Exception classes in ADT communication framework.
com.sap.adt.communication.message	Request/response message handling in ADT communication framework.
com.sap.adt.communication.resources	Resource and URI handling in ADT communication framework.
com.sap.adt.communication.session	Session handling in ADT communication framework.
com.sap.adt.communication.util	Utilities for ADT communication framework.

Figure 7-2. *ADT SDK starting page*

When you click one of the package names, you will get the details about the classes, interfaces, exceptions, or enumerators that are contained inside (Figure 7-3). You can of course navigate through those objects further to get more details about them and their uses (if provided). In some cases, but unfortunately not in all yet, you will also get example uses of the described element.

OVERVIEW	PACKAGE	CLASS	USE	TREE	DEPRECATED	INDEX	HELP

ALL CLASSES

Interface Summary

Interface	Description
IContentHandler<T>	Handler for processing communication message entities.
IContentHandlerRegistry	Registry for content handlers.
IContentHandlerResolver	Interface for resolution of content handlers.
IContentHandlingFactory	Factory for creating classes for content-handling related services.
IContentHandlingService	Utility for content handling.

Class Summary

Class	Description
AdtContentHandlingFactory	
AdtIanaLinkRelations	Provides constants for link relations define by IANA.
AdtMediaType	Provides constants for common Media Types (MIME Types) used for ADT.

Figure 7-3. *Package information in ADT SDK*

I personally wish that this SDK was full of usage examples and contained more classes or interfaces than it currently does, but in order for this to happen, we need more people creating extensions for ADT and putting pressure on SAP to update it correctly. Until then, we have to use what is available.

Enhanced Class Decompiler

Some of the software vendors provide the source code of their products to the community, and much of the software is open source. SAP software (the ABAP part) has historically been open source, and we could always see what was happening in the system and read and enhance the code when needed. That is why I was surprised that ADT is not this way.

At least this was my thinking, until I asked Ludwig Stockbauer-Muhr to give me some insights into his ADT plugin. He showed me the Enhanced Class Decompiler. This lovely plugin for Eclipse allows one to read the

ADT code. It made my day and I cannot imagine how I was writing plugins without it. I am sure that if you want to write your own, you will also love it. So let's go deeper into the topic of this plugin.

Installation and Configuration

You can find the Enhanced Class Decompiler plugin in the Eclipse Marketplace. In Figure 7-4, you can see that it is very popular, which makes me think I was not trying hard enough to find information about how to read compiled Java code. In a few moments you will understand why I was so happy to get the information about this plugin.

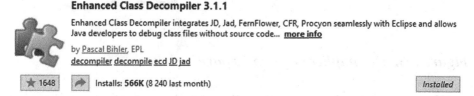

Enhanced Class Decompiler 3.1.1

Enhanced Class Decompiler integrates JD, Jad, FernFlower, CFR, Procyon seamlessly with Eclipse and allows Java developers to debug class files without source code... **more info**

by Pascal Bihler, EPL
decompiler decompile ecd JD jad

★ 1648   Installs: **566K** (8 240 last month)   *Installed*

***Figure 7-4.** Enhanced Class Decompiler in the Eclipse Marketplace*

First, install this plugin. During the installation process, select all available decompilers that appear on the screen. After a successful installation, restart Eclipse and go to Windows ➤ Preferences, as there are some settings that you need to change before you can use it fully. First, select Java ➤ Decompiler and set up the Default Class Decompiler (Figure 7-5). For me, CFR worked best, but this might be different for you, so try the others as well.

The most important point here is that you keep the Startup setting called Set Class Decompiler Viewer as the Default 'Java Class File' Content Type Editor enabled.

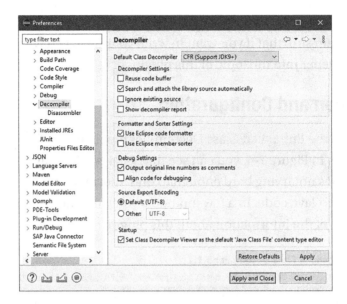

Figure 7-5. *Decompiler preferences page*

If you go one level deeper, to the Disassembler preferences page, you can choose what needs to be shown in the editor when opening decompiled class. For me, the most important setting is Show Source Line Number, which I deselect to have more readable code.

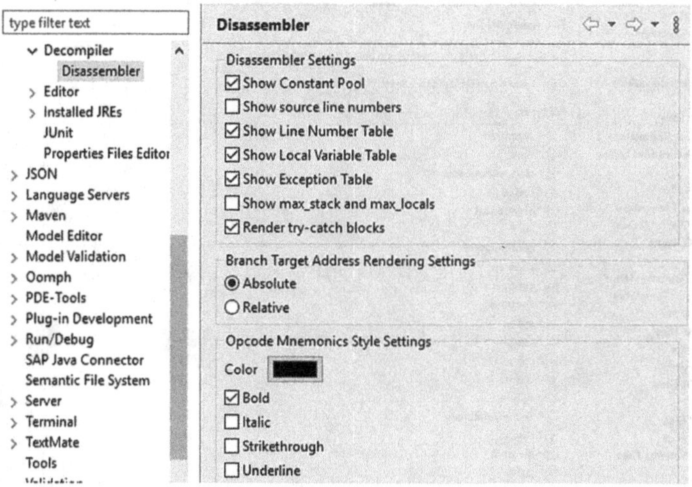

Figure 7-6. *Disassembler settings*

For the next step, we need to go to General ➤ Editors ➤ File
Association. In this preferences page, find two file types: *.class and
*.class without source (Figure 7-7). Select them and, in the Associated
Editors list, select Class Decompiler Viewer and click the Default button.
After this action, you can open and debug the code of all plugins installed
in Eclipse.

Figure 7-7.   *File Associations settings for *.class files*

Using the Decompiler

To see the power of the Enhanced Class Decompiler, create a new plugin project in Eclipse (Figure 7-8). This time we will not add any code to it. Name this project accordingly. I called it ABAP Dependencies. Use Next button and then click Finish.

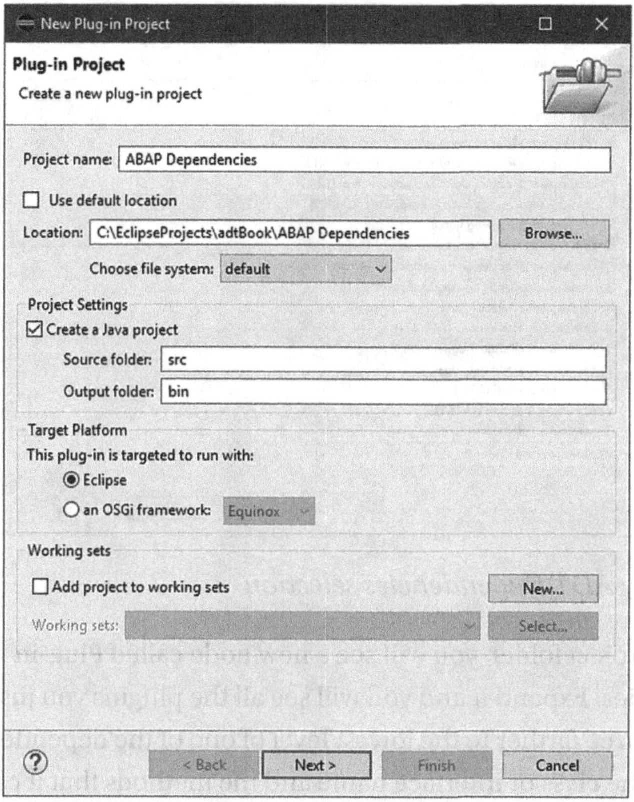

Figure 7-8. *New Project wizard: general project*

Find your new project in Project Explorer, open it, go to the META-INF folder, and open the MANIFEST.MF file. You will see the plugin details editor; switch to the Dependencies tab. While you are there, click the Add button and put com.sap.adt in the filter field (Figure 7-9). Use Ctrl+A to select all the found plugins and click Add. After a few seconds, all the selected entries will appear in the Dependencies tab. Now it is time to save the project and return to Project Explorer.

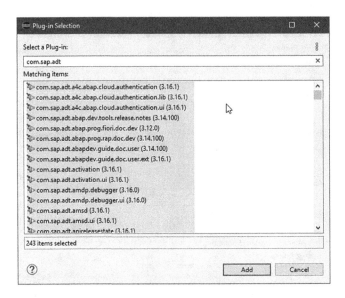

Figure 7-9. *ADT Dependencies selection*

In the project folder, you will see a new node called Plug-in Dependencies. Expand it and you will see all the plugins you just added. Expand the tree farther to the lowest level of one of the dependencies. You will notice the class or interface name and the methods that it contains (Figure 7-10). Double-click the class name.

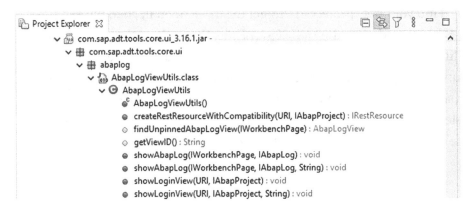

Figure 7-10. *Expanded dependency in Project Explorer*

You will see the decompiled code in the editor window (Figure 7-11). This can help you understand how SAP is using Eclipse and even learn how to use certain ADT objects that are described in SDK but don't have examples.

```
AbapLogViewUtils.class [CFR] 
94
95    public void showLoginView(URI uri, IAbapProject abapProject, final String textPreselected) {
96        final URI uriLog = uri;
97        final IAbapProject project = abapProject;
98        Job job = new Job(abapProject.getProject().getName()){
99
100           protected IStatus run(IProgressMonitor monitor) {
101               IRestResource resource = AbapLogViewUtils.this.createRestResourceWithCompatibility(uriLog, project);
102               try {
```

Figure 7-11. *Decompiled class content*

If your settings are not correct, or when you do not have the Enhanced Class Decompiler installed, you will get information from the class file editor stating that the source code was not found (Figure 7-12). The same will happen during debugging if you want to jump into the code of an object that is part of the ADT standard.

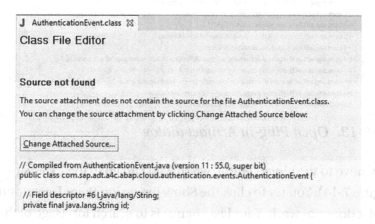

Figure 7-12. *Class opened without the Enhanced Class Decompiler active*

Real-Life Scenario

Being able to read the plugin vendor's code is really helpful, especially
when you want to extend this plugin with your own one but there is lack of
SDK and documentation. For example, you want to be notified about the
successful activation of an ABAP object. You use Ctrl+Shift+A to call the
Open Plugin Artifact dialog and write com.sap.adt*acti in the filter field
to get artifacts that could be useful (Figure 7-13). You find an extension-
point that looks like the one that could fit: com.sap.adt.activation.
ui.activationSuccessListener. Select it and open it.

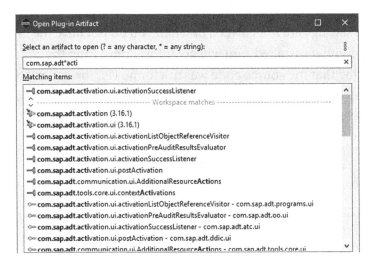

Figure 7-13. *Open Plug-in Artifact dialog*

You move to the plugin editor, where you can go to the Extension Points
tab (Figure 7-14). You try to click the Show Extension Point Description
link, but it does not work. Your last chance is to search for usage of this
extension point, which is why you click the Find References link.

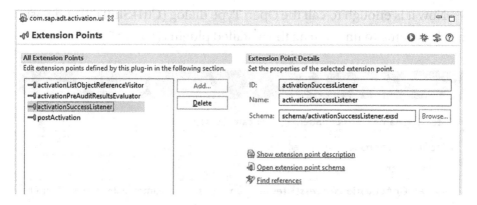

Figure 7-14. *Definition of the activationSuccessListener extension point*

In the Search view, you receive the place where this extension point is used (Figure 7-15). Double-click the entry.

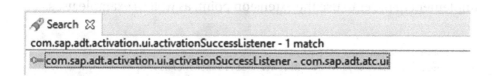

Figure 7-15. *Extension point usage list*

You move to the plugin editor again, but this time to the one that is using the extension point (Figure 7-16). You can see how you have to define the extension in your own plugin (which XML nodes are used by SAP). You can also see that it is implemented in the AtcOnActivationSuccessListener class.

```
375    <extension
376          point="com.sap.adt.activation.ui.activationSuccessListener">
377       <onActivationSuccess
378             class="com.sap.adt.atc.ui.internal.launch.worklist.AtcOnActivationSuccessListener">
379       </onActivationSuccess>
380    </extension>
```

Figure 7-16. *Extension point implementation*

427

Now it is enough to call the Open Type dialog (Ctrl+Shift+T) and paste the class name to find it in all the installed plugins (Figure 7-17).

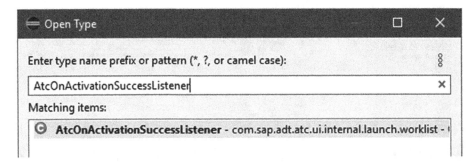

Figure 7-17. *Open Type dialog*

The decompiled source code of the class is displayed on the screen (Figure 7-18). You get information about the interface that you need to implement in order to use the extension point, as well as example uses.

```
    AtcOnActivationSuccessListener.class [CFR] ☒
  1 package com.sap.adt.atc.ui.internal.launch.worklist;
  2
  3 import com.sap.adt.activation.ui.IActivationSuccessListener;
  4 import com.sap.adt.atc.IAtcCheckableItem;
  5 import com.sap.adt.atc.ui.internal.launch.worklist.AtcOnActivationJob;
  6 import com.sap.adt.tools.core.IAdtObjectReference;
  7 import com.sap.adt.util.configuration.AdtConfiguration;
  8 import java.net.URI;
  9 import java.util.ArrayList;
 10 import java.util.List;
 11 import java.util.Locale;
 12 import org.eclipse.core.resources.IProject;
 13
 14 public class AtcOnActivationSuccessListener
 15 implements IActivationSuccessListener {
 16     private static final String DO_AUTOMATIC_ATC_RUNS_ON_ACTIVATION = '
 17
```

Figure 7-18. *Decompiled code of the AtcOnActivationSuccessListener class*

Exporting Source Code

The last functionality of the Enhanced Class Decompiler is the ability to extract a whole JAR file (the whole plugin). To do this, use the context menu of Project Explorer while you are in the Plug-in Dependencies node and choose Export Source. Unfortunately, you can only extract one JAR file at a time, so in order to have the fully extracted code of an ADT plugin, you need to manually extract more than 200 plugins.

The extraction is done to a ZIP file with the folder structure mirroring the package structure. After extracting it, you can read the source code in any text editor or IDE, such as Notepad++ or VSCode. Both editors allow you to search through all files in the folder, which can be used to quickly find references. This can be very useful but also takes a lot of time.

ADT Integration Examples

You have seen the SDK and you have installed Enhanced Class Decompiler, so now it is time to look at some of the ADT elements. This is, of course, just a small part of what is available in ADT, but we start with the basic objects that you will need to use sooner or later during extension of ADT.

In the next sections, I present you with a few objects and code snippets that you can use in your own plugin. All of this code can be also found in the book's Git repository.

Project

After installing ADT, the first thing you do is create an ABAP project. This virtual folder is very important, not only for navigation through the SAP system source code, but also for programming your own plugin that works with ADT. The project object will be the most common one that you will use.

Each Eclipse project implements the interface IProject, which is why you will find this interface in many of the ADT methods and inside many Eclipse classes. Thanks to that, it is not hard to get the object of an active project (the project of the active Eclipse editor). As during the plugin development, you will probably need it very often, so it's best to create a separate method to get an active ADT. The code in Listing 7-1 can be used to get the ABAP project type. You can cast it directly to IAbapProject type, but in most cases you will still need IProject.

Listing 7-1. Method for Fetching an Active ADT Project

```
public static IProject getActiveAdtProject() {
 try {
  IWorkbenchPage page = PlatformUI.getWorkbench()
      .getActiveWorkbenchWindow().getActivePage();
  IWorkbenchWindow window = page.getWorkbenchWindow();
  ISelection adtSelection = window.getSelectionService()
                        .getSelection();
  IProject project = ProjectUtil.getActiveAdtCoreProject(
              adtSelection, null, null,
              IAdtCoreProject.ABAP_PROJECT_NATURE);
   return project;
} catch (Exception e) {
   return null;
     }
}
```

If you know the project name you want to get, you can make it a bit faster and simpler, as it is enough to use the Resources Plugin static methods shown in Listing 7-2.

Listing 7-2. Getting a Project by Its Name

```java
public static IProject getProjectByName(String projectName) {
 try {
  IProject project = ResourcesPlugin.getWorkspace().getRoot()
                    .getProject(projectName);
  return project;
 } catch (Exception e) {
  return null;
 }
}
```

Another possibility is to ask the user to select a project for you, while using the plugin. This was implemented in the ABAP Favorites plugin by Ludwig Stockbauer-Muhr to handle the double-click behavior of the favorite object. The code itself basically calls the project selection dialog prepared by SAP (Listing 7-3).

Listing 7-3. Getting a Project Object Based on the Selection Dialog

```java
public static IProject getProjectFromProjectChooserDialog() {
    return AbapProjectSelectionDialog.open(
            PlatformUI.getWorkbench().
                    getActiveWorkbenchWindow().getShell(),
            null);
    }
```

Logon Service

When you open Eclipse, your plugins have direct access to all the Eclipse projects, as well as to ADT. This is also the case when you are not logged in to the ADT project. That's why it is important to know that you can check your plugin if you are already signed in. To do so, use the ensureLoggedOn method of the ADT logon service.

There are two logon services available: AdtLogonService and
AdtLogonServiceUI. They have small differences in usage. When you want
to check if users are logged on and show the standard logon dialog of ADT
if they are not, you should use AdtLogonServiceUI. Example code is shown
in Listing 7-4.

Listing 7-4. ADT Logon Using the User Dialog

```
public static void ensureLoggedOn(IProject project) {
 try {
   IAbapProject abapProject = project.getAdapter(
                        IAbapProject.class);
   AdtLogonServiceUIFactory.createLogonServiceUI()
           .ensureLoggedOn(abapProject.getDestinationData(),
           PlatformUI.getWorkbench().getProgressService());
     } catch (Exception e) {
   System.out.print(e.getMessage());
     }
}
```

If you know the user's password, you can use ADTLogonService
instead. To do this, you need to put the password in AuthenticationToken.
It is very simple, as you can see in Listing 7-5. If it fails, you can always call
the method that is using the standard user dialog for logon.

Listing 7-5. Logging On to an ADT Project Without the User Dialog

```
public static void logonWithPassword(IProject project,
                    String password) {
 IAdtCoreProject adtProject = project.getAdapter(
                    IAdtCoreProject.class);
 IDestinationData destinationData = adtProject
                    .getDestinationData();
```

```
try {
 if (!password.isEmpty()) {
    IAuthenticationToken authenticationToken =
                    new AuthenticationToken();

   authenticationToken.setPassword(password);
   AdtLogonServiceFactory.createLogonService()
            .ensureLoggedOn(destinationData,
                            authenticationToken,
                            new NullProgressMonitor());
    }
 } catch (Exception e) {
                ensureLoggedOn(project);
 }
}
```

Editor

Besides the project, one of the main objects in Eclipse is the editor. Each editor in Eclipse is a subclass of EditorPart. As you can see in Figure 7-19, there are several ADT editors, serving different types of objects. They all inherit from AbapSourceMultiPageEditor, which is a child of MultiPageEditorPart and a grandchild of EditorPart.

Figure 7-19. *Type hierarchy of AbapSourceMultiPageEditor*

The Eclipse platform provides an easy way to get the active editor. Listing 7-6 shows the basic way to do that, without checking the type of the editor. After determining the editor object, you can cast it according to your needs.

Listing 7-6. Getting an Active Eclipse Editor

```
public static IEditorPart getActiveEditor() {
 try {
     IEditorPart activeEditor = PlatformUI.getWorkbench()
        .getActiveWorkbenchWindow().getActivePage()
              .getActiveEditor();
    return activeEditor;
    } catch (Exception e) {
    return null;
    }
}
```

You can also get the position of the caret in the selected editor using the code in Listing 7-7. The position is always given as an offset of characters from the source code.

Listing 7-7. Getting an Offset of the Caret Position

```
public static int getCaretOffset(IEditorPart editor) {
 StyledText text =
             (StyledText)editor.getAdapter(Control.class);
 return text.getCaretOffset();
}
```

I told you just before that all ADT editors inherit directly from
MultiPageEditorPart. This means that a single editor can have
several pages (tabs). Normally, you'll notice this only when you edit
classes in ABAP, but from a programming point of view, for each ADT
editor, these pages are always there, even if there's only one. To get the
IABAPSourcePage object, which is the base object for the ABAP editors, you
need to use the code in Listing 7-8.

Listing 7-8. Getting an ABAP Source Page

```
public static IAbapSourcePage getAbapSourcePage(
                                    IEditorPart editor) {
 try {
  MultiPageEditorPart multiPartEditor =
                                    (MultiPageEditorPart) editor;
  IAbapSourcePage sourcePage = (IAbapSourcePage)
                              multiPartEditor.getSelectedPage();
  return sourcePage;
 } catch (Exception e) {
  return null;
 }
}
```

Once you get the source code page and the cursor position, you can use them by calling one of the methods of the scanner services. These may be very useful when you are creating a plugin around the ABAP source code. Scanner services implement the IAbapSourceScannerServices interface, which gives you a lot of information about the code. You then do not have to parse the ABAP code yourself. As an example, Listing 7-9 shows how to use the scanner services to get the statement's tokens based on the given cursor position.

Listing 7-9. Getting Tokens of the Current ABAP Statement

```
public static List<Token> getTokens(
            IAbapSourcePage sourcePage, int cursorPosition) {
  IDocument document = sourcePage.getDocument();
  IAbapSourceUi sourceUi = AbapSourceUi.getInstance();
  IAbapSourceScannerServices scannerServices = sourceUi
                        .getSourceScannerServices();
  int startOfStatement = scannerServices.goBackToDot(
                        document, cursorPosition) + 1;
  return scannerServices.getStatementTokens(document,
                                        startOfStatement);
}
```

Of course, this is only beginning of what you can do with the scanner services. You can also determine if a token is a keyword or comment, get the next or previous token, and get the statement for an offset (Figure 7-20). All of these methods enable you to do many checks on the ABAP code using the ADT built-in classes.

```
getStatementTokens(IDocument paramIDocument, int paramInt) : List<Token> - IAbapSourceScannerServices
equals(Object obj) : boolean - Object
findLeftOffsetWhereReparsingShouldBegin(IDocument paramIDocument, int paramInt, boolean paramBoolean) : int - IAbapSourceScanner
findLeftOffsetWhereReparsingShouldBegin(IDocument paramIDocument, int paramInt, boolean paramBoolean1, boolean paramBoolean2)
findRightOffsetWhereReparsingShouldEnd(IDocument paramIDocument, int paramInt1, int paramInt2, boolean paramBoolean) : int - IAbap
getClass() : Class<?> - Object
getInStringLiteralCharacter(IDocument paramIDocument, int paramInt, int[] paramArrayOfint) : Character - IAbapSourceScannerServices
getNextToken(IDocument paramIDocument, int paramInt) : Token - IAbapSourceScannerServices
getPreviousToken(IDocument paramIDocument, int paramInt) : Token - IAbapSourceScannerServices
getPreviousToken(IDocument paramIDocument, int paramInt, boolean paramBoolean) : Token - IAbapSourceScannerServices
getStatement(ITextEditor paramITextEditor, IDocument paramIDocument, int paramInt) : Token[] - IAbapSourceScannerServices
getSyntaxHighlightToken(IAbapSourcePage paramIAbapSourcePage, int paramInt) : ISyntaxHighlightToken - IAbapSourceScannerServices
goBackToDot(IDocument paramIDocument, int paramInt) : int - IAbapSourceScannerServices
goForwardToDot(IDocument paramIDocument, int paramInt) : int - IAbapSourceScannerServices
hashCode() : int - Object
isAbapTokenDelimeter(IDocument paramIDocument, int paramInt) : boolean - IAbapSourceScannerServices
isComma(char paramChar) : boolean - IAbapSourceScannerServices
isComment(IDocument paramIDocument, int paramInt) : boolean - IAbapSourceScannerServices
```

Figure 7-20. *Part of the IAbapSourceScannerServices methods*

Editors pages are also important because they give you the possibility to fetch the IDocument object. This object allows you to set the listeners for the code changes or to change the code in the editor from your plugin. It also allows you to convert the source code offset into line number if needed.

IAdtObject

The next important object type is IAdtObject. It allows you to get the most basic information about the ADT object that you are currently editing. You can fetch the name, description, type, link, or changed at and changed by information. To get the ADT object from the editor, you have to use the code shown in Listing 7-10.

Listing 7-10. Getting an ADT Object from the ABAP Editor

```
public static IAdtObject getAdtObject(IEditorPart editor) {
  if (editor instanceof IAbapSourceMultiPageEditor) {
    IAbapSourcePage abapSourcePage = (IAbapSourcePage) editor
                          .getAdapter(IAbapSourcePage.class);
```

```
if (abapSourcePage == null) {
    return null; }
  return abapSourcePage.getMultiPageEditor().getModel();
}
    return null;
}
```

There are of course more options if you know the exact type of object that is returned. Figure 7-21 shows the places where the IAdtObject interfaces are used. It should be clear that if you cast it to a specific object type, you could get much more information from it.

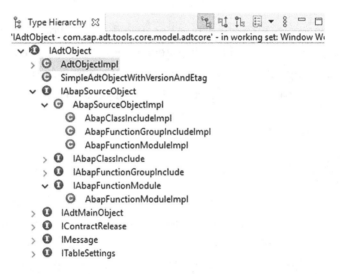

Figure 7-21. *Type Hierarchy of the IAdtObject interface*

ADT Repository Information System Search API

You might have a need to search for an object that is not opened yet. In this case, you need to use ADT Repository Information Systems' search API (ADT RIS). When you use ADT RIS, you only get the basic information about the objects. Their code is not loaded into ADT. This should be enough to decide if you want to do something more with the code, such as open it in the editor window.

Listing 7-11 shows an example search for a class using its name. A maximum of ten results are returned. Why ten results when you have given the full class name? It's because the name passed into the ADT RIS works as a pattern, so it may give you more results, like in the standard dialog for opening objects in ADT (Ctrl+Shift+A).

Listing 7-11. Example Use of AdtRisQuickSearch

```
public static IAdtObjectReference getClassReference(
              final IProject project, final String className) {
 List<IAdtObjectReference> res = null;
   try { res = AdtRisQuickSearchFactory.createQuickSearch(
                            project,
                            new NullProgressMonitor())
                     .execute(className, 10,false,"CLAS");
 } catch (OperationCanceledException |
           RisQuickSearchNotSupportedException e) {
    e.printStackTrace();
    return null;}

  for (final IAdtObjectReference ref : res) {
    if (ref.getName().equals(className))
          return ref;
    }
    return null;
}
```

As you can have more results, I added a check if the name of the fetched class equals the class name passed in the method parameters. This will ensure that you get an object reference to a proper class.

The result of the search will be a type of IAdtObjectReference. It is also widely used in the ADT world. This object reference gives you basic information about the object and allows you to use it in the navigation process.

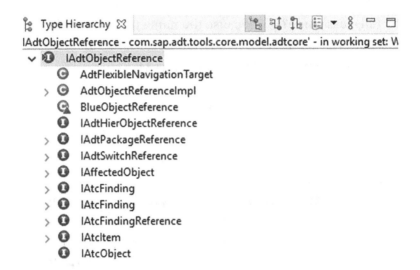

Figure 7-22. *Type Hierarchy of the IAdtObjectReference (partial)*

ADT Navigation

The navigation service factory allows you to navigate to ADT objects inside Eclipse. You can use IAdtObjectReference as input or use ADT Link. When you already have an object reference, you can simply create a navigation service and open the object using the code in Listing 7-12.

Listing 7-12. Opening the Object in the ABAP Editor

```
public static void openObject(final IProject project,
    final IAdtObjectReference adtObjectRef) {

    AdtNavigationServiceFactory.createNavigationService()
                    .navigate(project, adtObjectRef, true);
}
```

If you do not have the object reference, but do have the ADT
Link, you can use another method of the navigation service—
navigateWithExternalLink. The code in Listing 7-13 uses a regex
expression to replace the project name in the ADT Link before calling the
navigation service.

Listing 7-13. Opening an ADT Link

```
public static void openAdtLink(final IProject project,
                                    String adtLink) {
adtLink = adtLink.replace("(?<=\'/\'/)(.*?)(?=\'/)",
                            project.getName().toString());
AdtNavigationServiceFactory.createNavigationService()
                .navigateWithExternalLink(adtLink, project);
        return;
}
```

GUI Navigation

The last use of IAdtObjectReference is to call this object in SAP
GUI. There are some reasons why you might want to do that, such as to
run the object for tests or if the ADT Editor is not fully equipped with the
features of SE80 in your NetWeaver version, like table or structure editing.

This call is very similar to the call of the ADT Editor, but in this case, we
need to choose the workbench action. In the example in Listing 7-14, the
EXECUTE action of the WorkbenchAction is used. It will cause the object to
be run, like you could do from SE80. But you can also use other workbench
actions, such as EDIT, DISPLAY, or even CREATE.

Listing 7-14. Running an Object Using SAP GUI

```
public static void runObject(final IProject project, final
            IAdtObjectReference adtObjectRef) {

  AdtSapGuiEditorUtilityFactory.createSapGuiEditorUtility()
      .openEditorForObject(project, adtObjectRef, true,
              WorkbenchAction.EXECUTE.toString(),null,
              Collections.<String, String>emptyMap());
}
```

Calling the Backend

When you are creating an ADT plugin, you can decide whether you want to use only the APIs prepared by SAP or create your own call to the backend system. Before writing this book, I had never tried to call the backend directly. I wanted my ADT plugins to work without having to install additional elements on the backend, which in many cases developers are not allowed to do. But there can be several good reasons why you would call the backend: The data you need for your plugin is not available in ADT at the moment or you are building a custom solution for your company based on Eclipse.

There are two ways to call the backend from Eclipse. One is to use Java Connector, and the second is to use a RESTful API call. Both possibilities are brought to you by the ADT, so there is nothing to install additionally. The difference is in the way the backend is called and what you have to do in the backend, which I will explain very soon.

In order to show you how both ways are handled, I created a new plugin called Class Outline, which shows the same outline structure for the class that you had in SE24 or SE80 T-Code (Figure 7-23).

Inside this plugin, you will see how I handled both types of calls and a few other small things, to which I will come back later. The source code of the frontend for this plugin is available on GitHub via the book's product page, located at `https://github.com/Apress/abap-in-eclipse-java`. The backend code is available at `https://github.com/Apress/abap-in-eclipse-abap`.

In order to use the plugin, you need to clone the Java repository into your Eclipse installation and use `abapGit` to install the backend in one of your systems.

The idea behind the plugin is simple. It gets the old-style outline tree for a class and displays it as a tree, and then it navigates through the tree node with a double-click.

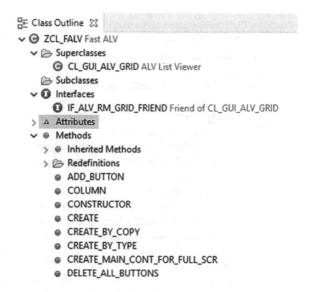

Figure 7-23. *Class Outline view*

When you call the plugin in debug or run mode, you can select which kind of call the view should make (Figure 7-24). Before you do this, let me guide you through the process of creating both types backend calls.

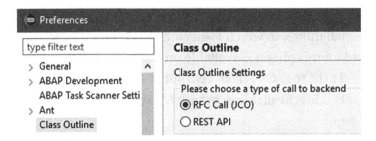

Figure 7-24. *Class Outline plugin preferences*

If you loaded the `ClassOutline` plugin code into Eclipse, you can look at its structure (Figure 7-25). The code for calling the backend is found in the `com.adtbook.classOutline.api` package. You will also find two subpackages there—`rest` (RESTful API) and `rfc` (Java Connector).

Figure 7-25. *Structure of the ClassOutline plugin*

Java Connector

I will start with the Java Connector, as I think this is easier for every ABAP developer to understand, especially if you have experience in RFC function module creation. I split the explanation into two parts: backend and frontend. The backend is done in ABAP, and the frontend is done in the Eclipse plugin.

Backend Process

In the case of Java Connector usage, the backend preparation includes creating the RFC function modules that will be used directly in Java. As in each RFC or API, make sure that you send only the needed information. That way, the exchange of information is much faster, especially when there's a slow network.

In order to serve the Java Connector call, I created two function modules:

- Z_ADT_BOOK_GET_TREE_FOR_CLASS

- Z_ADT_BOOK_GET_URI_FOR_NODE

Both function modules have a very simple interface. The Z_ADT_BOOK_GET_TREE_FOR_CLASS function module imports only the class name and exports the full class outline tree, which is of type SNODETAB (Listing 7-15).

Listing 7-15. Z_ADT_BOOK_GET_TREE_FOR_CLASS Signature

```
FUNCTION Z_ADT_BOOK_GET_TREE_FOR_CLASS
  IMPORTING
    VALUE(CLASS_NAME) TYPE SEOCPDKEY-CLSNAME
  EXPORTING
    VALUE(TREE) TYPE SNODETAB.
```

The second function module, Z_ADT_BOOK_GET_URI_FOR_NODE, takes the class name and the tree node row as input and returns the navigation URI for the given tree node (Listing 7-16). In this case, URI is a path to a specific element. In ADT, it is built on the /sap/bc/adt/ prefix, the type of object, its name, and the source code place and position. For example, /sap/bc/adt/oo/classes/zcl_falv/source/main#start=1304,9 URI points to line 1304 and column 9 of the main code of the ZCL_FALV class. The same URI is used in the ADT links that I described in the previous chapters.

Listing 7-16. Z_ADT_BOOK_GET_URI_FOR_NODE Signature

```
FUNCTION Z_ADT_BOOK_GET_URI_FOR_NODE
  IMPORTING
    VALUE(NODE) TYPE SNODETEXT
    VALUE(CLASS_NAME) TYPE SEOCPDKEY-CLSNAME
  EXPORTING
    VALUE(URI) TYPE STRING.
```

These signatures of the FMs are important for understanding the frontend part of the plugin, the code inside is not important at the moment.

Frontend Process

Java Connector (JCo) is not new to the SAP world. It has been used for a long time, which is why you may have already used it outside of Eclipse. If not, do not be worried. It is not hard to work with. Personally, I used the tutorial found on the SAP Community Wiki[1] and Matthew Billingham's code from his SAP Community blog post[2] to learn how to use it.

---

[1]Using Java Connector to call function modules: https://wiki.scn.sap.com/wiki/display/Snippets/How+To+Import+and+Export+data+to+Function+Module

[2]Matthew Billingham's blog can be found at https://blogs.sap.com/2020/06/05/a-few-code-snippets-while-developing-an-adt-plugin/

The most important thing is to know from which project you want to call the backend and what the RFC Function Module name is. The rest comes quite easy (Listing 7-17). You first need to get the destination ID from the project. To do so, you can use the code in Listing 7-18. Then you have to create the JCo destination, which is used to call your function in the backend. This JCoFunction object allows you to set the import and tables parameters and execute the function call. After execution, you can fetch the results of the call using the same object.

Listing 7-17. Java Connector Implementation of the getNewClassTree Method

```
public ClassTree getNewClassTree(String className,
                                    IProject project) {
  try {
    String destinationId = ProjectUtility.getDestinationID(
                                project);
    JCoDestination destination = JCoDestinationManager
                                .getDestination(destinationId);
    JCoFunction function = destination.getRepository()
                    .getFunction("Z_ADT_BOOK_GET_TREE_FOR_CLASS");
    if (function == null)
      throw new RuntimeException(
        "Z_ADT_BOOK_GET_TREE_FOR_CLASS not found.");

    function.getImportParameterList().getField("CLASS_NAME")
                        .setValue(className.toUpperCase());
    try {
      function.execute(destination);
      JCoTable classTree = function.getExportParameterList()
                                .getTable("TREE");
      return RfcClassTreeContentHandler.deserialize(className,
                                project, classTree);
```

447

```
        } catch (AbapException e) {
            System.out.println(e.toString());
            return null;
        }
  } catch (JCoException e) {
      e.printStackTrace();
      return null;
      }
}
```

Listing 7-18. Getting a Destination ID for the Project

```
public static String getDestinationID(IProject project) {
 String destinationId = AdtCoreProjectServiceFactory
     .createCoreProjectService().getDestinationId(project);
 return destinationId;
}
```

I moved the deserialization of the exporting parameter, called TREE, into separate method, called deserialize, in order to show you how this is handled (Listing 7-19). At first sight, you can see a loop over the rfcTable and the current row ID. If you are familiar with the tables with header lines in ABAP, this will be not great news for you, because you have to use the table object rfcTable to read the row entries. I guess that if this were programmed today, we would not have such similarities. Anyway, once the row is set, you can fetch the field value using the correct type and the name of the line field. For example, the PARENT, CHILD, and ID fields are Integer type, while the rest are String.

Listing 7-19. Reading the JCoTable Line Entries

```
public static ClassTree deserialize(String className,
                   IProject project, JCoTable rfcTable) {
 ClassTree newClassTree = new ClassTree(className, project);
 if (rfcTable == null)
   return null;
  for (int i = 0; i < rfcTable.getNumRows(); i++) {
   rfcTable.setRow(i);
   ClassNode classNode = new ClassNode(rfcTable.getInt(
                      ClassNode.fieldNameId));
   classNode.setChild(rfcTable.getInt(
                      ClassNode.fieldNameChild));
   classNode.setParent(rfcTable.getInt(
                      ClassNode.fieldNameParent));
   classNode.setType(rfcTable.getString(
                      ClassNode.fieldNameType));
   classNode.setName(rfcTable.getString(
                      ClassNode.fieldNameName));
   classNode.setText1(rfcTable.getString(
                      ClassNode.fieldNameText1));
   classNode.setText2(rfcTable.getString(
                      ClassNode.fieldNameText2));
   classNode.setText8(rfcTable.getString(
                      ClassNode.fieldNameText8));
   classNode.setText9(rfcTable.getString(
                      ClassNode.fieldNameText9));
  newClassTree.addChild(classNode);
 }
 return newClassTree;
}
```

Advantages of Java Connector

When you look at the steps that you need to follow in order to get the data from the SAP backend using JCo, you can understand that it is very easy. Additionally, there are plenty of standard RFC function modules that you can use without any additional effort on the backend side. For me, this is one huge advantage of using JCo.

RESTful APIs

The second way to fetch data from SAP is the consumption of RESTful APIs created in the backend. The nice thing is that SAP created a tutorial for this approach and published it in the SAP Community.[3] This tutorial is frequently updated (Figure 7-26). When I was reading it, I had a feeling that it was converted from an internal tutorial for SAP employees, as it looks like part of a training document. Nevertheless, it is very useful if you want to understand how to call the SAP backend from ADT using RESTful APIs.

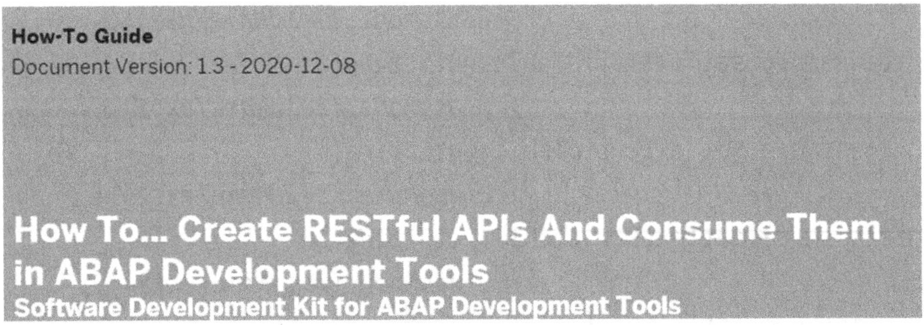

How-To Guide
Document Version: 1.3 - 2020-12-08

How To... Create RESTful APIs And Consume Them in ABAP Development Tools
Software Development Kit for ABAP Development Tools

Figure 7-26. *SAP guide for creating RESTful APIs for ADT*

---

[3]https://assets.cdn.sap.com/sapcom/docs/2013/04/12289ce1-527c-0010-82c7-eda71af511fa.pdf

Backend

This time, preparing the backend is more complex than it was with the JCo. That's because you need to prepare the Simple Transformation and resource class for each API, then do BAdI implementations to allow the discovery and registration of your resource classes. That all sounds complicated, but it is not in reality. It does take more time than just preparing RFC FM.

I am also sure that, instead of a Simple Transformation to handle the API XML body or the response, you can use the JSON format and the /UI2/CL_JSON class to serialize or deserialize it in ABAP. But this class is not available in all NW versions and it was updated through the years, so Simple Transformation may be a safer solution to deploy.

Simple Transformations

You may remember the signature of the RFC FMs that I showed you while preparing the JCo backend. Because I wanted to reuse these FMs in this RESTful API example, I had to prepare the simple transformations for the TREE parameter of the FM Z_ADT_BOOK_GET_TREE_FOR_CLASS, and the NODE parameter of the FM Z_ADT_BOOK_GET_URI_FOR_NODE. They are both based on the dictionary types, so it was quite easy and I used the XSLT_TOOL transaction to create them both.

While preparing the transformation for the class tree (Listing 7-20), I removed all the unused fields. This will limit the amount of data sent through the API to a minimum.

Listing 7-20. The Transformation Z_ADTBOOK_CLASS_TREE

```
<?sap.transform simple?>
<tt:transform xmlns:tt="http://www.sap.com/transformation-
templates" xmlns:ddic="http://www.sap.com/abapxml/types/
dictionary" xmlns:def="http://www.sap.com/abapxml/types/defined">
```

```
<tt:root name="SNODETAB" type="ddic:SNODETAB"/>
<tt:template>
    <CLASSTREE>
    <tt:loop ref=".SNODETAB">
      <SNODETEXT>
        <ID tt:value-ref="ID"/>
        <TYPE tt:value-ref="TYPE"/>
        <NAME tt:value-ref="NAME"/>
        <PARENT tt:value-ref="PARENT"/>
        <CHILD tt:value-ref="CHILD"/>
        <TEXT1 tt:value-ref="TEXT1"/>
        <TEXT2 tt:value-ref="TEXT2"/>
        <TEXT8 tt:value-ref="TEXT8"/>
        <TEXT9 tt:value-ref="TEXT9"/>
      </SNODETEXT>
    </tt:loop>
    </CLASSTREE>
  </tt:template>
</tt:transform>
```

I used the same approach as in the transformation creation to read the tree node information passed from the importing parameter NODE of the FM Z_ADT_BOOK_GET_URI_FOR_NODE (Listing 7-21). Note that it differs only a little from the previously described transformation.

Listing 7-21. The Transformation Z_ADTBOOK_CLASS_TREE_ NODE

```
<?sap.transform simple?>
<tt:transform xmlns:tt="http://www.sap.com/transformation-
templates" xmlns:ddic="http://www.sap.com/abapxml/types/
dictionary" xmlns:def="http://www.sap.com/abapxml/types/
defined">
```

```
<tt:root name="SNODETEXT" type="ddic:SNODETEXT"/>
<tt:template>
  <CLASSNODE>
    <ID tt:value-ref=".SNODETEXT.ID"/>
    <TYPE tt:value-ref=".SNODETEXT.TYPE"/>
    <NAME tt:value-ref=".SNODETEXT.NAME"/>
    <PARENT tt:value-ref=".SNODETEXT.PARENT"/>
    <CHILD tt:value-ref=".SNODETEXT.CHILD"/>
    <TEXT1 tt:value-ref=".SNODETEXT.TEXT1"/>
    <TEXT2 tt:value-ref=".SNODETEXT.TEXT2"/>
    <TEXT8 tt:value-ref=".SNODETEXT.TEXT8"/>
    <TEXT9 tt:value-ref=".SNODETEXT.TEXT9"/>
  </CLASSNODE>
</tt:template>
</tt:transform>
```

BAdI Implementations

The next step to publish the RESTful API for ADT is to create the BAdI
implementations. Two implementations are needed:

- `BADI_ADT_DISCOVERY_PROVIDER`: Responsible for
  making the resources on the SAP backend discoverable

- `BADI_ADT_REST_RFC_APPLICATION`: Used to register the
  resources and bind them to the controller classes

Controller classes are responsible for handling the API calls, which
means they parse the request and build the response for `GET`, `POST`, and
`PUT` methods. Before we look at creating the implementations for the two
BAdIs, let's look at how I created the controller classes.

Resource Controller Classes

I used the first controller class, ZCL_ADT_BOOK_CLASS_TREE_RES, to get the table with the class outline. Because I will use a GET method for the API call, I redefined it and I am calling the FM Z_ADT_BOOK_GET_TREE_FOR_CLASS, which you may remember from the JCo backend preparation.

When you go through the code in Listing 7-22, you should stop for a second on the implementation of the two important methods: GET_CLASS_NAME_FROM_URI and GET_CONTENT_HANDLER. I will explain their purposes shortly.

Listing 7-22. The Controller Class zcl_adt_book_class_tree_res

```
CLASS zcl_adt_book_class_tree_res DEFINITION
  PUBLIC
  INHERITING FROM cl_adt_rest_resource
  FINAL
  CREATE PUBLIC.

  PUBLIC SECTION.
    METHODS get REDEFINITION.

CONSTANTS: class_name TYPE seoclname
                    VALUE 'ZCL_ADT_BOOK_CLASS_TREE_RES',
           resource_type TYPE string VALUE 'SNODETAB'.
PRIVATE SECTION.
      CONSTANTS class_tree_transformation TYPE string
                    VALUE 'Z_ADTBOOK_CLASS_TREE' ##NO_TEXT.
    METHODS get_class_name_from_uri
      IMPORTING request TYPE REF TO if_adt_rest_request
      RETURNING VALUE(class_name) TYPE seoclname.
```

```abap
  METHODS get_class_tree
    IMPORTING class_name TYPE seoclname
    RETURNING VALUE(class_tree) TYPE snodetab.

  METHODS get_content_handler
    RETURNING VALUE(result) TYPE REF TO
                              if_adt_rest_content_handler .
ENDCLASS.

CLASS zcl_adt_book_class_tree_res IMPLEMENTATION.

 METHOD get.
  DATA(class_tree) = get_class_tree(
                      get_class_name_from_uri( request ) ).
  response->set_body_data(
        content_handler = get_content_handler( )
        data            = class_tree ).
 ENDMETHOD.

 METHOD get_class_tree.
  CALL FUNCTION 'Z_ADT_BOOK_GET_TREE_FOR_CLASS'
    EXPORTING
      class_name = class_name
    IMPORTING
      tree       = class_tree.
 ENDMETHOD.

METHOD get_content_handler.
 DATA(factory) = cl_adt_rest_cnt_hdl_factory=>get_instance( ).
 result = factory->get_handler_for_xml_using_st(
                  st_name   = class_tree_transformation
                  root_name = resource_type ).
ENDMETHOD.
```

```abap
METHOD get_class_name_from_uri.
  request->get_uri_attribute( EXPORTING name = 'class_name'
                                        mandatory = abap_true
                              IMPORTING value = class_name ).
ENDMETHOD.

ENDCLASS.
```

You can see that this class is not very complex, but there are some things that need to be explained. The content handler instance, which is created in the GET_CONTENT_HANDLER method, is needed to serialize or deserialize the body of the request (POST) or response (POST, GET).

There are a few predefined content handlers that you can create using the factory class CL_ADT_REST_CNT_HDL_FACTORY. In my example, I used the handler of the XML using simple transformation, which is based on the simple transformation name; the root name converts the internal table into XML.

The GET_CLASS_NAME_FROM_URI method gets the value of the URI[4] attribute class_name. As an example, in the case of the *\adtbook\ classtree\ZCL_FALV* URI, the adtbook is the root node, classtree is a collection, and ZCL_FALV is the value of the dynamic attribute class_name. If it's not clear where the value of the URI comes from, I will explain it when we look at the resource application class.

The second controller class is ZCL_ADT_BOOK_TREE_URI_RES. This class gets the URI (link) for the Class Outline tree node that will allow the navigation to that element. It is very similar to the previous controller class. That is why Listing 7-23 contains only the implementation of the two differing methods: POST and GET_URI_FOR_TREE_NODE. The POST method is used to pass the tree node data to the backend in order to retrieve the link to it. I did not want to build a very long URI for the GET method. I prefer to

---

[4]To read about URIs in REST API programming, check out https://restfulapi. net/resource-naming/

keep all this data in the body of the request, to be able to quickly adapt the structure and not be limited by the maximum length of the URI.

GET_URI_FOR_TREE_NODE is mentioned on purpose, so you know where the FM Z_ADT_BOOK_GET_URI_FOR_NODE is called.

Listing 7-23. Implementation of the Most Important Methods of the zcl_adt_book_tree_uri_res Class

```
CLASS zcl_adt_book_tree_uri_res IMPLEMENTATION.
  METHOD post.
    factory = cl_adt_rest_cnt_hdl_factory=>get_instance( ).
    DATA: node TYPE snodetext.
    request->get_body_data(
      EXPORTING
        content_handler = get_content_handler( )
      IMPORTING
        data            = node ).

    response->set_body_data(
      content_handler = factory->get_handler_for_plain_text( )
      data = get_uri_for_tree_node(
            node       = node
            class_name = get_class_name_from_uri( request ) )
    ).
  ENDMETHOD.
  METHOD get_uri_for_tree_node.
    CALL FUNCTION 'Z_ADT_BOOK_GET_URI_FOR_NODE'
      EXPORTING
        node       = node
        class_name = class_name
```

```
    IMPORTING
        uri        = uri.
  ENDMETHOD.
  ...
ENDCLASS.
```

Resource Application Class

The next type of a class that I needed to create is the resource application class. This type of class is responsible for registering the resources and binding them to the controller classes. Without this, it's not possible to propagate the request to a proper controller class.

The class itself is quite simple, as it inherits from the default implementation of the resource application class CL_ADT_DISC_RES_APP_BASE. All I had to do was redefine three methods:

- IF_ADT_REST_RFC_APPLICATION~GET_STATIC_URI_PATH

- GET_APPLICATION_TITLE

- REGISTER_RESOURCES

In the GET_STATIC_URI_PATH method, I had to pass the root node for all of my resources (/adtbook). GET_APPLICATION_TITLE also requires only a simple description of the discovery service. The most difficult-to-understand part of the resource application class (Listing 7-24) is the redefinition of the REGISTER_RESOURCE method. Although, for each resource controller class, I had to call two methods only to make them registered and bound, then I had trouble at the beginning understanding why I needed the root scheme, relation scheme, or category term. It started to be clear when I had to use them in order to discover the resources in the frontend part, that I could call from the backend.

Listing 7-24. The ZCL_ADT_BOOK_DISCOVERY_RES_APP Class

```abap
CLASS zcl_adt_book_discovery_res_app DEFINITION
  PUBLIC
  INHERITING FROM cl_adt_disc_res_app_base
  FINAL
  CREATE PUBLIC .

  PUBLIC SECTION.
  CONSTANTS root_scheme TYPE string VALUE
                      'http://abapblog.com/adt' ##NO_TEXT.
  CONSTANTS class_tree_uri TYPE string VALUE
                      '/classtree/{class_name}' ##NO_TEXT.
  CONSTANTS tree_node_uri TYPE string VALUE
                      '/treeuri/{class_name}' ##NO_TEXT.
  CONSTANTS root_rel_scheme TYPE string VALUE
                'http://abapblog.com/adt/relations' ##NO_TEXT.
  CONSTANTS xml_application TYPE string VALUE
                                  'application/xml' ##NO_TEXT.
  CONSTANTS application_title TYPE string VALUE
                'ADT Discovery for Class Outline' ##NO_TEXT.

  CONSTANTS:
      BEGIN OF category,
        classtree TYPE string VALUE 'classtree' ##NO_TEXT,
        treeuri   TYPE string VALUE 'treeuri' ##NO_TEXT,
      END OF category,
      BEGIN OF description,
        classtree TYPE string VALUE 'Class Tree' ##NO_TEXT,
        treeuri   TYPE string VALUE 'Tree URI' ##NO_TEXT,
      END OF description,
      static_uri    TYPE string VALUE '/adtbook' ##NO_TEXT.
```

```abap
    METHODS if_adt_rest_rfc_application~get_static_uri_path
                                                  REDEFINITION.
    PROTECTED SECTION.
      METHODS: get_application_title REDEFINITION,
               register_resources REDEFINITION.
    PRIVATE SECTION.
      METHODS register_tree_uri_resource
        IMPORTING
          registry TYPE REF TO if_adt_disc_rest_rc_registry.
      METHODS register_class_tree_resource
        IMPORTING
          registry TYPE REF TO if_adt_disc_rest_rc_registry.
ENDCLASS.

CLASS zcl_adt_book_discovery_res_app IMPLEMENTATION.

 METHOD if_adt_rest_rfc_application~get_static_uri_path.

   result = static_uri.

 ENDMETHOD.

 METHOD get_application_title.
    result = application_title.
 ENDMETHOD.
 METHOD register_resources.

  register_class_tree_resource( registry ).
  register_tree_uri_resource( registry ).

 ENDMETHOD.

 METHOD register_class_tree_resource.
```

```abap
DATA(collection) = registry->register_discoverable_resource(
 url             = ''
 handler_class   = ''
 description      = description-classtree
 category_scheme = root_scheme
 category_term   = category-classtree ).

collection->register_disc_res_w_template(
  relation = root_rel_scheme
  template = class_tree_uri
  description = description-classtree
  type = xml_application
  handler_class = zcl_adt_book_class_tree_res=>class_name ).

ENDMETHOD.

METHOD register_tree_uri_resource.

  DATA(collection) = registry->register_discoverable_resource(
      url             = ''
      handler_class   = ''
      description      = description-treeuri
      category_scheme = root_scheme
      category_term   = category-treeuri ).

collection->register_disc_res_w_template(
  relation = root_rel_scheme
  template = tree_node_uri
  description = description-treeuri
  type = xml_application
  handler_class = zcl_adt_book_tree_uri_res=>class_name ).
ENDMETHOD.

ENDCLASS.
```

Creating BAdI Implementations

All the backend code is ready, so it's finally time to show you the creation
of the proper BAdI implementation. I used Ctrl+Shift+A to access the Open
ABAP Development Object dialog and then opened BADI_ADT_REST_RFC_
APPLICATION. The Enhancement spot called SADT_REST_RFC_APPLICATION
was opened in the editor (Figure 7-27), as it contains the selected BAdI
definition. After right-clicking BADI_ADT_REST_RFC_APPLICATION, I chose
Create BAdI Implementation.

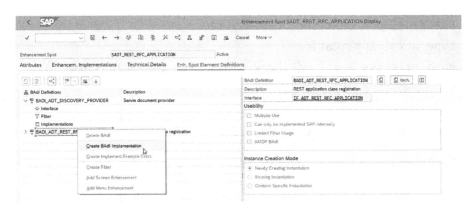

Figure 7-27. *Enhancement spot SADT_REST_RFC_APPLICATION*

In the first step, I was asked to create the enhancement
implementation. I gave it the name and description you see in Figure 7-28.

NPL(1)/001 Create Enhancement Implementation	×
Enhancement Implementation	Z_ADT_BOOK
Short Text	ADT BOOK Class Tree Rest API
Composite Enhancement Implementation	

Figure 7-28. *Z_ADT_BOOK Enhancement Implementation*

In the next step, I gave the BAdI Implementation a description and a name (Z_ADT_BOOK_RESOURCE_APP). I also set the implementing class to the previously created ZCL_ADT_BOOK_DISCOVERY_RES_APP (Figure 7-29).

≡	NPL(1)/001 Create BAdI Implementation	×
BAdI Implementation	Z_ADT_BOOK_RESOURCE_APP	
Description	ADT Book Class Tree Resource App	
Implementing Class	ZCL_ADT_BOOK_DISCOVERY_RES_APP	

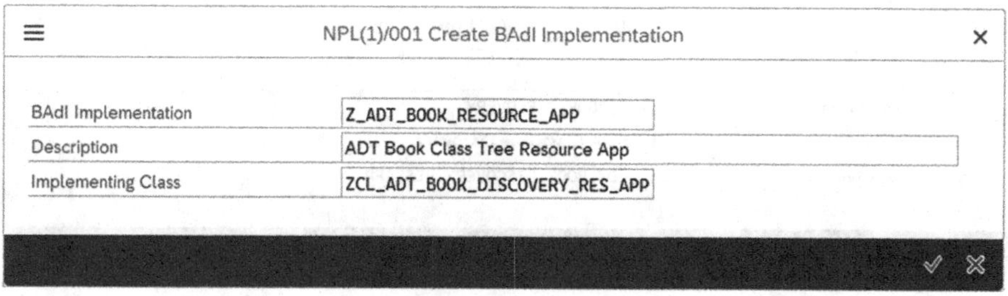

Figure 7-29. *Implementation of the BADI_ADT_REST_RFC_APPLICATION*

Finally, I set up the filter value for STATIC_URI_PATH to /adtbook/* (Figure 7-30). This will ensure that all calls from ADT that have a root node of URI set to /adtbook/* will be handled by my resource application class.

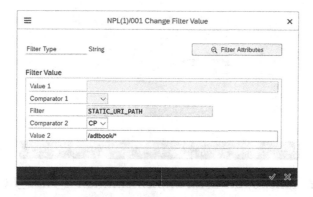

Figure 7-30. *Filter values for BADI Implementation Z_ADT_BOOK_RESOURCE_APP*

I had to create the BAdI implementation for BADI_ADT_DISCOVERY_ PROVIDER as well. I used the same enhancement implementation (Z_ADT_ BOOK) and the same implementing class as before (Figure 7-31).

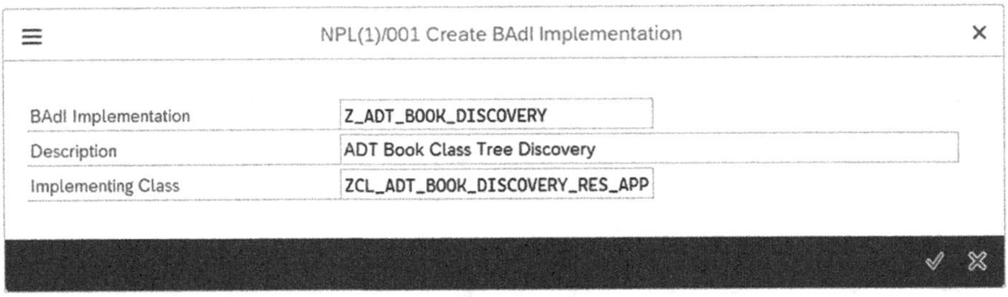

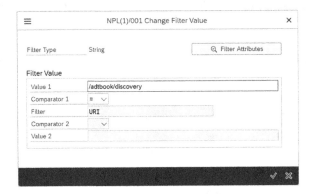

Figure 7-31. *Implementation of the Z_ADT_BOOK_ DISCOVERY*

The last step is to adapt the filter for this implementation. I set the value of the URI filter to /adtbook/discovery (Figure 7-32).

Figure 7-32. *Filter of the BAdI implementation Z_ADT_BOOK_ DISCOVERY*

After activating the enhancement implementation, the work on the backend is finally done.

Frontend

The frontend part is much faster to implement than the backend. When I saw SAP examples of implementing this, the backend side became clearer as well. But first I had to create the constants for the plugin discovery, root and relation schemes, category terms, and the URI parameter (Listing 7-25).

Listing 7-25. Declaration of the Class RestAPICaller Static Members

```
private static final String PLUGIN_DISCOVERY =
                                  "/adtbook/discovery";
private static final String URI_PARAMETER_CLASS_NAME =
                                  "class_name";
private static final String RELATION =
                    "http://abapblog.com/adt/relations";
private static final String SCHEME =
                                  "http://abapblog.com/adt";
private static final String CLASSTREE_TERM = "classtree";
private static final String TREEURI_TERM = "treeuri";
```

As you can see, these are exact copies of the constants created in the SAP backend. When you look at the beginning of Listing 7-26, note that I had to get the destination ID again from a project. After that, the story starts to differ from the JCo version.

Listing 7-26. The getNewClassTree Method of the RestApiCaller Class

```
public ClassTree getNewClassTree(String className,
                IProject project) {
String destinationId =
                ProjectUtility.getDestinationID(project);
URI classTreeUri = getURI(destinationId,
                        className,
                        CLASSTREE_TERM);
```

```java
IRestResourceFactory restResourceFactory =
     AdtRestResourceFactory.createRestResourceFactory();
IRestResource classTreeResource = restResourceFactory
    .createResourceWithStatelessSession(classTreeUri,
                                         destinationId);
try {
 IResponse response = classTreeResource.get(null,
                                        IResponse.class);
 ClassTree classTree = new RestClassTreeContentHandler(
                          className, project)
                    .deserialize(response.getBody(),
                                     ClassTree.class);
 return classTree;
 } catch (ResourceNotFoundException e) {
   System.out.println(e.toString());
   return null;
 } catch (RuntimeException e) {
   System.out.println(e.toString());
   return null;
 }
}
```

First of all, to call the API, I had to prepare its URI. It will be used to get the class tree table from the backend. One possibility is to build the URI from a template (/adtbook/classtree/{class_name}) and I guess that would be the fastest way. But one of the rules of RESTful APIs is that the URI must be discovered; this is done in the getURI method (Listing 7-27). Once that's done, I created a stateless session for resources using AdtRestResourceFactory and I called the get method of the session object. This call will invoke the get method of the controller class zcl_adt_book_class_tree_res in the backend.

Listing 7-27. The getURI Method of the RestApiCaller Class

```
private URI getURI(String destination, String className,
                   String categoryTerm) {
  IAdtDiscovery discovery = AdtDiscoveryFactory
  .createDiscovery(destination, URI.create(PLUGIN_DISCOVERY));

  IAdtDiscoveryCollectionMember collectionMember = discovery
                .getCollectionMember(SCHEME, categoryTerm,
                                     new NullProgressMonitor());

  IAdtTemplateLink templateLink = collectionMember
                        .getTemplateLink(RELATION);
  IAdtUriTemplate uriTemplate = templateLink.getUriTemplate();
  String uri = uriTemplate.set(URI_PARAMETER_CLASS_NAME,
                      className).expand();
  return URI.create(uri);
}
```

After a successful call, the results are stored in the response body. You can fetch them using the getBody method of IResponse. The response will be an XML file, which needs to parsed. I am doing that in the RestClassTreeContentHandler class, which you can check in the GitHub repository, but you will not find anything special there.

You may remember that, to get a link for the Class Outline tree node for the controller class, I decided to use a POST method. Listing 7-28 shows how this is handled in the frontend. Basically, I had to do the opposite of what I did with the getNewClassTree method. That means I had to serialize the tree node into XML that was set as a body of the POST method. In the end, I retrieved a simple string with the link to the node in the body of the response, which I then passed to the ADT navigation service in the TreeDoubleClickListener class.

Listing 7-28. The getUriForTreeNode Method of the RestApiCaller
Class

```
public String getUriForTreeNode(TreeNode treeNode) {
 String destinationId =
      ProjectUtility.getDestinationID(treeNode.getProject());
 URI classTreeUri = getURI(destinationId, treeNode
                      .getClassName(), TREEURI_TERM);
 IRestResourceFactory restResourceFactory =
      AdtRestResourceFactory.createRestResourceFactory();
 IRestResource classTreeResource = restResourceFactory
      .createResourceWithStatelessSession(classTreeUri,
                                          destinationId);
 try {
  IResponse response =
      classTreeResource.post(null, IResponse.class,
      new RestClassNodeContentHandler()
          .serialize(treeNode.getSourceNode(),
                     Charset.forName("UTF-8")));
      return response.getBody().toString();
 } catch (ResourceNotFoundException e) {
  System.out.println(e.toString());
  return null;
 } catch (RuntimeException e) {
  System.out.println(e.toString());
  return null;
 }
}
```

Advantages of the RESTful API

You can see that it is more complex to create a RESTful API than a simple RFC call using Java Connector. However, there are some advantages to having RESTful API in place:

- It can be called from any platform or development language that supports REST API, as the API interface is standardized.

- It does not need any additional connector (SAP Java Connector, SAP .Net Connector, etc.).

- You can add new functionalities to collections and they will not interrupt existing ones.

- You do not have to know and hardcode the URI, as it is discoverable.

Of course, these advantages matter the most with commercial projects or big community projects. For small projects or for the sake of the compatibility with the older SAP backends, I would use JCo for ADT plugin creation.

Summary

I know that this last chapter has not been the easiest one to follow, especially the part about the RESTful API. It took me the most time to prepare and to write it. I hope after reading it, you know how to start the development of the ADT plugin with a backend data call. I hope also that you liked the information about the SDK and the Enhanced Class Decompiler. They really are game-changers.

Thank you for reading this book. I'll be waiting for your own ADT plugins to appear in the Eclipse Marketplace.

APPENDIX A

Shortcut Cheat Sheet

Type	Command	Shortcut
Debugger	Toggle Soft Breakpoint	Alt+B
	Refresh ABAP Breakpoint Activation	Ctrl+Alt+B
	Set a Line Breakpoint in the ABAP Editor	Ctrl+Shift+B
	Inspect ABAP Variable	Ctrl+Shift+I
	Step Into	F5
	Step Over	F6
	Step Return	F7
	Resume	F8
	Jump to Line	Shift+F12
	Run to Line	Shift+F8
Code Quality	Profile ABAP Development Object	Alt+F9
	Profile ABAP Application	Ctrl+F9
	Run ABAP Test Cockpit	Ctrl+Shift+F2

(continued)

Type	Command	Shortcut
Navigate	Navigate Through the Editor Navigation History	Alt+Left/Right
	Navigate Through the Tabs of the Class Editor Between Global Class, Local Class, and Test Classes	Alt+Page Up/ Page Down
	Open in Last Used Project	Alt+Shift+P
	Switch Editor Window	Ctrl+F6
	Step Quickly Through the Editor Markers, Like Tasks, Bookmarks, Error Markers, ATC Findings, etc.	Ctrl+ ; / :
	Easily Open Eclipse Views or Trigger Command via the Quick Access Input Field	Ctrl+3
	Show the Compare with Project Menu	Ctrl+Alt+C
	Open ADT Link	Ctrl+Alt+O
	Show the Open In Project Menu	Ctrl+Alt+P
	New ABAP Project	Ctrl+Alt+Shift+P
	Display a List of All Open Editors	Ctrl+E
	Close the Active Editor Tab	Ctrl+F4
	Easily Switch Between All Eclipse Views	Ctrl+F7
	Easily Switch Between The Perspectives	Ctrl+F8
	Maximize the Active Editor or Viewer to Full-Screen Mode	Ctrl+M
	Navigate Through the Editor Tabs Forward and Backward	Ctrl+Page Up/Page Down
	Open ABAP Development Object	Ctrl+Shift+A
	Close All Editor Tabs	Ctrl+Shift+F4
Run	Run ABAP Object	F8
	Run ABAP Application (Console)	F9
SAP GUI	Run an ABAP Development Object	Alt+F8
	Open SAP GUI	Ctrl+6

(continued)

Type	Command	Shortcut
Source Code	Move the Selected Codelines Up/Down in the Editor	Alt+Up/Down
	Package Check	Ctrl+Alt+F5
	Create Logpoint...	Ctrl+Alt+L
	Duplicate Codelines Before/After the Selected Codeline	Ctrl+Alt+Up/Down
	Delete the Previous Word in the Editor	Ctrl+Backspace
	Delete the Selected Codeline	Ctrl+D
	Delete the Next Word in the Editor	Ctrl+Delete
	Check ABAP Development Object	Ctrl+F2
	Activate	Ctrl+F3
	Create New Development Object	Ctrl+N
	Delete the Content from the Cursor Position to the End of the Line	Ctrl+Shift+Delete
	Add a Newline above the Current Line and Position the Cursor in that Line	Ctrl+Shift+Enter
	Activate Multiple ABAP Development Objects	Ctrl+Shift+F3
	New ABAP Repository Object	Ctrl+Shift+N
	Navigate To (Matching Statement)	Ctrl+Shift+P
	Occurrences in File	Ctrl+Shift+U
	Unlock Object	Ctrl+U
	Scroll Line Up/Down Without Changing Cursor Position	Ctrl+Up/Down
	Navigate To Implementation	F3
	Add a Newline Below the Current Line and Position the Cursor in that Line	Shift+Enter
	Navigate To Declaration	Shift+F3

(continued)

Type	Command	Shortcut
Source	Add Comment	Ctrl+<
Code	Remove Comment	Ctrl+>
Comments	Toggle Comment	Ctrl+7
Source	Format Block	Ctrl+Alt+Shift+F
Code	Indent	Ctrl+I
Format	Format	Ctrl+Shift+F
	Format Block	Ctrl+Shift+F1
	Format	Shift+F1
Source	Toggle Block Selection	Alt+Shift+A
Code	Extract Local Variable	Alt+Shift+L
Refactoring	Extract Method...	Alt+Shift+M
	Rename...	Alt+Shift+R
	Delete Unused Variables (Selection)	Alt+Shift+U
	Delete Unused Variables (All)	Alt+U
	Quick Fix	Ctrl+1
	Assign to Attribute	Ctrl+2, F
	Assign to Local Variable	Ctrl+2, L
	Rename in File	Ctrl+2, R

(continued)

Type	Command	Shortcut
Source Code Support	Show Method Information	Alt+F2
	Toggle ABAP Editor Breadcrumb	Alt+Shift+B
	Compare with Last Used Project	Alt+Shift+C
	Toggle Mark Occurrences	Alt+Shift+O
	Reduce Font Size	Ctrl+-
	Increase Font Size	Ctrl+=
	Quick Outline	Ctrl+O
	Show in Quick Assist View	Ctrl+Shift+1
	ABAP Where-Used List	Ctrl+Shift+G
	Quick Hierarchy	Ctrl+T
	Show ABAP Language Help	F1
	Open Element Info	F2
	Show ABAP Type Hierarchy	F4
Unit Tests	Run ABAP Unit Tests	Ctrl+Shift+F10
	Run ABAP Unit Tests with Coverage	Ctrl+Shift+F11
	Run ABAP Unit Tests With...	Ctrl+Shift+F12
	Preview ABAP Unit Tests	Ctrl+Shift+F9

Index

A

ABAP ADT Extensions
  automatic logon, 319–321
  Eclipse Marketplace, 317
  project settings, 317, 318
ABAP Code Completion
  settings, 235
ABAP Code Insight, 290–292
ABAP Continuous Integration
  coloring projects, 284, 285
  dashboard, 288
  Eclipse Marketplace, 283
  job configuration screen, 286
  preferences, 288–290
  source code state widget, 287
  suppressions view, 288
  view, 286
ABAP coverage, 91
ABAP Element Info views, 86, 87
ABAP Exception view, 79
abapGit
  Eclipse plugin, 278
  repositories, 278–281
  staging, 281, 282
ABAP Internal Table view, 79, 80
ABAP Language Help
  view, 83, 84

ABAP project
  Cloud Project
    authentication, 26
    connection settings, 22
    project explorer, 24
    project name, working sets,
      and favorite packages, 24
    service instance details, 23
    service key, 25
    settings overview and
      language selection, 23
  on-premise project
    logon to system, 18
    perspective switch, 20
    project explorer view and
      favorite packages, 20
    project name, 19
    SAP Logon Pad entry, 17
    SAP system connections, 16
  types, 15
ABAP repository trees, 50–54
ABAP source code editor
  breadcrumbs, 128
  editor tabs, 124, 125
  internal editor tabs, 130, 131
  overview ruler, 128
  source code, 129

Printed in the United States
by Baker & Taylor Publisher Services